QUESTIONS OF TRADITION

Tradition is a central concern for a wide range of academic disciplines interested in problems of transmitting culture across generations. Yet the concept itself has received remarkably little analysis. A substantial literature has grown up around the notion of 'invented tradition,' but no clear concept of tradition is to be found in these writings; since the very notion of 'invented tradition' presupposes a prior concept of tradition and is empty without one, this debunking usage has done as much to obscure the idea as to clarify it. In the absence of a shared concept, the various disciplines have created their own vocabularies to address the subject. Useful as they are, these specialized vocabularies (of which the best known include hybridity, canonicity, diaspora, paradigm, and contact zones) separate the disciplines and therefore necessarily create only a collection of parochial and disjointed approaches.

In contrast, the essays in this volume deal in diverse ways with the complexities of cultural transmission and collectively ask, what is tradition when it is not invented? The first essays, rooted in anthropology, art history, and museum studies, are grounded in real case studies that help to challenge and inform the more abstract discussions in the second half of the book devoted, broadly, to intellectual history, philosophy, and politics. Until now, there has been no concerted attempt to put the various disciplines in conversation with one another around the problem of tradition. Combining discussions of the idea of tradition by major scholars from a variety of disciplines with synoptic, synthesizing essays, *Questions of Tradition* will initiate a renewal of interest in this vital subject.

MARK SALBER PHILLIPS is a professor in the Department of History at Carleton University.

GORDON SCHOCHET is a professor in the Department of Political Science at Rutgers University.

Questions of Tradition

*Edited by Mark Salber Phillips
and Gordon Schochet*

UNIVERSITY OF TORONTO PRESS
Toronto   Buffalo   London

© University of Toronto Press Incorporated 2004
Toronto   Buffalo   London
Printed in Canada

ISBN 0-8020-4498-0 (cloth)
ISBN 0-8020-8272-6 (paper)

Printed on acid-free paper

National Library of Canada Cataloguing in Publication

Questions of tradition / edited by Mark Salber Phillips and
   Gordon Schochet.

   Includes bibliographical references.
   ISBN 0-8020-4498-0 (bound). – ISBN 0-8020-8272-6 (pbk.)

   1. Tradition (Philosophy)   I. Phillips, Mark, 1946–   II. Schochet,
   Gordon J., 1937–   III. Series.

   B105.T7Q47 2004   148   C2004-901670-9

University of Toronto Press acknowledges the financial assistance to its
publishing program of the Canada Council for the Arts and the Ontario
Arts Council.

University of Toronto Press acknowledges the financial support for its
publishing activities of the Government of Canada through the Book
Publishing Industry Development Program (BPIDP).

To the memories of
Felix Gilbert
and
Peter Laslett,
who first taught us to think about
questions of tradition

Contents

Part II

Preface

MARK SALBER PHILLIPS AND

GORDON SCHOCHET

The idea of 'tradition' has led multiple lives, with results that have enriched and confused general discussions of this essential concept. From the perspectives of anthropology or popular culture, for instance, tradition generally suggests established folkways, often seen as threatened by the pressures of modernity or (more recently) as persisting in various ways through processes of hybridization. In this usage, which is broadly characteristic of the social sciences, tradition is identified with enduring social practices, and tacitness is often regarded as its signature.

Philosophy, religion, law (in some of its aspects), and intellectual history, on the other hand, tend to understand tradition in terms of strikingly different assumptions. Far from identifying tradition with the inarticulacy of practice, scholars in these fields confront highly self-conscious bodies of ideas as they are transmitted over time. Of course, what Michael Polanyi called 'tacit knowledge' enters very importantly into traditions of knowledge as well – as recent historians of science have done so much to show. Nonetheless, the fundamental problems of continuity and change necessarily take on a different shape in relation to genealogies of ideas rather than the persisting influence of custom.

In both realms, questions of tradition are often bound up with the problem of authority, which has created further possibilities for confusion or misprision. Whether the subject is the persistence of custom or the evolution of ideas, our interests can be framed in essentially historical terms, making tradition a matter for descriptive rather than prescriptive discussion. Thinking about the idea of tradition in these terms permits us to conceptualize some aspects of the large and complex problem of cultural transmission – the ways in which practices and beliefs persist over time and become integral and often definitive parts of the cultures that surround and preserve them.

In some contexts, however, 'tradition' may be invoked not simply to call attention to or to recognize historical continuities of this kind but to mark the authority they carry – and even to endorse and sustain it. In this form, the idea of tradition is more prescriptive than historical and takes on strong ideological meanings. Among other things, these prescriptive associations pointedly illustrate the ways in which appeals to tradition have often become symbolic battlegrounds in the political life of modernity, places where those who see themselves and their causes as progressive spar with opponents who defend long-standing institutions or identities that they hold dear.

These ideological inflections have also played large parts in academic understandings of tradition. Investigating processes of continuity and change is at the core of many of our disciplines, and in this sense, the analysis of tradition (by whatever vocabularies we prefer to call it) has long been one of the central preoccupations of the human sciences. Additionally, however, there has been a very important prescriptivist and conservative social science account of tradition that warns of the dangers of rapid change. Theorists ranging from Alexis de Tocqueville to Michael Oakeshott have claimed that societies are held together and partially constituted by fragile networks of accumulated practices and institutions and, therefore, that substantial departures from those traditions constitute terrible threats to the health of human society.

The prominence of this ideological usage has made it difficult at times for other kinds of discussions to proceed without incurring the suspicion that *any* interest in tradition must necessarily rest upon similar political foundations. The taint of *traditionalism*, in other words, has seemed to cling to almost any discussion of the idea of tradition, whatever its overt intention or political engagement. For academic analysis, it seems fair to say, the consequence has been the effective loss of 'tradition' as a central term – though hardly as a central *problem* – in the vocabulary of the human sciences. And this loss has been confirmed rather than remedied by the important and influential work of Hobsbawm and Ranger on *The Invention of Tradition* (1983). For two decades, in fact, it has seemed extraordinarily difficult to think about the idea of tradition except in the deconstructive framework of pseudo-traditionality. Meanwhile tradition in its wider sense has remained undervalued, underutilized, and certainly undertheorized.

This volume seeks to remedy that situation by underlining the importance of tradition as a necessary focus of study for a wide range of historical and social scientific disciplines. Behind all the papers lies the common conviction that the time has come to engage with this subject in larger and more constructive terms than those permitted by the recent obsession with invention and manipulation. We also recognize, however, that the term has multiple meanings and that its very centrality works against any attempt to seek an all-encompassing definition of tradition – an effort, in any case, more likely to be an exercise in legislation than discovery. Instead, we have begun with the far more modest task of exploring current understandings within individual disciplines, taking this as a step towards an expanded, cross-disciplinary discussion.

Following an introductory chapter by Mark Salber Phillips, the volume is divided into two sections, the first dealing with traditions as understood and studied by anthropologists, art historians, and museum curators, and the second devoted, broadly, to intellectual history, philosophy, and politics. Each section is capped with a review essay that draws together the individual essays and puts their concerns in a wider frame. The first review essay is by James Clifford, the second by Gordon Schochet.

In his opening essay, Phillips discusses some central themes in the history of the idea of tradition and criticizes the recent dominance of ironic and demystifying understandings of tradition, arguing that the very idea of 'invented tradition' makes little sense without a prior conception of 'tradition' as such. He also points to the ways in which various writers or schools have outlined their ideas of tradition without any recognition of other, parallel discussions in related disciplines.

The next three essays deal in various ways with the conflicts between the traditions and conventions of anthropology and collecting, on the one hand, and the traditions and cultural products of Native peoples, on the other. Andrea Laforet outlines a conflict of traditions within the concrete setting of negotiation of cultural repatriation agreements between the Canadian government and Aboriginal peoples. She shows how Native traditions regarding property and orality conflict with a radically different set of traditions regarding property and public display embedded in the practices of the museum as an institution.

A related clash between Western and Native traditions about the display and study of objects is the focus of Ruth B. Phillips's chapter. Her contribution provides an account of an Iroquois campaign to withdraw masks regarded as sacred from public exhibition or reproduction. Observing the change in conditions of display over a period of time, Phillips seeks to historicize the issue, without denying the authenticity of the demand.

In the next essay, Christopher B. Steiner examines the confrontation between tradition and modernity in both the history of 'African art' and in its contemporary evaluation in the academy, the museum, and the art market. Collectors, Steiner says, disparage the incursion of modernity into African art, and museums follow their lead, emphasizing the aesthetics of *things* and the epistemic problems of provenance and function. They tend to leave the academic art historian – who is often caught up in the denigration of tradition – to do conceptual battle with a world that is eager to recycle traditions.

Mieke Bal's subject is the practice and the photographic representation of the Dutch *Zwarte Piet* Christmas tradition. Bal, who writes as an insider but with the distance of an observer, finds the tradition offensive since it perpetuates racial stereotypes, but her analysis reveals the difficulties inherent in intentional attempts to alter a tradition to accord with changes in other social practices and attitudes. She surmises that a tradition may be altered or abandoned when it fits so badly with a culture's sense of its own reality that retaining it would be too painful but that such a change is unlikely to come about by official fiat or stipulation.

In the final essay in this section, James Clifford comments on the themes raised by the previous essays in relation to the crucial contemporary issues of decolonization and globalization. He uses his notion of 'articulation' to explain assertions of 'indigenous traditionalisms' and to account for the fact that people are generally more willing to organize in behalf of local traditions and customs than for more universal goals such as human rights.

In the opening chapter of Part II, Michael McKeon takes the English Enlightenment's attack on tradition as his starting point for an analysis of the relations between the tradition and ideology. Using Michael Polanyi's concept, he employs the 'tacit knowledge' implicit in 'ideology' and 'the aesthetic' to examine the differences between the pre-Enlightenment cultures of tradition and what he calls 'our cultural modernity,' which is more self-consciously 'ideological' than 'traditional.' When societies begin the process of rendering their implicit beliefs explicit and struggle to free themselves from received tradition,

McKeon argues (following Clifford Geertz), they not only undermine tradition, they effect its replacement by ideology.

Daniel T. Rodgers discusses the 'traditions of liberalism' and their hold on American social beliefs and on the historiography of American politics. Accounts of the practices of nineteenth-century liberal politics and the ideology of 'classical liberalism,' he argues, have combined to give us a false picture of America as a liberal society by 1900. Brief analyses of economic, legal, religious, and familial conditions reveal a much more complex – and much less 'liberal' – world than the one usually presented. It turns out that rather than itself comprising a tradition as we are often led to believe, liberalism consists of multiple traditions, all of which must be studied and engaged.

One of the most frequently encountered instances of the appeal to tradition is its pairing with law, which David Lieberman examines in the next chapter. Law inevitably draws upon and reflects the past, in the process, flattening it out and providing it with a usable coherence. This is especially true of the common law, which often proclaimed itself to be the distillation of English legal customs as well as the embodiment of their gradual and accumulated change. Ranging from Sir John Davies in the seventeenth century, to Jeremy Bentham and William Blackstone in the eighteenth, to Oliver Wendell Holmes and modern jurisprudential theorists, Lieberman discusses the role of custom in the law, the problems of the unwritten and the written law, the alleged relationships among reason, custom, and law, and the importance of *stare decisis*, the formalized practice of binding courts to the decisions of their predecessors.

Georgia Warnke in the next essay analyses the relationship of ethical knowledge to tradition in modern, multicultural societies. She begins with a puzzle in Jane Austen's *Pride and Prejudice* – how was Elizabeth so readily able to overcome her objections to Darcy? – which she solves by using the notions of 'thick concepts' and 'confidence' from Bernard Williams's *Ethics and the Limits of Philosophy*. Like Elizabeth, Warnke suggests, we should recognize that our own beliefs and ethical principles, no less than those of our neighbours, come from our traditions. This realization, combined with a 'confidence' in the validity of those beliefs, should enable us to enter into conversation with those who differ from us and to lower our voices as well as our expectations.

Patrick H. Hutton investigates the work of Philippe Ariès, a distinguished historian of mentalities, who strongly believed in the power of tradition to hold societies together. According to Ariès, traditions survived by adapting to changed circumstances. In the twentieth century, that adaptation took the form of a retreat from the public to the private realm, a retreat that Ariès spent much of his professional life documenting. He saw modern society as an amalgam of the strands of many persistent traditions, and in this, according to Hutton, he stood in pointed opposition to the view that traditions are invented.

In the final essay, Gordon Schochet, commenting on the chapters in Part II, argues that there is an unavoidably political aspect to tradition, both in the way it functions and in the way it is invoked. Distinguishing between the 'external' *identification* of tradition and its 'internal' *use*, he says that tradition calls attention to boundaries, to the limits of the permissible and the extent of the required. While he agrees in part with the Weberian distinction between traditional and law- and reason-based societies and recognizes that traditions may be manipulated, he insists that they continue to play important roles and are essential parts of what holds all societies together.

In its first incarnation, this volume was a conference held at Rutgers University in November 1997. The conference, entitled 'Questions of Tradition,' was sponsored by *The Journal of the History of Ideas*, and we remain indebted to the *Journal*, its Board, and especially to Donald Kelley, the Editor, Jerome Schneewind, and Joseph Levine for their encouragement and support, without which neither the conference nor this book would have existed. We also are indebted to the then newly organized International Society for Intellectual History, which soon became a co-sponsor of the conference, and to its director, Constance Blackwell. Much of the success of that initial conference was due to the hard work of Neil Miller, our conference coordinator, and to the vital assistance offered by Robin Ladrach, the Managing Editor of the *Journal*.

The conference enjoyed the support of the Rutgers University's Research Council, which designated it as its social science conference for 1997–8 and generously awarded a grant that covered much of the travel expenses of the participants. Richard Foley, then Dean of Faculty of Arts and Sciences of Rutgers University, New Brunswick, provided further financial assistance.

Green College of the University of British Columbia generously funded a year-long 'thematic lecture series' which allowed us to continue the process begun at Rutgers the previous year. The support of Green College not only created the opportunity for a number of the contributors to present revised versions of their papers, but it also provided a partial subvention of the publication costs. We are deeply grateful to Richard Ericson, Principal of Green College, and to Mark Vessey, then Acting Principal, for this crucial help in the gestation of the project. Important additional support also came from the Dean of the Faculty of Arts of the University of British Columbia and from the Research Development Initiatives program of the Social Sciences and Humanities Research Council of Canada.

Finally, we are indebted to the anonymous readers for University of Toronto Press, whose suggestions about the structure and organization of the volume were very helpful, and to our editors at the Press, Kristen Pederson, Jill McConkey, and Barb Porter, for their guidance and good cheer.

The conference was an exciting occasion and we happily and gratefully acknowledge the contributions of our other participants: Suzanne Blier, William Connell, Anthony Grafton, Donald Kelley, Suzanne Klengel, Alkis Kontos, Joseph Levine, Phyllis Mack, Vladimir Malachov, Jacob Meskin, Ann E. Moyer, James Muldoon, Kirstie McClure, Mary Poovey, David Harris Sacks, Naoki Sakai, Gabrielle M. Spiegel, Siep Stuurman, and Yael Zerubavel. Special thanks are owing to Natalie Zemon Davis, who took on the particularly arduous role of general commentator and who, in that capacity, did so much to weave together a wide variety of themes and disciplines.

QUESTIONS OF TRADITION

Introduction

What Is Tradition When It Is Not 'Invented'? A Historiographical Introduction

MARK SALBER PHILLIPS

> Remember the days of old, consider the years of many generations: ask thy father, and he will show thee.
>
> Deuteronomy 32.7

> Even if you are Catholic, if you live in New York you're Jewish. If you live in Butte, Montana, you are going to be goyish even if you are Jewish.
>
> Lenny Bruce

In general usage the concept of tradition has the widest currency, yet in most academic disciplines it has come near to disappearing in serious use. A few studies do exist, but considering the importance of the idea, scholarly analyses of the history and present meaning of the concept of tradition remain remarkably few. 'If there had been other comprehensive books about tradition and traditions,' Edward Shils wrote in his 1981 book *Tradition*, 'this book would have been a better one.'[1] Two decades after the publication of Shils's book, the situation is not remarkably different.[2]

Much of the reason for this neglect is ideological. On both ends of the political spectrum, there has been a widespread assumption that anyone concerned with tradition would not simply be showing an interest in a conceptual problem but demonstrating a commitment to a particular politics in relationship to it. Of course, this confusion between the problem of tradition and the politics of traditionalism has not meant that we have simply ignored the issue of cultural transmission; but at a time when 'tradition' so often seems to be employed either as a vapid catchall or an ideological banner, it is not surprising that much of the discussion has flowed into newer and generally narrower channels. Instead of 'tradition' – a term possessing great historical depth – we have adopted a host of more specialized vocabularies that appear to be free of the stigma of traditionalism. 'Discourse,' 'canonicity,' 'memory,' 'diaspora,' 'hybridity,' 'the history of concepts'[3] – these and similar terms in use across a variety of disciplines have become our most recent tools for talking about tradition's domain. New vocabularies of this kind often bring a sharper sense of particular issues, but something is also lost when we scatter into separated inquiries, without a sense that all of these discussions share some common concerns. In fact, as a brief survey of the major views on tradition will show, it is striking how much each discussion has kept to itself, avoiding any reference to other ways of construing the central terms and problems.

In contemporary scholarship, there remains one particular usage that has been widely employed across a number of disciplines. This is the idea of 'invented tradition,' a term introduced by Eric Hobsbawm, Terence Ranger, and their collaborators in a well-known volume called *The Invention of Tradition* (1983). The popularity of this debunking usage seems only to confirm the apparent consensus that for scholarly purposes at least we need no longer (or perhaps *can* no longer) speak of tradition except in tones of irony. I want to reexamine this idea of 'invented tradition' (along with its related term 'memory') as the starting point for a brief sketch of a larger history of the concept – one that 'invented tradition' seems to both presuppose and preempt. This historiographical exercise is not meant to produce a new consensus on the meaning of tradition; the point, rather, is simply to provide a background to the particular studies that follow, each of which pursues its own engagement with the complex problem of cultural transmission.

Invented Traditions and *Lieux de mémoire*

Like any coinage that acquires quick popularity, the idea of 'invented tradition' is often loosely used, and most of those who have adopted it seem content to let the (notional) oxymoron do the work of definition. Even in Hobsbawm's original formulation, however, it is difficult to know clearly what is distinctive about the phenomena he and his collaborators drew together under this rubric:

> The term 'invented tradition' is used in a broad, but not imprecise sense.
> It includes both 'traditions' actually invented, constructed, and formally

instituted and those emerging in a less traceable manner within a brief
and dateable period – a matter of a few years perhaps – and establishing
themselves with great rapidity ... It is evident that not all of them are
equally permanent, but it is their appearance and establishment rather
than their chances of survival which are our primary concerns.[4]

Hobsbawm goes on to say that invented traditions are governed by
'overtly or tacitly accepted rules ... of a ritual or symbolic nature'
whose repetition implies continuity with the past. 'A striking example
is the deliberate choice of a Gothic style for the nineteenth century
rebuilding of the British parliament, and the equally deliberate decision after World War II to rebuild the parliamentary chamber on
exactly the same basic plan as before.'[5]

The rituals and symbols of modern public life constitute the core
of Hobsbawm's interests. *The Invention of Tradition* is essentially a
book about the public rituals of modern, secularized society, though
Hobsbawm admits that such 'inventions' have probably occurred in all
times and places. How, then, do we distinguish the 'instant formaliza-
tions' that constitute such modern 'inventions' from the 'genuine'
uninvented traditions that they mimic and replace? Hobsbawm's first
answer – rapid formation of new symbolic complexes, regardless of
their longevity – does not seem sufficient, since the formula seems as
applicable to the early history of the Dominicans or the Jesuits as to
Baden-Powell's Boy Scouts. We could, of course, simply agree that Sts
Dominic and Ignatius, along with Luther, Wesley, and General Booth,
all stand as magnificent examples of inventors of tradition, but then we
seem to be rapidly approaching the notion that most if not all traditions could be seen as invented, at least in their beginnings – a thought
that must surely be followed by the realization that any lasting tradition must be in a process of continual reinvention.

In practice, however, for Hobsbawm the division between invented
and uninvented traditions seems to rest on the idea that tradition must
be both unselfconscious and invariable. 'The object and characteristic
of "traditions," including invented ones, is invariance. The past, real or
invented, to which they refer imposes fixed (normally formalized)
practices, such as repetition.' In this way tradition is apparently distinguished from custom, which 'cannot afford to be invariant, because
even in 'traditional' societies life is not so.' It follows from the static
quality that Hobsbawm ascribes to tradition that innovation is essentially incompatible with the inflexible regime of tradition, even if what

is at stake is innovation in the *service* of tradition. Thus Hobsbawm remarks that movements for the defence or revival of traditions mark a break in continuity which signals that a tradition must be in the process of becoming an invented one. 'On the other hand the strength and adaptability of genuine traditions is not to be confused with the "invention of tradition." Where the old ways are alive, tradition need be neither revived nor invented.'[6]

This is either circular or plainly untrue. It goes without saying that where old ways are fully alive they do not need reviving, but modern history is full of moments in which cultural continuities were in the gravest doubt, and it is also full of spectacular successes for those who struggled, through processes that mixed revival and invention, to renew their languages and cultures.[7] A simple opposition between 'genuine' and 'invented' traditions is unworkable. It corresponds to nothing we know about the transmission of culture, either in the conditions of the modern West or elsewhere.

Hobsbawm's remarks about adaptability seem to contradict the idea that invariance is the identifying mark of tradition; they also reflect the assumption that to be genuine, tradition must be involuntary and unconscious – as though, for instance, two millennia of Christian traditions have been simply the deposit of unreflective custom. The result of this stress on the involuntary features of tradition is a hostility to the work of intellectuals, a stance that disallows some of the most interesting questions one might ask about the ways in which traditions are created and renewed.

Let me briefly sum up a few of the problems that seem to be raised by the idea of invented tradition. First, in the absence of any serious consideration of tradition as such, 'invented' traditionalisms of the sort that are the real subject of Hobsbawm's book inevitably become defining for the category of tradition as a whole. This blurring together of tradition as such with a (putatively) bogus traditionalism lends itself to a notion that tradition is necessarily static or reactionary, never adaptive, constructive, or creative.

Second, with respect to the specific processes of 'formalization' to which Hobsbawm dedicates his introduction, it is worth asking whether deliberately anti-traditional gestures should not also be seen as constituting 'inventions of tradition.' Martin Luther's doctrine of *sola scriptura*, to name a historical example of the greatest importance, was explicitly a radical attack on the authority of tradition, yet if we are going to use the language of 'invention,' who would qualify better than Luther? It seems important to recognize that traditions can be constituted or reconstituted on the basis of acts of rupture as well as of renewal – and Luther's Reformation consisted of both.

Third, it seems necessary to question the opposition of modernity and tradition which underlies so much discussion of tradition. Oscar Wilde's quip that the youthfulness of America is its oldest tradition has its analogue here. Though the Enlightenment is often taken to represent the attack of reason on tradition, Enlightenment rationalism can be seen as the oldest tradition of modernity. As Shils writes: 'The tradition of reason became a major contender against substantive traditionality for the suffrage of the human race.'[8] A similar view of modernity as tradition is advanced by the philosopher John Michael when he argues that in the face of contemporary heterogeneous societies, those 'traditions in the West best suited to negotiate heterogeneity are the traditions of a certain enlightened strain of modernity.'[9]

Fourth, the last two points bear on the idea that genuine tradition is somehow inarticulate, 'opaque to reason,'[10] the domain of ingrained custom, not conscious articulation. As already noted, this assumption leads to hostility towards the work of intellectuals in the field of tradition. When the presence of conscious articulators is taken as an indicator of the ideological artifice and mimicry that mark 'invented' traditions, the historian is discouraged from asking questions about how and when traditions move beyond the circumstances of their origins. If some traditions become so weak as to need self-conscious acts of resuscitation, others surely, begun by design, take root and flourish. The spread of the syncretistic pow wow movement among the Native peoples of North America testifies to this possibility, as does the brilliance of modern Hebrew literature – a spectacularly successful instance of cultural invention.[11]

If we rule out self-conscious intellectual articulation, we also obscure the many ways in which the activities of intellectuals themselves are both governed by and constitutive of traditions. Traditions of interpretation are certainly no less important a part of our subject than traditions governing other social practices; indeed, for many, the primary meaning of 'tradition' has always been the preservation and elaboration of a body of authoritative texts. But even when more modestly conceived, teaching is fundamental to the work of tradition: the very notion of *disciplina*, after all, is inseparable from the idea of 'handing on' or 'handing down,' which is the definition of tradition. In this light (as I will argue below) Thomas Kuhn's discussion of the role of paradigms in establishing and transmitting the essential features of scientific practice stands as perhaps the most influential discussion of tradition in recent times.

I cannot take leave of 'invented tradition' without noting its close relationship to the current vogue for 'memory,' a coinage introduced at the very same moment and intended to answer many of the same questions. As a collective project, Pierre Nora's *Les Lieux de mémoire* (1984) bears a number of resemblances to Hobsbawm's, and its central term ('sites of memory') functions in parallel fashion to address forms of attachment to the past within modern societies assumed to be purged of genuine traditionality. Our interest in 'sites of memory,' Nora argues, is a function of a particular historical moment in which we are conscious of a deep rupture with the past, leaving 'memory' to be artificially celebrated around specially selected social sites. Whether they be physical locations, shared images, or other forms of commonplace, these 'lieux de mémoire' allow contemporary cultures to invoke – but not genuinely to experience – continuity with the past. 'Even as traditional memory disappears, we feel obliged assiduously to collect remains, testimonies, documents, images, speeches, any visible sign of what has been.' The result, says Nora, is that we have sites of memory because the 'milieux de mémoire,' the genuine contexts in which memory was real and unquestioned, have disappeared.[12]

If both projects assume the antinomy of modernity and tradition, however, differences arise from their contrasting responses to the politics of disenchantment. 'Invented tradition' carries with it an implication of manipulation or imposition; it is a kind of false consciousness veiling exercises of power. 'Lieux de mémoire,' on the other hand, stands for a widely experienced dissociation from the past. Nor can this inauthenticity be remedied (as in Hobsbawm) by a bracing application of historical truth, since for Nora the unmasking impulse itself is largely to blame. Indeed, the historical self-consciousness of modern societies has played a crucial part in undercutting the possibility of genuine memory, leaving us only with the artifice of commemorated sites. Because it is a critical practice, history stands opposed to memory, which it seeks to replace or destroy. 'The remnants of experience still lived in the warmth of tradition, in the silence of custom, in the repetition of the ancestral, have been displaced under the pressure of a fundamentally historical sensibility.'[13]

Thus Nora takes the familiar dichotomy of modernity and tradition and imposes upon it the polarity of history and memory, making his-

torical study itself – especially in its modern, reflexive form – the powerful agent of our collective loss. He asks us to consider the difference
between 'real memory' (which he calls 'the secret of so-called primitive
or archaic societies') and history, which is the way in which 'our
hopelessly forgetful modern societies'[14] represent the past. History is
sceptical and – especially in the present moment of reflexivity – highly
self-conscious. Real memory, by contrast, is unselfconscious and per-
petually actual. It 'ceaselessly reinvents tradition' remaining (like
Hobsbawm's custom) 'in permanent evolution, open to the dialectic of
remembering and forgetting.'[15]

Eight years after initiating the collection, Nora offered a concluding
chapter that sheds more light on the relation of memory and tradition.
In this important retrospect, Nora wrestles with the fact that the idea of
'lieux de mémoire,' which he claims was 'forged as a tool for maintaining critical distance,' had itself become a central part of the vocabulary
of commemoration.[16] Curiously, the final chapter is written with an
ironic bite that in many ways is more reminiscent of Hobsbawm's
work than of the elegiac tones of his own Introduction. Reexamining
what he calls the passage from the historical to the remembered and
from the remembered to the commemorative, Nora now focuses
sharply on the disintegration of the nationalist assumptions of French
historiography. 'Owing largely to the work of the schools over time,
history, in its primary sense – essentially an expression of the nation,
just as the nation essentially expressed itself through history – became
the framework and matrix of our collective memory.' Even scientific
history, he writes, 'consisted in the rectification and enrichment of this
tradition of memory.' Although it was intended to be critical, 'it was in
fact only a deepening of that tradition.' The ultimate goal of historical
study was 'identification through filiation,' which Nora also calls 'verified memory.'[17]

Against the official tradition of the political nation, expressed in its
schooling and its state monuments, Nora marks the advent of a new
tide of commemoration. Memory marks the 'advent of historical consciousness of defunct traditions, the reconstitutive recovery of phenomena from which we are separated and which are most directly of
interest to those who think of themselves as the descendants and heirs
of such traditions.' 'Official history' could afford to ignore these traditions, 'because the "national group" was generally constructed by sti-
fling them or reducing them to silence, or because they did not emerge
as such into history. Now that such groups are being incorporated into

national history, however, they feel an urgent need to reconstruct their traditions with whatever means are available, from the most ad hoc to the most scientific, because for each group tradition is part of its identity.'[18]

Clearly this formulation of the problem represents a considerable shift, not only in tone but in conception, from the Introduction. In that first formulation the separation of history and memory was attributed to the working of an ironic consciousness – a consciousness, that is, belonging not simply to this group or that group, but to historical thought in general. The reflexivity of historical consciousness, he explained in a famous phrase, introduces an element of doubt, 'running a knife between the tree of memory and the bark of history.'[19] This sort of elegant Hegelianism is absent from the final chapter, replaced by a much franker politics that recognizes what was accomplished when centrist histories were imposed while others were 'stifled' or 'silenced.' From this perspective the failure of 'official history' to maintain its hold means that those who were formerly excluded are now in a position to insist on finding their own likeness in the past that is represented to them. As a man of the older dispensation, Nora, of course, has no enthusiasm for this version of 'verified memory,' and he assumes that the traditions of those who were formerly excluded must have lapsed into inauthenticity. Even so, he does not deny the urgency these groups feel about connecting themselves to their past or that there is material at hand for its reconstruction. Tradition, it seems, once dismissed from the schoolrooms of the French nation, has returned by the back door.

Invented tradition and memory are just the most recent chapters in a long history of conceptualizations of the problem of tradition. It is certainly beyond the scope of the present Introduction to attempt anything like a genuine history of this central idea, but it may be helpful to sketch a few of its important elements. An outline of this sort may help us to see some relationships between a variety of terms that make up the vocabulary of tradition and perhaps in this way will lead to a more historically self-conscious understanding.

Tradition in Jewish and Christian Contexts

Secular-minded theorists seldom take note of the long and rich history of discussions of tradition in both Jewish and Christian religious thought.[20] Nonetheless, most of our varied understandings were first adumbrated in a religious context. In rabbinic Judaism, the idea of tradition took the form of a body of orally transmitted truths – the Oral Torah – that originated with Moses in Sinai and was passed down from generation to generation. This knowledge was codified in the Mishnah, which is the core of Talmud.[21] (This idea of a second revelation was revived by Renaissance neo-Platonists like Pico, who subscribed to the idea of an elite and secret 'perennial philosophy.') The Jewish idea of tradition also takes the form of a chain of interpretation. This is the implication of the important practice of *midrash*, a kind of commentary by which inspired texts are reread to make the content more explicit and more relevant to particular circumstances in the present.

In the earliest Christian usages, *traditio* refers to a 'handing on,' the delivery of God's truth to His people through the apostles. In time, though, tradition came to stand for the continuity of orthodoxy in the Church. Thus tradition and scripture together give access to the whole truth of divine revelation. 'What [the apostles] spoke in brief form,' wrote Gregory the Great, '[the orthodox theologians of the church] expanded to greater length ... by gathering together the statements of many who had gone before and expanding these more profoundly in what they added to them.'[22] The relationship of scripture and tradition, however, has never been easy to fix, and church historians have usefully distinguished two views of tradition, which came into relief in the late Middle Ages and the Reformation. The more conservative view saw tradition simply as the body of authoritative interpretation of Scripture. But others gave a wider meaning to tradition and argued that there existed, to quote Jaroslav Pelikan, 'a second channel of apostolic revelation through which parts of the original message had been handed down apart from Scripture.'[23]

Luther's doctrine of *sola scriptura* made tradition a central issue for the Reformation. Luther stripped away many traditions he considered to be without scriptural basis, but he also condemned the Anabaptists as dangerous individualists for their radical application of his anti-traditional stance. On the other side of the controversy, the Catholic position as defined at Trent stopped short of flatly declaring the parallelism of Scripture and tradition, but decreed that both were to be accepted with an equal feeling of respect.[24] Nor did the issues highlighted by the Reformation disappear in later centuries. For the followers of reform, the question of what was to guide the reading of Scripture gave rise to a long tradition of Protestant hermeneutics, while on the Catholic side it is hardly an accident that the most important rethinking of the issue came from John Henry Newman, a celebrated convert from Anglican Protestantism to the Roman Church.

Newman's *Essay on the Development of Christian Doctrine* (1845; rev. 1878) propounds a view of the 'development of doctrine' as a way of coming to terms with the obvious changes in Christian observance since the times of the primitive Church. Polemically his aim is to ward off Protestant critics who (like Newman himself in an earlier stage) would exploit this history to undermine the claim of Rome to apostolic authority. Against this view, Newman urges that Christians need to understand the necessary development of ideas if they are to make sense of the evidence of eighteen centuries of their history.

As Newman sees it, variation and development are part of any great idea, and he eloquently describes the process by which ideas grow through contestation and assimilation. 'The multitude of opinions formed concerning it in these respects and many others will be collected, compared, sorted, sifted, selected, rejected, gradually attached to it, separated from it, in the minds of individuals and of the community. It will ... introduce itself into the framework and details of social life, changing public opinion, and strengthening or undermining the foundations of established order.' Over time, the idea will have grown into an ethical code, a system of government, or a theology, but all this, for Newman, will still be nothing more than the exfoliation of the original idea, 'being in substance what that idea meant from the first, its complete image as seen in a combination of diversified aspects, with the suggestions and corrections of many minds, and the illustration of many experiences.'[25]

For Newman, development is no less a feature of the inspired truths of Christianity than of other systems of thought. He argued that 'from the structure of the human mind, time is necessary for the full comprehension and perfection of great ideas; and that the highest and most wonderful truths, though communicated to a world once for all by inspired teachers, could not be comprehended all at once by the recipients, but, as being received and transmitted by minds not inspired and through media which were human, have required only the longer time and deeper thought for their full elucidation.'[26] In making the case for development, however, he also had to ward off the possibility that later doctrines might be taken as corruptions of earlier truths. Thus the problem of authentic continuity of doctrine was all important to his argument. To answer this challenge, Newman offers seven 'notes' ('tests' in the earlier editions) by which continuity might be judged and discriminated from 'corruption.' These have been conveniently summarized as follows: '1. Preservation of the original type: in effect, preserving the quality of the original impact of some new thing. 2. Continuity of known principles. 3. Power to assimilate alien matter to the original idea. 4. Logical connectedness. 5. Being anticipated early in a partial way here and there. 6. A conserving attitude to the past: taking steps to preserve an old idea in a new form. 7. Chronic vigour: i.e., lasting in a healthy state for a long time.'[27]

One of the ideas that Newman was anxious to show had enjoyed a continuous presence in Christian tradition was that of papal authority. 'If Christianity is both social and dogmatic,' he wrote, 'and intended for all ages, it must humanly speaking have an infallible expounder. Else you will secure unity of form at the loss of unity of doctrine [i.e., the Church of England], or unity of doctrine at the loss of unity of form'.[28] Newman's view that the unity of tradition implies (and is superintended by) authority is a reminder that the prescriptiveness of tradition, however open to revision or elaboration it may be, always carries some implication of *authority*. In this regard it is interesting to compare Newman's views with those of a commentator who emerges from a very different religious tradition, one in which the policing of tradition by an 'infallible expounder' had long ceased to be possible. In Gershom Scholem's explorations of the history and theology of Kabbalah, we find a notion of tradition in which only the texts finally have authority, and tradition, though utterly central, is remarkably free. Indeed, though it may seem oxymoronic, Scholem's theology has been called 'anarchistic.'[29]

Scholem presents the spontaneity and multiplicity of interpretation as the inseparable companion to the absoluteness of revelation. 'In Judaism, tradition becomes the reflective impulse that intervenes between the absoluteness of the divine word – revelation – and its receiver. Tradition thus raises a question about the possibility of immediacy in man's relationship to the divine, even though it has been incorporated in revelation ... Can the divine word confront us without mediation? ... does the divine word rather not require just such mediation by tradition in order to be apprehensible and therefore fulfillable?' For rabbinic Judaism, Scholem answers, the answer is that 'every religious experience after revelation is a mediated one.'[30]

The consequence of this position, both historically in terms of the development of rabbinic Judaism and philosophically in terms of

Scholem's own epistemology, is to figure the search for truth in the mode of commentary. 'Not system but *commentary* is the legitimate form through which truth is approached.'[31] And yet for Scholem, although he is fully aware of the danger, it does not follow that the result will be a closed, repetitive, and inward-looking spirit. On the contrary, speaking for the Kabbalistic tradition which he both explicates and rejuvenates in his work, he argues that the absoluteness of Revelation is also the basis for its infinite interpretability. The result is an uncontrollable pluralism of interpretation that Scholem describes as constituting 'the authority of commentary over author.'[32]

'Precisely because tradition perceives, receives, and unfolds that which lives in the word,' Scholem writes, 'it is the force within which contradictions and tensions are not destructive but rather stimulating and creative.'[33] As such statements indicate, every definition of tradition is simultaneously a vision of community – a setting of limits, larger or smaller, on the circle of those who share its memory or its truth. Thus if in theological terms Scholem's optimistic and anarchic vision of tradition depends on the absoluteness of Revelation, in human terms it rests on a shared commitment to the prescribed sources of that tradition. 'For those who stand within the tradition it is easy to see the organic unity of these contradictions, precisely because it presents a dialectic relationship in which the word of revelation is developed. Without contradictions it would not perform this function.'[34]

Tradition Secularized

Theological understandings of tradition have been relatively well discussed, if only among historians of religion and generally within the boundaries of particular religious traditions. With regard to secular understandings, on the other hand, the customary opposition of (inertial) tradition and (dynamic) modernity has left the impression that modernity alone required explanation. Surprisingly little has been said about the historical process by which nonreligious usages emerged that gave tradition an important place in secular understandings of politics and culture. It seems evident, however, that the idea of tradition was redirected towards new uses in the latter part of the eighteenth century and first part of the nineteenth. The outcome was that tradition became articulated as a self-conscious posture towards history and politics, forming the basis for programs of both conservatism and reform. Building on this ground, a theory of tradition subsequently became an essential component of classical social theory as well as of some aspects of literary modernism.

Up to the end of the eighteenth century, theological arguments continued to define the primary meaning of the term, but the word was also used in a secular context to mean knowledge handed down by oral or folk transmission. This contrast to the exactness of the written record meant that tradition carried the sense of evidence that is generally weak or unreliable. Only occasionally did an interest in folkways bring a more positive valuation, so that oral transmission might also be seen as preserving knowledge that, different though it was from written testimony, possessed an authenticity of its own.

The philosophical inquirers of the Enlightenment, with their interest in the manners of 'rude nations,' often warned against the unreliability of national legends. 'Conjectures and opinions formed at a distance,' wrote Adam Ferguson, have little authority. Even where 'at first they contained some semblance of truth, they still vary with the imagination of those by whom they are transmitted, and in every generation receive a different form. They are made to bear the stamp of the times through which they have passed in the form of tradition, not of the ages to which their pretended descriptions relate.'[35] Ferguson's primary emphasis is clearly on the unreliability of transmission, but his statement also carries the core of the notion that 'traditionary' narratives might testify to another kind of truth. Similarly, David Hume cautioned against speculative writers who 'are apt to push their researches beyond the period, in which literary monuments are framed or preserved; without reflecting, that the history of past events is immediately lost or disfigured, when intrusted to memory and oral tradition.' But (though ever the sceptic in matters of religion) he comes closer to the enlarged, modern meaning of tradition when he writes of the innovations of the Civil War period: 'Every man had adjusted a system of religion, which, being derived from no traditional authority, was peculiar to himself.'[36]

In Anglo-American writing, Burke is generally taken as an originating figure who gave birth to a new concept of tradition. Such a judgment probably gives too much credit to the self-image of the age as a time of historical rupture. The central conceptions here derive from the moral sciences of the Scottish Enlightenment, which made custom and usage seem the foundation of historical and political knowledge.[37] Hume, Smith, Millar, and others undermined the Machiavellian myth of the great legislator, fostering instead a belief that historical change is shaped by the indirect consequences of social as well as political action. Nonetheless, Burke was clearly a crucial figure in the coalescence of an essentially secular vision of tradition.

Burke himself, it is important to note, did not explicitly use the term, yet he gave the idea vivid expression as a key weapon in the struggle against revolutionary rationalism and universalism. It was the arrogance of the revolutionaries, he charged, to treat society as a *tabula rasa* on which they were free to write at will. His own idea of society was, by deliberate contrast, resolutely local, and he frankly celebrated the value of customary 'prejudice,' which Burke considered the deposit of history and experience. The consequence was a vision of society in which the present generation were seen as custodians of a legacy – a partnership between the living, the dead, and those yet to be born.

In Burke, the processual sense of tradition derived from the Scottish Enlightenment incorporated a powerful element of counterrevolutionary traditionalism, with its nostalgia for the days when Europe was governed by the idea of the Church and the idea of the gentleman. Burke, in fact, was more concerned to urge us to revere what is traditional than to define tradition as such. Mortmain, entail, natural growth, partnership, contract, the succession of generations – any of these ways of figuring continuity might have been made the basis for a description of the way traditions function, but mixed together in the urgency of his arguments, the rapid play of metaphor creates the sense of something largely resistant to definition, yet pervasively present in our world. The consequence is that tradition is best understood not as a thing in itself, but as a manner of experiencing the world. Like sympathy or sublimity, it is a sentimental construction, and, as such, it is far from being limited to the institutions of law or government. It enters, rather, into the whole texture of social life, and is best expressed in the workings of manners and opinions, which for Burke as for his Scottish contemporaries constituted the most fundamental level of historical experience. Among Burke's many followers, both conservative and progressive, tradition would become a way of giving a name and, especially, an authority to this new conception of mediated, half-conscious change.

It is crucial, of course, that this complex of ideas began to take shape at a time when national and ideological conflict brought questions of loyalty and identity to the forefront. In this context, the emerging idea of tradition brought a reassuring emphasis on the fundamental stability of the collective experience over long periods of time. Not only was change gradual, it was also mediated by persistent social habits that lay well beneath the surface of ordinary politics and almost beyond the reach of conscious interference. Like the idea of public opinion, which was its presentist and liberal-minded counterpart, tradition could serve as an integrative framework for programs of political action as well as analysis; it not only connected a vision of the past to a putatively shared present, but it also assimilated very disparate forms of experience under the common banner of national spirit.

Tradition and Modernity

In the construction of nineteenth-century European social theory and in much of the sociological tradition deriving from it, tradition comes into prominence as a foil to the idea of modernity. In this new context, which includes Marxist sociologies as well as liberal ones, tradition comes to be seen as a point of origin, rather than a process. Accordingly, traditional customs and attachments may be eroded or attenuated to make way for modernity, or they may prove surprisingly resistant to the incursions of modern political or economic practices. But since tradition matters primarily for its contrastive value, it is always modernity, not traditionality, that requires specific analysis. Even in a thinker of the stature of Max Weber, traditionality functions essentially as a residual category.[38]

Thus in Weber's theory of action, rational action is defined by the actor's weighing up of means and ends, his consciousness of alternative means, his sense of the relative importance of different ends. Traditional action, on the other hand, is defined as oriented 'through the habituation of long practice.' Strictly traditional behaviour, he goes on to say, 'lies very close to the borderline of what can justifiably be called meaningfully oriented action, and indeed often on the other side. For it is very often a matter of almost automatic reaction to habitual stimuli which guide behaviour in a course which has been repeatedly followed.'[39] Similarly, in his analysis of authority, Weber defines rational-legal authority as a form of domination resting on the belief that rules are enacted by due process and based on fundamental legal precepts. In contrast, traditional authority exists when legitimacy is 'believed in on the basis of the sanctity of the order and the attendant powers of control as they have been handed down from the past, "have always existed." The person or persons exercising authority are designated according to traditionally transmitted rules. The object of obedience is the personal authority of the individual, which he enjoys by virtue of his traditional status.' With the same circularity of definition, he goes on to say that under a system of traditional authority, the commands of the ruler are legitimized 'partly in terms of traditions which themselves directly determine the content of the comment and the objects and extent of authority,' and in part on the chief's free personal decision 'in that tradition leaves a certain sphere open for this.'[40]

Even some of Weber's most ardent disciples have had to acknowledge the vagueness and generality of his concept of tradition, and it is clear that his real effort is drawn to defining the more dynamic features of social action, such as charismatic and rational-legal authority.[41] This same pattern of attention is clearly present in the large literature on modernization, in which 'tradition' is the foil to a theory of development and 'traditional society' functions as a polite replacement for an older evolutionist vocabulary laden with racial overtones. For this and other reasons, modernization theory came under severe attack in the 1970s.[42] Our habit of pitting modernity against tradition is so ingrained however, that the rejection of 'modernization theory' has also meant the near disappearance of 'tradition' from the vocabulary of the human sciences, except in the ironic usage with which I began. Only among those influenced by hermeneutics has a different, more positive view of tradition been pursued.

Dialogues with Tradition: Gadamer

Much of the sociological and anthropological discussion of tradition has been carried on as though tradition primarily concerned the unselfconscious continuance of social institutions and practices, often in nonliterate societies. In contrast, philosophers and literary theorists engaged with questions of hermeneutics think of tradition primarily in terms of traditions of interpretation in religion, philosophy, or literature. Textual readings, rather than social customs, provide the model for their theory of understanding. Indeed, for the leading hermeneutical philosopher of recent times, Hans-Georg Gadamer, the 'linguisticality of understanding' means that 'the essence of tradition is to exist in the medium of language.'[43]

For Gadamer, traditions of interpretation are not simply things for the hermeneuticist to study; rather, tradition names an essential condition that makes understanding possible. Gadamer (drawing upon

Heidegger) argues that knowledge depends upon a 'fore-structure of understanding' and is governed by the anticipation of completion. This is the essence of the process that metaphorically is described as the hermeneutic circle:

> The circle, then, is not formal in nature. It is neither subjective nor objective, but describes understanding as the interplay of the movement of tradition and the movement of the interpreter. The anticipation of meaning that governs our understanding of a text is not an act of subjectivity, but proceeds from the commonality that binds us to the tradition. But this commonality is constantly being formed in our relation to tradition. Tradition is not simply a permanent precondition; rather, we produce it ourselves inasmuch as we understand, participate in the evolution of tradition, and hence further determine it ourselves.[44]

True to his own vision of tradition, Gadamer presents himself as both an inheritor and a critic of earlier hermeneutical writings. Against Dilthey, in particular, he insists that nineteenth-century hermeneutics mistook its task by thinking of the 'circle' as a methodological instrument. In contrast, his own view amounts to seeing the circle as 'an element of the ontological structure of understanding.'[45] He is also critical of the assumption, which he finds in both Enlightenment and Romantic thought, that sets tradition and reason in a necessary opposition. Instead, he seeks a rehabilitation of the idea of 'prejudice,' which like tradition itself becomes a prime way of making reference to the historicity of understanding. To do justice to man's 'finite, historical mode of being,' Gadamer asserts, it is necessary to acknowledge that there are legitimate prejudices. Thus 'a truly historical hermeneutics' would ask 'what is the ground of the legitimacy of prejudices?'[46] Since Gadamer does not seem to be arguing that all prejudices are equally legitimate, however, the historian might want to press the philosopher for more help with this task. What makes some prejudices legitimate, we might ask, and therefore an essential object for historical questioning?

For Gadamer, an important task of hermeneutics is to reflect on the modes of understanding included in the social sciences. Once we are freed from the Enlightenment assumption of the absolute opposition of reason and tradition (or prejudice), we can understand the human sciences themselves as operating within the circle of tradition. Historical research does not stand 'as in an absolute antithesis to the way in which we as historical beings relate to the past.' Rather, we are always situated within traditions, and for this reason, 'we do not conceive of what tradition says as something other, something alien.'[47] This may seem to fly in the face of the fact that so much of the history of the human sciences has involved a deliberate distancing from received traditions. But for Gadamer, the inescapableness of tradition means that the human sciences can never be reduced to objective, methodological rules. The refined historical consciousness of modern Europe should not think of itself as having escaped the conditions that have always constituted the human relationship to the past.[48] Even in the most 'objective' historical research, 'the real fulfilment of the historical task is to determine anew the significance of what is examined'[49] – a truth that perhaps does not do away with the need to speak more closely to the relationship between the forms of understanding cultivated by historical investigation and the broad consciousness of historicity that has become a mark of modern life.

In responding to Gadamer's theory of tradition, it may be useful to distinguish two levels of discussion. On the one hand, he addresses the idea of tradition as a necessary structure of understanding and – in reaction to Dilthey's methodologism – he considers this a matter having to do in the broadest possible sense with our mode of being in the world. On the other hand, he also asserts that traditions always have reference to specific contents, since traditions are always situated in the communality of experience and belief of actual cultures. This more limited and more conventional meaning of tradition is open to an obvious charge, namely that it conceals from itself an authoritarian and conservative politics that is implicit in its definition of community. In short, the question of 'how wide the definition of the we'[50] is always crucial to the politics of tradition.

Returning to the first, more general, level of discussion, it is clear that Gadamer's view of tradition draws considerable strength from his deep concern for language as the essential human attribute that defines our way of experiencing the world.[51] In this commitment, Gadamer joins forces with a widespread movement in the human sciences that takes language as the defining feature of human experience. The 'linguistic turn' has meant that a good deal of social theory has addressed itself to the communicative functions of language and hence to the relations between the individual speaker and the language community. Viewed in this light, language is not an instrument possessed by an individual subject, but an already-existing, intersubjective 'web' which the individual acquires by growing up into a speech community. But of course, though language precedes the individual speaker, it is also changed by the use speakers give to it, just as the speech community is itself constituted by language.

For thinking about tradition, this view of language is enormously suggestive. (One has only to contrast it with Burke's vocabulary of inheritance or nineteenth-century talk of 'national spirit' to feel its appropriateness.) It is striking, indeed, that we can take many theoretical descriptions of the power and importance of language and mentally substitute the idea of tradition. Charles Taylor, for example, writes that 'language is fashioned and grows not principally in monologue, but in dialogue, or better, in the life of the speech community ... The language I speak, the web which I can never fully dominate and oversee, can never be just *my* language, it is always largely *our* language.'[52] For Taylor, language is 'a pattern of activity by which we express/realize a certain way of being in the world, that of reflective awareness, but a pattern which can only be deployed against a background which we can never fully dominate, and yet a background that we are never fully dominated by, because we are constantly reshaping it.[53] In the same vein, Gadamer himself writes, 'we are always already biased in our thinking and knowing by our linguistic interpretation of the world. To grow into this linguistic interpretation means to grow up in the world. To this extent, language is the real mark of our finitude. It is always out beyond us.'[54]

'Language' and 'tradition' are not, of course, simply interchangeable concepts, but it does seem evident that for our times language provides the best setting for thinking about tradition. Certainly, the 'web' of language gives us (always there is an 'us') something more compelling than the sacred hermeneutic of Luther, the contract across generations of Burke, or the false consciousness of Hobsbawm. And yet at this point, it may also seem as if we have gone from one extreme to the other: from the reductive idea of 'invented tradition' that is unusable because it trivializes its subject to a philosophical expansion that may in the end be equally unusable because it swallows the whole world. If tradition is generalized to this degree, becoming something embedded in language and present in every hermeneutic act, it becomes increasingly difficult to assign it any specific meaning not already present in the idea of interpretation or communication. Certainly, historians will want to ask themselves how such an idea of tradition can be made operative in any specific way.

Gadamer is not very helpful at this level of questioning. On the contrary, his universalization of hermeneutics specifically aims to overcome the close connection between hermeneutics and the methods of historical investigation that was the fundamental theme of Dilthey's work. Insofar as Gadamer's 'ontologization' frees us from the individualism and mentalism of Dilthey's 'Verstehen,' it will help us towards a deeper investigation of history. But it has to be admitted that the move to overcome method also makes Gadamer's understanding of tradition more remote from the ordinary concerns of the human sciences in their encounters with specific histories.

Tradition and Innovation in the History of Science

The prestige of the natural sciences has long meant that science serves as the standard of comparison in discussions of the history and sociology of knowledge. Perhaps it is not surprising, then, that the most widely influential theory of the transmission of knowledge of recent years comes from a historian of science. What is more remarkable, perhaps, is that Thomas Kuhn's paradigm theory has not been recognized as an important contribution to the literature on tradition[55] – a testimony to the fact that (even in the face of Kuhn's wide influence) the sciences continue to stand as the archetypes of anti-traditional modes of inquiry.

Kuhn's *Structures of Scientific Revolutions* (1962) is so well known that its proposals need little rehearsing here. From the point of view of an interest in the vocabulary of tradition, however, it is instructive to look to a slightly earlier publication in which Kuhn first announced his idea of paradigms. 'The Essential Tension: Tradition and Innovation in Scientific Research' (1959) was a key essay in the development of Kuhn's theories, and Kuhn later signalled the significance of the piece by reusing the title for his collected papers, which (modifying the subtitle) he called *The Essential Tension: Selected Studies in Tradition and Change*. But 'Essential Tension' proved to be a key moment not only because it introduced the fertile concept of paradigms, but also because in retrospect this moment of initiation also seemed to retain a clarity of definition that was later lost. Looking back, Kuhn noted:

The concept of paradigms proved to be the missing element I required in order to write the book, and a first full draft was prepared between the summer of 1959 and the end of 1960. Unfortunately, in that process, paradigms took on a life of their own, largely displacing the previous talk of consensus. Having begun simply as exemplary problem solutions, they expanded their empire to include, first, the classic books in which these accepted examples initially appeared and, finally, the entire global set of commitments shared by the members of a particular scientific community.[56]

In subsequent writings, Kuhn did his best to return 'paradigm' to this original meaning of 'exemplary problem solutions,' while finding new terms for the 'global set of commitments,' or what he calls here the 'previous talk of consensus.' The confusion arose, he confessed, because 'paradigm' should only have been used to refer to one key element of the larger 'disciplinary matrix,' not to all its elements at once. Having narrowed and clarified the definition of paradigms in this way, he continued to insist on their cognitive importance. The conventional emphasis on scientific theory and theory-derived rules, Kuhn argued, falsely represents the ways in which scientific education works. 'Acquiring an arsenal of exemplars, just as much as learning symbolic generalizations, is integral to the process by which a student gains access to the cognitive achievements of his disciplinary group.'[57] Adopting Michael Polanyi's idea of 'tacit knowledge,' Kuhn writes that the scientist learns 'by doing science rather than by acquiring rules for doing it.'[58]

As this restatement of the importance of paradigms indicates, questions of education and authority – key elements in a theory of tradition – were always an important part of Kuhn's investigations. Here again the essay on 'The Essential Tension' is particularly instructive. Kuhn's point of departure is his desire to question the widespread view that science progresses simply through the cultivation of habits of 'flexibility and open mindedness.' Against this facile celebration of creativity in science, Kuhn insisted on the deep importance of commitment to tradition; 'only investigations rooted in the contemporary scientific tradition are likely to break that tradition and give rise to a new one. That is why I speak of an "essential tension" implicit in scientific research.'[59] Very often, Kuhn continues, the scientist must 'simultaneously display the characteristics of the traditionalist and of the iconoclast.' This might be an implausible combination to ask for in a single individual, but Kuhn concludes that the scientific community as a whole must foster both.

New Vocabularies and the Broad Scope of Tradition

Kuhn's theorization of the history of science seems a good place to bring this brief survey to a close. This is certainly not because discussions of cultural transmission still rest where Kuhn left them. On the contrary, recent years have created a wealth of new vocabularies to deal with particular features of the broader problem, and many of these terms – *invented tradition, memory, hybridity, canonicity, diaspora* – have quickly established themselves in current use. To follow out these many branches of discussion would, however, be far more than this Introduction could accomplish and is a task best left to the more theoretical portions of the essays that follow. But there is another reason for closing at this juncture, since in a number of important ways Kuhn's theory and its reception point to a key issue motivating this survey, namely the problems that arise when issues of cultural transmission are pursued in the absence of a central and vigorous discussion of tradition.

I have been arguing that Kuhn was in fact the most influential recent theorist of tradition but has not been recognized as such. In this context, it seems plausible to suggest that the inflation of the term 'paradigm' that Kuhn came to regret might have been avoided if his work had been both conceived and received as a contribution to a broader project concerned with transmission of tradition. Reciprocally, those in other fields who rushed to adopt the apparently novel idea of paradigms (invariably, as Kuhn complains, in the looser, global meaning that he later sought to retract) might have considered more carefully had Kuhn settled earlier on the less seductive term 'disciplinary matrix' – one not far removed, it should be said, from the already familiar idea of 'disciplinary tradition.'

Despite his powerful interest in explicating the process of 'tradition and innovation,' Kuhn did not, of course, draw upon other bodies of scholarship concerned with parallel issues of transmission. (A brief reference to Polanyi gives the only hint of this possibility.)[60] But Kuhn is hardly alone in carrying on his project in essential isolation from other, parallel literatures. Thus Shils's attempt at a comprehensive analysis of tradition contains no reference that I can find to Kuhn, to Gadamer, or to Scholem. On another flank, Alasdair MacIntyre seems to be alone in recognizing the importance of Newman, while not a single one of the names just mentioned finds its way into the index of *The Invention of Tradition.*

There is no saying, of course, what the enlarged conversation about tradition might look like and where it might evolve. Even so, it seems reasonable to suppose that one effect will be to dissolve the simple binary of tradition and modernity which for so long has distracted those who have tried to come to grips with this concept and which still underwrites the presumed ironies of 'invented tradition.' Once this false opposition is set aside and the problem of tradition ceases to be defined as a resistance to modernity, tradition becomes again a means of raising essential questions about the ways in which we pass on the life of cultures – questions that necessarily include issues of authority as well as invention, practice as well as interpretation. In this enlarged framework, it should become possible to encourage hitherto separate discussions to speak more closely to each other: to appreciate with Kuhn the traditionalism of science and with Scholem the inventiveness of commentary, to grasp the place of tacitness in the practices of the laboratory as well as in the textures of politics, or to recognize a power of tradition not only in works of art or religion, but in the ways everyday understanding is shaped by the community of language.

NOTES

1 Shils, *Tradition* (Chicago, 1981), vii. A simple keyword search in my university's library (a collection of moderate size) produced something over 5000 volumes with 'tradition' in the title. Even a cursory look at the results, however, would be enough to indicate that most usage is as empty as it is ubiquitous. 'Tradition and innovation,' 'tradition and change,' 'tradition and modernity' – titles of this sort can be found by the hundreds, all too often providing a rationale for bundling together loose collections of miscellaneous essays.

2 One successor to Shils is David Gross, *The Past in Ruins: Tradition and the Critique of Modernity* (Amherst, MA, 1992). Gross's work was the subject of a symposium in *Telos*, 94 (1993–4).

3 I note, for instance, that in Lentricchia and McLaughlin's important handbook of recent literary theory, there are substantial articles on a variety of topics such as 'Culture' and 'Canon,' but 'tradition' does not warrant even an index entry. See *Critical Terms for Literary Study,* ed. Frank Lentricchia and Thomas McLaughlin (Chicago, 1990; 2nd ed. 1995).

4 Hobsbawm, 'Introduction: Inventing Traditions,' in E. Hobsbawm and T. Ranger, eds, *Invention of Tradition* (Cambridge, 1983), 1.

5 Ibid., 1–2.

6 Ibid., 8.

7 The first two essays in Hobsbawm's book, dealing with parallel periods of breakdown and renewal of tradition in Scotland and Wales, illustrate this problem and some of the ways in which a more flexible understanding of tradition can help to avoid it. In the first, Hugh Trevor-Roper gleefully debunks the pseudo-traditionalism of late eighteenth- and early nineteenth-century Highland myths promoted by men like Walter Scott. The result is an entertaining historical romp, yet in truth the essay adds very little to our understanding of a society that, as Scott himself famously said, had undergone a transformation so rapid 'as to render the present people of Scotland a class of beings as different from their grandfathers as the existing English are from those of Queen Elizabeth's time.' *Waverley: or 'Tis Sixty Years Since* (London, 1892), 447. On the other hand, Prys Morgan's parallel essay on 'The Hunt for the Welsh Past in the Romantic Period,' treats the dilemmas of Welsh culture broadly and with sympathy. Though Druidical 'revivals' and other myths of Welsh life offer abundant material for debunking, Morgan stresses the generally successful adaptation of institutions like the *eisteddfod* to modern purposes.

8 Shils, *Tradition*, 23.

9 John Michael, 'Tradition and the Critical Talent,' *Telos*, 94 (1993–4): 58.

10 The phrase is John Michael's, who while endorsing the idea of modernity as a specific tradition of some groups in the West, nonetheless holds to the view of tradition as inarticulate or inarticulable.

11 See Robert Alter, *Hebrew and Modernity* (Indianapolis, 1994).

12 Pierre Nora, 'Between Memory and History: Les lieux de Mémoire,' *Representations* 26 (1989): 13. I quote by preference from the first, more poetic, translation of Nora's program. Two further versions have appeared: *Realms of Memory; Rethinking the French Past*, 3 vols., ed. L. Kritzman and tr. A Goldhammer (New York, 1996), and *Rethinking France*, ed. D. Jordan and tr. M. Trouille (Chicago, 2001).

13 Nora, 'Between Memory and History,' 7.

14 Ibid., 8.

15 Ibid.

16 Nora, *Realms of Memory*, 3: 609.

17 Ibid., 3: 626.

18 Ibid.

19 'Between Memory and History,' 10.

20 Note for example the absence of the religious understanding of tradition in Raymond Williams's entry in *Keywords*. More surprising, however, is the

relative neglect of theological positions by Edward Shils, an erudite scholar with a deep interest in religious traditions.

21 See Jacob Neusner, *The Oral Tradition in Judaism: The Case of the Mishnah* (New York, 1987).

22 Quoted in Jaroslav Pelikan, *The Christian Tradition: A History of the Development of Doctrine*, 4 vols (Chicago, 1971), 1: 337.

23 Ibid., 4: 121.

24 On the history of tradition in religious thought, see Yves Congar, *Tradition and Traditions*, tr. M. Naseby and T. Rainborough (London, 1966); Jaroslav Pelikan, *The Vindication of Tradition* (New Haven, 1984), as well as his *Christian Tradition*, cited above. For a good summary of Reformation doctrines, see Alaister E. McGrath, *Reformation Thought* (Oxford, 1988); for the Tridentine period, see Congar, *Tradition*, 169–76.

25 *Essay on the Development of Christian Doctrine*, ed. C.F. Harrold (London, 1949), 35. On Newman, in addition to Congar, see Aidan Nichols, *From Newman to Congar: The Idea of Doctrinal Development from the Victorians to the Second Vatican Council* (Edinburgh, 1990), and Nicholas Lash, *Newman on Development: The Search for an Explanation in History* (London, 1975). Among modern philosophers interested in tradition, MacIntyre is explicit about his debt to Newman, whom he calls 'a far more important theorist of tradition' than Burke, and rightly points to the neglect of Newman by secularist thinkers. See *Whose Justice, Which Rationality* (Notre Dame, 1988), 353.

26 Newman, *Essay*, 28.

27 See Nichols, *Newman*, 51; Newman's own briefest summary precedes the enumeration of the seven notes: 'There is no corruption if it retains one and the same type, the same principles, the same organization; if its beginnings anticipate its subsequent phases, and its later phenomena protect and subserve its earlier; if it has a power of assimilation and revival, and a vigorous action from the first to last.' *Essay*, 159.

28 Newman, *Essay*, 83.

29 See David Biale, *Gershom Scholem: Kabbalah and Counter History*, 2nd ed. (Cambridge, MA, 1982), 94.

30 Scholem, 'Revelation and Tradition,' in *The Messianic Idea in Judaism and other Essays* (New York, 1971), 292.

31 Ibid., 289.

32 Ibid., 291.

33 Ibid., 297.

34 Ibid.

35 Adam Ferguson, *Essay on the History of Civil Society* (Edinburgh, 1966), 76.

36 Hume, *History of England*, 6 vols (Indianapolis, 1983 [1778]), 1: 3, and 6: 3.

37 Though I am far from discounting the importance of the common law tradition, I am uneasy with John Pocock's idea of 'the common law mind.' See
Politics, Language, and Time: Essays in Political Thought and History, rev. ed.
(Chicago, 1989). In my view, the Enlightenment's critique of politics is both
more proximate and more fundamental to Burke's thought. I have explored
these issues, and their implications for the construction of historical narrative, in *Society and Sentiment: Genres of Historical Writing in Britain, 1740–
1820* (Princeton, 2000).

38 Shils protests that this is not true, and in justification he points to Weber's
extensive knowledge of the non-European world. But the real question concerns the status of Weber's conceptual categories, not the extent of his erudition. See Shils, *Tradition,* 293.

39 Weber, *Theory of Social and Economic Organization,* ed. T. Parsons (New York,
1947), 115–16.

40 Ibid., 341.

41 Parsons defends Weber's definition of traditional action from the sense that
it might appear simply a kind of automatism, but admits the general difficulty of definition: 'There seems to be an inherent difficulty in adequately
describing a *total* concrete system of action by the one term traditional in
the sense involving norms, which probably accounts for the suggestion of
"habit" in Weber's definition.' Parsons, *Structure of Social Action* (New York,
1937), 646–7.

42 For the critique of modernization theory from one who formerly subscribed
to this view, see S.N. Eisenstadt, *Tradition, Change, and Modernity* (New
York, 1973). See also Dean Tipps, 'Modernization Theory and the Comparative Study of Societies: A Critical Perspective,' *Comparative Studies in Society
and History,* 15 (1973): 199–226.

43 *Truth and Method* (London, 1975), 389. 'Linguistic tradition is tradition in the
proper sense of the word – i.e. something handed down' (389). For the sake
of keeping this Introduction to a manageable limit, I have chosen to concentrate on Gadamer, who has certainly enjoyed the widest influence. In a
longer consideration, one would certainly want to consider the very important work of Alasdair MacIntyre.

44 Ibid., 293.

45 Ibid.

46 Ibid., 277.

47 Ibid., 282.

48 Ibid., 283.

49 Ibid., 282.

50 I take this expressive phrase from David Hollinger's essay with the same

title, ' "How Wide the Circle of the We": American Intellectuals and the Problem of the Ethnos Since World War II,' *American Historical Review*, 98 (April 1993): 317-37.

51 'Language is the fundamental mode of operation of our being-in-the-world.' *Philosophical Hermeneutics* (Berkeley, 1976), 3.

52 'Language and Human Nature,' in *Philosophical Papers*, 2 vols (Cambridge, 1985), 1: 234.

53 Ibid., 1: 232.

54 *Philosophical Hermeneutics*, 64.

55 There is no reference to Kuhn's work in Shils, nor in Gross.

56 *Essential Tension: Studies in Scientific Tradition and Change* (Chicago, 1977), xix.

57 'Second Thoughts on Paradigms,' in *Essential Tension*, 307.

58 *Structure of Scientific Revolutions* (Chicago, 1962), 191. Kuhn's view of the importance of tacit knowledge acquired through practice parallels Michael Oakeshott's influential discussions of political traditions. See *Rationalism in Politics, and Other Essays* (New York, 1962).

59 *Essential Tension*, 227.

60 A second was added in the Postscript appended to the 2nd edition (1962).

Part I

Chapter One

Narratives of the Treaty Table: Cultural Property and the Negotiation of Tradition

ANDREA LAFORET

Although established to resolve outstanding claims to land, contemporary treaty negotiations between the government of Canada and Canadian Aboriginal[1] peoples now include historical objects of Aboriginal origin. In the early 1990s the collections of federal and provincial museums became subject to negotiation as part of the comprehensive claim of the Nisga'a, an Aboriginal people whose homeland is located on the Nass River in northwestern British Columbia. As the primary federal repository for objects of Nisga'a origin, the Canadian Museum of Civilization (CMC)[2] joined the Nisga'a treaty discussions in 1993 and participated in them until the conclusion of the final agreement on Culture and Heritage in April 1998. Treaty negotiations are intended to resolve deceptively simple, practical questions about resources and governance. Through the discussions relating to cultural objects the Nisga'a treaty negotiation became a place of encounter between the Nisga'a and Western approaches to conceptualizing the relationship between objects and history. More specifically, it brought into close juxtaposition elements of Nisga'a tradition and those elements of Western tradition that support the museum as an institution and inform its daily practice.

In this paper I explore the concepts that emerged as essential to both traditions and reflect on them as bodies of understanding and practice whose relationship will be further defined as the Nisga'a Final Agreement[3] is implemented. In this, I am also reflecting on my own experience. As Director of Ethnology at the Canadian Museum of Civilization I was responsible for the direction of research and scholarly interpretation of Aboriginal culture and post-contact history within the museum. I was also the representative of the museum at the treaty table. This role was somewhat anomalous within the general framework of treaty negotiations. Since 1990 the Canadian Museum of Civilization has been a Crown corporation, with a Board of Trustees accorded sole authority under the Museums Act to dispose of objects from the museum's collection. Rather than delegate the representation of the museum's interests to federal negotiators working for the Federal Treaty Negotiation Office, as federal government line departments were required to do, the board insisted that a member of the museum staff be at the negotiating table.

The 'Preamble' of the Nisga'a Final Agreement states, 'Whereas the Parties acknowledge the entitlement of the *Simgigat* and *Sigidimhaanak* (hereditary chiefs and matriarchs) to tell their *Adaawak* (oral histories) relating to their *Ango'oskw* (family hunting, fishing, and gathering territories) in accordance with the *Ayuuk* (Nisga'a traditional laws and practices).' For the Nisga'a this statement was an important affirmation of a core feature of their past and contemporary culture, made in vivid memory of a time[4] when the feasts that were the required context for the telling of such histories were forbidden by law. The *adaawak*, and the telling of *adaawak*, validate the ownership of Nisga'a lands and the social order those lands have supported for centuries. They are essential components of Nisga'a historical practice. *Ayuuk*, a code unwritten at the time of the treaty's negotiation, embraces Nisga'a tradition, in both concept and practice.

The mandate for the Canadian Museum of Civilization's collection is expressed in the Museums Act:[5] 'The purpose of the Canadian Museum of Civilization is to increase, throughout Canada and internationally, interest in, knowledge and critical understanding of and appreciation and respect for human cultural achievements and human behavior by establishing, maintaining and developing for research and posterity a collection of objects of historical or cultural interest, with special but not exclusive reference to Canada.' According to this, the collection itself is both an object of endeavour and an assemblage that mandates endeavour, and its primary purpose is to be a vehicle for the generation and preservation of knowledge. The trustees' authority to sever objects from the collection is envisaged as a means of enhancing the collection, through the occasional disposal of an object of lesser value, or more distant relationship to the museum's mandate, in order to acquire an object of greater value or closer relationship. The Museums Act does not provide for the disposal of large portions of the museum's collection that are central to its mandate to preserve, generate, and disseminate knowledge about the human history of the various peoples of Canada.

At the time the Nisga'a negotiation began, assumptions governing museum practice in relation to Aboriginal objects had already been challenged by requests for the repatriation of objects from museums throughout North America, and museums were moving from being fairly staid repositories of cultural objects from the past to being sites of active negotiation of tradition and, in particular, of the degree to which objects in museums were part of continuing or renewed Aboriginal and Native American cultural practice.[6] The idea that objects in a centralized collection were ideally available for study by all contrasted painfully with the perception, articulated by many Aboriginal people, that objects in collections were immured, out of reach, and the parallel idea, often articulated by non-Aboriginal people outside the museum profession, that only those objects actually on exhibit were truly accessible. Formal discussion between the Nisga'a and the Canadian Museum of Civilization began at a time when 'the sacred' constituted a dominant theme in repatriation discussions at large. Early calls for repatriation of museum collections focused on objects such as Plains medicine bundles that originated and were used entirely in the context of the relationship between human and supernatural beings and were protected from general use. This was also a theme of discussions leading to the recommendations of the Task Force on Museums and First Peoples co-sponsored by the Assembly of First Nations and the Canadian Museums Association.[7] The Canadian Museum of Civilization Board of Trustees adopted these recommendations in principle soon after they were tabled in 1992. Although just one of several themes of repatriation debates that have also included the treatment of human remains, objects of cultural patrimony, and the need of societies for access to a wide range of objects from their past, the fact that respect for the sacred has a general value for people of many cultural perspectives recommends it as a theme on which members of Euro-Canadian and Aboriginal societies may find common ground. This influenced the outcome of the Nisga'a negotiations, providing to the museum's administration a rationale for returning to the Nisga'a approximately one-third of the objects in the museum's collection documented as having originated with a Nisga'a person or community. The Nisga'a Final Agreement provides for the outright return to the Nisga'a of approximately 107 objects associated with traditional curing and for possession of those objects remaining with the Canadian Museum of Civilization to be shared between the Nisga'a and the museum. These remaining objects, many of which have a place in Nisga'a lineage histories, are to be cared for in ways that respect Nisga'a traditional laws and practices (*ayuuk*), as well as the statutory mandate of the Canadian Museum of Civilization.

During the negotiations, Nisga'a and Western concepts of knowledge in relation to objects and time emerged as a second theme of the discussions, providing implicit frames of reference in which Nisga'a and museum personnel,[8] respectively, placed particular statements about the importance of objects. Although never fully articulated – a society's detailed conceptualization of its relationship to time is very seldom open to a succinct summary of practice and belief – these two frames of reference gradually became part of the operational environment of all the negotiators at the table.[9] The discussions at the treaty table became an encounter between the Nisga'a tradition, identified as the orally transmitted body of knowledge and laws known as Nisga'a *ayuuk*, and the museum's interpretation of the Western tradition, embraced by the Museums Act and identified in the treaty as the Canadian Museum of Civilization's statutory mandate, but more accurately seen as an aggregate of written policies and unwritten practices, supported by deeply held values. The term 'tradition' has come to be rather hazardous in anthropology. Too often and too loosely used in regard to indigenous societies to identify all cultural practices, regardless of their temporal period or social impact, it has come to connote something both monolithic and incapable of change without loss of authenticity. In writing here of the Nisga'a and Western traditions as bodies of concept and practice relating to knowledge of the past that may well be in a process of constant change, but have, nonetheless, both historical depth and current force, I am referring to something closer to Hobsbawm's idea of 'custom.'[10]

The following synopsis highlights concepts fundamental to approaches to the past on the northern Northwest coast and in the museum. Informing and transcending these specific elements are contrasting ideas about property, time, and the relationship between object and narrative.

Objects and Ideas on the Northern Northwest Coast

Most of the published literature on the northern Northwest coast treats themes common to the Nisga'a and their neighbours, the Coast Tsimshian and Gitksan.[11] While internal distinctions concerning Nisga'a works of art or cultural practices may be made in various texts, there is very little in the way of focused representation of the place of Nisga'a objects in Nisga'a culture alone. In fact, there is relatively little literature devoted solely to Nisga'a society per se.[12] With this in mind, I have set out, below, elements of a perspective that may apply generally to the Tlingit, Nisga'a, Gitksan, Coast Tsimshian, and some of their immediate neighbours, without presuming to delineate a Nisga'a perspective in precise terms.

Geography

The salient events of narratives (*adawaak*, for the Nisga'a) underlying the generation and use of crests happened in localities directly associated with the people who generated the objects. The place names are both features of the narratives and markers for historical knowledge. The narratives also delineate attributes of the lands held by houses (corporate lineage groups), and serve to connect those houses publicly and unalterably with those lands.

Family/Lineage

Northern coast kinship has a matrilineal structure, and Nisga'a society, in particular, is organized in four clans, Gisk'aast (Killer Whale), Laxgibuu, (Wolf), Ganhada (Raven), and Laxsgiik (Eagle).[13] The *adaawak*, or narrative histories belonging to houses of these clans, are fundamental to Nisga'a history and definition of society.

Mandate

The history of specific crest objects and the mandate for their use are furnished in narratives of encounters between human ancestors and particular supernatural beings. For the general origin and use of raven rattles, there is also a mandating narrative, although it is not located in a particular lineage. Shamanic objects are mandated by the encounter with supernatural beings from which a shaman derives his power, and although the role and capacities of a shaman have sometimes been transferred from one generation to another, the narratives are more specifically defined as personal narratives with a scope limited to the lifetime of one person.

Crests

The different languages and societies of the northern coast have different terms related to the idea of crest. The Tlingit concept, *at.oow*, has been defined by Nora and Richard Dauenhauer as 'an owned or purchased thing,'[14] with the caution that the words mean something different from what might be expected by someone uninstructed in Tlingit culture. A 'thing' may be a mountain or place, an image from an oral narrative on a clan hat or tunic, a song, a story from the life of an ancestor, or an ancestor. The purchase may have been made with money, an action, or, very often, an ancestor's life. Beyond this, and most important, is that the subsequent display and use of the *at.oow* by its owner and the accumulation of lineage history which results from its public use are vastly different from what happens with a commodity – or an object of cultural heritage – in Western society. The object remains in use as long as it is physically viable and may be replaced, when necessary, by another. The new object may or may not have precisely the same features as its predecessor but will have the same meaning and function. The object may be singular but may also be part of a group of objects linked by relationship to lineage history rather than form or practical function.

Inter-Being Relationships

In each category a connection between a human and animal-supernatural being provides the context for the generation of the object, for its interpretation, and may also have significant implications for its proper handling. Animal-supernatural beings have not only capacities that exceed human capacities but also greater knowledge of the world and its structure. A significant aspect of an encounter with a human being is the imparting of some of this knowledge. The human being carries it back with him to his own society.

Inter-Generational Connections

The passing of crest objects from one generation of title-holders to another according to lineage rules is foreordained and part of the crest object's identity (and possibly chiefly power regalia); shamanic objects are taken out of use and sequestered in the shaman's grave following his or her death.

Objects and Ideas in the Museum

In the Western tradition the conceptualization of the relationship between objects and the past is grounded in very different ideas. The museological narrative draws from the Western tradition and contains elements that are all more or less familiar to those who work in museums, if seldom combined in a coherent statement. Although in identifying these I have drawn upon the work of Pearce, Hooper-Greenhill, Kirshenblatt-Gimblett, among others, all of these concepts inform the Canadian Museum of Civilization's perception and implementation of its mandate.

The Object

The object is singular and secular; whatever its capacity to symbolize spiritual truth, it has an entirely physical existence. It is property in the legal sense, capable of transfer through monetary transaction. Once accepted into the collection, it is considered to be divorced from its original function.

The Collection

An assemblage of objects[15] that is more than the sum of its parts, the collection is at the heart of the museum's claim to a capacity to interpret and represent the past. Although the Geological Survey of Canada had acquired material from Aboriginal societies between 1879 and 1909, most of the collection now in the Canadian Museum of Civilization was acquired between 1910 and 1930. The collections made for the original Victoria Memorial Museum after the establishment of the Department of Anthropology in 1910 were adjuncts to a research program sketched by the first Director of Anthropology, Edward Sapir, in the journal *Science* in 1911.[16] Ethnographic and linguistic work undertaken within this program was intended to document the cultures – at that time seen to be static arrays of features rather than ever-changing sets of practices and understandings – of Aboriginal people, who were under substantial threat and predicted to decline to the point of disappearance. It can be argued, with Clifford,[17] that ethnography itself is a form of collecting, but Sapir and his colleague Marius Barbeau saw the collecting, both of information and objects, as a form of preservation, as well as an affirmation of enduring value, in the face of otherwise inevitable loss.

By 1915 the major collections in Europe and the United States were already in place. The competitive collecting phenomenon that built those collections was beginning to fade, but many of the collectors, such as George Emmons and Charles Newcombe, were still at the height of their careers, and substantial private collections were being assembled.

Canadian museum collections were among the last to be made through direct collecting. Sapir and Barbeau saw themselves as pulling valuable cultural material out of the commercial flux and into a condition of stasis.

Geography

The value of the object transcends its associations with particular places. Its value may be recognized internationally. Whatever its origin, its current locale is urban. Objects accumulate in value as they are centralized within a political entity, for example, the nation, province, or municipality.[18]

Preservation

Preservation is a symbolic (and sometimes practical) defiance of entropy that links the object with Western ideas of time. Within the museum objects are time embodied. The past is conceived in terms of a linear chronology[19] that can in theory be applied unendingly back in time. Even though in popular practice the internal differentiation of the past beyond a certain point – for example, 'a hundred years ago' – becomes less and less important to anyone but scholars with an interest in a particular period, in an overall linear framework every object can be seen as the physical representation of a moment that will never come again. Any object from the past can suggest volumes of unspoken knowledge about that moment to the museum visitor, with the museum exhibit unlocking enough of this knowledge to confirm the potential of much more. The Western approach to time, shared by laymen and scholars alike, is distinguished by an arbitrary barrier between past and present[20] as well as a constant juxtaposition of the general and specific where time is concerned.

Knowledge

In 1912 Sapir gently discouraged a proposal by the collector Charles Newcombe to trade objects not represented in the museum's collection for 'duplicates,' saying that there was no such thing as a redundant object[21]: 'As regards duplicates, you realize yourself that part of the purpose of a scientific museum is to house a considerable number of duplicates of any type of object in order to make it possible to determine the range of variation of that type, also the extent to which it is truly typical.'

The museum narrative of preservation is based on an equation between object and knowledge that has deep roots in European thought and has become embedded in the culturally formatted matrix of common sense which underlies specific definitions of what it is important to know. Pearce affirms that 'collected material ... stands at the heart of modernist knowledge, both as evidence of particular truths, and as demonstrating what constitutes evidence, itself the underpinning narrative upon which the other stories depend. Collections, therefore, do not merely demonstrate knowledge, they are knowledge.' Further, 'material must be observed and arranged in order to yield up its inherent knowledge, and important material must be preserved in order to continue to demonstrate the truths that are asserted.'[22] Universality and system are two essential elements of knowledge in relation to museum objects. The extension of the concept of object to 'objectified' information, such as texts and other forms of cultural data,[23] has a long history in the scholarly practice of the CMC.

Contrasting Traditions

The encounter at the treaty table between the Nisga'a and Western traditions illuminates fundamental differences in the imaginative connections made by the two societies between objects, on the one hand, and narratives, on the other. In the northern coast lineage histories, crest object and narrative (and song) have complementary functions in the reenactment of the knowledge of past generations in the present to ensure that it *becomes* the knowledge of the present generation and is acknowledged as the property of the present lineage chiefs.

A lineage history consists of the narrative, plus the totem pole or poles, the songs, the names, chiefly prerogatives and crest properties, and the explication at a feast of the territories and their use. All of these elements are brought together in the functioning of a chief at a feast. None of the elements composing a lineage history is expected to stand alone. A Gitanyow totem pole consists of carved elements representing people, supernatural beings, and events from the narrative history, but it is incomplete without the songs which are sung and the narrative which is told when it is erected. Poles may stand singly or in groups, with all of the poles in the group together signifying a history.[24] The figures on the pole represent different elements or internal narratives of the lineage history but do not, in themselves, compose a linear narrative. The concept of linear time has little place in formal Gitanyow social organization, although present-day Gitanyow may make use of the concept in everyday life. As a Gitanyow chief succeeds his predecessor, he assumes the prerogatives, names, responsibilities, and authority of his ancestors. The Gitanyow approach to time and the past, insofar as the principal elements of social organization are concerned, may be comparable to the West African system of 'stereotypic reproduction,'[25] in which title-holders are considered to replace their predecessors in a very exact sense.

Although objects and narratives are complementary in the way in which they are used, in the histories of northwestern British Columbia the object is drawn from the narrative and not vice-versa. A 'likeness of' a robe covered with ermine and marten skins and trimmed with the hooves of unborn caribou, worn by a prince killed during a historic journey of the Gilt-winth (Wolves) of Kitwancool (Gitanyow) becomes the robe of the Wolf clan.[26] The shape, history, and subsequent role of the object are set by the narrative. By implication, as long as the narrative endures, the object can be replaced. In contrast to the museological paradigm, the narrative is unchanging; the object is not.

While the Western imagination allows narratives[27] to create time in an expansive way, objects are considered to hold time in a reductive way. Human stories, events, and entire eras can be contained silently in a single object. Through a process of associating the object with contextual information drawn from other kinds of data sets (as well as from analysis of its own internal composition), a scholar may draw its stories from it. This is a concept essential to archaeology. In a paper published in the early 1980s that almost uncannily touches upon many issues of concern today, John Ewers, an anthropologist distinguished for his study of Native American societies of the Plains, provides a personal narrative of his own study of Plains artifacts from the twin points of view of art and ethnohistory. His work to draw an anthroplogical narrative from objects and collections of objects began in the 1930s with the collections of the American Museum of Natural History and the Heye Foundation (now the National Museum of the American Indian). At that time standard ethnography was far more tied to the explication of objects associated with 'traditional' culture than it is today, and the narrative drew its scope from the object, and from that extended object, the collection. Ewers wrote, 'I learned early in my career that studies of Indian art and material culture tend to become both broader and deeper through examination of the holdings of a goodly number of museums. As I look back on those pioneer studies of Plains Indian art and artifacts conducted by Clark Wissler and his colleagues and published in the *Anthropological Papers of the American Museum of Natural History* during the first quarter of this century, I can see that their greatest limitations are the result of too exclusive reliance upon the collections of that one museum.'[28] In this framework, the scope of the narrative is proportional to the collections studied. Ewers's perspective and work are characteristic of a particular period in the history of ethnological research. Although it is assumed that the knowledge acquired through research will in some degree be cumulative, it is accepted that the character of the insights generated by research and the narratives that result will vary with the perspective of individual scholars and as concepts and methods evolve from one generation of anthropologists to another.

The development within museum practice of the relationships among artifact, science, and knowledge has been increasingly historicized through analysis of European approaches to collections since the Renaissance[29] and, more directly pertinent to the museum's history, the work of Boas and others.[30] The museum's collection is a particularly formalized expression of the imaginative connection, fundamental to the habitus[31] of Europeans and North American people whose cultures derive from Europe, between living members of the population and objects surviving from the past. A research collection is animated by the idea that the full value of an object can be realized only in association with contextual information. In correspondence with the British Columbia ethnographer James Teit, Sapir affirmed the priority of scientific collecting over curio hunting, repudiating the antiquarian model used by collectors such as George Heye,[32] a New York philanthropist who was then in the process of assembling a very large collection. Between 1910 and 1930 the National Museum of Canada purchased both old and new objects. Sapir and Barbeau both documented the identities of the makers, when they were known, as well as the vendors.[33] To the scholar of material culture, objects, in association with documentation, hold promise of illuminating the past within specific, delimited temporal components, and for many scholars who have ignored or survived the long period in anthropological fashion when the study of material culture was discounted, the value of the collections lies in the insight they may provide into the originating societies.[34] In making all objects, whatever their origin, universally accessible to scrutiny, museums reinforce an idea, often honoured in the breach, of knowledge as fully open and available to anyone who cares to seek it.

To summarize, the northern Northwest coast paradigm draws the object from the historical narrative while the Western paradigm draws the narrative from the object; but these differences define fields of emphasis, not exclusive, arbitrary positions. A relic of the true cross is an object drawn from the Christian narrative. Neither scholarship, nor print, nor the progressive objectification characteristic of Western science impedes the creation of objects based in Western historical narratives. Correspondingly an arbitrary application of the northern Northwest coast paradigm would suggest that objects now in museums could be carved anew by members of Aboriginal societies and the originals left as a permanent record, but while this strategy is not ignored at the treaty table (the Nisga'a included replication of museum objects in their claim) it is considered a fall-back solution. It is also possible that an overwhelming desire to reunite objects and narratives is the contemporary legacy of the colonialism that interrupted their complementary relationship and threatened both with extinction. In a discussion of the Nisga'a perspective at a Repatriation Forum in August 1998,[35] Nisga'a negotiator Harry Nyce made it clear that the Nisga'a lineage chiefs maintained a strong interest in maintaining the relationship between lineage titles and the crest objects associated with them.

For scholars interested in the Northwest coast it comes as no surprise that *at.oow* and comparable objects in northern coast societies derive meaning from historical narratives and validity from public display at feasts. Museums have seen themselves as places in which knowledge relating to this can be assembled and celebrated. However, certain elements of the Western perspective that appear to accommodate other modes of knowing inadvertently mask the disparity that exists between these two systems of knowledge. For example, the concept of context, expressed in the idea of documentation and the affirmation of its necessity to the museum's role in the preservation of knowledge makes a space for recognition of the place of the object in the northern coast system of knowledge without providing for its continuing actualization within this system. This is reinforced by the idea that the authority of a museum specimen is proportional to its degree of separation from its original function.

Another element is the sense that the Western concept of scientific study is fundamentally liberating and must, therefore, be accommodating of diverse intellectual concerns.[36] For someone raised to see as positive the ideas that knowledge is secular and universally available, and that anyone can overcome the constraints of class and economic disadvantage to gain authority through scientific study, it is hard to grasp in a visceral way that, to someone for whom the knowledge associated with certain objects is lineage property, these impacts of the Western system might not be positive, and the levelling of objects within a collection might be incomprehensible or even offensive. Ironically, the scholarly purpose of collecting, and certainly of maintaining collections in the present, is to preserve the system of knowledge supporting the object as much as the object itself. Until the recent return of wampum and medicine bundles by some North American museums, it has been virtually unknown for museums to contemplate the possibility that this may be achieved only by relinquishing certain objects and the Western concepts of knowledge and property that validate their retention in a public collection.

The idea that an object, once identified by inclusion in a museum collection as critically related to the past, must endure as long as possible has also gone unquestioned in the museum. However, some Aboriginal societies see the object as a transitory reflection in physical form of enduring, nonmaterial knowledge. In 1986 Gloria Cranmer Webster, then Curator of the U'mista Cultural Centre at Alert Bay, British Columbia, addressed a meeting of museum curators and conservators and said,

> we know what conservators do or try to do; that is, preserve objects for as long as possible. But, diametrically opposed to this is the general Indian view as I know it, which is that objects are created to be used and when those objects are damaged or worn out, they are thrown away and new ones are made. This applies to everything from small masks to large totem poles. For example, many Indian people feel that once a pole has served its purpose it should be allowed to go back into the ground. I think this attitude has a lot to do with the way Indian people look at the objects. The objects themselves are not important; what matters is what the objects represent. They represent the right to own that thing, and that right remains even if the object decays or is otherwise lost.[37]

Comparable principles have since been articulated by other Aboriginal people, but even at that time there were indications that for some Aboriginal people from the Northwest coast the original object had a value even after it had been succeeded. The University of British Columbia Museum of Anthropology and the Vancouver Museum both have in their collections pieces of the original Thunderbird figure from the top of the pole erected in Alert Bay by Chief Wakas in 1893. The Thunderbird figure was replaced in 1966, but two different members of Wakas's family saved the head and belly of the bird. Ms Cranmer Webster went on to say, 'So, somewhere between these two opposed views is our Cultural Centre and probably others like it. We spend enough time in the museum world to appreciate the importance of saving and preserving material, but we often do it in communities where the other point of view prevails.'[38]

This divergence in views concerning the essential nature of specific objects also bears on concepts of property. While concepts of knowledge represent a huge pool lying under treaty negotiations, concepts of property constitute the pivot of decision making. For the museum, the physical object is at the heart of property, where the collection is concerned. The idea that an object, once purchased, becomes the property of the institution is fundamental to the museum's operation. On the north coast, the most important aspects of property are nonmaterial and lie in the rights to produce and use objects that represent historical event and privilege. The north coast and museum paradigms employ contrasting ideas of property to arrive at concepts of symbolic capital that have vastly different implications for the ideal biography of an object and its separability from particular persons. The concept of 'inalienable wealth,' as outlined by Weiner,[39] is a factor here, but it is too simple and all-encompassing to illuminate fully the original, post-contact, and current situations of these objects. Aboriginal and non-Aboriginal treaty negotiators come together to discuss collections that were assembled through financial transactions, many of them part of a series of transactions occurring between Aboriginal vendors and collectors over many years. While the conversion of cultural objects to saleable material may be discussed at the treaty table as an unsought and unwanted consequence of colonization, the concept of commodity may not be separated easily from the concept of cultural property. In the course of one of the many sets of negotiations in which the Canadian Museum of Civilization is now engaged,[40] it was proposed to both the First Nation and the museum that the entire body of museum objects originating with the First Nation no longer be considered as commodities. The First Nation and the Museum would each have title to a portion of the collection, but neither would sell the objects remaining in its care. Although both the First Nation and the Museum had concepts that could roughly be described as 'inalienable wealth,' and neither intended to sell the material, they did not consent, on the grounds, quite real in Canadian law, that ownership implies the right to transfer title.[41]

One overriding consequence of the competitive process of collecting, of the possibility of converting objects to money, and of the endeavour to assemble 'complete' collections is that in many Aboriginal communities there is very little left. George Dorsey of the Field Museum could write to Charles Newcombe in 1903 about a region of the western United States that was 'cleaned out' of certain kinds of artifacts, and Newcombe could write in the same year about the need to consider the purchase of new baskets from the Fraser Valley since there were no good old ones left, and Franz Boas could comment that feast bowls symbolically invoked by a Kwakiutl chief at Fort Rupert were actually in museums elsewhere,[42] but no one – not Boas, not Newcombe, and certainly not Dorsey – appreciated the importance for the preservation of community knowledge and well-being of Aboriginal people (or anyone else) of having objects from the past always at hand in the present. Although this imbalance could be addressed through redistributive mechanisms other than outright transfer, the argument is made, at the table and elsewhere, that the only means of addressing the impact of the colonial initiative is to reverse the transactions that brought the museum its claim to ownership.

Conclusion

The encounter between traditions that came into focus at the Nisga'a treaty table is now replicated at many treaty tables across Canada. The full implications of Aboriginal and Western traditions of knowledge for repatriation, and the impact of repatriation on those traditions, can only develop as the agreements are implemented. To affirm that the relationships between object, person, society, time, and narrative prevailing in an Aboriginal society in the eighteenth century have force and validity today can mandate the return of objects, but in the face of the internal diversity and wide geographic distribution of the populations of many contemporary First Nations, a seamless reintegration of those objects into past modes of being is unlikely. Similarly, the museum's affirmation of the value of those objects to knowledge is unlikely to dictate that they will be understood and used within museums in precisely the ways envisaged by their nineteenth-century collectors.

In *The Location of Culture* Homi Bhabha has written of 'a movement away from a world conceived in binary terms, away from a notion of the people's aspirations sketched in black and white.'[43] The 'terms of cultural engagement,' he writes, are 'produced performatively,' and 'The representation of difference must not be hastily read as the reflection of *pre-given* ethnic or cultural traits set in the fixed tablet of tradition. The social articulation of difference, from the minority perspective, is a complex, on-going negotiation that seeks to authorize cultural hybridities that emerge in moments of historical transformation.'[44]

Tradition is also maintained, or changed, through performance. Even before the terms of the Nisga'a treaty were broached, specific projects in which First Nations and museums worked together were having an impact on certain of the concepts long held to be fundamental to the museum's role. Most frequently challenged was the assumption that everything, once acquired by a museum, was subject to a secular gaze; the AFN/CMA Task Force recommendations of 1992 were augmented in 1999 by a statement in the ethical guidelines published by the Canadian Museums Association: 'In specific cases, it may be appropriate to restrict access to certain objects, to honour the protocols and ceremonies of that community regarding storage, treatment, handling and display, or to facilitate special access as appropriate.'[45] Issues of interpretation, particularly the connection between the exhibition of objects of Aboriginal origin and relationships between 'self' and 'other' were fairly readily articulated and addressed through the 1990s in collaborative projects between museums and Aboriginal communities. Challenges to the idea that preservation is a paramount responsibility of museums are just beginning to be appreciated and assessed. The concept that objects in museum collections are taken out of time, to be preserved forever, if possible, is at the heart of the museum's mandate. While challenges to preservation may come through repatriation where burial or other means of disposal are considered culturally appropriate, in most instances of repatriation the goal is continued preservation. Preservation may become an issue at any point where the continuing role of historic objects in Aboriginal tradition is negotiated. For example, the decision on the part of the University of British Columbia Museum of Anthropology to lend regalia acquired by the museum back to the originating artists so that they could be used in performances challenged the idea that objects must lose their original function when they enter a collection and generated a corresponding concern about the propriety of subjecting the object to damage.[46] An object in use is not suspended in time.

Both scholars and institutions are grappling with suggestions that the values of Western knowledge fundamental to their own training, such as universal access to information, objective study, and undifferentiated rights of men and women to conduct research, may be inappropriate when applied to certain domains of knowledge in some Aboriginal societies. In recent years, as the concept of collecting and the idea of collections have been examined with increasingly precise focus, the idea of the collection as an enhancement of a national self or the product of appropriation has come to be a topic of urgent discussion.[47] This is not to say that there is instant or universal agreement on these issues. Museums can be hives of dissension and are often sites for constant, sometimes sharp, encounters of differences in philosophy. Where the issues are acknowledged, and people are struggling to work with them, they may be seen within the institution as problems limited to specific sectors of a museum's function rather than challenges to the institution as a whole. Their effect, however, is likely to be very broad.

The Western and north coast systems of knowledge may be held apart by hidden structures and concepts that have implications and effects beyond their surface meaning, but this is not to say they are completely irreconcilable. There have been recent scholarly attempts to reach across the gap, and in the *Delgamuukw* case, in which the Gitksan, neighbours of the Nisga'a in northwestern British Columbia, sued the governments of Canada and British Columbia for return of their traditional lands, the courts became a site for the negotiation of these issues. In 1997 the Supreme Court of Canada's decision that there should be a new trial in *Delgamuukw* included a requirement that in assessing the merits of Aboriginal claims to land, 'the laws of evidence must be adapted in order that [oral histories] can be accommodated and placed on an equal footing with the types of historical evidence that the courts are familiar with, which largely consists of historical documents.'[48]

Intended to mark a moment of historical transformation, the Nisga'a treaty identifies its signatories as forever connected and forever apart.

Its terms are permanent, some of them protected under section 35 of the Constitution Act.[49] As time and continued interaction allow for the exploration of meaning through performance of which Bhabha writes, the features that made the two traditions so distinctive at the outset of the treaty discussions may change. Just as the operation of Nisga'a *ayuuk* within the Canadian Museum of Civilization may lead to new protocols for recognition and care of objects related to lineage histories, the construction of a cultural centre in the Nass Valley to hold returned items will, according to an approach the Nisga'a have designated 'the Nisga'a common bowl,' create a permanent public repository for what has been traditionally mandated to be known and handled by individuals or within lineages. What has been public in large museums is becoming private, and what has been private in Aboriginal communities is, to a degree, at least, becoming public.

The Nisga'a Final Agreement is now law in Canada, and its affirmation of the validity of the recitation of narratives fundamental to the Nisga'a practice of history has full legal protection. The Museums Act continues to affirm the place of the collection at the heart of the museum's preservation of knowledge of the past. However, the negotiation of the treaty has illuminated and emphasized culturally divergent ideas about the connection between objects and history at work in Nisga'a society and in the museum. Its implementation may find both the Nisga'a and the museum engaging in new practices that, both intentionally and unintentionally, bridge that divergence.

NOTES

1 In Canada the terms 'Aboriginal people' and 'First Nations' have replaced 'Indian.' While the term 'Native' still has some currency as an adjective, 'Native American' is not used.

2 The Canadian Museum of Civilization originated as a department of the Geological Survey of Canada and through the twentieth century has been known successively as the Victoria Memorial Museum, the National Museum of Canada, and the National Museum of Man. It was renamed the Canadian Museum of Civilization (CMC) in the 1980s. Since 1990 the CMC has been a federal Crown corporation with a Board of Trustees appointed by the Prime Minister's Office and an arm's-length relationship to the federal government. In the course of discussions between the museum and federal negotiators it was eventually agreed that the legislation attending the implementation of the treaty would address any discrepancy between

the board's role in repatriation negotiations and the role established by the Museums Act.

3 The Nisga'a Final Agreement, which became law 11 May 2000, is a tripartite agreement, binding the government of Canada, the province of British Columbia, and the Nisga'a Nation. It defines rights and obligations relating to a wide range of issues, including the disposition of land in Nisga'a traditional territory, the jurisdiction of the Nisga'a Lisims Government, established by the treaty, taxation, the fishery, wills and estates, and issues relating to culture and heritage beyond repatriation.

4 A clause forbidding the potlatch was added to the Indian Act in 1885. It was in force until 1951. For a discussion of its impact, see Douglas Cole and Ira Chaikin, *An Iron Hand upon the People: The Law against the Potlatch on the Northwest Coast* (Vancouver and Seattle, 1990).

5 An Act Respecting Museums, House of Commons of Canada, Bill C-12 (1989), 4.

6 As a result of specific discussions with the originating communities, the Canadian Museum of Civilization returned two medicine Plains bundles in 1988 and 1989, respectively, and three wampum to the Six Nations Confederacy in 1991. In the United States, the Native American Graves Protection and Repatriation Act was passed in 1990, providing for the repatriation of human remains, sacred objects, and objects of cultural patrimony from federally funded museums.

7 *Turning the Page: Forging New Partnerships between Museums and First Peoples.* A Report jointly sponsored by the Assembly of First Nations and the Canadian Museums Association (Ottawa, 1992).

8 Museum personnel addressing the issues directly or indirectly also included then Executive Director George F. MacDonald and members of the Board of Trustees.

9 I am indebted to Harry Nyce, the principal Nisga'a negotiator for culture and heritage, and to Brian Martin, the negotiator for the Federal Treaty Negotiation Office in Vancouver, for reading this paper in its formative stage and offering helpful comments.

10 Eric Hobsbawm, 'Introduction: Inventing Tradition,' in Eric Hobsbawm and Terence Ranger, eds, *The Invention of Tradition* (Cambridge, 1983), 2.

11 Exceptions are Stephen McNeary, 'The Traditional Economic and Social Life of the Niska of British Columbia,' unpublished report (Ottawa, 1974); Edward Sapir, 'A Sketch of the Social Organization of the Nass River Indians,' *Museum Bulletin* 19 (1915); and Nisga'a Tribal Council, *Bringing Our Ancestors Home: The Repatriaton of Nisga'a Artifacts* (New Aiyansh, 1998).

12 In an unpublished PhD dissertation, 'The Tsimshian Crest System: A Study Based on Museum Specimens and the Marius Barbeau and William Beynon

Field Notes' (University of British Columbia, 1973), Marjorie Halpin has drawn on the very extensive unpublished field notes of Barbeau and his colleague William Beynon to articulate the relationship of different types of objects from the Tsimshian-speaking peoples to streams of knowledge and action in Tsimshian society. In *Shattered Images: Dialogues and Meditations on Tsimshian Narratives* (Ottawa, 1987) John Cove has explored the relationship between narrative and knowledge in early nineteenth-century Tsimshian society. However, with the exception of Wilson Duff, ed., *The Histories, Territories and Laws of the Kitwancool* (Victoria, 1959), none of the published works concerning northern coast peoples places the objects owned by a particular family or lineage in the context of their history and use according to the perspective of the people concerned.

13 This list and the spelling of terms for clans have been taken from Nisga'a Tribal Council, *Bringing Our Ancestors Home: The Repatriation of Nisga'a Artifacts* (New Aiyansh, 1998), 17.

14 Nora Marks Dauenhauer and Richard Dauenhauer, eds, *Haa Shuka, Our Ancestors. Tlingit Oral Narratives. Classics of Tlingit Oral Literature,* vol. 1 (Seattle and London, 1987), 25.

15 For definitions of the collection see Susan Pearce, *On Collecting* (London and New York, 1995), 20–2, 24.

16 Edward Sapir, 'An Anthropological Survey of Canada,' *Science,* n.s. 34 (July–December 1911): 789–93.

17 James Clifford, 'On Collecting Art and Culture,' in *The Predicament of Culture: Twentieth Century Ethnography, Literature and Art* (Cambridge, MA, 1988), 230.

18 Eilean Hooper-Greenhill places the inception of this geographic organization (and the disciplinary museum itself) in postrevolutionary France, where 'the Louvre in Paris ... would represent a faithful reflection of all European art and each European city would do so on a smaller regional scale ... Thus a vast intersecting museological gaze was established that judged and surveyed collections in the regions of France and the conquered domains.' *Museums and the Shaping of Knowledge* (London and New York, 1992), 185.

19 As Anthony Grafton has shown, European ideas of chronology have their own complicated history. 'Chronology and Its Discontents in Renaissance Europe: The Vicissitudes of a Tradition,' in Diane Owen Hughes and Thomas R. Trautmann, eds, *Time Histories and Ethnologies* (Ann Arbor, 1995), 139–66.

20 Cf. David Lowenthal, *The Past Is a Foreign Country* (Cambridge, 1985).

21 Letter from Edward Sapir to C.F. Newcombe, 21 December 1912. Sapir Correspondence, Canadian Museum of Civilization Archives.

22 Pearce, *On Collecting*, 111.
23 See Ira Jacknis, 'The Ethnographic Object and the Object of Ethnology in the Early Career of Franz Boas,' in George W. Stocking, Jr, ed., *Volksgeist as Method and Ethic: Essays on Boasian Ethnography and the German Anthropological Tradition*, History of Anthropology vol. 8. (Madison, 1996), 186.
24 Duff, ed., *Histories, Territories and Laws of the Kitwancool*.
25 D.J.Y. Peel, 'Making History. The Past in the Ijesha Present,' *Man*, n.s. 19 (1984): 113.
26 Duff, ed., *Histories, Territories and Laws of the Kitwancool*, 16.
27 Paul Ricoeur has stated, 'time becomes human to the extent that it is articulated through a narrative mode, and narrative attains its full meaning when it becomes a condition of temporal existence.' *Time and Narrative*, vol. 1 (Chicago 1984), 52. The schematic discussion here of the relationship between object, time, and narrative teeters on the edge of a huge discourse in Western philosophy, to which Ricoeur's three-volume work provides an entry point.
28 John C. Ewers, 'The Use of Artifacts and Pictures in the Study of Plains Indian History, Art and Religion,' in Anne-Marie E. Cantwell, James B. Griffin, and Nan A. Rothschild, eds, *The Research Potential of Anthropological Museum Collections: Annals of the New York Academy of Sciences*, 376 (1981): 248.
29 For a discussion of this process, see Hooper-Greenhill, *Museums and the Shaping of Knowledge*.
30 Jacknis, 'The Ethnographic Object,' 189.
31 After Pierre Bourdieu, *Outline of a Theory of Practice* (Cambridge, 1977), 76: 'a socially constituted system of cognitive and motivating structures.'
32 Sapir–Teit correspondence, February 1915, Canadian Museum of Civilization.
33 This principle may often be honoured in the breach, however. One can contrast Sapir and Barbeau's actions and intentions with Sally McLendon's comment that, although, as she has demonstrated with reference to the notes of California collector Grace Nicholson, it is possible to locate within the general ethnographic record documentation for certain, otherwise isolated, objects in museums, 'one cannot expect to rely on a single archival source or assume that a given museum's archives will document its own collection.' 'Preparing Museum Collections for Use as Primary Data in Ethnographic Research,' in Cantwell, Griffin, and Rothschild, eds, *Research Potential of Anthropological Museum Collections*, 225. Additional support is furnished by Stanley Freed's wry account of his discovery that a famous (and well illustrated) Plains pipe bowl had floated so free of the original

documentation as to have been wholly manufactured for exhibit purposes. 'Research Pitfalls of Museum Specimens,' in Cantwell, Griffin, and Rothschild, eds, *Research Potential of Anthropological Museum Collections*, 229–30.

34 The relative priority of object and information within museums is the focus of continuing debate. Arguing that the ethnographic object is created by the ethnographer through detachment from its original context and subsequently reconnected to a context formulated as information, Kirshenblatt-Gimblett contrasts the statement by Vico that objects are 'manifest testimony,' carrying 'greater authority than texts, even contemporaneous ones,' with George Brown Goode's mid-twentieth-century pronouncement that 'an efficient educational museum may be described as a collection of instructive labels, each illustrated by a well-selected specimen.' 'Objects of Ethnography,' in Ivan Karp and Steven D. Lavine, eds, *Exhibiting Cultures: The Poetics and Politics of Museum Display* (Washington and London, 1991), 394.

35 Repatriation Forum, co-sponsored by the University of British Columbia and the Smithsonian Institution, UBC, 17 August 1998.

36 Hooper-Greenhill has outlined the historical relationship between state seizure of the deposed nobility's privately owned art works, the development of openly accessible public collections in late eighteenth-century France, and the subsequent development of close relationships between museums and government. Although certainly affected by these events, museum curators are generally guided by a more circumscribed historical perspective and ideas that have become schematic and generalized. *Museums and the Shaping of Knowledge*, 188–90.

37 Gloria Cranmer-Webster, 'Conservation and Cultural Centres: U'mista Cultural Centre, Alert Bay, Canada,' in R. Barclay, M. Gilbert, J.C. McCawley, and T. Stone, eds, *Symposium 86: The Care and Preservation of Ethnological Materials, Proceedings* (Ottawa, 1986), 77.

38 Ibid.

39 Annette Weiner, 'Inalienable Wealth,' *American Ethnologist* (1985): 210.

40 First Nations following the Nisga'a into the treaty process also included repatriation in their list of subjects to be negotiated. In 2001 the Canadian Museum of Civilization was negotiating repatriation with more than thirty First Nations across Canada.

41 Marc Babington, personal communication.

42 Letter from Franz Boas to his children, 14 December 1930, Boas Family Papers, American Philosophical Society, cited in Douglas Cole, *Captured*

Heritage: The Scramble for Northwest Coast Artifacts (Vancouver and Toronto, 1985), xiii.

43 Homi Bhabha, *The Location of Culture* (London, 1994), 14.

44 Ibid., 2; italics in original.

45 Canadian Museums Association, *Ethics Guidelines 1999*, 14.

46 Miriam Clavir, Elizabeth Johnson, and Audrey Shane, 'A Discussion on the Use of Museum Artifacts by Their Original Owners,' in R. Barclay, M. Gilbert, J.C. McCawley, and T. Stone, eds, *Symposium 86: The Care and Preservation of Ethnological Materials, Proceedings* (Ottawa, 1986), 80–9.

47 Susan Pearce has identified three approaches to collecting: the systematic, where the 'intention is to create complete sets which will demonstrate understanding achieved;' the fetishistic, in which the collector obsessively gathers as many objects as possible and is, in turn, created by them; and the souvenir , where the individual creates a romantic life-history through an 'object autobiography' (*On Collecting*, 32). Pearce makes the point that many collections will operate in all these modes at the same time. Similar features of systematic collecting are scholarship, which museums generally support, antiquarianism, which they generally see as undesirable, and connoisseurship, which can exist both as part of scholarly endeavour and in support of other aspects of the museum's symbolic capital. While museologists are turning more and more attention to collecting as a phenomenon, few are prepared to see collections in Jean Baudrillard's terms as pools reflecting the narcissism of their owner-creators: 'La collection est toujours un processus limité, récurrent, son matériel même, les objets, est trop concret, trop discontinu pour qu'elle puisse s'articuler en une réelle structure dialectique (au contraire, par exemple, de la science, de la mémoire, qui sont elles aussi collection, mais collection de faits, de connaissances).' *Le système des objets* (Paris: 1968), 114.

48 *Delgamuukw, also known as Earl Muldoe, suing on his own behalf and on behalf of all the members of the Houses of Delgamuukw and Haaxw (and others suing on their own behalf and on behalf of thirty-eight Gitksan Houses and twelve Wet'suwet'en Houses ...) Her Majesty the Queen in Right of the Province of British Columbia and The Attorney General of Canada*, 11 December 1997, 45.

49 Canada, Constitution Act (1982), section 35.3.

Chapter Two

Disappearing Acts: Traditions of Exposure, Traditions of Enclosure, and Iroquois Masks

RUTH B. PHILLIPS

Smithsonian exploration and field work has become almost a tradition among the Six Nations near Brantford on the Grand River.

William N. Fenton, 1941[1]

These pieces were not meant to be taken out of human activity. They're not meant to be put in vaults, or in metal cases. They are to be used in our spiritual practices.

Doug M. George, 1995[2]

One of the most striking changes in ethnographic and art museum representations of Native North American peoples at the turn of the twenty-first century has been the disappearance from public display of object types long celebrated as canonical forms of art and material culture. As the result of carefully orchestrated campaigns by community representatives, Zuni *Ahayu:da* (or 'war gods') have been returned to the Zuni for reburial, wampum belts have been repatriated to the care of Iroquois confederacy chiefs, Coast Salish rattles and masks have been moved to restricted store rooms, female museum staff have been asked to stop handling categories of Plains medicine objects specific to men, and research on human remains and associated burial objects has been curtailed.[3] Collectively, these 'disappearing acts' represent a grand refusal of key Western traditions for the production and disposition of knowledge. They set limits on classic methods of study – objectification, comprehensiveness, and critical analysis – and they erode the ideal of universal access to knowledge created by technologies of exposure and display in museums, archives, and universities. Contestations such as this engage a wide range of questions around tradition that have both general relevance to the large issues discussed in this book and specific resonance within the history of colonialism and post-colonialism.

In this paper I will discuss one of the most successful and far-reaching of these projects of removal, the Iroquois campaign to stop the public display of the *Ga:goh:sah*, or False Face masks; their reproduction in painted, photographic, or sculptural form; and the academic study of the masks and related ceremonies.[4] It would be easy to interpret such negotiations as battles between censorship and academic freedom, or as pressure on the museum, as an archetypical Western institution, to yield the ground of its enlightened (but uninterrogated) modernity to a reactionary traditionalism. I offer this case study as an opportunity to complicate this kind of interpretation. I will argue that the ethics and politics of pluralism require that museums and academic institutions attend seriously and respectfully to requests that render some objects in-visible. I will also argue, however, that responses to and resolutions of conflicts must be grounded in accurate understandings of the specific histories of collecting, display, and representation that have led to the current situation – even though the creation of such histories invokes the same Western technologies of exposure that are under attack. Attempts to suppress historical inquiry into the ways that indigenous traditions have changed over time – and particularly, in this case, in relation to the value of display, representation, and seeing – will ultimately frustrate attempts to reach understanding.

When episodes of museum contestation are examined carefully, the cases, the labels, the lights, the taxonomics, and the security systems of museums come to be seen as integral to traditions that are as culturally specific as are those of the Iroquois. Although privileged under colonial regimes of power, they can no longer be taken for granted. We need to denaturalize the fundamental expository practices of the museum and the academy and to develop more reflexive understandings of the premises that underlie them. At the same time, we need to recognize the organic nature and contemporary vitality of indigenous traditions even when this entails restrictions on traditions of academic inquiry. The positioning of traditional ritual practices within contemporary multicultural societies is, in other words, a dialogic process involving a continuing negotiation between two systems of knowledge management.

Finally, my argument will go beyond the museum and the academy as self-contained sites of representation. As interdisciplinary work in

visual studies and visual anthropology has shown, the system of exposition and exposure to which public museum displays belong extends
well beyond its walls. *Both* museum collecting, display, and academic
discourse *and* contemporary rearticulations of indigenous traditions
are intimately joined to underlying processes of souvenir and art market commodification, as well as to the mass circulation of mechanically
reproduced images and texts in journalism, advertising, film, children's literature, and popular performance. Western and indigenous
traditions for the *disposition* of knowledge must therefore be analysed
within specific *economies* of knowledge. Although it has not often
enough been acknowledged, postcolonial critiques of museum representation are generated within this broader arena and must therefore
be examined systemically and not as isolated incidents of institutional
transgression.[5]

Museums, Modernity, and Native North Americans

The case of the Iroquois *Ga:goh:sah* is representative of the contestations that have taken place in museums around the world as the result
of postcolonial activism. As background to the discussion, it will be
useful, then, to review briefly the role that museums have played as
agents of colonialism in the inscription of modernist ideology. A key
aspect of this ideology is its construction of the traditional as oppositional to the modern.[6] For Native North Americans the specific trope
that became an article of faith under settler colonialism for non-
Natives of all political persuasions is that of the Disappearing Indian.[7]
The first challenge that faces indigenous activists, therefore, is the refutation of this doctrine and the affirmation and demonstration of the
survival *within* modernity of indigenous traditions that have been represented as lost or fragmented. The dialectical construction of tradition
and modernity also implies essentialist notions of identity and authenticity, requiring Native North Americans, like other colonized peoples,
to argue explicitly for the authenticity of the hybrid and the syncretistic. As the Iroquois case study will show, contestations have regularly
been complicated and confused by the disunity and factionalization of
indigenous communities, a situation that is itself a result of colonial
policies that encouraged missionization by competing Christian sects,
that legally prohibited indigenous spiritual practices and ceremonies,
and that suppressed traditional forms of governance.

As a large and growing literature shows, museums have historically played a central role in the inscription of specific tenets of modernist ideology instrumental to the implementation of such policies. The great period of museum and collection building that began in the mid-nineteenth century coincided almost exactly with the formulation and implementation of official assimilationist policies in the United States and Canada between about 1880 and 1940. Ethnological exhibits organized according to the principles of cultural evolutionism and art museum installations of 'primitive art' informed by idealist and formalist theories conveyed to broad publics the racially determined hierarchies of history, culture, and art generated within the academy.[8] Together, these anthropological and aesthetic discourses contributed to a specifically modernist version of primitivism which ascribed interest, value, and beauty within indigenous cultures exclusively to 'traditional' objects, defined in turn as those that appeared to display the minimum of Western influence. Authenticity and value were, thus, located in an irretrievable pre-contact past, while the hybrid cultural forms that characterize post-contact and contemporary indigenous peoples were devalued as contaminated and inauthentic.[9] At the same time, in appropriating the cultural artifacts of indigenous peoples into their public displays museums and galleries overwrote indigenous systems of classification and knowledge management with those of the West.

It must be stressed that this rather bald account describes the simplified messages conveyed by public museum exhibitions through their installations and their privileging of certain kinds of objects during much of the twentieth century. It does not refer to the new consultative and collaborative culture that has been developing in many museums during the past two decades,[10] nor to the far more complex and mediated understandings of artistic and cultural process achieved by ethnologists and art historians in their detailed studies and field diaries. But because the exhibition paradigms of art and artifact developed during the first half of the twentieth century have cast such long shadows, lingering on in major urban museums decades after the disciplinary formations that gave them birth were rejected within the academy itself, they have remained legitimate targets for contestation in many places. The taxonomies, life groups, and ethnographic presentism of the early twentieth-century anthropology exhibit have remained in place into the twenty-first century at major institutions such as the Smithsonian's National Museum of Natural History,[11] while the connoisseurship, 'rare art tradition' model associated with the modernist construct of Primitive Art, lives on in the Rockefeller Wing of the Metropolitan Museum of Art in New York.

Art Historical and Ethnological Encounters with Iroquois *Ga:goh:sah*

The appropriation of Native American objects into the Western art system did not occur until the 1930s, late in the sequence of such primitivist redefinitions.[12] This process, like earlier appropriations of 'tribal' objects, was driven by the inexorable logic of modernism's universalist presumptions which predicted the presence of art in all cultures. The inscription of the Western discourse of art on world cultures, furthermore, recapitulated its own hierarchical classification of fine and applied arts. To construct a global art gallery it was necessary to discover genres that fitted the fine art categories of sculpture and painting.

The specific canon of Native North American art that emerged during the middle decades of the twentieth century was predicated in important ways on a prior process of ethnographic collecting. Virtually every *Ga:goh:sah* that has appeared in an art exhibition was temporarily lifted out of an ethnographic collection in order to make its appearance as fine art. (This secondary appropriation is typical of Native American objects in general, few of which were initially acquired by primitivist art collectors.) By the 1930s there were well over 1500 False Face masks in ethnological collections in Europe and North America.[13] This is a huge number when one considers that during the late nineteenth and twentieth centuries, when most of the masks were collected, the membership of the Longhouse (the practitioners of traditional Iroquois spirituality) was probably not much greater than twice that number.[14] The number of collected masks evidences, on the one hand, a 'scramble' for False Face masks comparable to the competition for northwest coast totem poles and other object types regarded as centrepieces of turn-of-the-century museum displays, and, on the other, an active Iroquois commercial production of masks for outsiders.[15]

Iroquois *Ga:goh:sah* have attracted an inordinate amount of scholarly attention ever since Lewis Henry Morgan's first published account of 1852.[16] No fewer than thirty professional field ethnologists, including J.N.B. Hewitt, M.R. Harrington, Arthur Parker, and Frank Speck, have written about them. The study of the masks and their rituals has been central to the long and distinguished scholarly career of William Fenton, the dean of twentieth-century Iroquoianists. He has produced over fifteen publications focusing on questions of the ethnohistory, typology, and ritual practices associated with the masks as understood from both non-Native and Iroquois perspectives. His massive 500-page monograph, *The False Faces of the Iroquois*, was published in 1987, fifty years after the appearance of his first article.[17] The question of why, among all things made by Iroquois, False Face masks have so consistently been singled out by Western connoisseurs as high art is closely tied to their prominence in ethnographic study and collecting. The importance attributed to these masks by the late nineteenth- and early twentieth-century ethnographers who collected most of what is in museums today exemplifies a tight interdependence of art theory and ethnography that long predates the advent of a modernist discourse of primitive art. In both art and anthropological practice the genres and styles of 'art' were key diagnostics of the level of civilization attained by a given society. For ethnographers, as for art critics, 'true sculpture' – that which is divorced from any functional purpose – was the most highly evolved form of plastic art. Its inclusion was therefore indispensable to any study based on evolutionist principles, and particularly for any ethnographer desirous of displaying 'his' people in the most favourable possible light. The entry 'Sculpture' in the Smithsonian Institution's influential *Handbook of American Indians North of Mexico* states this position clearly:

> The sculptural arts in their widest significance may be regarded as including the whole range of the nonplastic shaping arts, their processes and products; but as here considered they relate more especially to the higher phases of the native work, those which rise above the mere utilitarian level into the realm of esthetic expression, thus serving to illustrate the evolution of sculpture into fine art.[18]

The *Ga:goh:sa* belong to one of the most important medicine societies of the Iroquois. (That other medicine societies of equivalent ritual importance are not as well known to the general public is undoubtedly due to the fact that they do not make use of masquerades.) The masks represent forest spirits who put their powers at the disposal of human beings for the prevention and curing of illness. They bring healing to individuals and also drive away disease on behalf of the whole community at important annual ceremonies.[19] According to Iroquois origin stories, this great benefit was achieved by the Creator after a contest with *Hadui*, the World Rim Dweller and the most powerful of the False Faces, who challenged the Creator to a test of their relative powers. In proving his superiority the Creator caused a mountain to slam into *Hadui*'s face, breaking his nose and twisting his features. The physiognomies of the various types of masks are, thus, purposeful inversions and exaggerations of human forms. By their deeply grooved wrinkles and shiny metal eyes the 'Common Face' masks are seen to be forest beings, the possessors of other-than-human powers; the mask type that represents *Hadui* himself displays the broken and distorted features that resulted from the great battle.[20]

The intentional and intensely meaningful distortions of the False Faces have been problematic for most Western observers, who are accustomed to idealized anthropomorphic religious iconographies. In the accounts of Jesuits and other early contact-period travellers who witnessed their public appearances they are invariably described in terms that denote ugliness, paganism, and the diabolical, such as 'hideous' (1687), 'clumsy,' 'antic,' 'hobgoblin' (1751), 'idolatrous,' 'frightful,' 'awry' (1741), and 'ghastly' (1779).[21] Early twentieth-century ethnographic descriptions continued to employ this vocabulary of the grotesque, although rationalized and objectified by means of a new contextualization within mythological narratives.[22] As I have noted, ethnographic collectors enthusiastically collected False Face masks not only because they illustrated Iroquois beliefs and rituals, but also because they were preeminent examples of 'sculpture.' But it was not until the primitivist impulse within modern art had reached a certain stage that the *Ga:goh:sah* became celebrated as aesthetic creations. The specific history of primitivism in North America was also instrumental. One result of the initial engagement of the turn-of-the-century European modernists with African and Oceanic art had been the assignment of a special prominence to masks, as objects that can be easily decontextualized, hung on the wall, and made available for aesthetic contemplation.[23] During the 1930s and 1940s a number of prominent surrealists who spent the war years in temporary exile in New York began to promote genres of Native North American art that seemed to them to embody dream experience, the urges of the unconscious, primal archetypes, and the mythic.[24] During these decades, too, nationalist artistic projects in the United States and Canada drew attention to indigenous arts as alternatives to European artistic traditions.

Large, anthropomorphic, wooden carvings with deeply carved and dramatically distorted features, streaming hair, and shining metal eyes, the *Ga:goh:sah* embodied the mid-twentieth-century modernist ideal of primitive art far better than other aesthetically elaborated Iroquois objects, which tend to be small and intimate in scale or hybrid in style and made of 'craft' materials such as fibres, beads, or hide. It is not surprising to find that False Face masks were prominently featured in every book or exhibition catalogue on Native American art published since the 1930s – a convention that has changed only in the last few years.[25] As we have seen, a constellation of apparently disconnected and even, at times, contradictory positions ranging from idealist aesthetics to cultural evolutionism to aesthetic expressionism had combined to make their canonization inevitable.

The first art publications on Native American art appeared in 1931 and 1941 to accompany the first large exhibitions on the subject, the *Exposition of Indian Tribal Arts* (subtitled the 'First exhibition of American Indian art selected entirely with consideration of esthetic value'), and the Museum of Modern Art's 1941 exhibition *Indian Art of the United States*.[26] In both texts the False Faces are described in terms that remain closely tied to ethnological accounts, despite the self-proclaimed aesthetic orientations of the two exhibitions. In the earlier of these, for example, Oliver LaFarge gave a dramatic account of the *Ga:goh:sah* as 'awful beings' wearing 'grotesque masks' that were 'made terrible by great staring eyes.'[27]

A recognizably formalist language is more evident in the publications of the 1960s. In the most widely circulated such text, Frederick Dockstadter's *Indian Art in America*, the author noted the 'plastic quality of the carving and the dramatic portrayal of the features.'[28] In the spate of exhibition catalogues and books on Native American art published in the 1970s this language is further elaborated. One major survey catalogue describes the *Ga:goh:sah* as 'among the most virile and spectacular works of art created by the Iroquois.'[29] The language of expressive form is, perhaps, most fully developed in a Denver Art Museum publication of 1979, in which Richard Conn wrote of one mask:

The carver who produced this mask sought to convey the powerful aspects of his subject. Copper rings about the eye holes invoke the searing quality of the spirit's eyes; the vigorous carving of the planes and hollows of the forehead is emphasized by precisely painted red lines that echo the shape and color of the mouth. The dynamic design perfectly embodies the forceful personality and indomitable might of the spirit.[30]

Numerous further examples could be given, including one from my own earlier work.[31] With this kind of close formal reading curators and writers tried to transpose the experience of Native American art from an object that was to be understood as an illustration of a mythic narrative to one that could be contemplated in more purely aesthetic terms. In doing so they were promoting the art museum's mandate to act as a special kind of space in which the gaze plays freely over objects. As Svetlana Alpers has noted, 'the taste for isolating this kind of attentive looking at crafted objects is as peculiar to our culture as is the museum as the space or institution where the activity takes place.'[32]

False Faces and Popular Visual Culture

Iroquois and other Native Americans make little distinction between ethnographic and aesthetic projects of collecting and display. In this sense the distinction between 'art' and 'artifact' paradigms of the object has been a preoccupation of Western, not indigenous, writers. The high compliment that, as Clifford has written, our culture pays to others by recognizing their objects as art has often missed its mark, and both types of museum display have appeared equally invasive to colonized peoples.[33] The Carribean-Canadian writer M. Nourbese Philip has expressed the process as a ritual litany – 'identify, describe, catalogue, annotate, appropriate' – whose purpose is ultimately to control 'the Other, against which are arrayed the forces of reason, rationality, logic and knowledge as possessable and certifiable.' I want to add to this list the forces of capital and commerce. The commodification of the *Ga:goh:sah* began, as has already been noted, with the production of masks by traditional carvers for ethnologists and private collectors, a production that has continued to the present, most actively by the Iroquois-owned Iroqrafts company of Oshweken, Ontario. This production supplied needed income for impoverished reserve economies. Fenton writes that, 'by 1930 picking old masks and carving new ones for collectors was a regular practice, and collecting was expected behavior of visiting ethnologists. I recall vividly the puzzlement of persons who showed me old masks and wondered why I simply wanted to photograph them.'[34] During the twentieth century Iroquois artists and performers have also incorporated the masks into their work. In the 1920s Esther Deer, or Princess White Deer, a successful dancer from Kahnawake, used a *Ga:goh:sah* in one of her acts at the *Ziegfeld Follies*. A publicity photograph of the 1920s shows her holding the mask next to her face in an image that very strongly recalls an icon of twentieth-century photography, Man Ray's *Noire and Blanche*, of 1926.[35] During the 1980s and 1990s Joe Jacobs and other noted contemporary Iroquois sculptors continued to incorporate images of the masks in their soapstone carvings, for which they were criticized by some other Iroquois.

Perhaps the most widely publicized example of this kind occurred in 1996 during the presentation of the annual National Aboriginal Achievement Awards, nationally televised by the Canadian Broadcasting Corporation. Native actor Tom Jackson, star of a popular CBC television series, performed an almost identical juxtaposition to Princess White Deer's, playfully holding a *Ga:goh:sah* over his face before making one of the awards. In one letter of protest, an Iroquois correspondent wrote that 'this misuse of our sacred masks is akin to someone serving sacramental wine and consecrated hosts at a cocktail party.'[36] John Kim Bell, the founder of the Canadian Native Arts Foundation, which organizes the awards and the ceremony, and himself a Mohawk from Kahnawake, defended the show by affirming a distinction between active masks, carved according to correct ritual procedures, and the masks used on the program, which he described as 'tourist replica knock-offs, which are made and sold by the hundreds by Iroquoian people.'[37] This debate, which has been conducted in terms of conflicting interpretations of Iroquois tradition, needs to be understood against the background of a much more extensive twentieth-century history of the mechanical reproduction of images of *Ga:goh:sah* of which the 1996 telecast was only the most recent and – thanks to the power of television – most widely seen example. I would like now to fill in several chapters of that history.

From the nineteenth century, the primary mandate of the public museum has been the education (and, as Bennett and Duncan argue, socialization) of an audience defined in ever broader and more democratic terms.[38] In addition to the representations they produce in-house, museum ethnologists have regularly collaborated in commercial projects such as world's fairs and publications. During the twentieth century, then, False Face masks and their images have been inserted into commercial circulation through the entrepreneurial activities of Iroquois themselves, through authorized public–private collaborations with museum curators, and through other, unauthorized appropriations. Most of these projects have left only ephemeral traces. The following examples do not, therefore, represent a systematic sampling, but they serve to rough in a commercial context of popular visual culture essential to the understanding of contemporary contestations.[39]

One of the largest early twentieth-century non-museum displays of Native North American objects was installed in the grill room of the Hotel Astor in New York City, named the 'Hall of the Americas.'[40] The printed guidebook to the Hall, illustrated by photographs of the installations and museum-like catalogue entries for the artifacts, clearly states the combination of nationalist, sentimental, and commercial motives behind its creation. It also foregrounds the professional museological authorization for its artifact displays (which, like those of the museums, were bought from a trading company). 'Leading officers of the American Museum of Natural History and the Ethnological Bureau in Washington' it states, supplied busts of Indians taken from life casts as well as ethnographic photographs, which served as an attraction to foreigners and other visitors at the same time that they commemorated 'the noble red man.' As the guidebook notes, 'Being deeply interested in the history of our country, the creation of an American style of decoration appealed to [its designer] strongly.'

The Hall was divided into eight sections that roughly followed the standard ethnographic culture area map, one of which was dedicated solely to the Iroquois, identified in the guidebook as 'the most famous of all groups of Indian tribes.' Guests entered through a foyer decorated with artifacts of the early settler era of old New York and then, 'having so far examined the relics of the white men who drove the Indian back from the shores of the Atlantic to the desert fastnesses of the far west, one passes to the room where historical relics of vanished or fast-vanishing tribes have been made the sole attraction.' The Hall is intended as a *lieu de mémoire* in Nora's sense; here in the midst of bustling urban life people could 'pause to remember at times that the wigwam of the Indian once stood on the very ground now occupied by our great cities.' Like the museum, it was also intended to serve as a locus of the displaced authenticity of indigenous people, since on the reservation 'the progress of civilization has stripped him of his most attractive characteristics.'[41]

In the middle of the Hall, in the section devoted to the Iroquois, seven *Ga:goh:sah* were prominently displayed (see figure 2.1). As in the other sections, life busts (wearing Plains feather bonnets) were mounted on pedestals, and framed photographs were set into the wainscoting – although most showed feather-bonneted Plains Indians, it having proved impossible to find more than two 'authentic' images of Iroquois life. The ethnographic objects were arranged in the trophy formation used in world's fairs and expositions. Among the moose

2.1 Page from the guidebook to the Hotel Astor Hall of the Americas, Times Square, illustrating the trophy-like installation that included Iroquois *Ga:goh:sah* on display between about 1904 and 1937. Courtesy University of Virginia Art Museum.

head, snowshoes, bags, ladles, and other objects that made up the Iroquois trophy three *Ga:goh:sah* were suspended like captured shrunken heads. The special interest associated with these masks is suggested by the second grouping of five masks displayed on an adjacent wall. The masks are glossed in the guidebook as follows:

> The most peculiar objects are two hideous masks beset with hair and smeared with red and black paint. They belong to the outfit of medicine men, who, up to the present day, prey upon their kinsmen by pretending to have power over the many demons and witches which threaten the life of the Iroquois. Opposite the moose head, hanging on the balcony, are several other masks, one of which is fearfully distorted.

In this passage, despite the careful academic and museological framing of the American Indian Hall, a serious slippage has occurred. The standard anthropological account has given way to the untrammeled popular imagination, and older tropes of the primitive and the savage have surfaced, demonizing the Iroquois medicine society in a language that harks back to the *Jesuit Relations*.

Other examples can be given of anthropologically authorized popularizations of the *Ga:goh:sah*'s that also diverge, though in different ways, from the representations of the museum or academic ethnologist. For example, the text of *Indians of America*, a children's book published in 1935, reflects the more liberal attitudes towards Indians that began with the Collier years and the Roosevelt administration. The book credits 'well known anthropologists at the Heye Foundation in New York,' for their help.[42] Its stated aim is to counter the 'bloodthirsty' and warlike image of the Indian by emphasizing an understanding of 'their life before these troubles began.' 'The famous benevolent society of the Iroquois,' the child readers are told:

> was known as the Ja-di-gon-sa meaning 'False Face Society.' Members wore carved false faces, some of which were extremely hideous, with large noses and twisted mouths. They believed these faces gave them power to do good, the deed being of greater benefit if the benefactor was masked and unknown.[43]

While this account does not demonize the masks in the manner of the Hotel Astor publication, the language of the grotesque with which the masks are described and its desire to 'arouse your interest in a vanishing race' remain fixed within familiar aesthetic and temporal boundaries.[44]

The appropriation of images of False Face masks, among other objects, to the interests of private corporate enterprise is even more comprehensively realized in a 1956 publication issued by the Canadian Pulp and Paper Association entitled *National Asset – Native Design*. The twenty-page, large-format paperback is lavishly illustrated with examples of Canadian Aboriginal art and French Canadian folk art.[45] The National Museum of Canada and some of the most authoritative and respected figures in the Canadian cultural world are prominently credited as collaborators in its production, including Canada's premier ethnologist, Marius Barbeau, his son-in-law, artist Arthur Price, and the well-known painter A.J. Casson, who designed the publication.[46] Effectively, the booklet presents two parallel texts, one written and the other visual. The written text is a history of and a paean to the pulp and paper industry, while the visual text consists of photographic and painted images of Canadian indigenous and folk art that fill the margins of the pages. The two texts are connected only in the opening passage, entitled 'Native Design': 'This book, which concerns a great national asset, is illustrated with native Canadian folk designs,' it begins. 'The indigenous art used herein is an adornment well suited to the story of a great native enterprise that enriches the life of every Canadian whether in the vast hinterland, in the teeming cities, or in the pleasant countryside.' Since 'Indians of the forests' made many of the objects, they can serve as 'reminders' of the even greater importance of the forest to the modern nation. And, just as the indigenous objects served as tools, historical records, or 'means of expression and communication,' 'the products of Canada's leading industrial enterprise fulfil much the same purpose as these designs served some hundreds of years ago: for Canada is a world leader in the manufacture of pulp and paper, the currency of civilization and the handmaid of commerce.' The final paragraph sounds again the note of appropriated indigeneity: 'primitive design and folk art has ever served to lend character to national culture and to national art. So, perhaps, the illustrations herein may help to widen the adaptation of native art to architecture, to furniture, to textiles, to metals, to industrial design, to fine art, and to wherever craftsmanship can add distinction and value to the products of Canada.' The four *Ga:goh:sah*'s that appear midway through the book are, then, completely divorced from any specific ethnographic context. Rather they are positioned as a prelude to the progressivist and assimilationist settler narrative of Canadian history in which the dynamic, industrial Anglo-Canadian economy is asserted to be the natural successor to the primitive Aboriginal (and French-Canadian) economies that preceded it. Their arts, like their lands, become a resource to be legitimately exploited by the newcomers.

When we turn to the many unsanctioned commercial appropriations of False Face masks we find that the attachment of romantic, derogatory, or opportunistic significations to the *Ga:goh:sah* was accomplished with even greater disregard for ethnographic or indigenous meanings than in the previous examples. A *Ga:goh:sah* appears in one of the plates of *Le plus bel album du monde pour les industries de luxe*, a portfolio advertising a French Art Deco jewellery design firm published during the late 1920s.[47] The tag attached to a made-in-Japan souvenir doll representing a False Face masker states: 'GOOD LUCK / MEDICINE MAN / INDIAN DOLL / Protects You Against All Evil Spirits / While Driving – At Work – At Play.' The reverse side reads: 'An interesting American Indian custom was the wearing of hideous masks by their Medicine men. They believed that by wearing the face of a particular animal or one representing an evil spirit they could prevent bad luck.'[48]

Sometime during the 1970s or 1980s Nabisco Canada distributed a series of cards about North American Indians in boxes of cereal. As in baseball cards, one side bore an image and the other a set of vital statistics. One of the cards shows a *Ga:goh:sah* with a particularly twisted face and the terse caption, 'Seneca Indian Mask (Northeast United States).' On the reverse is a map locating the Seneca within North America, and the text: 'This mask made by the Seneca Indians represents a spirit of the forest whose face became twisted out of shape as a punishment for boasting. Thus, a warning for both children and adults.' The format of the card conveys a bogus ethnographic authority through its museum-like map and label, while the format of the set miniaturizes, infantilizes, and trivializes indigenous people by creating the illusion of their collectibility. (The top corner of the map side bears the admonition, 'Punch hole here / Collect all twenty cards,' appealing directly to the obsessive psychology of the collector described by Baudrillard.)[49] Most seriously, the interpretive text distorts out of all recognition the meanings the masks have for Iroquois people.

Numerous other such unmediated commercial appropriations have occurred, but let me end with one particularly blatant example. A 1952 issue of the *National Geographic* contained a full-page advertisement for The Travelers Insurance Company featuring a large, highly naturalistic drawing of a masked *Ga:goh:sah* shown in a ritual posture crawling toward the viewer, turtle shell rattle in hand (see figure 2.2). It was headed 'Iroquois scare-devil,' and the text below read:

Iroquois medicine men wearing horrible masks like this crawled into the tribe's lodges twice a year – jumping and moaning and rattling their turtle-shell noisemakers.

As a part of the ceremony, they scattered ashes on the floor. And that particular Iroquois dwelling was supposed to become a safe place in which to live.

A wonderful idea – chasing out evil spirits that might later harm you and your family. But it won't work for you any better than it did for the old-time Iroquois.

But mishaps around the house, or personal injury accidents anywhere, needn't be a heavy burden on your pocketbook. Just call in your Travelers agent and let him tell you about Travelers Accident Insurance.[50]

As in the Nabisco Indian 'baseball cards' the fragmentation of the narrative results in disinformation. Not only has the *Ga:goh:sah* become completely detached from the significations attached to it as an ethnographic artifact, but the context in which the ad occurs – in a magazine whose readers could be presumed to take a sympathetic interest in cultural differences – makes its sarcastic and scornful tone particularly shocking.[51]

Commercial exploitations of this sort and museum installations are at opposite ends of what I would term a 'spectrum of responsibility' to originating communities. Although museums also decontextualize ethnographic artifacts in order to reinsert them into non-Native narratives, the new significations assigned to them have been controlled by processes of research that connected them through fieldwork and, more recently, a range of collaborative strategies, to indigenous systems of meaning. Commercial commodification loosens these controls to differing degrees. During the twentieth century, as the power of mechanical reproduction and consumerist commodification grew to reach ever-expanding audiences, Iroquois activists increasingly identified the museum as the site where the initial gesture of display and interpretation occurs and therefore as the originating point of the semiotic chain that ends in such offensive and uncontrolled examples of

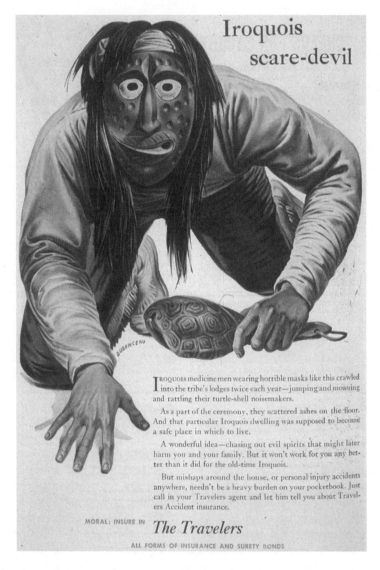

2.2 Advertisement for the Travelers Insurance Company published in the *National Geographic* in 1952 (vol. 101, no. 3). The illustration of the *Ga:goh:sah* masker in one of the postures adopted during ritual appearances is based on ethnographic photographs published during the first half of the twentieth century. Courtesy Royal Ontario Museum.

commercial exploitation. It is one of the many contradictory features of this history, however, that once images become disseminated in popular visual culture it is virtually impossible to call them back. Paradoxically, it may be museums – both the older institutions and the newer Native-run centres – that can most effectively respond to and critique the fictions and fantasies of popular culture.

Debating Removal, Replication, and Reproduction

In the mid-1970s and 1980s, as part of a renewed political activism in Native North American communities, Iroquois groups in the United States and Canada began to create written policies on False Face mask display and to approach museums with formal requests for changes to public exhibits. In a longer historical perspective, the disappearance of the *Ga:go:sah*'s that resulted can be seen as one of a series of strategic removals from and insertions into spaces of display that articulate proto-colonial, colonial, and emergent postcolonial phases in Iroquois relations with European North Americans. As numerous accounts make clear, during the early years of contact the public appearances of the *Ga:goh:sah*'s in Iroquois villages could be viewed by any outsiders who happened to be present. One effect of the destabilization of Iroquois life that followed upon the political defeats, population losses, and land appropriations of the early nineteenth century was the division of communities into traditionalists, or Longhouse members, and followers of a variety of Christian sects.[52] As a result the public and communal nature of False Face masquerades gradually became more private and sectarian. During the first half of the twentieth century, as we have also seen, anthropologists were able to observe ceremonies, to interview faith keepers, and to gain the collaboration of Iroquois who believed in the importance of salvage anthropology as offering a valuable means of preserving a record of their historical cultures. In recent decades, however, the resurgence of traditional practice and belief and a determination to control unauthorized and exploitative uses of the masks have combined to close off access for researchers and other outsiders to all ceremonies of the Society of Faces and the Longhouse.

For many traditional Iroquois the making available of *Ga:goh:sah* to spectatorial scrutiny and pleasure, which is the museum's central mandate, had always been a potentially dangerous activity and, to some extent, a contravention of ritual correctness. For them, masks that have been properly prepared are 'alive' and full of power. They must be offered tobacco and fed with corn mush. Viewing must be restricted and carefully managed by specialists, for without proper treatment the masks can cause illness and trouble the dreams of those who come in contact with them – including museum visitors. During the twentieth century Iroquois consultants pointed out the need to care for masks in museums to the ethnologists with whom they worked, and some museums made arrangements for ritual specialists to come at intervals to perform necessary rituals. William Fenton's report that 'when carvers make a False Face mask for a museum they speak to it and tell it it is going to "a place where people come in and out to look"' is evidence not only of how unnatural museum display is from an Iroquois point of view, but also that the viewing of the masks was not, per se, forbidden.

Part of the confusion in the museum world results from the variations in the policies and requests brought forward by different Iroquois organizations and communities. The National Museum of Canada (now the Canadian Museum of Civilization) was one of the first to be approached. 'In various visits we have had from Longhouse Iroquois leaders,' wrote the Iroquoian Ethnologist at the National Museum to his director in 1975,

> The point has been quietly though forcefully made that we should not be displaying 'living' false face masks in the Iroquois Hall ... The Iroquois consider the masks highly sacred and even 'dangerous' objects that should be on view only at the time of curing rituals. The issue has come up from time to time, and I think we ought now to give serious consideration to the possibility of substituting replicas.[53]

Five years later, in 1980, the masks were removed and replaced with fibreglass casts.[54] The use of replicas, however, was explicitly rejected in a statement developed in the early 1980s by the Grand Council of the Hodenosaunee, or Iroquois Confederacy, which represents most of the New York State Iroquois communities.[55] Its current policy statement identifies the masks as 'essential to the spiritual and emotional well-being of the Hodenosaunee,' and states that any interference with them is a violation of religious freedom. It denies that any distinction exists between ritually and commercially carved masks and forbids the public exhibition of all masks. It also forbids all forms of reproduction or the distribution of any kind of information. The language is explicit:

The exhibition of masks by museums does not serve to enlighten the public regarding the culture of the Hodenesaunee, as such an exhibition violates the intended purpose of the mask and contributes to the desecration of the sacred image.

In addition, information regarding medicine societies is not meant for general distribution. The non-Indian public does not have a right to examine, interpret nor present the beliefs, functions and duties of the secret medicine societies of the Hodenosaunee. The sovereign responsibility of the Hodenosaunee over their spiritual duties must be respected by the removal of all medicine masks from exhibition and from access to non Indians ...

The Council of Chiefs find that there is no proper way to explain, interpret, or present the significance of the medicine masks and therefore ask that no attempt to be made by museums to do other than to explain the wishes of the Hodenosaunee in this matter.

Finally, the statement requests the return of all masks to the 'proper caretakers among the Hodenosaunee' because 'it is only through these actions that the traditional culture will remain strong and peace be restored to our communities.'

A number of large American museums, notably the Smithsonian's Native-run National Museum of the American Indian (NMAI), are guided by this statement. The NMAI has made special provision for the closed storage of its masks. The Mohawk community at Kahnawake, though not formally part of the Grand Council, has taken a position similar to that of the Grand Council. During the 1988 showing of the controversial exhibition *The Spirit Sings: Artistic Traditions of Canada's First Peoples,* the Kahnawake Mohawk brought an unsuccessful lawsuit against the Glenbow Museum to remove a False Face mask on loan from the Royal Ontario Museum. Although the courts did not uphold the request, the mask was voluntarily removed before the show's second venue, the Canadian Museum of Civilization, and replaced with a replica made by the late Chief Jacob Thomas. As the result of these and other actions, over the past fifteen years or so, *Ga:goh:sah*'s have been removed from most of the major museums in North America.[56]

The question of replication and the closely related question of commercial art market production remain, however, subjects of debate within the Iroquois community, confusing museum officials in their efforts to respect Aboriginal views on the display of sacred objects.[57] Both the ethnographic literature and interviews with modern-day faith keepers establish quite clearly a distinction between active and inactive masks which, in the view of some Iroquois ritual specialists, would permit the viewing of replicas and reproductions. The initial solution adopted by the National Museum of Canada to replace masks with replicas was posited on this distinction. The museum of the Woodlands Cultural Centre on the Six Nations Reserve has removed from view all of its live masks, but displays a False Face mask still attached to a tree trunk because, as an incomplete carving, it is not yet alive. The museum's director, Tom Hill, has written that 'we do believe, however, that it remains important to discuss their creation which can successfully be conveyed without putting the mask on display.'[58] The museum's Policy on Sacred and Sensitive Material states: 'Only images of masks which have not been "blessed" or have not been used in any ceremonial function will be presented in any Centre sponsored display. Such a display will be approved by the appropriate traditionalists,' and, further, 'Mask classifications will not be based on ethnographic or museological standards but standards which are appropriate to the traditional community.' This policy conforms with the teaching of Chief Jacob Thomas, who was both a faith keeper of the False Face Society at Six Nations and a member of a prominent family of mask carvers. In a 1982 CBC television documentary Chief Thomas was filmed as he carved masks on a living tree and in his studio. He explained:

> My grandfather was also a carver and there were many carvers in those days ... It took me time before I did get to know the art of it ... Now I do carving most of the time and I have a lot of standing orders. It's mostly for commercial, but we don't bless the mask for commercial purposes.[59]

The narrator further explains that 'The full ritual which gives a medicine mask its powers and the annual feeding of the mask to sustain these powers could never be shown to outsiders. But part of the ritual can be shown, the physical carving of a mask in the old way, from a living tree.' The reproduction of images and the publication of ethnographic information also remain controversial. The National Museum of the American Indian recently refused my request to publish a reproduction of a painting of False Face ceremonies in its collection made in the 1930s by Seneca artist Ernest Smith as part of a project designed to strengthen traditional material culture overseen by Seneca ethnologist Arthur Parker. Similarly, my request for a copy of the guidebook to the Hotel Astor's Hall of the American Indian from the University of Virginia's Bayly Museum, which now owns the masks that were displayed there, was reviewed in relation to the Grand Council's policy. Yet in reserve communities whose leaders have taken the most categorical positions, such as Kahnawake, images of False Face masks are to be found painted on the walls of a local tourist village and reproduced in advertisements published in the annual Pow Wow program.

The issue of reproduction hits most directly at principles of free dissemination of information at the heart of post-Enlightenment Western academic traditions. The two positions can be represented by two reviews of William Fenton's encyclopedic monograph, published in 1987 just as the debates summarized here were becoming public and heated. Both of the reviewers, ethnohistorian Bruce Trigger and Six Nations Mohawk writer Joel Montour, are well informed and sensitive to the complexities of the issues. Trigger praised Fenton for his success in accomplishing 'the anthropological task of presenting Iroquois culture on its own terms' and for offering 'as complete insight as it is possible for outsiders to acquire into Iroquois beliefs and rituals and how these have survived and adapted to changing conditions.'[60] Montour took the opposite view, arguing that the information, gathered decades earlier, contributes to the picture of a culture frozen in time. Where Trigger judged the book as transcending stereotypes and offering a respectful historical record useful to Iroquois and outsider alike, Montour urged the need to acknowledge the shifting of meaning over time and the importance of representing 'living expression and individual application.' Montour's objections were based not so much on objections to breaches of ritual secrecy – he states that he did not grow up in the Longhouse – but rather on the anthropologist's use of what Carlo Ginzburg calls the 'evidential paradigm.'[61] 'The emphasis on material culture as *sine qua non*,' Montour remarked, 'negates individual interpretation and style ... the reality is that we seek to understand other cultures by their material presence ... but it is still the view of outsiders looking through a window fogged by their own breath.' For Montour, Fenton's material culture methods and ethnohistorical perspective weaken the vitality of contemporary practices, which he wants to privilege, while Trigger's allegiance to Western academic traditions lead him to affirm the value of historical understandings and generalizable insights into cultural process produced by anthropological work.

Disappearing Acts as Postcolonial Strategy

Anthony Grafton remarked during the conference that led to this volume that a museum is a place where you put things behind glass to protect them from people, where once people had to be protected from them. On one level, the motivations behind the disappearing acts of the Iroquois and other indigenous people can be read as efforts to protect people from certain objects whose power has been denied by the premises of secular modernity. That is, they can be read as attempts to return to earlier traditions that turn out not, after all, to be lost. In this sense Iroquois goals are diametrically opposed to those of modernist and postmodernist artists who celebrate mechanical reproduction, following Walter Benjamin, as a means of destroying the art object's aura and with it a precinct of class privilege. For Iroquois and other Aboriginal people it is precisely the destruction of aura – understood as essence or power – that needs to be prevented. Iroquois efforts to limit access to the *Ga:goh:sah* are directed at the preservation and restoration of those ineffable qualities and inherent powers that technologies of scientific and formal exposition and analysis, as well as of mechanical reproduction, seek to render transparent. Furthermore, as a large body of work by anthropologists and art historians has clearly established, very few non-Western peoples have developed a discourse of the visual art object as autonomous and commodifiable parallel to that of the West. In most world cultures the aesthetic has traditionally been located among a range of patterned behaviours that can be kinetic, auditory, olfactory, gestural, performative, and/or visual. Visual aesthetic production, furthermore, has often been incidental to the work of the ritualist, the healer, the hunter, or the maker of clothing. The expressive and cognitive tradition related to the treatment of objects being invoked by Iroquois activists is, then, holistic and spiritual rather than specialized and secular.

When, in contrast, Iroquois activists attempt to suppress the reproduction of texts and images, they are trying to find solutions for modern realities for which there can be no appeal to historical traditions. Their goal here is to terminate the long history of colonial surveillance of Iroquois society and to throw off the still-lingering, inquiring gaze of the outsider. Disappearing acts are intended to disable the axis of knowledge and power that was activated during the colonial period through academic and popular projects of representation.[62] It would be naive to think that in the early twenty-first century any people on the face of the earth can avoid the necessity of negotiating the Western 'art-culture' system, as Clifford terms it,[63] that has been inscribed by centuries of colonial rule, economic integration, and global mass communication. At the same time, however, the incomplete and partial nature of the Western inscription is becoming increasingly apparent.

Eight years ago, when I was preparing the lecture that eventually turned into this paper, I had the opportunity to ask Mohawk elder Ernest Benedict's advice about whether or not I should show slides of the *Ga:goh:sah*. He replied that the matter was difficult and still unresolved within the Iroquois community. Then he told me a story. 'I heard about a carver,' Benedict said, 'who gave permission to some people who wanted to photograph masks, because, as the carver said, "The masks can take care of themselves." When the pictures were developed,' the punchline went, 'they came out black.' Benedict's story, I think, is more than an assertion of the living power of False Face masks. It is also a metaphor for the ultimate inadequacy of the 'pictures' made by outsiders, be they ethnographic texts or formalist descriptions, to capture the reality of the masks as understood by cultural insiders.

I began this essay by remarking on how Iroquois protests usefully reveal the traditions of knowledge management that operate in the academy and the museum. Eight years ago I decided not to show any slides. I have now come to a different decision. Although I do not illustrate ritually active masks, I do display some of the secondary representations of the masks because of their importance to the postcolonial scholarly project. The very power and centrality of the visual in the Western tradition makes the critique of visual images a necessary part of the work scholars need to perform in order to develop critical understandings of the histories of representation and misrepresentation that are colonialism's legacy.[64] In her book *Double Exposures* Mieke Bal has powerfully analysed the need to perform such acts of critique with discretion, judgment, and sensitivity to framing so that we do not end up reinscribing that which we are attempting to critique.[65]

Traditional Iroquois, like other Native Americans, regard the whole universe as animated by powers that must be respected. All kinds of objects – and images – can potentially share in these powers. My own attempt to separate the issue of sacred power from that of resistance to surveillance remains an example of Western analytical practice. In order to write this paper I have had to use Fenton's book. Nor will the issue of reproduction be resolved by individual acts of intervention in the museum. As I was working on an earlier draft of this paper someone taped to my office door a xeroxed *New York Times* article describing an attempt by Seneca leaders to stop the sale of *Ga:goh:sah* at a Sotheby's auction.[66] The article was illustrated with five clear photographic reproductions. Indigenous people will, no doubt, continue to confront us with other ways of thinking about the issue. The Saulteaux-Ojibwa artist Robert Houle did this, for example, in his 1992 installation 'Mohawk Summer 1990' when he painted on one wall, in reverse lettering, the words 'sovereign,' 'longhouse,' 'landclaim,' and 'falseface.' Houle has said that this work – dissonant, oppositional, and expressive of an almost perversely inverted reality, is a '[metaphor] of contemporary Mohawk life.' His elegant conceptual piece and punning use of language ties the False Face mask to a fully integrated notion of Iroquois social life and insists that culture cannot be divorced from larger political concerns about power and self-government. But Houle's artistic statement is made in an art gallery, suggesting, with equal urgency, the indispensability of the museum to the negotiation of competing traditions in the contemporary world.

NOTES

1 'Museum and Field Studies of Iroquois Masks and Ritualism,' *Explorations and Fieldwork of the Smithsonian Institution in 1940* (Washington, DC, 1941), 100.
2 Quoted in 'Slow but Steady Progress Reported in Return of Artifacts to Indians,' *The Indian Trader* (November 1995). George was referring to an Iroquois request to the New York State Museum for the return of masks. The quotation begins: 'A concern the Museum has is that since these items are so great historically, what assurances can we offer that they be preserved?'
3 See T.J. Ferguson and B. Martza, 'The Repatriation of Zuni *Ahayu:da*,' *Museum Anthropology*, 14, no. 2 (1990): 7–15; W.L. Merrill, E.J. Ladd, and T.J. Ferguson, 'The Return of the *Ahayu:da*: Lessons for Repatriation from Zuni Pueblo and the Smithsonian Institution,' *Current Anthropology*, 34, no. 5 (1993): 523–67; George H.J. Abrams, 'The Case for Wampum: Repatriation from the Museum of the American Indian to the Six Nations Confederacy, Brantford, Ontario, Canada,' in Flora E.S. Kaplan, *Museums and the Making*

of 'Ourselves': The Role of Objects in National Identity (London, 1994); and
Zena Pearlstone, *Katsina: Commodified and Appropriated Images of Hopi Super-
naturals* (Los Angeles: Fowler Museum of Cultural History, 2002); and Ruth
B. Phillips and Elizabeth Johnson, 'Negotiating New Relationships: Canadian Museums, First Nations, and Cultural Property,' in John Torpey ed.,
Politics and the Past: On Repairing Historical Injustices (New York, 2003),
149–68.

4 The names for these masked beings differ in the languages of the six modern Iroquois nations. I use the Seneca name as given by Fenton.

5 For recent discussions of the methods and goals of visual studies and visual
anthropology see W.J.T. Mitchell, 'Showing Seeing: A Critique of Visual
Culture,' *Journal of Visual Culture*, 1, no. 2 (2002): 166–7; Nicholas Mirzoeff, '
Introduction,' in *An Introduction to Visual Culture* (New York: Routledge,
1998); and Marcus Banks and Howard Morphy, 'Introduction: Rethinking
Visual Anthropology,' in Marcus Banks and Howard Morphy, eds, *Rethink-
ing Visual Anthropology* (New Haven, 1997). For model studies of museum
and popular 'seeing,' see Annie Coombes, *Reinventing Africa: Museums,
Material Culture and Popular Imagination* (New Haven, 1994); and Nicholas
Mirzoeff, *Visual Culture*, chap. 4.

6 See, among others, Tim Barringer and Tom Flynn, eds, *Colonialism and the
Object: Empire, Material Culture and the Museum* (New York, 1998); Annie
Coombes, *Reinventing Africa*; Thomas Richards, *The Imperial Archive:
Knowledge and the Fantasy of Empire* (London, 1993); James Clifford, *The
Predicament of Culture: Twentieth-Century Ethnography, Literature and Art*
(Cambridge, MA, 1988), and *Routes: Travel and Translation in the Late Twenti-
eth Century* (Cambridge, MA, 1997); Nicholas Thomas, *Entangled Objects:
Exchange, Material Culture, and Colonialism in the Pacific* (Cambridge, MA,
1991) and *Possessions: Indigenous Art/Colonial Culture* (London, 1999).

7 See Brian W. Dippie, *The Vanishing American: White Attitudes and U.S. Indian
Policy* (Middletown, CT, 1982).

8 See George W. Stocking, Jr, ed., *Objects and Others: Essays on Museums and
Material Culture* (Madison, 1985); James Clifford, 'On Collecting Art and
Culture,' in Clifford, *Predicament*; Sally Price, *Primitive Art in Civilized Places*
(Chicago, 1989); Shelly Errington, *The Death of Authentic Primitive Art and
Other Tales of Progress* (Berkeley, 1998); Susan Hiller, ed., *The Myth of Primi-
tivism: Perspectives on Art* (New York, 1991); and Shepard Krech III and Bar-
bara A. Hail, eds, *Collecting Native America, 1870–1960* (Washington, DC,
1999).

9 See my 'Why Not Tourist Art: Significant Silences in Native American
Museum Representations,' in Gyan Prakash ed., *After Colonialism: Imperial*

Histories and Postcolonial Displacements (Princeton, 1995); Johannes Fabian, *Time and the Other: How Anthropology Makes Its Object* (New York, 1983); and Errington, *Death of Authentic Primitive Art.* See also Robert Young, *Colonial Desire: Hybridity in Theory, Culture, and Race* (London, 1995).

10 For an overview of these developments see Laura Peers and Alison Brown, eds, *Museums and Source Communities* (New York, 2003).

11 The Smithsonian's plans to change this exhibit were halted by budget cuts during the early 1990s. Two particularly important examples of new permanent installations that reflect extensive consultation with indigenous communities, the First Peoples' Hall at the Canadian Museum of Civilization, opened in 2003, and the new National Museum of the American Indian in Washington is opening in September 2004.

12 Christian F. Feest, 'From North America,' in William Rubin, ed., *Primitivism in Twentieth-Century Art: Affinities of the Tribal and the Modern* (New York, 1985), and W. Jackson Rushing III, *Native American Art and the New York Avant-Garde, 1910–1950* (Austin, 1995).

13 William Fenton tabulated the major museum holdings of carved and husk face masks he studied, which number 1,509. *The False Faces of the Iroquois* (Norman, OK, 1987), 20–1.

14 I derive the number of masks from Fenton's comprehensive table of 'Museums Visited and Mask Collections Seen and Studied,'*False Faces*, 20–1. The immense projects of ethnological collecting that began in the mid-nineteenth century tailed off rather abruptly around 1930, and Fenton's 'sample' was exhaustive. On the museum collecting of the period see William Sturtevant, 'Does Anthropology Need Museums?' *Proceedings of the Biological Society of Washington* 82 (1969): 619–50. Sally Weaver estimates that between the 1860s and the 1960s Longhouse membership in the largest community, the Six Nations Reserve in Ontario, was roughly 23 per cent of a population that fluctuated between 3,000 and 4,500 in the period 1860 to 1930. 'Six Nations of the Grand River,' in Bruce Trigger ed., *Handbook of the North American Indian*, vol. 15: *The Northeast* (Washington, DC, 1978), 527, 530. I add to this figure the same percentage of the roughly 10,000 Iroquois living on other reserves. See *Handbook*, vol. 15: *The Northeast* ('St Lawrence Lowlands Region').

15 See Douglas Cole, *Captured Heritage: The Scramble for Northwest Coast Artifacts* (Seattle, 1985); Janet Catherine Berlo, ed., *The Early Years of Native American Art History* (Seattle, 1991); Diana Fane, Ira Jacknis, and Lisa M. Breen, *Objects of Myth and Mystery, American Indian Art at the Brooklyn Museum* (Seattle, 1991); and Krech and Hail, eds, *Collecting Native America*.

16 Report on the fabrics, inventions, impalements, and utensils of the Iroquois,

made to the Regents of the University, January 22, 1851, Assembly Document No. 122, *New York State Cabinet of Antiquities Annual Report* 5, 66–117 (Albany, 1852).

17 'Ga:goh:sah' translates as 'face,' as it does in all the other Iroquois languages except for Onondaga, which uses a form of the name *Hadui*. The scholarly studies are tabulated and enumerated by Fenton in *False Faces*, 87–9.

18 W.H. H[olmes], *Bulletin of the Bureau of American Ethnology*, 30, Smithsonian Institution, Washington, DC (1907–10), 2: 490.

19 The *Ga:goh:sah*s appear on three different kinds of occasions: the semi-annual Traveling Rites, the Midwinter Festival, and private ceremonies. Fenton, *False Faces*, 267.

20 The strategy used by Iroquois carvers recalls Robert Thompson's discussion of the Yoruba anti-aesthetic as an inversion of ideal standards of beauty, or a 'sanctioned expression of artistic ugliness,' adopted for highly specific expressive purposes. See 'Aesthetics in Tropical Africa,' in Carol F. Jopling, ed., *Art and Aesthetics in Primitive Societies: A Critical Anthology* (New York, 1971). As Fenton further explains, however, the relationship between the forms of a mask and the being it represents through time is not fixed. Older Common Faces can eventually come to represent *Hadui*, a phenomenon that almost exactly parallels the changing identities of masks among the Liberian Dan documented by Eberhardt Fisher, 'Dan Forest Spirits: Masks in Dan Villages,' *African Arts*, 11, no. 2 (1978): 22–7.

21 For a compilation of these early descriptions see Fenton, *False Faces*, 72–82.

22 For an important historical perspective on the application of the term 'grotesque' to non-Western art, see Frances S. Connelly, *The Sleep of Reason: Primitivism in Modern European Art and Aesthetics, 1725–1907* (University Park, PA, 1999).

23 Within cultural evolutionist discourse a distinction was made between carving and the higher form of sculpture. The less tool-like a carved implement was the more sculptural it became. The 1907–10 *Handbook of the American Indians*, for example, noted a 'strong sculptural tendency' in 'the stone pipes, ornaments, and images of the mound-builders of the Mississippi valley, the carvings of the pile-dwellers of Florida, the masks, utensils, and totem poles of the N. W. coast tribes, and the spirited ivory carvings of the Eskimo. Sculpture, the fine art, is but a higher phase of these elementary manifestations of the esthetic.'

24 Fenton has written that his first articles on the masks in the late 1930s and early 1940s 'reached a wide audience outside of ethnology and promptly went out of print .Masks evidently hold an especial fascination for a wide

range of people in the creative arts, whereas shamanism has implications for medicine and professions concerned with the human psyche.' *False Faces*, 13–14.

25 The False Faces, furthermore, are represented by multiple examples in contrast to other types of objects which appear as unique pieces. The books surveyed included Oliver LaFarge et al., *Introduction to American Indian Art* (Glorieta, NM, 1985 reprint [1931]); Frederic H. Douglas and Rene D'Harnancourt, *Indian Art of the United States* (New York, 1941); Frederick J. Dockstadter, *Indian Art in America: The Arts and Crafts of the North American Indian* (New York, n.d.); Wolfgang Haberland, *The Art of North America* (New York, 1968); Ralph T. Coe, *Sacred Circles: Two Thousand Years of North American Indian Art* (London, 1976); Evan Maurer, *The Native American Heritage: A Survey of North American Indian Art* (Chicago, 1976); Walker Art Center, *American Indian Art: Form and Tradition* (New York, 1972); Richard Conn, *Native American Art in the Denver Art Museum* (Denver, 1979); Norman Feder, *American Indian Art* (New York, 1982); Christian F. Feest, *Native Arts of North America* (New York, 1980); and Glenbow Museum, *The Spirit Sings: Arts of Canada's First Peoples: A Catalogue of the Exhibition* (1987).

26 On the MoMA exhibit see W. Jackson Rushing III, 'Marketing the Affinity of the Tribal and the Modern,' in Janet Catherine Berlo, ed., *The Early Years of Native American Art History* (Seattle, 1992), and for the Exposition of Indian Tribal Arts see Molly H. Mullins, 'The Patronage of Difference: Making Indian Art "Art, Not Ethnology,"' in George Marcus and Fred Myers eds, *The Traffic in Culture: Refiguring Art and Anthropology* (Berkeley, 1995), 166–98.

27 Oliver LaFarge et al., *Introduction to American Indian Art*, 160–1. The MoMA catalogue is more restrained, noting that the False Faces were 'exceptions' to the general simplicity of Iroquois crafts, and mentions in passing only their 'twisted and exaggerated features and ... profusion of wrinkles.' Douglas and D'Harnancourt, *Indian Art*, 154, 157.

28 *Indian Art in America*, caption accompanying plate 223. The book illustrates the collections of New York's old Museum of the American Indian, now the National Museum of the American Indian.

29 Coe, *Sacred Circles*, 85. When ethnologists contributed to art catalogues, as has often occurred, they sometimes contested a narrowly aesthetic presentation of the masks. In an important 1972 exhibition catalogue Robert Ritizenthaler was asked to contribute one essay on False Face masking alone and another, of the same length, to cover all the rest of 'Woodland Indian Art.' He ended the essay on the masks with the statement: 'When worn by actors performing their rites before an appreciative audience of members of

their own society the masks then constitute an entity that vanishes when they are kept in a museum or simply regarded as art objects.' Walker Art Center, *American Indian Art*, 47.

30 *Native American Art*, 47. Of another mask Conn wrote that its 'lively sense of rhythm and design maximizes the emotional impact of this striking mask.' *Native American Art*, 48.

31 In the catalogue caption to the mask (which, as discussed below, was later removed from the show at the request of Mohawk representatives) I wrote that the False Faces 'are portrayed in a plastic and expressionistic style quite unlike the restrained naturalism that marks effigy clubs and utensils. Sharp contrasts are set up between concave and convex forms, smooth surface and deeply grooved wrinkles, and the shiny metal insets against the darkened wood.' *The Spirit Sings*, 46.

32 See 'The Museum as a Way of Seeing,' in Ivan Karp and Stephen D. Lavine, eds, *Exhibiting Cultures: The Poetics and Politics of Museum Display* (Washington, DC, 1991), 26.

33 'On Collecting Art and Culture,' 215–51. See also Berlo, *The Early Years*; Janet Catherine Berlo and Ruth B. Phillips, 'Our (Museum) World Turned Upside-Down: Re-presenting Native American Arts,' *Art Bulletin*, 77, no. 1 (1995): 6–10; Joan Vastokas, 'Native Art as Art History: Meaning and Time from Unwritten Sources,' *Journal of Canadian Studies*, 21, no. 4 (1986): 7–36; Ruth B. Phillips, 'Art History and the Native-Made Object: New Discourses, Old Differences?' in W. Jackson Rushing III, ed., *Native American Art in the Twentieth Century* (New York, 1999).

34 *False Faces*, 454. Undated photographs in the collection of the Woodland Cultural Centre at Brantford, Ontario, show False Face masks displayed for sale at the craft shop run by the Jamieson sisters on the Six Nations Reserve.

35 Both photos are reproduced in Ruth B. Phillips, 'Performing the Native Woman: Primitivism and Mimicry in Early Twentieth-Century Visual Culture,' in Lynda Jessup, ed., *Antimodernism and Artistic Experience: Policing the Boundaries of Modernity* (Toronto, 2001).

36 The letter was written by Kanatiio (Allen Gabriel) to the *Ottawa Citizen*, 20 April 1996, H6.

37 *Globe and Mail*, 17 April 1996, A8.

38 See, for example, Tony Bennett, *The Birth of the Museum: History, Theory, Politics* (New York, 1995); Carol Duncan, *Civilizing Rituals: Inside Public Art Museums* (New York, 1995); Eilean Hooper-Greenhill, *Museums and the Shaping of Knowledge* (New York, 1992); and Aldona Jonaitis, *From the Land of the Totem Poles* (Seattle, 1988).

39 I am greatly indebted to Dr Trudy Nicks of the Royal Ontario Museum,

who has generously shared her long-term research into popular visual culture representations of Indians and who has brought many of the examples cited in this essay to my attention.

40 The hotel was located at Times Square between 44th and 45th streets. Designed by Clinton and Russell, it opened in 1904.

41 *Hotel Astor Indian Hall*, designed and executed by A. Malcolm, 164 Fifth Avenue, New York (25 pp., unsigned, undated, and unpaginated). I am grateful to Mary Jo Ayers of the Bayley Art Museum, University of Virginia, which received the masks displayed at the Hotel Astor together with a copy of the publication from Nancy, Lady Astor, in 1937.

42 The credits name Charles Turbyfill, Dr Blossom, and Prof. Coffin specifically.

43 Lillian Davids Fazzini, *Indians of America* (Racine, WI, 1935), 2.

44 Ibid., 7.

45 Published by the Canadian Pulp and Paper Association, Sun Life Building, Montreal, November 1956. Lithographed by Sampson-Matthews Limited in Toronto.

46 Barbeau and other ethnologists working for the National Museum of Canada engaged repeatedly in similar projects aimed to promote industrial applications of Canadian Native art and to encourage prominent Canadian artists to adopt Native themes in their work. See Harlan I. Smith, *An Album of Prehistoric Canadian Art* (Ottawa, 1923), and Sandra Dyck, 'These Things Are Our Totems': Marius Barbeau and the Indigenization of Canadian Art and Culture in the 1920s (MA thesis, School for Studies in Art and Culture, Carleton University, 1995).

47 See *Art Deco Jewelry Designs in Full Color, Idées Paris* (Dover reprint, New York, 1993), plate 24.

48 Private collection, Toronto.

49 'The System of Collecting,' in John Elsner and Roger Cardinal, eds, *The Cultures of Collecting*, trans. Roger Cardinal (Cambridge, MA, 1994).

50 *National Geographic*, 101, no. 3.

51 See Catherine A. Lutz and Jane L. Collins, *Reading National Geographic* (Chicago, 1993).

52 See Anthony F.C. Wallace, *The Death and Rebirth of the Seneca* (New York, 1969.)

53 Memo from Michael K. Foster to Dr Barrie Reynolds, Chief Ethnologist, Canadian Ethnology Service, 10 March 1975, File E7-6R, Canadian Ethnology Service, Canadian Museum of Civilization. I am grateful to Judy Hall for her help in reconstructing this history.

54 Memo from Sandra Gibb, Senior Exhibits Coordinator, 9 April 1980. The

masks were removed on 14 April. The exhibition was taken down ten years later when the museum moved to its new building.

55 These are the Onondaga, Tuscarora, Tonawanda, Seneca, and Akwesasne reservations. According to Fenton, a letter articulating this policy was first sent to museums known to have False Face masks by the Grand Council in March 1981. I cite a statement sent to me by Peter Jemison in 1996.

56 The specific arrangements made by different museums vary, depending on their discussions with different Iroquois consultants. At the McCord Museum of Canadian History in Montreal, for example, Iroquois representatives recommended that they be stored face to the wall. At the National Museum of the American Indian in New York a special room with restricted access has been set aside for them.

57 Akwesasne Mohawk elder Ernest Benedict responded to a question on this subject by noting that the Grand Council had discussed the matter and was divided. Personal communication, October 1994.

58 Letter of 8 February 1995 from Tom Hill to Michael Ames, Director of the University of British Columbia Museum of Anthropology, museum files.

59 *Spirits Speaking Through: Canadian Woodland Artists*, Spectrum Series, Canadian Broadcasting Corporation.

60 'The False Faces of the Iroquois,' *Canadian Historical Review* 69 (1988), 256.

61 'Clues, Roots of an Evidential Paradigm,' in Carlo Ginzburg, *Clues, Myths and the Historical Method* (Baltimore, MD, 1989), 95–125.

62 Surveys of the history of non-Western art, furthermore, are the products of such processes of surveillance.

63 'On Collecting Art and Culture,' 215.

64 For Mirzoeff, for example, 'a history of visual culture would highlight those moments where the visual is contested, debated and transformed as a constantly challenging place of social interaction and definition in terms of class, gender, sexual and racialized identities.' *Visual Culture*, 4.

65 See Mieke Bal, 'Postcards from the Edge,' in *Double Exposures* (New York, 1997).

66 Rita Reif, 'A Law, a Legacy, and Indian Art,' *New York Times*, 6 November 1995, 39.

Chapter Three

The Tradition of African Art: Reflections on the Social Life of a Subject

CHRISTOPHER B. STEINER

My impetus for writing this essay dates back to a debate that took place in 1993 at a conference at Dartmouth College on the subject of textiles and cross-cultural trade in Africa and Southeast Asia. Invited to respond to a set of papers that dealt with the history and ethnography of textile commerce in the modern world system, I began my discussion by addressing a graduate student's essay on the manufacture of madras cloth in India for the Kalabari market in Nigeria.[1] The Kalabari are a riverine people inhabiting the inner delta of the Niger at the southern tip of Nigeria. Originally fishermen, they became important middlemen in the Atlantic trade of the eighteenth and nineteenth centuries, selling Western imports such as guns, alcohol, and brassware to the African interior and exporting African produce to the coast.[2] Though living in a region with a rich repertoire of narrow-band and other hand-loom weaving, the Kalabari have never possessed indigenous weaving technology. The clothing which is most typically associated with Kalabari ethnicity and identity is made of special fabrics called *pelete bite* and *fimate bite*. Neither of these cloths is woven by the Kalabari, but rather they are produced by a unique form of subtractive textile modification that consists of removing selected threads from imported Indian madras cloth in order to create or, as it were, reveal a new and different design.

The author whose paper I was discussing focused on field research conducted on the Indian side of the trade, where she demonstrated quite convincingly that there was a very restricted range of aesthetic variation in the type of madras cloth that the Kalabari were willing to purchase – i.e., certain colours and pattern arrangements were simply better suited to the 'cut-and-pull' method of textile modification, and these specific cloths were selected over the occasional innovations that itinerant Indian merchants attempted to introduce to their Kalabari clientele. I began my remarks on the relationship between the Indian manufacturers of madras cloth and their Kalabari consumers by noting that 'what is most striking about the relationship between these two worlds is the relatively conservative nature of its interactions – that is, the calculated lack of innovation on either side of the commercial equation.'[3] Kalabari tastes and aesthetic standards, I continued, 'are relatively rigid, and innovations on the part of Indian textile suppliers are generally met with rejection from traditional Kalabari consumers.'[4]

Much to my surprise, my remarks concerning Kalabari 'conservatism' were met with disapproval by one of the leading authorities on Kalabari art and culture, Professor Joanne Eicher of the University of Minnesota, who was also participating in the Dartmouth conference. Contrary to my interpretation, Eicher argued that the Kalabari are highly inventive and creative producers of culture who continually construct new fashions and clothing ideas and innovate all the time in their designs for *pelete bite* and *fimate bite*. I stress that I was truly startled by this reaction because in my mind the portrait I was painting of the Kalabari – a portrait that I still maintain accurately reflected the data in the paper I was commissioned to discuss – was one of a people who had heroically resisted cultural assimilation in the modern Nigerian nation-state, and whose unique form of textile modification successfully served as a currency of cultural autonomy in defiance of outside pressures.[5] Rather than accept trade cloth whole, or 'as is,' and rather than bow to the multitude of Western fashion possibilities proffered by the international world market, the Kalabari remain highly selective in their choice of attire and stick to a 'conservative' value system which favours one specific type of ethnic dress over everything else. So while I would not deny that the Kalabari are quite innovative *within* their tradition, the tradition itself is a 'conservative' reaction to the 'liberal' whimsies of modern African fashion and clothing markets.

Indeed, as I suggested in my original conference commentary, the conservatism of the Kalabari is an example of a particular type of ethnic or social boundary marking that finds interesting parallels to the aesthetics of dress and fashion in seventeenth-century France – where conservatism and restraint acted as the very signs of class membership and social identity. Writing in 1695, for example, the Duchesse d'Orléans noted her profound distaste for the current craze in the proliferation of new styles of dress and the rapidly changing fashion innovations in France:

> I don't know why people have so many different styles of dress. I wear Court dress [*le grand habit*] and a riding habit; no other; I have never worn a *robe de chambre* nor a mantua; and have only one robe de nuit for getting up in the morning and going to bed at night.[6]

This unexpected connection between conservatism in fashion in late seventeenth-century Europe and the conservatism of Kalabari dress in the modern Nigerian nation-state revolves around some very fundamental ideas regarding the role of dress in marking boundaries of class and ethnicity respectively. It has less to do with tradition versus change as it does with mapping identity and difference within the homogenizing process typical of early and late industrial capitalism. Neither practice is either blindly conservative or a so-called invented tradition, but rather each is a calculated strategy to both maintain and create cultural and political autonomy within contexts of rapidly changing social conditions.

At this point – of what was actually turning into an interesting but heated debate on the intersections of tradition and modernity in the context of Kalabari fashion and social identity – Joanne Eicher's longtime colleague, Tonye Erekosima, an indigenous Kalabari scholar with whom she has worked for over twenty years, stood up in *my* defence to argue that the Kalabari are really quite conservative when it comes to ceremonial dress and public fashion. 'There is a fundamental conservatism which underlies Kalabari traditional attire,' he said. Clearly, over the course of two decades of collaborative research and writing on Kalabari clothing and aesthetics the questions of tradition and innovation had never been worked out between these two scholars, let alone perhaps even broached as an imperative problem.

My debate, then, with one of the leading North American scholars on Kalabari textiles and culture was not founded on any fundamental disagreements about the ethnographic 'facts,' but rather was based on a profound and revealing misunderstanding regarding the use of the concept of 'tradition' itself. While I was speaking of conservatism within the entire realm of contemporary fashion in West Africa, Eicher was speaking of innovation narrowly within the Kalabari practice of textile modification and fashion choices. At the end of the day, it may be fair to conclude that neither of us was 'wrong'; we simply approached the issue from two radically different starting points. The question which remains, however, is how can two individuals trained more or less in the same disciplines look at a similar body of ethnographic materials and draw nearly diametrically opposed conclusions?

These two different conclusions, and the details of the discussion and dispute that ensued at the Dartmouth conference, led me to question the intellectual and symbolic baggage that accompanies terms like 'traditional' and 'conservative' on the one hand, and 'innovative' and 'creative' on the other. These words, I am now quite convinced, have become hopelessly linked in the parlance of Africanist art history and anthropology to a broader bipartisan ideology of conservative versus liberal politics. Simply using the word 'conservative' to describe the attitudes of an African people raises today the spectre of old school politics and the reactionary discourse with which it is so often characterized. While the terms 'innovative' and 'creative' often sit more comfortably with the modern politics of change in Africa – as well, of course, with the ideologies of progressive liberalism in academia within which these concepts have been generated – there are instances when the terms 'conservative' or 'traditional' simply *do* fit the data and should be used without having to bring with them all the emotionally weighted passion of political ideology.

While creativity and novelty are important in so many contexts of African art production and reception, conservatism and tradition also serve valuable functions. Thus, by privileging innovation over tradition in Africanist scholarly discourse we may in fact be reading African art, fashion, or aesthetics through the aperture of postmodern Western sensibilities and in so doing missing key aspects of indigenous meaning and attitudes. In the remainder of this essay, I will attempt to explore the discourse of 'tradition' and 'modernity' within the fields of African art history and anthropology by examining two of the many worlds that African art objects occupy. First, I consider the history of 'tradition' in the language or parlance of Africanist scholarship. When and why did this concept come to be associated with the peoples and material cultures of Africa? Second, I examine the world of African art collection and display. Why have collectors and museums clung so steadfastly to terms like tradition and traditional, while Africanist scholars (such as Eicher) have tried so hard to distance themselves from the very same concepts and words?

Intellectual Routes of Tradition

> Until recently, tradition has been a term to think with, not to think about.
>
> (Dan Ben-Amos)[7]

For Edward Tylor, writing at the turn of the last century, tradition was defined as 'past knowledge that had accidentally survived.'[8] Tradition, from this perspective, was viewed as a useless or quaint relic of the past. Tylor and other early anthropologists of the period had inherited this view of tradition largely from nineteenth-century social theorists who viewed tradition negatively, either as a distinguishing feature of small-scale, peasant, and communal societies, or simply as the opposite condition of modernity or the highest evolutionary stage of civilization. Thus, for Maine the distinction was between status and contract; for Tönnies it was between *Gemeinschaft* and *Gesellschaft*; for Durkheim it was mechanical solidarity versus organic solidarity; while Marx spoke of the differences between realization in pre-capitalist societies and alienation under capitalism.[9] In all of these cases, tradition was characterized as a set of inflexible native rules and customs through which all pre-modern individuals were contained and supposedly dominated by the larger social group.

This image of tradition as a kind of conservative dogmatism in which individuals in society are bound to the past as slaves to custom did not die during the course of the twentieth century. Indeed, it is still a popular concept that serves as a defining feature of many non-Western cultures. Witness, for example, Mircea Eliade's classic definition of traditional society from his 1959 book *Myth of the Eternal Return*:

> For traditional societies all the important acts of life were revealed *ab origine* by gods and heroes. Men only repeat these exemplary and paradigmatic gestures ad infinitum ... an object or an act becomes real only insofar as it imitates or repeats an archetype. Thus, reality is acquired solely through repetition or participation, everything which lacks an exemplary model is 'meaningless.'[10]

While this rigid and inflexible notion of tradition remains popular, by the 1920s, particularly in American anthropology, the term 'tradition' became somewhat more encompassing of all societies as it grew to be synonymous with the term 'culture' itself. For Robert Lowie, writing in the 1930s, culture *was* 'the whole of social tradition.' And for Margaret Mead, writing at about the same period, culture was 'the whole complex of traditional behavior.'[11] Even within British social anthropology, which had long resisted any models or definitions of culture, A.R. Radcliffe-Brown drew an explicit connection between culture and tradition in the late 1940s when he wrote:

> The reality to which I regard the word 'culture' as applying is the process of cultural tradition, the process by which in a given social group or social class language, beliefs, ideas, aesthetic tastes, knowledge, skills and usages of many kinds are handed on ('tradition' means 'handing on') from person to person and from one generation to another.[12]

Following the Second World War, concepts of 'change' and 'transformation' captivated the model makers of anthropology. In particular, the Manchester School under the direction of Max Gluckman attempted to shift much of the focus of British social anthropology from a predominant concern with systems, stasis, and continuity to an emphasis on process, change, and schisms. But in all of this literature, tradition continued to be viewed uncritically as a kind of reverse state of modernity. Thus, during this period, 'transitional' societies usually were dissected and 'taken apart in an attempt to identify the modern versus the traditional elements.'[13] If one could peel away the layers of cultural 'impurities' stacked on by Western modernism, it was believed, one could finally hope to uncover a true, authentic traditional culture.

The independence of African nation-states and the parallel emergence of development studies during the early 1960s fuelled the birth of a new pairing of terms: 'tradition and innovation' or, as it was also sometimes called, 'continuity and change.' Victor Turner's classic monograph *Schism and Continuity in an African Society* (1957) and William Bascom and Melville Herskovits's edited volume *Continuity and Change in African Cultures* (1959) both epitomize the issues and concerns of this emerging genre. The juxtaposition of 'old' and 'new' in all of these works was intended to stress the simultaneous (and perhaps even contradictory) permanence and mutability of African societies. While much of this literature finds its origins in the social and political sciences, beginning sometime in the same period a tremendous number of publications and exhibitions on African art were also using phrases such as 'tradition and innovation' or 'continuity and change' in reference to the art of various 'tribes' or peoples. A 1974 exhibition at the Crocker Gallery in Sacramento, typical of this period, was consequently entitled *Tradition and Change in Yoruba Art*. And, more recently, a section on twentieth-century art in Herbert Cole's 1989 Smithsonian exhibition *Icons: Ideals and Power in the Art of Africa* at the National Museum of African Art was labelled 'Change and Continuity.' In Africa itself, several exhibits of the work of contemporary African artists have also used these juxtaposed terms to emphasize both the tension and persistence between past and present in modern African art – for example, *Tradition and Modernity: An Exhibition of Ceramics by Benjo Igwilo*, a 1996 exhibit at the University of Nigeria; and *Sokari Douglas Camp: Between Tradition and Modernity*, a 1998 exhibition at the National Gallery of Namibia. In most of these publications and exhibitions, the words 'tradition' or 'continuity' were meant to draw attention to a putatively unchanging and more 'authentic' past, while 'innovation' and 'change' were meant to acknowledge both the presence of Africa in the modern world and the presence of the modern world in Africa. As Barbara Johnson notes in the conclusion to the catalogue for her 1986 exhibition *Four Dan Sculptors: Continuity and Change*, 'the Dan culture has been a conservative one, controlled by the elders and placing value on continuing the traditions of the past ... There are fewer of the old Dan carvers left today to provide the continuity once required by the whole Dan culture. Inevitably, as the culture changes with the times, the art will change too.'[14]

Although such efforts to juxtapose tradition with innovation, or continuity with change, were probably intended as useful counterarguments to the myth of a timeless and ahistorical Africa, they often created a tremendous disservice to the term 'tradition' itself. Rather than fold the dynamics of history and change *into* the concept of tradition, this pairing of terms created a polarity between old and new, static and dynamic. As historian Jan Vansina reflected in his biographical work *Living with Africa*, 'ever since the beginning of my career the term [tradition] had been anathema. I loathed expressions such as 'traditional life' or 'traditional times' because they implied that before the arrival of the Europeans nothing had ever changed.'[15] The association of tradition with a kind of 'primitive' and 'timeless' past not only has been problematic to many Africanist scholars but, more important perhaps, it has also offended many Africans themselves. As sociologist Norbert Elias once pointed out in the preface to a catalogue of his collection of African art: 'Nothing could be more fallacious and more irritating to the peoples of Africa themselves than the regret some Europeans seem to feel about the passing of the old order in Africa.'[16]

By the late 1970s and early 1980s, there was an attempt to rescue the term 'tradition' from the doldrums of some of this outdated nomenclature. In particular, Eric Hobsbawm and Terence Ranger's 1983 edited volume *The Invention of Tradition* argued that tradition could, under certain circumstances, be interpreted as 'modern' if we acknowledged that contemporary political and social issues might be framed 'as if' they were rooted in the past. Tradition in this sense is evacuated of all meaning and becomes a mere epiphenomenon or mask hiding the 'real' social conditions and causes underlying current struggles, issues, and concerns.

While the literature on the 'invention of tradition' had a significant impact in the early 1980s on the fields of African art history and anthropology, the rubric of 'continuity and change' continues to be a seductive metaphor. Indeed, during the past two decades the concept of 'continuity and change' seems to have enjoyed a resurgence, particularly, for some reason, in graduate student theses. Thus, during this period one could find this expression in numerous dissertation titles, for example: 'The Blacksmiths of Kano City: A Study in Tradition, Innovation and Entrepreneurship in the Twentieth Century' (Philip J. Jaggar 1978), 'Tswana Design of House and Settlement: Continuity and Change in Expressive Space' (Graeme Hardie 1981), 'Continuity and Change in Mampurugu: A Study of Tradition as Ideology' (David C. Davis 1984), 'Adugbologe's Children: Continuity and Change in a Yoruba Woodcarving Industry' (Norma Wolff 1985), 'Yoruba Theater: A Case Study in Continuity and Change' (Diedre Badejo 1985), 'The Aesthetics of Action: Continuity and Change in a West African Town' (Kris Hardin 1987), 'Continuity and Change among the Maasai People' (Paul C. Hutchins 1987), 'Dance Uniforms: Tradition and Innovation among Isaiah Shembe's Amanazaretha' (Karen H. Brown 1995), 'Tuareg Jewelry: Continuity and Change' (Kristyne Loughran 1996), 'Continuity and Change: An Archaeological Study of Farming Communities in Northern Zimbabwe, AD 500–1700' (Gilbert Pwiti 1996), and 'Change and Continuity in the Architecture of the Kibidoué Neighborhood' (Julia A. Risser 1996). The thrust of most of these works was to capture the contradictions in contemporary art and cultures. As Norma Wolff states in the introduction to her dissertation on the production of contemporary Yoruba carvings:

This is a study of the persistence of the Adugbologe art tradition in which the contemporary woodcarvers adapted the artistic concepts and production techniques historically associated with their lineage group to respond to new economic opportunities in the acculturated society. Like most art industries of this type which utilized traditional art forms, *the formal attributes of the art objects produced are marked by both continuity with the past tradition and change away from it.*[17]

Although 'tradition' still appears offset by words like 'change' and 'innovation,' there has also been a concerted campaign to expunge the word tradition altogether from the literature on African art and culture – or at the very least to place it in quotation marks, along with such other problematic terms as 'primitive' and 'tribal,' which are equally awkward and loaded but seemingly difficult to remove entirely from the discourse of the field.[18] Putting the word tradition in quotation marks seems to me a sleight-of-hand that sidesteps inquiry into the role of stasis in structuring and anchoring the past in terms of the present. Is it not possible that there are indeed traditional or conservative practices and visual expressions in Africa that derive significance and meaning because of their very real and immutable qualities?

Both the tempering of the word tradition by counterposing it to more progressive words like change and innovation, and the more recent bracketing of the term tradition by placing it in quotation marks stems from a legitimate reaction to the misuse and abuse of the term 'traditional' in African studies – especially in the fields of history, political science, anthropology, and art history. Tradition has become a 'dirty' word in such disciplines primarily because it has so often been constructed in opposition to modernity. Modernity, unlike tradition, is presented, according to this argument, as a system of thought and social structuring in which it is believed that there is such a thing as an independent self that can decide on its own what it wants – that is, a self that can, by opposing the putatively restrictive world of traditional embeddedness, achieve autonomy and self-sufficiency. The notion of tradition emerging from a discourse that counterposes everything traditional to everything modern is clearly something that needs to be challenged. But to react by dismissing altogether any notion of traditional or conservative practices appears, in my view, to be throwing the baby out with the bath water.

Studying the history of the collection and exhibition of African art in Europe and North America during the twentieth century may shed some light on the general academic displeasure with terms like tradition and traditional. For, while scholarship on African art has increasingly distanced itself from using 'tradition' as an organizing concept or framework of research, museums and collectors have embraced the concept again and again. Indeed, much of the African art market today is predicated on the assumption that traditional art is authentic, while modern art is commercial, touristic, and generally of poor quality.[19] If it is fair to say that academia has largely rejected tradition, then one could also argue that the art market has rejected the modern with the same forcefulness and determination.

The tension between these two perspectives can be felt very clearly in a critical review of a 1993 exhibition at the University of Witwatersrand in Johannesburg entitled *African Barber Posters and Hairstyles: Tradition and Change*. While celebrating the exhibit's commitment to aesthetic expressions of modernism and the contemporary world, the reviewer rebukes the African art collectors for their aesthetic snobbery and their hostility toward all that is new in African visual culture:

> No culture is static. Only *conservative* African-art collectors hang onto the notion of an uncontaminated culture from which authentic pieces issue ... The idea that purity does exist in African art was challenged [in this exhibition] and, one hopes, replaced by a notion that this art or activity is part of an ever-changing continuity. This makes *conservative* collectors distinctly uncomfortable.[20]

One of the results of this split between scholarship and collecting is that museum exhibitions of African art since the turn of the twentieth century have tended to display the same set of narrowly defined canonical objects again and again. In each case, the exhibit is publicized as a major new event, and a first of its kind, but upon closer inspection we detect that little has changed. As we will see below, this process may not be an example of the 'invention' of tradition as much as it is perhaps a 'recycling' of tradition.

The Recycling of Tradition

Plus ça change, plus c'est le Memsahib.

(Ogden Nash)

African art was the talk of the town in New York City during the summer of 1996. The opening at the Solomon R. Guggenheim Museum of the blockbuster exhibition *Africa: The Art of a Continent*, which originated at the Royal Academy of Art in London the previous year, sent the press and the public scurrying to discover a remarkable array of 'traditional' artworks from Africa and in the process disentangle the 'deep' and 'dark' mysteries that still appear to shroud the art of the continent.

Even before the exhibition's American debut, some rather swanky publications (ones that do not normally dabble in 'primitive' art) featured extensive articles on different aspects of African art history and collecting. In May, for example, *Departures*, the magazine for American Express Platinum cardholders, ran a feature story on the history of African art connoisseurship and appreciation.[21] In columns interspersed with glossy advertisements for Range Rover, Bottega Veneta, and the Four Seasons Hotels and Resorts, the article explains the difference between 'ethnographic' and 'aesthetic' approaches to the display of African art. While the former, we are told, draws upon the dry and humdrum disquisitions of science, the latter appeals to passion and the tender appetite of the senses. Perhaps not surprisingly, given the nature of the magazine's readership, the article concludes with a discussion of how, where, and why to buy African art in such cities as Paris, New York, and Los Angeles. Bargains, cardholders are assured, are still to be found in the as yet largely 'untapped' market for nonfigurative traditional arts, including pottery, basketry, textiles, and furniture. In other words, discriminating consumers of African art are advised to avoid any figurative art that might in any way be 'modern' and instead focus on anything 'traditional' – whatever its form or materials. The rewards of collecting 'traditional' art, Platinum cardholders are told, are investment returns that can be very lucrative and worthwhile. The celebrated (and somewhat unique) example of the sale of Harry Franklin's Bangwa memorial figure for $3,410,000 at Sotheby's in 1990 is offered as a stunning illustration of the kind of yield one can get on a $29,000 investment.

The connection between *Africa: The Art of a Continent* and the possible resurgence of a slumping African-art market is made even more apparent in *Art & Auction*'s May cover story entitled 'Out of Africa: A New Show at the Guggenheim Presents the Continent's Creations as the Aesthetic Equals of Western Artworks.' Here, conversations with both dealers and collectors stress the importance of appreciating 'traditional' African works as *objets d'art*, not ethnographic specimens. In reflecting on the significance of the Guggenheim exhibition and its emphasis on 'art' rather than 'artifact,' art dealer Maureen Zarember, director of New York's Tambaran Gallery, remarks that 'The show takes African art out of the curio cabinet and puts it in a museum where it belongs ... People in America need to learn how to see African art as *art*.'[22] This 'aesthetic' treatment of African objects, the author notes in passing, 'has greatly pleased dealers like Zarember,' who hope 'that it will help stimulate the public's appreciation of the vast riches of the continent.'[23]

One of the primary stated objectives of the Guggenheim exhibition is to separate African artifacts from their cultural context so that they can 'be judged' simply as art. This theme is made particularly clear in an interview with the show's curator, artist Tom Phillips, when he says: 'We're not trying to beat people over the head with the idea of Africa ... We're simply inviting them to look at objects made on the continent as works of art equal in aesthetic quality to Western artworks.'[24] 'Ethnological museums may prize inferior quality,' Phillips stated in another interview, 'but we are the Royal Academy, an aesthetic institution. We show art.'[25] Indeed, much of the discourse generated by exhibition organizers and media critics alike focuses on the notion that until now African art has largely been ignored by the art world and relegated to the 'anti-aesthetic' netherworld of ethnographic representation.

But critics still seem to agree that the exhibition's explicit emphasis on African art's 'aesthetic' merit outweighs any of the epistemological problems raised by its exceedingly ambitious scope. It is touted as having redressed the negative stereotypes of 'primitive' African art, and in a kind of mass apologia begs pardon for the sins of previous generations. Indeed, concludes one reviewer, the show might well have been subtitled 'Cecil Rhodes Atones.'[26]

In the *Boston Globe*, *Africa: The Art of a Continent* is described as 'an overdue apology' for an art that 'has been neglected, abused, or treated as automatically inferior "primitive" work in the West.'[27] It is characterized as 'visually stunning' and exalted as 'a compelling argument for the rightful presence of this work in a fine-art setting.'[28] In an article for the *New York Times* entitled '"Primitive" No More, African Art Finds a Proper Respect,' one critic commented, 'Until now, African pottery, wooden carvings and textiles had been viewed essentially as handicraft because, it was argued, the religious, military, sexual or decorative functions of the works suggested that they had not been created as art, to be appreciated for their own sake.'[29] And writing in the *Financial Times*, William Packer declared jubilantly that 'This is great art, all of it, and this is one of these rare exhibitions that change perception and understanding forever ... We shall never look at African art in our old innocent, patronizing naïveté again.'[30]

These enthusiastic evaluations of the Guggenheim show neglect the scores of exhibitions in past decades that have approached African art with equal, if not greater, sensitivity to 'aesthetic' quality and worth. In 1935, over sixty years before the Guggenheim 'benevolently' opened its doors to African art, James Johnson Sweeney, curator of the exhibition *African Negro Art* at the Museum of Modern Art, declared that 'today the art of Africa has its place of respect among the aesthetic traditions of the world.'[31] In the same year, the *New York Times* reported that 'An African spring in the galleries of New York ... argues a considerable and increasing public interest in a contribution to the world's store of art which, until recently, has been relegated principally to museums of anthropology and archaeology.'[32] Sound familiar? 'Here is an art of major proportions,' wrote one critic in reaction to the 1935 MoMA exhibition, 'an art which can stand comparison with the great sculpture of the past, Chinese, archaic Greek and Mayan.'[33] And in *The Magazine of American Art*, Alain Locke arrived at this conclusion: 'The current exhibition of the Museum of Modern Art, aside from being the finest American showing of African art, reveals it for the first time in its own right as a mature and classic expression.'[34]

New York in 1935–6 was indeed swept away by African art, not only by the exhibition at MoMA but also by the display of Louis Carré's collection of Benin art at the Knoedler Gallery, the presentation of the Ratton collection at the Pierre Matisse Gallery, and an exhibition of some 120 African sculptures in wood, ivory, and bronze at the Jacques Seligmann Galleries. 'There is a decided trend in the direction of African art which is apparent on the exhibition calendar this season.'[35] Decades before department stores like Bloomingdale's even thought of coordinating their merchandise displays with the theme of museum blockbuster shows, New York was already consuming the idea of Africa in the overlapping worlds of culture, commerce, and high society. 'It's smart to be primitive today,' reported the New York *American* in spring 1935. 'Perhaps our homes and clothes have gone so far as possible in sophistication, and have begun all over again reverting to deepest Africa for ideas in fabrics, fashions, and decoration.'[36] Fashion and art collecting were inextricably linked. 'A vogue for African primitive art ... is sweeping our town,' observed one writer for the *World-Telegram*. 'Helena Rubinstein collects African idols. This evening she is giving a primitive dinner in her apartment at 895 Park Avenue. The main dishes and refreshments will be carried out in a dark motif.'[37]

But 1935 was neither the first nor the last year that African art would take New York by storm. African art was for the 'first time' displayed as 'art' at Robert Coady's Washington Square Gallery in the spring of 1914, and then at Alfred Stieglitz's Photo-Secession Galleries later that same year.[38] The *New York Times* published a spirited review of the Stieglitz exhibit, heralding African art as 'brilliantly barbaric.'[39]

In 1923 a review in the same newspaper, this time of Stewart Culin's exhibition of African art at the Brooklyn Museum, brandished the exuberant headline 'Wide Vogue Gained by Art of Africa.'[40] Four years later, following an exhibition of Raoul Blondiau's collection of Belgian Congo art at J.B. Neumann's New Art Circle Galleries, New York critics declared that African art had at last 'made it' in the art world. Again, the *New York Times* wrote: 'That the black people of "savage" Africa produced sculpture and craftswork that place examples of their workmanship among the most prized creative treasures of the world's art museums and collectors is no secret to those who have been initiated into a knowledge of their accomplishment in wood, ivory and metal.'[41]

Two years later, in 1929, Marya Mannes wrote that 'Now the interest in old African art has reached the proportions of a craze.'[42] And, as in the recent 'craze,' the link between exhibition and marketplace was quickly apparent. 'Collectors realize,' Mannes continued, 'that here is a new and probably limited field to be exploited and enjoyed before it sinks into the inevitable ... oblivion of all collecting fads.'[43] Every decade, apparently, New Yorkers manage to rediscover African art yet again. In reviewing some of the published reactions to exhibitions of African art in New York City from 1914 to the present, I am amazed to see how many times it has been declared that African art has finally 'made it,' and how often it has been validated by its exhibition at a major cultural institution. In 1927 it was said that 'The founding of special museums of negro art in several European art centres and the opening of African wings in some of the less conservative museums elsewhere have finally added official recognition after a decade or more of personal discovery and appreciation.'[44] And in 1996 we read again that 'The most important aspect about the arrival of 'Africa' at the Guggenheim [is] the fact that African art is actually appearing *as art* in a major museum.'[45] In spring 2000, Paris was shocked by the introduction of *arts premiers* (a euphemism for the indigenous arts of Africa, Asia, Pacific, and the Americas) into the Louvre Museum. While some curators at the Louvre protested that the museum was not a universal museum intended to represent the interests of all of France's immigrants – thereby criticizing President Jacques Chirac's initiative as politically motivated – others welcomed the new arrivals in the Louvre. With the same enthusiasm and decisiveness that was voiced in New York nearly a century earlier, Jacques Kerchache, a renowned French collector of African art and a close friend of the president's, noted that 'The era of disdain is over. "Primitive art" has finally entered the Louvre.'[46] Just as in earlier decades, the exhibition of African art in world-class museums was meant to signal to its visitors that other people's arts might be equal to their European counterparts, as well as being a gesture of Europe's and America's benevolent generosity toward other world cultures. As Stephane Martin, director of the public section of the Louvre told the French newspaper *Le Figaro*, 'We wanted to show that sculpture known as primitive can measure up to some of the greatest Western works of art.'[47]

Finally, later in the summer of 2000 the *New York Times* hailed an exhibit of African art at the Metropolitan Museum of Art, pointing out once again its long-fought battle to share space with canonical works that occupy the floor space of the Met: 'That "Art and Oracle" is where it is at the Met represents a hard-won vote of confidence and augurs well for a new flowering of attention to African art, than which no art is greater, in New York.'[48]

The following passage from Martin Freidman's review of 'The Traditional Art of Africa's New Nations,' an exhibition held in 1961 at the Museum of Primitive Art in New York, might easily have been culled from the pages of today's press: 'Certainly the vital art of [Africa] has now gained universal recognition. There is no longer a question of having to argue for its aesthetic existence.'[49] But over three decades later, the argument remains almost the same. Some might blame this repetitive cycle on the ignorance and cultural insensitivity of the American public. Until museum-goers can drop their racist blinders and accept African art as great *art*, so the argument goes, there will be a need to (over)emphasize 'aesthetic' merit, hyperbolize universal validity, and generally claim more superiority over past interpretations.

While I would agree there is some truth to this reasoning, more interestingly I would suggest the need to validate exhibitions of African art by disparaging previous efforts hinges on a certain element of 'discovery' which has always been integral to the reception of African art.[50] Like Africa itself, obscured in the Western imagination by the enigma of the 'dark continent,' the art of Africa has been validated in museum exhibitions by its association with mystery and the unknown. Too much information, such as the 'tedium of ethnographic details' contained in some exhibition labels, is said to interfere with the public's 'authentic' communion with the soul of African aesthetic expression. Appreciation of African art, according to this point of view, is not based on knowledge and understanding but rather on the 'discovery' of the unexplored – which, by definition, can only emerge out of the intellectual void created by cycles of collective amnesia.

The excitement felt in New York in 1935 was based on the public's genuine 'discovery' of something foreign and new; never before had an African art exhibition of such major proportions been mounted in a New York museum. But once the deed is done, novelty has to be artificially remanufactured. History must be rewritten; memories must be erased. In his writings on the cultures of collecting, James Clifford has argued that those who first 'discovered' primitive art claimed to have arrived on the scene just in the nick of time – salvaging the last 'authentic' objects on the eve of colonialism, missionary conversion, and acculturation.[51] In making his argument, Clifford invokes the famous phrase from the reign of Louis XV: '*Après moi le déluge!*' If *collecting* African art in the field has been premised on the assumption that everything that came afterward was tainted by change and contact, then one might say that the display of African art, beginning in the early years of this century, has been premised on the assumption that everything that came before was insensitive and disparaging. Until *this* exhibition, the argument goes, African art remained unappreciated (or even worse, maligned) by Westerners – an art form relegated to the 'dusty bins' of ethnographic storerooms. But now, through great personal insight, exceptional conviction of taste, and leaps of cultural relativity, the art of Africa has been assigned its proper place amid the world's great art traditions. In this case, to rephrase the words of the *ancien régime*, one might say that the philosophy behind many African art exhibitions of the twentieth century has been: *Avant moi la dérision!*

The problem is that most of the objects in exhibits such as *Africa: The Art of a Continent* are the same ones that were featured in earlier shows. Some of the works of art that began their tour in London for the 1996 exhibit, for example, had already travelled to New York in 1935, and many have been on the road ever since. Because the canon of African art, with its emphatic focus on 'traditional' ritual objects of precolonial manufacture, is so restricted in scope (even when you include Ancient Egypt and North Africa), the pool of qualifying works that can be featured in a major exhibition is exceedingly small. As a result, old objects have to be reclothed in the fashion of new interpretive trends.

Conclusion: Old Wine, New Bottles?

> When the collector takes time to visit an ethnographic museum, or attends a private view of a tribal art exhibition at a culture centre or gallery, sipping wine amongst fellow guests, he or she is surrounded by the wonders of a world now extinct or near-extinct, and will have cause to dwell upon what has now been lost in the tides of acculturation.[52]

One of the problems facing the future direction and growth of African art production is the dogmatic connection between style, region, and tradition. According to this model – often referred to in the literature as the 'one tribe, one style' model – the art of every ethnic group is associated with a narrow range of stylistic features, and deviation from these canonical norms is generally rejected by collectors and museums alike. This means that any innovations on the part of African artists that deviate too far from the accepted 'norm' for that particular ethnic group or region are judged to be inauthentic and unsaleable. Thus, artists dependent upon Western market demand are doomed to repeat outsiders' definitions and perceptions of their own so-called traditions.

While there may be some correlates to this pattern of repetition within the Western art canon, perhaps a more interesting and unexpected parallel exists in the French wine industry today. A recent editorial in *Wine Enthusiast* magazine points out that each year many fine French wines are denied their commercial rank or status because they fail to fit the taste expectation of their particular region. 'A wine can be refused its *labelle*,' the author of the article explains, 'because it is not typical, which means that the producer is not making a wine in the expected style of the appellation.' He goes on to further note that the appellation panels, which are made up of winegrowers and wine professionals, have a 'fixed idea of what a wine style should be ... So when a wine comes along that doesn't taste typical to them, it can be rejected.' Even though some winemakers 'can be making more exciting wines than the norm for the appellation, they are not typical. So the search for typicity in a wine can often stifle innovation.' In lamenting the industry's narrow and banal quest for only the typical wines of each region, the author concludes 'But wait a minute. There's something here that smacks of tablets of stone, of the dead hand of tradition.'[53]

Isn't this precisely the kind of thinking that underlies the intellectual rift between academics and collectors in the realm of African art? To move back for a moment from French wine to African art – specifically Yoruba spiritual carvings – the parallels between these arguments become clear when we consider what is perhaps one of the most famous examples in African art of what might be called an indigenous transgression of 'traditional' art. In 1973, Marilyn Hammersley Houlberg published a field photograph showing a young Yoruba schoolteacher carrying in the front folds of her cloth dress a bright red plastic doll. The factory-made doll was being treated in the same manner as the more commonly seen wooden statues that Yoruba mothers care for to honour their deceased twin(s). These small, naturalistic wooden carvings, known as *ere ibeji*, have been prized by Western museums and collectors for many years. Depending on their display context they may be viewed either as works of 'art' or as ethnographic 'artifacts'; but in any case the wooden figures are considered authentic material manifestations of Yoruba religious practices. The photograph of the woman carrying the plastic doll, which was subsequently reproduced in various other African art publications – most notably Susan Vogel's 1988 exhibition catalogue *Africa Explores* – created something of a controversy and division in the field. For while many African art historians embraced the plastic *ibeji* as an exciting sign of a 'modern tradition,' some scholars and certainly most collectors challenged the cultural integrity and authenticity of the plastic doll. Writing in praise of the plastic doll, John Picton noted, 'by challenging the very notion of the "traditional," the red plastic doll with blue eyes (and squeaker) enhances our understanding of whatever it is, whether artifact or performance or process, we consider as art and/or consider art to be.'[54] Critics, on the other hand, challenged the veracity of the photograph, claiming that the image was either staged or represented a cultural anomaly that did not reflect 'typical' Yoruba practices. In other cases, critics argued that although some Yoruba may indeed substitute plastic dolls for carved wooden *ibeji*, the synthetic substitutes have no place in exhibitions of Yoruba 'art' – a category that largely has been constructed by Westerners in the first place. In all cases, critics of the plastic doll have been guided by their intrinsic assumption that modern African material-culture art has little economic value. 'Collectors of Yoruban art,' reported the *Los Angeles Times* in a recent review of a Yoruba beadwork exhibit, 'tend to think that the older the piece the better, and some of the earliest Yoruban works excavated at the ancient city of Ife have sold for upward of a million dollars.'[55]

Thus, in the end, the problem of tradition for those who study African art is not simply a matter of rethinking the 'invention of tradition' paradigm – that is, what is tradition when it is not invented? But rather the problem is even more complicated as we try to sort out an academic discourse on tradition that has been constructed largely in reaction to an art market and museum paradigm that has excluded any expressions of modernity. The result is a peculiar tension between a commercial art world that capitalizes on the recycling of traditions and an academic universe that disparages tradition in favour of anything new or different.

NOTES

1 Sandra Evenson, 'Indian Madras Cloth and the Kalabari' (paper read at the conference on 'Cloth, the World Economy, and the Artisan: Textile Manufacturing and Marketing in South Asia and Africa, 1780–1950,' Dartmouth College, 23–5 April 1993).

2 Nigel Barley, 'Pop Art in Africa? The Kalabari Ijo Ancestral Screens,' *Art History*, 10, no. 3 (1997): 369.

3 Christopher B. Steiner, 'Textiles and the Modern World System: A Commentary' (paper read at the conference on 'Cloth, the World Economy, and the Artisan: Textile Manufacturing and Marketing in South Asia and Africa, 1780–1950,' Dartmouth College, 23–5 April 1993), 2.

4 Ibid., 3.

5 See Christopher B. Steiner, 'Technologies of Resistance: Structural Alteration of Trade Cloth in Four Societies,' *Zeitschrift fur Ethnologie*, 119 (1994): 75–94.

6 Cited in Michael M. Edwards, *The Growth of the British Cotton Trade, 1780–1815* (New York, 1967), 48.

7 Dan Ben-Amos, 'The Seven Strands of "Tradition": Varieties in Its Meaning in American Folklore Studies,' *Journal of Folklore Research*, 21, nos. 2–3 (1984): 104.

8 Ibid.

9 See Alice E. Horner's helpful discussion in 'The Assumption of Tradition: Creating, Collecting, and Conserving Cultural Artifacts in the Cameroon Grassfields (West Africa)' (unpublished PhD dissertation, University of California, Berkeley, 1990), 5.

10 Mircea Eliade, *The Myth of the Eternal Return: or, Cosmos and History* (Princeton, 1971), 29.

11 Cited in Horner, 'The Assumption of Tradition,' 9.

12 Cited in ibid., 10.

13 Ibid., 11.

14 Barbara Johnson, *Four Dan Sculptors: Continuity and Change* (San Francisco, 1986), 56.

15 Jan Vansina, *Living with Africa* (Madison, 1994), 229–30.

16 Norbert Elias, *African Art: From the Collection of Professor Norbert Elias* (Leicester, 1970), 4.

17 Norma Hackleman Wolff, 'Adugbologe's Children: Continuity and Change in a Yoruba Woodcarving Industry' (unpublished PhD dissertation, Indiana University, 1985), 2; my emphasis.

18 See Sally Price, *Primitive Art in Civilized Places* (Chicago, 1989), 1–2; Susan Vogel, *Africa Explores: 20th Century African Art* (New York, 1991), 35–7; Suzanne Preston Blier, 'Truth and Seeing: Magic, Custom, and Fetish in Art History,' in Robert H. Bates, V.Y. Mudimbe, and Jean O'Barr, eds, *Africa and the Disciplines: The Contributions of Research in Africa to the Social Sciences and Humanities*, (Chicago, 1993), 152–6.

19 See Christopher B. Steiner, *African Art in Transit* (Cambridge, UK, 1994); Christopher B. Steiner, 'Authenticity, Repetition, and the Aesthetics of Seriality: The Work of Tourist Art in the Age of Mechanical Reproduction,' in Ruth B. Phillips and Christopher B. Steiner, eds, *Unpacking Culture: Art and Commodity in Colonial and Postcolonial Worlds* (Berkeley, 1999), 87–103; Christopher B. Steiner, 'The Taste of Angels in the Art of Darkness: Fashioning the Canon of African Art,' in Elizabeth Mansfield, ed., *Art History and Its Institutions: Foundations of a Discipline* (London, 2002), 132–45.

20 Karel Nel, 'Review of *African Barber Posters and Hairstyles: Tradition and Change*, exhibition at Gertrude Posel Gallery, University of Witwatersrand, Johannesburg,' *African Arts*, 27, no. 2 (1994): 77; my emphasis.

21 John Windsor, 'Africa on a Pedestal,' *Departures*, 39 (May/June, 1996): 63–4, 66, 68.

22 Steven Vincent, 'Out of Africa,' *Art and Auctions*, 43, no. 10 (1996): 125; emphasis in original.

23 Ibid., 125.

24 Ibid., 122–4.
25 Windsor, 'Africa on a Pedestal,' 68.
26 Deborah Solomon, 'The Gugg Goes to Africa,' *New York Times*, 14 June 1996, 16.
27 Christine Temin, 'The Art of Africa: After Centuries of Condescension and Neglect, the Western Art World Is Starting to Pay Attention,' *Boston Globe*, 10 December 1995, 18.
28 Temin, 'The Art of Africa,' 35–6.
29 Alan Riding, '"Primitive" No More, African Art Finds a Proper Respect,' *New York Times*, 29 October 1995, 43.
30 Quoted in ibid., 43.
31 James Johnson Sweeney, *African Negro Art* (New York, 1935), 3.
32 H.I. Brock, 'Black Man's Art: From Africa Come Primitive Objects That Reveal a Story of a Culture,' *New York Times*, 5 May 1935, 23.
33 *The Republican* [Springfield, MA], 'African Negro Sculpture at the Museum of Modern Art,' 31 March 1935, 25.
34 Alain Locke, 'African Art: Classic Style,' *The Magazine of American Art*, 28, no. 5 (1935): 271.
35 'African Sculpture Show Illustrates One of the Oldest Art Traditions,' *Art Digest*, 10, no. 7 (1936): 5.
36 Alice Hughes, 'Modern Mode Goes African,' *American*, 18 April 1935, 6.
37 'New Vogue for a Primitive Art,' *World-Telegram*, 26 April 1935, 10.
38 See Virginia-Lee Webb, *Perfect Documents: Walker Evans and African Art, 1935* (New York, 2000).
39 'The Sun of Africa on Paper,' *New York Times*, 20 November 1914, 7.
40 'Wide Vogue Gained by Art of Africa,' *New York Times*, 2 September 1923, 16.
41 Sheldon Cheney, 'Darkest Africa Sends Us Art,' *New York Times*, 13 February 1927, 7.
42 Marya Mannes, 'African Art in the Rubinstein Collection,' *International Studio* (May 1929): 55.
43 Ibid., 55.
44 Cheney, 'Darkest Africa,' 7.
45 Vincent, 'Out of Africa,' 127; emphasis in original.
46 Alan Riding, 'Bowing to Pressure, the Louvre Goes Primitive,' *International Herald Tribune*, 14 April 2000, 22.
47 'Paris Louvre Launches Ethnic Exhibition to End Art Snobbery,' *Agence France Presse*, 13 April 2000.
48 Holland Cotter, 'Divine Form and Spirit,' *New York Times*, 28 April 2000, E33.

49 Martin Friedman, 'New Africa's Old Art,' in Hilton Kramer, ed., *Perspectives on the Arts* (New York, 1961), 89–96.

50 See Steiner, *African Art in Transit*, 131–4.

51 James Clifford, *The Predicament of Culture: Twentieth-Century Ethnography, Literature and Art* (Cambridge, MA, 1988).

52 Nicholas Barnard, *Living with Folk Art: Ethnic Styles from around the World* (Boston, 1991), 65.

53 Roger Voss, 'Typical, Not Tradition-Bound,' *Wine Enthusiast* (September 2000): 24.

54 John Picton, 'On the Invention of "Traditional" Art,' in Moyo Okediji, ed., *Principles of 'Traditional' African Culture* (Ibadan, 1992), 3–4.

55 Kristine McKenna, 'Communicating with the Gods: A UCLA Exhibit Translates the Spiritual Language of Yoruban Beadwork,' *Los Angeles Times*, 18 January 1998, B3.

Chapter Four

Zwarte Piet's *Bal Masqué*

MIEKE BAL

tradition
– the handing down of information, beliefs, and customs by word of mouth or by
example from one generation to another
– an inherited pattern of thought or action (e.g. a religious practice or a social
custom); a convention or set of conventions associated with or representative of
an individual, group, or period <the title poem represents a complete break
with nineteenth-century ~ *– F.R. Leavis*>
– cultural continuity in social attitudes and institutions

The ultimate uncertainty of the past makes us all the more anxious to validate that things were as reputed. To gain assurance that yesterday was as
substantial as today we saturate ourselves with bygone reliquary details,
reaffirming memory and history in tangible format.

David Lowenthal (1985: 191)

Whoever has approved this idea of order ... will not find it preposterous
that the past should be altered by the present as much as the present is
directed by the past.

T.S. Eliot (1975 [1919])

Concept or Ideology?

They dance, jump about, play the fool. Colourful, festive, full of surprises, they turn boring, grey, early-winter days into a period of party-
ing. They knock on windows, while inside, near the hearth, children
sing the season's songs. Sometimes, without anyone leaving the room,

the door opens a notch and a handful of candies are thrown in. They used to threaten and shake their birch branches, but these days they mainly reassure kids by giving them candy. Reassurance is called for. This alone is what deserves attention. Fascination and reassurance – hence, a play with anxiety – are what underlie the Dutch *Sinterklaas* and *Zwarte Piet* (Black Peter) tradition. It is a tradition that seems to me to be a typical cultural configuration of sentiments towards 'race' and other differences among people as they are instilled in children.

The Zwarte Piet tradition, which serves as my case study here, has astounded many who were not brought up with it. Over a period of years, the British photographer Anna Fox came to the Netherlands to make portraits of these figures playing the black-faced fools. Her photographs explore the multiple ambiguities of that need for reassurance. As a quasi-ethnographer, she selected for her fieldwork a country close to hers, yet utterly foreign with respect to this particular tradition, which has been maintained for so long against all odds. This position of the artist-observer, hovering between closeness and utter foreignness, where the customary sense of 'the exotic' is replaced with a sense of astonished understanding, comes close to being a revision – not a rejection – of that academic tradition akin to cultural analysis, namely ethnography.[1] Ethnography studies traditions. Fox photographed this one. Her photo series is both subject and object of analysis in this chapter. While this series is the star, I cast a few paintings by Velázquez, Regnault, and Aptekar in supporting roles.

As images, instances of visual art in a performance of cultural analysis as critical pursuit, Fox's photographs derive their striking power from the way their maker succeeds in conveying the ambiguities inherent in the tradition.[2] But, in making her intervention, Fox deploys another tradition, this time from 'high art' instead of 'popular culture': that of the portrait. This double engagement with tradition turns her photographic project into an instance of theory-practice intertwinement. In this sense, her project is parallel to Coleman's play with the inextricable bond between – yet not collapse of – performance and performativity; to Bourgeois' activity of making images as transhistorical translation; and arguably, also, to the exhibition around but emphatically not *on* the Judith theme. For Fox, too, makes cultural objects that propose by visual means an intervention akin to what academics would do if they were aiming to conduct an explicit cultural critique. Her ensemble of Zwarte Piet photographs takes our notion of 'image' even further. Here, *mise-en-scène*, framed and framing, performing (the tradition as well as the analysis of it) and performative (striking the viewer), image comes to embody cultural analysis itself, as a powerful form of critique that overcomes the gap between academic and artistic work.

As I will argue below, Fox's work revitalizes the concept of *tradition*. As an instance of working with or through a particular tradition, it can be seen as propping itself up on a modified interpretation of T.S. Eliot's reflections on tradition in art.[3] But, I will also argue, her work probes, in an anti-traditionalist attitude or vision, what tradition in general is and does. Travelling between high art and popular culture but without endorsing the separation between these two overlapping domains, her photographic series will be our guide in this chapter. For it facilitates understanding yet another 'travel' of concepts, the one between the subject of analysis (the artist, but also the academic looking at the art) and the analytic work itself, as well as the place of the relevant concept in that analytic work.

For when it comes to justifying the work that humanists do to the world at large, tradition is involved in each and every piece of academic work, along with either a self-evident alibi or a bone of contention. By choosing the concept of tradition as the focus of this essay, I aim to shed the instrumental handiness of concepts. *Tradition* is not a 'tool' for analysis. It is not a mini-theory that helps us to understand the artistic object. It is more like an ideology. Concepts have this dubious aspect to them. Here, by foregrounding one concept easily recognized as problematic in itself, I hope to demonstrate an intercourse with it that refrains from taking anything for granted. I also aim to eliminate from cultural analysis the still-rampant Althusserian idea that critical analysis can stand outside its object of critique.[4]

Two different kinds of tradition are played off against each other in these portraits. The first is the tradition of and from which Eliot speaks in his famous paper, which laid the ground for a consideration of works of art on their own terms through an activity called 'close reading.' The second is the seemingly 'natural,' common-sense 'way things always were' – which is, as often as not, 'invented.'[5]

Eliot posed a dialectic between tradition – as in, say, poetic, romantic, baroque, or Western – and the individual contributions and creations artists make within traditions. The dialectic is that between originality, the dominant aesthetic in Eliot's days, and imitation or emulation. Several consequences of Eliot's view have since been rightly criticized and rejected. One is the idea that within that dialectic, literary texts should be read primarily in terms of their originality, and that, when read closely, they will yield their uniqueness and thus gain an autonomy from all other, contextual aspects, one of which is the author, whose 'individual talent' makes the text. We no longer believe that works of art can be considered out of context, that they can 'speak for themselves.' Moreover, although the New Criticism, whose founder Eliot was, has firmly rejected what was called 'the intentional fallacy,' the appeal to authorial intention has never ceased to haunt criticism.

Tradition, moreover, is one of those word-concepts that, like 'text' or 'culture,' is used in ordinary discourse as well as analytical, critical commentary. It also often has political agendas inscribed in it. This situation has methodological implications that I will spell out below. Here I aim to make a stronger case than has been made thus far for the acknowledgment and endorsement of the position of the subject of cultural analysis – say, the academic student of culture – within the field under scrutiny. To get a clear grip on what such a word-concept can mean for a cultural analysis that does not allege for itself an illusory meta-critical distance but that stays self-consciously within the cultural realm under examination, I will suspend judgment, yielding to the cultural field that is also the target of critique, and raise questions rather than supply answers. The tradition I want to examine, and from which I cannot disentangle myself, is that of Zwarte Piet.

The Past Is a Foreign Country

Zwarte Piet triggers my oldest memory of fear. While during the rest of the year the house I grew up in was a safe haven into which, at the onset of darkness, I quickly fled to escape the growing shadows of strangers on the street, in late November and early December that haven was visited by spooks that I never saw but who left their traces: candy, a warning note, a slightly misplaced shoe. I knew who they were, and that they were benign. Their presence was thrilling, a promise of mystery, candy, presents. But somehow, they scared me, and that spoiled the fun, the security, the confidence. I was afraid to pass the basement door on my way to the kitchen, afraid to go upstairs during the day. It took half a lifetime for me to stop looking under my bed before daring to lie on it.

Perhaps the inevitable anguish that defines the life of a small child was simply channelled – hence, held in check – by the traditional visit of Zwarte Piet, thus liberating me from it for the rest of the year.[6] Channelled, yes; specialized. And there, of course, lies the problem, the tradition that is today's embarrassment. For in the small, all-white town where I grew up, the black-faced clowns – in charge of gauging good and evil and challenging the closure of the family by pouncing on windows, handing out sweets, and knowing everything about our daily sins – marked my first encounter with racial difference, in the guise of a scary masquerade.[7]

Dutch society, like all societies, has traditions, some of which bring an embarrassed blush to your cheeks. The Easter bunny brings Easter eggs, brightly coloured, hidden in the garden. The 'pagan' Christmas tree looms over the tiny figurines representing the story of the birth of Jesus. And, during that part of the year when American children are trying to overcome their fear of darkness brought on by the gloom of the shortening days and the increasing cold, by dressing up and going out at Halloween, the Dutch are preparing for the annual visit of Sinterklaas.

All traffic in Amsterdam is stopped on the day the long-haired, white-bearded Bishop of Toledo sails into that city, past the Saint Nicholas Church, named after him, the patron saint of Amsterdam. On that same afternoon in late November, he simultaneously enters all Dutch cities on a white horse, surrounded by servants, black-faced fools, many of whom are young, white women, who jump about handing out candy from a burlap sack to dutiful children, shaking their birch branches to frighten the naughty. The very bad children might be put into the sack after it is empty and taken back to Toledo, only to be returned to their families the following year. I was bad, but never that bad – apparently.

This tradition is not the kind Eliot had in mind. It belongs, rather, to what is perhaps best exemplified by the 1983 collective volume *The Invention of Tradition*, whose programmatic title has triggered a flurry of criticism of the concept of and appeal to tradition, a critique that, by now, has itself become a tradition.[8] The traditions targeted in that book's critical essays are primarily cultural rather than strictly artistic. This makes the polemic all the more urgent. In the case study here, the widely cultural and narrowly artistic domains come together, as the artist probes, borrows, the guise of an ethnographer, only to mess up the neatness of her 'field.'

In *The Invention of Tradition*, the argument goes that traditions are conservative by nature and have no basis in cultural reality. They are artificially maintained, serve dubious political purposes, and suppress alternative traditions. Rather than being traces of a past to be cherished with nostalgic longing, traditions are inventions, fictions of continuity necessary for a conception of history as development or progress. A critique of traditions along these lines is frequently heard in more progressive cultural circles, including academic ones. The Dutch Zwarte Piet tradition most certainly qualifies for such a critique.

Much of this critique of tradition is justified, and it should be made continuously, especially as long as mainstream traditions are privileged over alternative ones. Traditions that promote group formation and identity can be dubious when structured on an inside/outside binary, especially when celebrated by the dominant groups in a social environment. But they cannot be dismissed so easily when faced with the evident need of – *traditionally!* – marginalized groups in danger of cultural dispersal to promote social cohesion. And, whereas the roots of traditions are not always where their advocates claim them to be – hence, the accusation of their fictitious status, as 'invented' – the attempt to eliminate or privatize traditions is, in many cases, illusory, idealistic, or, worse, as oppressive as the tradition itself.[9]

That the Zwarte Piet tradition is the product of invention seems obvious. Perhaps not quite, or not *only*, because – as Hobsbawm and Ranger point out and condemn – governmental and other powers use tradition to manipulate people's memories, but, my guess is, *also* because of that. It turns out not to be so easy to recover the interests underlying the invention or its agents. But children live it, they don't question it, and thus the tradition shapes their minds. In answer to my typical child's question 'Where does all this come from?,' I received a number of different replies. It was rumoured that the Bishop of Toledo had once rescued children from being cooked in a huge cauldron. This was true: the evidence was engraved in stone, in a relief on the church named after him near the Central Station in Amsterdam. His fondness for children gave him eternal life. Each year he came back, to *our* country, to *our* town, to celebrate *his* birthday by giving *us* children presents. I was very lucky to live in the very place he visited. We only had to answer his questions when he came to our school, and sing for him. His golden book contained a record of how good and bad we had been during the year.

And, then, less benign if only because of their looks, Zwarte Piet: all the saint's servants are called by the same generic name. Many in one? Three versions of the story explained his/their blackness. The coexistence of the diverging explanations helped accommodate incongruities.

The clowns, dressed in colourful fool's garb, were Moors, I was told, who accompanied the bishop from Spain, where they had been ever since the Moors came from Africa to fight the Christians. They were veritable athletes, prancing on roofs and climbing down chimneys. Or, in another version of the story, they weren't Moors at all; they had become black from the chimney soot; 'even though you're black as soot ...,' we used to sing. That explained the smudges, the white hair-lines, the white behind the ears that we began to notice as we grew from toddlers into primary-school children.

No more questions asked; none answered. The symbolism of white equals good, black equals evil, was not spoken aloud; we just sang 'even though.' The song continued, I don't remember quite how, but probably with something hair-raising like 'in your heart, I know you're good.' But this thing about fighting Christians didn't bode well for their backgrounds. Perhaps they were once devils and had become benign daredevils through the salvaging influence of the saint. That was the third explanation of their blackness. A confused and confusing explanation, it remained implicit, providing just that touch of moral-ism that was needed to produce the right sentiment in children. And, precisely because that sentiment was tinted with morality – more strongly, than, say, the American Santa Claus tradition is – both race and class, and less explicitly, gender, remained subject to a taxonomy of values inhibiting true equality. Black equals evil, equals devil, come what may. So much for the moralizing, educational background of the tradition. Who invented it, and for what purpose? For it's still here, now.

On the rare occasions when I saw a black person, I said, or at least thought: a Zwarte Piet who missed the boat and has to spend the year here. Poor guy! Even if the guy was a girl. The irony of the fantasy never struck me. During the years when I 'believed in Sinterklaas' – up to the age of seven or eight – I never spoke to a black person, nor did one ever come to our house. None of the students at school were black; but, then, none were boys either. By the time I saw through the masks – the line between the black face and the white hairline, the piece of string that attached Sinterklaas' beard, the day the golden staff made of cardboard broke – I felt the sadness of broken dreams.

Even then, I vaguely sensed that my childhood was about to end. One complex knot of sentiments replaced another, equally theatrical, speaking to the ambitions of a girl growing up. Soon *I* might be asked to be Zwarte Piet. If only I weren't so clumsy with my body, growing faster than I could gracefully handle, I could be legit as a tomboy! In a convoluted way, for me, as a white girl, black also connoted freedom (figure 4.1).

Like all European societies, Dutch society has changed. Today it is not as easy to play the black-faced fool to a crowd of racially and ethnically mixed Amsterdamers, facing descendants of the very people who, long ago, in a colonialist past, inspired the tradition that now slaps them in the face (then, it did worse). Bolder and less fearful than I was then, today's white Dutch children of kindergarten age, although surrounded by black children, persistently call out 'hi Zwarte Piet' to black people they meet on the street, not realizing, of course, how it might feel to hear that greeting several times a day.

Then a historical moment came and went. I was a young mother, trying to raise my children as best I could, in a culture where 'black' was no longer so exceptional. Aware of the problematic nature of this particular tradition, one year the Dutch tried to allow the Zwarte Piets to paint their faces red, blue, or green. It was a crucial moment – and it failed. Nobody liked it. Now they're black again. Too bad. An opportunity to continue a tradition but adapt it to changing times – out the window, down the drain. Perhaps this was too acute a confrontation with the inventedness of the tradition to allow the acceptance of its reinvention. The last time I checked, in December 1999, the policemen in Amsterdam still conscientiously held back traffic so that black-faced fools could impress Dutch kids.

Of course – I thought as I wrote this essay – today no culture would invent such a racist tradition. I hope. But my critical reader did not agree, and I fear he may be right.[10] This tradition is particularly troublesome because 'sophisticated,' with racism being worked over by classism (Zwarte Piets are servants) and sexism (they are feminized). The clownish behaviour even flirts with the traditional question raised in the sixteenth century, and again in the eighteenth, and then right up to the time of abolition, of whether blacks were quite human. No relativizations of the deeply racist ideology that underlies this tradition are possible. So why are the Dutch still so attached to it?[11]

I have a hypothesis, a tentative one that probably explains only part of that attachment. Let me speak in the 'we' form here.[12] We know only too well that this tradition is problematic. It flaunts its infraction of the sacred rule of our time: watch thy step, thou shalt be careful, tolerant, broadminded, non-discriminating, in short, *good*, regarding race, class,

4.1 Family snapshot with Zwarte Piet.

and gender. Although the Dutch tend to poke fun at North American moralism, dismissing it as 'political correctness,' I perceive Dutch culture as profoundly moralistic, *especially* in its more progressive corners. Perhaps, I suppose, it is precisely the deeply moralist, hence condescending, aspect of present-day Dutch liberalism that demands the preservation of this awkward tradition.[13] It is like a multi-purpose language-game.

Do I want the tradition to be abolished? Of course I do, but that might not be an effective way of dealing with the remnant racism in Dutch culture. It might help the 'aboriginal' Dutch such as myself, more than it would today's mixed culture. I don't think it would be good to abolish it in a single, swift gesture of erasure. What I suggest is that this painful, unacceptable tradition is needed just a bit longer, to allow a continued questioning of the psychological ideology that underlies its critical alternative. In what is all too eagerly called 'a postcolonial society,' political parties of dubious principles may fight lost battles to close frontiers, but even they would not dare to come up with a public figure such as Zwarte Piet. Maintaining an old tradition is a different story.

It remains a headache for the schoolteachers who have to tell the stories, explain the history, and answer the questions of children each of whom relates differently to the tradition, to the past from which it came, to the representations it embodies, and to the sentiments it promotes. Young parents today try to prevent their children believing in the story that my parents so earnestly wished to instil. More likely than not, their children have friends of colour or are coloured themselves. But, letting go of an old tradition, invented as it obviously has been: no way!

It's just as bizarre as the performance of Mozart's *Magic Flute* in the open-air theatre of Santa Fe. There, aboriginal Americans in the audience watched singers dressed up as Indians, feather headdresses and all, while looking out over the plains their ancestors had once hunted and where their grandparents had grown up, on the 'rez.' It's as bizarre as when 'aboriginal' Dutch see Muslim women being kept in their place as they walk, headscarf and all, a few steps behind their men; and as bizarre as it seemed to 'aboriginal' straights when they saw gay displays on boats, for which traffic was also stopped, during the 1998 Gay Games in Amsterdam. For weeks afterwards, readers wrote to the papers about it, but when it actually happened, the population came out in full force to greet the event. It was one of those moments when Dutch culture lived up to its liberal reputation a bit more than usual. That tradition, also invented, must stay. But it, too, must be examined, and its subterranean rhizomatic connections with Zwarte Piet and other contradictory behaviour, analysed.[14]

Cultural relativism then? No. The situation is just different when the game is being played by the 'qualitative' (i.e., predominant) majority, who plays it because it proves its 'aboriginal' rights. True, true, Zwarte Piet is and remains a deeply problematic tradition; there are no two ways about it. That's obvious. It has all the flaws: it is fictitious, oppressive, and conservative. But it is here that Anna Fox's photographs, as works of art to be close-read, come in. As a productive alternative to abolishing the tradition, to trashing it, Fox's series engages this tradition from the vantage point of artistic traditions of an altogether different kind.

For her photographs are not obvious. They neither naturalize, endorse, nor indict the Zwarte Piet tradition; nor do they dismiss it offhand, showing how awkward it looks to her British eye. For there is no easy way for nationals of any Western country to point the finger at their neighbour's racism without a good dose of self-reflection. In the end, Fox's is *not* a classical ethnographic project. It only uses ethnography as a third tradition, to question the self/other structure that ethnographers of the keenest sort have themselves questioned.

In looking at this photo series of the Zwarte Piet tradition, I would like to take a seemingly conservative view, retrieving some of the elements of Eliot's New Critical program that have been lost but shouldn't have been. I think the most valuable contribution of New Criticism has been its admittedly naïve focus on the text itself. This aspect of New Criticism – the close reading of tradition-bound works but without assuming that art is autonomous – remains valuable, and has been lost. Recovering it, and thus bringing renewed attention to the tradition in relation to which the works signify, is my methodological guideline in my discussion of Fox's photographs. The close reading of works of art, freed of a naïve belief in the autonomy of art and enriched by the additional attention to the kind of intertextual relations to which embedding traditions also belong, is a most valuable contribution to understanding *how* those works relate to traditions, and what they do to them. In other words, close reading makes traditions dynamic, transforming not a given but an aspect of an ongoing cultural process.

Instead of indicting or endorsing the Zwarte Piet tradition, Fox's images probe many of the tensions it harbours, exploring what it means to hold on to what at a rational level must be rejected. They question what it means for specific individuals to perform, rather than watch, the representation of the very past on which, for better or for worse, contemporary Dutch society rests. From a position both inside and outside the context within which this tradition functions, Fox probes and sympathizes, lingers within positions of identification, then moves out playfully to show the problems, before moving in again.[15] The images take me on a journey to tradition land, where the past sits like a wandering rock in the present, and back again, loaded with new baggage. The images solicit a variety of identificatory moments, all implicating the viewer, who is gently prompted to go, through the detour of that foreign country – the past – to a place in the present where perhaps she has never been before. A place where foreign countries are no longer relegated to the past.[16]

Revisiting Tradition

The reason the Zwarte Piet tradition is really impossible is also the reason it cannot be dismissed too easily. Both Dutch culture and the meaning of Dutchness are changing. To keep in touch with that culture's past, it is no longer enough to be taken to the Rijksmuseum by one's parents and shown what once constituted the glory of Dutch art. What matters most at any present moment – hence, also today – is to watch over, indeed, cherish, a culture's changeability. The past can be neither dismissed nor repressed. Elsewhere, I have argued that if a culture is to fully incorporate constructive changes and to allow for the potential of changing more, it is of vital importance not to eradicate its memories, the traces of its problematic past.[17]

In *Double Exposures*, I develop this argument through a detailed reading of installations in the American Museum of Natural History (AMNH). I analyse the tensions between the museum's desire to address contemporary audiences and its obligation to preserve the past that is the focus of this particular kind of museum. Many of the choices made in that past are today perceived as blatantly racist. Their consequences can be softened, but not quite eradicated. More subtle forms of representation, tainted by racism and often more recent, are harder to frame. Museum representation remains an arena of ongoing adjustment.

That tension was very difficult to negotiate, especially since that museum is a childhood favourite of many native New Yorkers. As I have been told on several occasions, they get seriously nervous whenever cultural critics like myself 'mess with *my* [meaning 'favourite'] museum.' Part of the problem I faced in that analysis had to do with my own background. I acknowledge the implication that, as a non-American, I was touching delicate sentiments. Yet that and similar museums are today facing a predicament structurally similar to the one the Dutch face with Zwarte Piet.

The problem is, indeed, structural. And it is this that justifies the choice of our Dutch case – equally importantly, inflected by an art work from a national of another European country – for the present discussion of travelling traditions. How to present display material from a colonial past – specifically, racially informed visions of African peoples – to an audience the majority of whom are young, impressionable schoolchildren and many of whom are of African descent? The AMNH, as it is arranged today, although constantly updated and critically rethought, still encourages its visitors to make biological identifications – to literally enter a pact of self-understanding.[18] Like native New Yorkers, the Dutch do not like to be confronted with their inner contradictions. Yet, like them, they must be; forced by social reality and intellectual and moral debate; forced, also, by artistic practices which, like critical philosophy, examine their context.

But, if one wants to deal with the problems that both reside in and 'colour' the social relations of the present, it is as unproductive to forget the past as it is to reiterate it unthinkingly. Recent debates on the importance of keeping the memory of the Holocaust alive and the difficulty of representing that past have made this clear.[19] Memory is not just something that happens passively to people; it is an act that intervenes in the present, gives it shape, body, and direction.[20] Forgetting entails repression, and what is repressed tends to return, often with a vengeance. The Dutch, for example, have not been very good at handling the utterly bizarre chronology of their colonial war in Indonesia, which began soon after Holland was liberated from Nazi-German oppression.[21] Nor have the French dealt well with their *Guerre d'Algérie*. Both cultures would benefit in the present from a serious 'working through' of that past, and from bringing that work to bear on today's ambivalences. They need to revisit the past, not as tourists or frightened children, but as critical ethnographers. Art, like Fox's, can be the best rough guide for such a visit.

For this reason, I see the cultural importance of the portraits in

Fox's series not as an uncritical endorsement, or as a finger-pointing, distance-taking indictment. In the light of the need to neither repress nor simply continue problematic traditions, I see them instead as interventions in a larger European culture, where each country has its own past but today faces similar challenges. Ambivalence characterizes Fox's photographs, just as ambivalence characterizes the Zwarte Piet tradition. But they are two different forms of ambivalence. The former makes the latter less easy to live by.[22] Through images that revitalize the tradition *and* its ambivalences, by making these more explicit through the subtleties of visualization that frame it, Fox's work produces *an act of cultural memory*. An act that the viewers of her work can perform – as a performance of the work's performativity.

The concept that orients my analysis here, then, is double-edged, in two ways. It bears on the tenacity of cultural conservatism, and thus questions the potential for change and the efficacy of cultural analysis; and it explores, simultaneously, the relative social value of specific traditions. The specifics, or contents, of a tradition are neither progressive and wholesome, nor reactionary and harmful, by definition. Moreover, the question is for whom their possible effects are either good or bad. Dictionary definitions do not pronounce on such questions, as the lemma in Longman, quoted above, demonstrates. Looking at the word-use of 'tradition,' one imagines the social cohesion involved in the first definition – the handing down of information, beliefs, and customs – along with the tendency to conservatism in the second – a convention or set of conventions – which makes the break in the Leavis example sound liberating. The third definition – cultural continuity in social attitudes and institutions – can be seen as lending itself to both.

But, unlike such definitions, Fox's photographs draw attention to the *activity* that cultural memory necessitates. Replete with a many-layered history, the images constitute just such an act of cultural memory as any productive engagement with the past for the sake of the present requires. Tentatively, I submit, this 'memory-acting,' or memory-enacting, is the result both of an engagement with a word-concept – tradition – that travels – here, through past and present – and of the wavering attitudes towards tradition itself, whereby the impossibility of an arrogant cultural disentanglement in the name of political progressivity is acknowledged. Fox's images can only be understood in their effectivity as cultural critique on the condition that they are read closely – but not autonomously. They can only be read in relation to the three traditions they deploy and subvert. Let me highlight a few of their aspects.

The images are portraits, indeed. What can that mean? Portraiture in itself is a deeply ambivalent tradition. Like racist typology, portraiture as a visual discourse produces and reflects a long-standing interest in the articulation of human variety. Portraiture foregrounds individuality. But it also provides tools with which to speak of the sameness in difference and the difference in sameness, both at once. This ambivalence of portraiture is what makes it so suitable to offer a 'counterpoint *within*,' to the racism of the Zwarte Piet tradition.[23]

The tradition of portrèaiture critically engages the tradition of black-faced fools, from within a position of productive complicity. The generic character, Zwarte Piet, is decomposed into as many individual faces, each begging to be looked at in detail, named, and understood in terms of what its subject is doing dressing up like this. In the face of a tradition that lumped fantasmatic black men under one generic name as if slavery were still alive, individualizing them according to a class-bound tradition that dates back to the 'Golden Age' of which Dutch culture is so proud is already an act of display that does not simply reiterate. As has been argued, the history of the portrait as a traditional genre is closely linked with specific social historical developments; hence, portraits carry the meanings that, via this context, have accrued to the genre.[24]

In these four photographs (figures 4.2–5), the specific features of the portrait that stand out are the posing and the dark background. In conjunction with Zwarte Piet's traditional white collar, these features strongly recall traditional Dutch portraiture of the seventeenth century, the period of the joint successes of colonialism, slavery, and capitalism. It is the dark background of the wealth that enabled the bourgeoisie, rooted in an individualism that is still with us today and that underlies the genre's greatness, to rise to power. A power, incidentally, maintained even today, in the name 'Golden Age,' still used, without self-consciousness, by academics.[25]

The photographs as portraits thus refer to – without reiterating – a tradition in art that was always-already problematic. Portraiture was not, of course, only a Dutch tradition. But it was particularly suitable for the emerging Protestant merchant class in my country. Spain, the country with which the Seven Provinces had been warring for so long at the time of their 'Golden Age' – and not coincidentally the mythical origin of the Zwarte Piet tradition – was also the artistic rival of the

Low Countries. This is not only a fact of art history; it is also a demonstration of the intricacies between art and other social and political processes.

Velázquez's 1650 portrait of the black painter Juan de Pareja is alleged to be the first full *portrait* – in the aesthetic tradition of that genre – of a 'man of colour' in Western art (figure 4.6). Until that moment, black people had only held supporting roles. As servants, of course, but, sometimes even as elements in a still life. Rembrandt's *Two Black Africans* (signed and dated 1661) is a good foil for Velázquez's work (figure 4.7).[26] The heads in this painting are closer to the kind of racist ethnographic typification of which print and paint media in the nineteenth century were so fond than to the genre that aimed to individualize its subjects. It depicts the figures for their strangeness, their difference from white individuals, and in that function they are both like each other and like innumerable other representations of black people. In contrast, Velázquez's portrait individualizes, also through the pride of pose and facial expression that comes with the genre. It was more than just a portrait; it was the portraitist's business card, an advertisement for the latter's skills in the genre. It is, in other words, the product of Velázquez's steadfast application of his extraordinary skills to the mastering of the variation of human types.

The painting not only served as an exercise and demonstration for the later portrait of Pope Innocent X. In order to obtain the commission for the Pope's portrait, Velázquez devised a ruse that provides us with an extraordinary anecdote. Pareja, also Velázquez's slave, took the painting and showed it to his master's friends, who were able to judge the painter's skills from a comparison of model and representation. The ruse was successful. The master received the commission and, six months later, freed his slave, who became a painter in his own right.[27]

Forecasting Pareja's future, the painter gave his model the pose he himself had taken in his most famous painting, *Las Meninas*. If we take this case as an allegory, then painting, and tradition, have the power to change themselves from within, and also to change social reality. This is how art can be truly performative, and how tradition can turn against itself. Velázquez, we can thus say within the context of this essay, revisited the tradition within which he was making his career, to turn it around while also holding on to it. But let's not get carried away here. Idealizing Velázquez's ruse and its subsequent double outcome would blind us to the ambivalence inherent in portraiture. By sending Pareja to Rome with his own portrait, the master offered him up for identifica-

4.2–4.5 Anna Fox, *Zwarte Piet*, Numbers 1, 3, 2, and 14, from colour photographs made in The Netherlands between 1993 and 1998.

4.6 Diego Velázquez, *Portrait of Juan de Pareja*, 1650, oil on canvas.

4.7 Rembrandt van Rijn, *Two Black Africans*, 1661, oil on canvas.

tion *as* the object of representation; not for identification *with* him. The story remains an allegory, but, as such, demonstrates something that spills over from the confines of individual intention – from the individualism that portraiture, emphatically, labours to promote. The master may have wished to glorify himself, but his act of individualizing was effectively continuous with Pareja's emancipation.[28]

Again: Performing Performativity

In addition to engaging with portraiture, Fox's photographs, like tourists travelling to a neighbouring country, engage with another significant practice of performance: theatre. For, despite the fact that the figures in her images masquerade as powerful, they are not. The casual, less-than-fancy backgrounds that shimmer through the artistic darkness – the radiator, the edge of a formica table – are indexes of the class background within and for which the Zwarte Piet play is staged. They recall the urban school as the theatre for Coleman's children. Yet the subjects are dignified. Not because their portraits are being made, but because, individualized as they are, and unlike the black subjects of the Western artistic tradition who remained confined to their subservient roles, but like Juan de Pareja, they appear masters of their poses. The ambivalence of the genre and its history is thus inscribed in each image.

A well-known portrait of a black man by Henri Regnault, from 1870, titled *Head of a Moor*, offers an interesting parallel example of the intersection of portraiture and theatre (figure 4.8). The comparison demonstrates the subtleties of such generic allegiances, and the impossibility of using concepts as labels. In Regnault's work, the perspective from below makes the figure look heroic. His gaze – directed outside the image, to the wings so to speak, whereas traditional portraits tend to have the sitter look at the viewer – and the red mantle he dons, which has clearly been chosen for its colouristic effect, both strongly suggest theatricality. But, as a portrait, it is emphatically *not* performing an appeal to identification. The way colour is used emphasizes blackness, so that it can only be seen as 'othering,' the opposite of identification. This is done not only by the facial colour itself – which is black in a way that black people rarely are, setting off the whites of the eye, in turn emphasized by the sideward look – but also by the bright yellow on the left and the deep crimson garment, elements that make this a colour picture in more senses than one. Theatrical performance does not come, here, with critical performativity. In this sense, Regnault's

4.8 Henri Regnault, *Head of a Moor*, c. 1870, oil on canvas.

work stands in contrast with Velázquez's individualizing portrait, but also with Coleman's deployment of theatricality.

In a move comparable to Bourgeois' 'emendation' of Bernini's *Teresa*, American artist Ken Aptekar revised Regnault's painting *preposterously*. In a show that critically worked over a number of pieces belonging to the collection of the Corcoran Gallery of Art in Washington, DC – as an instance of precisely the double-edged engagement with tradition that I am exploring in this chapter – Aptekar used Regnault's painting twice, as if to compensate for the lack of black subjects in the collection; at first sight, a gesture of identity politics.[29]

This is a portrait, and as a minimal intervention in the tradition for which it stands, it has been reversed (figure 4.9). The artist has kept only the most essential part of the face, cropping the portrait and eliminating the bright colours. The powerful sense of facing from the self/other portrait can be seen here, quite fully, even though the figure looks to one side. Most important, by way of interdiscursive polemic, the painting has become monochromatic, to avoid the picturesque colouring of the source. By being painted in one colour, burnt umber, the face regains its nuances, and the visibility taken away by the excessive contrast – which recalls the cultural politics of 'invisibility blues' of which Michele Wallace wrote so powerfully – is reinstated.[30]

In addition to making other slight changes to the source paintings in his show at the Corcoran, Aptekar mounted glass plates over them, on which he wrote short texts. Sometimes these were autobiographical mini-narratives; sometimes they were quotes, for example, from comments made by museum visitors. These words drove the point home that visual images are always overwritten by cultural discourses. The text written over this particular painting was not long, not narrative; it was a snippet from audience responses:

Strength. Determination. Power.
And that's a little like myself.
Carrie Parker, age 15

The text endows the features of the face with the positive feedback that their former invisibility could hardly have been given. Yet the quoted teenager made these remarks in response to Regnault's, not Aptekar's, painting. Heroism, in Regnault's painting, served a purpose that Velázquez's portraiture also did – but not *qua* portrait. The visitor responded to the pose and the perspective, the *mise-en-scène*.

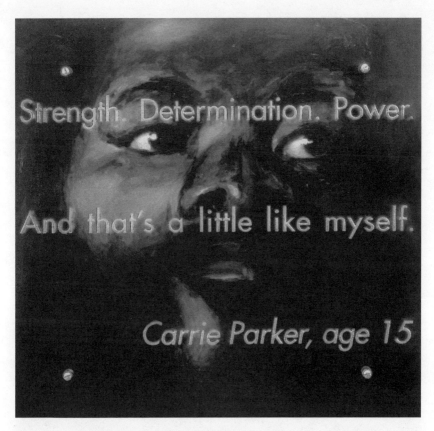

4.9 Ken Aptekar, *Strength. Determination. Power.* 1997, oil on wood, bolts, sand-blasted glass.

Moreover, her statement connects the audience to the figure through the explicit identification, based *not* on skin colour but on the features the figure as a person emanates. The figure in the painting is retrospectively given the 'Strength. Determination. Power.' that he always had, yet could not be given in the *portrait as such* by Regnault, because the use of colour there made his facial features invisible. Carrie Parker, young, female, contemporary, gives the figure these positive features as much as she takes them from him for her own benefit: 'And that's a little like myself.' Her comment demonstrates the importance of the loving gaze that affirms the subject of the interaction that language most basically is. Parker's response demonstrates the way external

After his license was suspended,

I drove my older brother to bars

in Detroit where whites didn't go.

I tried to be cool, sitting down

in a booth with my ginger ale.

My brother unzipped his gig bag,

raised his trumpet, and sat in with

the best of the be-bop bands.

4.10 Ken Aptekar, *After his license was suspended*, 1997, oil on wood, bolts, sand-blasted glass.

images 'key' the self to the values presented, to the skin as the shape of the self.

Identification is also the basis of Aptekar's other portrait made after this Regnault, *After his license was suspended* (figure 4.10). This work was also executed monochromatically, so as not to yield to social pressures to make skin colour a distracting and defining element. The burnt umber of *Strength* has been replaced with an overall blue that denaturalizes colour altogether while alluding to the many senses of the word 'blue.' Aptekar does here to the tradition of depicting black people as emphatically black – ethnographically – what Dutch culture tried to do, and didn't like, when it experimented with Red, Yellow, and Blue Piets. This denaturalizing effect is emphasized by the frame that has been added, and made to 'hang' askew. *After his license* offers one of those autobiographical mini-stories about the artist's past, this time about his adolescence; he can drive and goes out late at night, goes to bars and listens to music:

> After his license was suspended, I drove my older brother to bars in Detroit where whites didn't go. I tried to be cool, sitting down in a booth with my ginger ale. My brother unzipped his gig bag, raised his trumpet, and sat in with the best of the be-bop bands.

The story tells about a Jewish boy delving into black culture on a touristic trip to a tradition hitherto unknown to him.

The thrill of transgressing is audible – 'I tried to be cool' – and the pride the boy felt when his older brother managed to participate in 'the best of the be-bop bands' conveys the past 'feel' of the story more than the past tense does. The musical phrase 'the best of the be-bop bands,' with its alliteration and short drumming words, leaves an echo of be-bop as if we had been there too. This is identity poetics, not politics, at least not the kind of politics that separates and judges. The moment puts the autobiographical subject on the threshold of adulthood, on the threshold of a culture at a time of *de facto* segregation, on the threshold, again, where self and other meet. The threshold is the frame. The question raised here, both poetically and effectively, is: Is a frame a boundary that keeps distinctions in place, or a meeting point where a frame-up yields to an embrace?

The various thoughts I have attempted to address to tradition so far converge in this move beyond identity politics. To be or not to be: the question of identity is omnipresent and relative, explored in its tenacious difficulty and made to appear easy. I allege Aptekar's reworking of Regnault's traditional painting, which suggests an intercourse with the word-concept of tradition and with those dubious values, in the case of race-based cultural distinctions, that are attached to the particular tradition out of which the Dutch Zwarte Piet grew and within which it cannot but remain rooted.

'Good' messages are not available; they are deceptions of simplicity. There are many unsettling, worrying, anxiety-inducing messages running through our culture – and here, I use 'our' in a broader sense, one that connects Dutch with other European and North American cultures. One way or another, these unsettling messages relate to the way the individual's voice is erased by authority both within the family – which, after all, is shaped and confirmed by institutions – and within institutions. The diagnosis is sharp, but full of compassion in the literal and lived sense, too full to be a complaint. The interaction between public institutional pressures and their effect on the personal, private life that comes back to haunt public culture is scrutinized as well as put forward, literally, into the viewer's space. By integrating audience response, it makes explicit what art can do, what even fifteen-year-olds can do to *it*, when they respond to art's performativity by offering their counter-performance.

This, perhaps, makes empowerment the central theme of Aptekar's project. An empowerment that is also the goal of a cultural analysis of the kind I have been trying to put forward through my engagement with this art. But, for art to empower, it must be performative. Using theatricality, not to deceive or to impose sentimental identification by means of these reworkings of Regnault's portrait and the tradition it deploys, Aptekar enlists Carrie Parker as an actor, performing – in the two senses of that word. Performing on the stage – the museum – her speech act of self-empowerment.

Theatrical Portraiture

The two conventions of theatre and portraiture that have now accrued to our concept of image are reactivated in Fox's work. They come together in their working through of this painful tradition informed by moralism. My hypothetical explanation of the Dutch attachment to this tradition is based on the notion that moralism, even progressive, anti-racist moralism, is less a critique of the tradition than an integral part of it. This collusion is inevitable. Aptekar's works acknowledge that fact, and have this aspect in common with Fox's photographs.

By virtue of their emphatic interdiscursive relationship with portraiture, Fox's photographs command an individualizing attention that takes the masquerade as part of the subject's individuality. As part of it, along with other parts; but sometimes, also, as synecdoche, as the part standing for the whole, making the rest of the individuality invisible through figurativity. Masquerade, then, comes to stand for a new, disabused form of individuality, in the way Coleman's theatricality came to embody a new form of authenticity.

Fox's portraits thus become a critique of portraiture from within, a critique of its ruthlessly power-based individualism. But they replace that individualism with one that does not obscure the individual's allegiances and collusions. These updated portraits ask us to look through the disguise, the similarity, the assumption of generic identity that the collective name Zwarte Piet, the costume, and the black-facing offer us – at first sight. The subjects are women, but in the photographs, nothing of their traditional gear helps us to notice their gender; no breasts, no feminine clothing, no ornaments, no poses. We are just looking at faces, painted for disguise, and yet, in most of the photographs, we see women.

We see they are white; many have blue eyes. Still, in some cases I hesitate: is the woman with the blue bonnet, red hood, and white lace collar who looks me straight in the eye, white or black (figure 4.2)? To me, and to the friends to whom I showed the photographs, she 'looks black.' This commands a closer look. I scrutinize the image with an incurable, acquired, ideological magnifying glass. From my stock of prejudices, I glean all the features I have learned to associate with black people, and here I am, detailing the racist taxonomy learned so long ago in geography books at the age when I was also still a little scared of Zwarte Piet. This is how the photographs implicate their viewers; the past, they say, is not out there; it is here, today. And, to some extent – which I can neither master nor eradicate – it is inside me.[31]

And, while I am doing this, knowing that I am doing it, I also see the whiter edges around the subject's eyes, indexes of racial uncertainty, the hand that refuses to assert racial truth. Then I notice the smudge of black paint on the woman's upper lip. This smudge works like a wink, as if she is pulling my leg. 'I am not who you think I am,' the figure seems to say.[32] Is this a black woman playing a white woman playing a black man? What she is, here, *is not* the point; *that* is the point. The game she plays involves me, who I am, as much as it involves the she that she does not want to reveal herself to be. This is how Fox, by crossing portraiture and Zwarte Piet, and soliciting theatricality, denaturalizes tradition. The theatrical space opened up here is the space where culture doesn't simply exist – but happens.

What this image does to my awareness of the race-consciousness within me also happens with gender. We see women, all different. Or do we? Is the proud-posing person in the purple mantle, whose wig or bonnet has slipped backwards to reveal, intentionally or by accident, a white hairline, a woman or a man (figure 4.3)? Through the defiance in her gaze and on her lips, the figure's gender becomes so emphatically ambiguous that I wonder if this is a man posing as a woman posing as a man. And so, again, I realize that sometimes you do not know – and sometimes it does not matter. Sometimes, in other words, it is possible to reject compulsory identification *as*, and to replace it with identification *with*, another. The posing itself, the choice of and the mastery over the way each person is represented in this series, determines whether one is of a particular sex or gender – or whether s/he is playing the in-between. In this series, gender, like race, is emphatically an event, an effect, not a cause or an origin of social positions. Hence it is bound to the subject choosing to act it, and not an excuse to naturalize social positions and the inequities that come with them.[33]

Each woman is different from every other. But this individuality does not entail distance. Despite resembling the paintings in Dutch museums in some way, they are also very close, very personal, looking me straight in the eye, and inviting me to share the pride, boredom, fun, fatigue, resignation, fear, insecurity, comfort, or discomfort that playing the role entails, despite also resisting the precise reading necessary for such identification. The Zwarte Piet in the Italian Renaissance pose – in bright red and blue and pristine white, with a Zwarte Piet clad in yellow in the background – looks the way I dreamed I would look when I knew I would not be chosen to be Zwarte Piet because of my inability to muster that confident prettiness (figure 4.4).

This woman, who looks so utterly confident in her Renaissance role and who raises the issue of naturalizing role-playing in general, emanates the success which, for me, defined the class identity of those whose station was just a notch above mine. Having been raised with the ambivalent class consciousness characteristic of upward-striving, lower middle-class families (the target audience of Zwarte Piet in an era of the commercialization of tradition), as a child I would not have been aware that the woman emanated for me the successful imperson-ation of a class position superior to mine. But I would have sensed it. It would have been part of the drill: the learning of categories and power positions that came with them; *that* is the main task of children. Even the well-starched, well-ironed collar and the gold bands decorating the costume demonstrated the perfection I knew I would never achieve. The blue eyes are the most secure symptom of the travesty. But the pose of perfection – the head inclined just enough to be a flattering facial representation yet held proudly and easily at the same time – and the self-confidence of the facial expression are emphatic enough to reveal the artificiality of the pose caught in the act of its success. The acting itself, its visible performance, suggests this is not a wealthy girl from among my classmates, but a lower middle-class woman posing as an upper middle-class woman posing as a lower-class man.

Accordingly, the strategies of this play are different from the two other, ambiguous portraits I have been responding to. While the transvestite undermining of racial and gender identities that creates a space of uncertainty deploys an emphatically artificial conception of theatricality to achieve this effect, this portrait probes the limits of realistic theatre, or of that form of theatre that encourages the audience to forget its own nature and naturalize the spectacle instead. This seems to me to be a highly effective cultural intervention on the part of the artist-cum-model. Subtly approaching class by questioning naturalizing realistic representation, this photograph definitively implicates all viewers – willingly critical or not – in the tensions and ambiguities that representation brings with it, thus undermining its drilling educational effect from within.

My favourite Zwarte Piet in this series looks the way I would have looked given the chance, and seeing her, I know my case was hopeless, even if hers is not. Her hat is as brown as her stained face and eyes. Here, the brown, set off against the shiny, black nylon curls of the wig and the dark background and black costume, recalls that black isn't black, but just a symptom of a dichotomy that barely covers a physical reality (figure 4.5). The brown has been less than well applied by a brush, the result is as artificial as the colour of the lipstick. Nor is the white white, if the stained collar is any indication. The girl's costume is a bit shabby, her make-up sloppy. This most monochromatic of the portraits – as monochromatic as Velázquez's *Portrait of Juan de Pareja* – is also the most emphatic in its de-naturalizing of colour on the level of representation. Caught up in a whirlwind of maintained and decomposed traditions, I wonder why this portrait captivates me, and which share of its effect is the woman's, which the artist's, which the character's, and which my own.

The deep ambiguity here, which holds in its sway all the other ambiguities, is a psychological one. Her body, clad in black, barely visible, the shoulder with its fraying collar, tells a hundred stories. Straighten your back, her mother must have told her when, growing too tall too quickly and sprouting breasts before her classmates did, she/I tended to hunch her/my shoulders. Hold your head proud instead of looking down, she would have heard, when she didn't know she was soliciting her own status as wallflower that she so dreaded. She looks bravely, lips slightly parted, as if she were about to overcome her shyness and actually speak. Her entire face and body are held back just a fraction, perhaps stiff, expressing both the act of posing for the merciless eyes of the camera and the public, and the pain it inflicts on her. Her face speaks to me of fear and bravery; insecurity and the desire to overcome it. Fear, not of Zwarte Piet, but of playing the part in public. This is what I would have liked to be at one time in my life: a tomboy posing as a good feminine girl posing as an exuberant black man. The middle term is the price to pay for the empowerment of the first and the last elements of this theatrical, triple identity.

Trans-gender, trans-racial, and trans-personality travesty merge inextricably here to perform the kind of intersubjective process that constitutes cultural life. This, then, the least successful Zwarte Piet, is the closest you get to a self-portrait of me as viewer. My own performance as viewer, subjective and unpredictable as it is, thus also belongs to the performance of this work. Tomboy, transvestite, black-faced clown: playing the part of what you are not fulfils a deep desire. Like getting yourself dirty, or doing dirty deeds. Like mastering fear rather than mastering others. Like coping with the entanglements of this tradition rather than *simply* rejecting it, as if you owned it.

Dirty Art

I have been talking about complicity in this essay. But casting that complicity in the past alone is another form of disingenuous disavowal. Fox's art, again, helps counter that tendency. For it compels me to acknowledge that I enjoy these photographs. This is an effect of aesthetic as 'binding,' and through that aesthetic effectivity the photos hit me, performatively, with something in myself. They confront me with a tradition of which I have been too fond to simply shed the memories of it. Meanwhile, they confront me with a tradition that makes me blush with embarrassment. There is something shameless about these images. How can I negotiate them with the help of a concept – tradition – that itself has dirty hands? The variant of travel involved here seems to me, at best, to be that of tourism. Am I, can I only be, an exploitative, superficial tourist?

Regardless of the contingency of the cultural status of traditions and the value placed upon their historical specifics, it is not easy to determine the attitude of cultural agents today towards traditions that many consider unproductive for a dynamic society. For even harmful traditions cannot simply be wished away. The kind of critique that a politically alert cultural analysis can usefully bring to bear on traditions cannot cleanly disentangle itself from the cultural fabric in which the critique itself is embedded. And this cultural fabric is replete with tradition. To probe this issue, I have critically engaged with an extremely dubious yet perniciously persistent tradition in the country where I grew up and still live – and where the age-old tradition continues to thrive.

My goal was to question, through this example, both the easy dismissal of traditions and their unquestioned maintenance. Avoiding moralizing and partisanship, I discussed the Zwarte Piet tradition as a member of a culture that appears unable to let go of it, even in the face of increasing pressure to do so. I did this through a body of images that present themselves as a critical representation of that tradition, espouse another tradition to do so, and are made from a point of view exterior to the culture of the former (Zwarte Piet), while sharing the latter (portraiture). Taking my standpoint firmly in the present and looking first at the tradition's meanings and effects for contemporary (Dutch) culture, I considered the presence of the past in that present. In addition, I considered the status of traditions – both in art and in Dutch culture at large – that make up the fabric of Dutch society. I argued that traditions are neither dismissible fictions nor acceptable truths. Instead, I seek to understand their workings so that the culture can engage them, critically, where needed.

I said I would suspend judgment. Judgment here is to be understood in the two senses it usually takes – condemnation or valuation. Progressive criticism tends to indict cultural practices such as traditions, for their pernicious political conservatism. The more traditional (!) criticism of the venerable humanistic tradition implicitly or explicitly values the object of study. Any cultural object worthy of attention is by definition 'great,' or at least worthy of attention, according to the standards of the artistic canon and its collaterals or side effects. These two traditions – one of anti-traditional critique and the other of traditionalism – were suspended in this chapter. Instead, I aimed to practise an analysis that is anti-tradition*alist*, that argues against the two academic traditions that know, or think they know, the outcome of their search. Risking the objectionable position of endorsing yet another dubious tradition, I proposed to act like a tourist, at least in one respect.

Tourists bring souvenirs home, but they are very much aware of the fact that they enjoy from the outside, and are not close enough to judge, the cultures they visit. And, whereas tourism is officially much snubbed by progressive academics, it is what every student of cultural objects practises – all the time. Tourists are superficial visitors, exploitative and contributing to the ruination of the culture they admire. They know it, and they still do it, alleging their contribution to the local economy, which they know to be not so local. The position of the tourist is embarrassing. Maybe it is that embarrassment that makes cultural analysis potentially effective.

In this discussion, I have visited Fox's photographs, and through them, my own past as a foreign country. The four photographs I have discussed in detail here represent for me, in the keenest possible way, the ambiguities and tensions of the Zwarte Piet tradition. Through that tradition, they deploy, decompose, critique, and exploit other traditions, such as photography, ethnography, portraiture, and theatre. Contending, like Aptekar, with a work that itself contended with a tradition, Fox has captured these tensions – not so she can document them, but as a way of working through, and working with, the space they open up. Within that space, the tradition can be used, for better or for worse, to probe a culture in flux, a culture that is tragically locked up in itself yet unable to maintain the illusion of self-identity.

A culture is not condemned to forever maintain – let alone celebrate, in a profoundly nostalgic sentiment – its racist roots. On the contrary, it is, by definition, changing.[34] This changing quality does not mean change is automatic; the direction it takes is the subject of the continuous struggles among the subjects of that culture. Just think of South Africa. Art is not a slavish imitation of reality; that, too, is only too obvious. Nor is it cut off from reality as has sometimes been argued; much of present-day cultural practice is still entangled in the difficulty of articulating a position for art that is socially involved yet capable of doing its own job. It cannot be easily defined. Much recent work on representations of race, artistic as well as academic and critical, has demonstrated the importance of the efforts to keep trying.

Grosso modo, it is fair to say that in the history of Western art, black subjects have been represented the way they were treated in social reality: as marginalized or neglected; made ugly, sometimes monstrous, even comical; or idealized, always a projection screen for white painters' fears and desires.[35] But, as I have argued elsewhere, progressive cultural critics have tended to reiterate such abuse in the very gesture of indicting it.[36] Such representations, including the criticism addressed to them, are neither imitations of, nor disconnected from, social imagery and traditions. Art today cannot but interact with that embarrassing tradition if it is to be effective in its interventions in changing culture. Only by neither repressing nor reiterating the past can we live with a present brought forth by that past, and that still harbours it, whether we like it or not.

Like Velázquez's, Regnault's, and Aptekar's paintings, each in their own temporal landscape, Fox's photographs are both disabused and optimistic. Humorous and tender, ironic and identifying, they are powerful in the way they offer art as a means to face the need to interact head-on. This is the chief aspect of the interaction that the portrait as genre has become: rather than pretending to settle what an individual is – a lone power broker – the portrait of this postmodern variety proposes the individual as framed by time and history but able to exercise the performativity that a theatrical authenticity solicits. Fox's images stand here for a practice of cultural analysis that manages to avoid the two most predictable attitudes to which a project like this might succumb: the endorsement of reiteration and the moralism of indictment.

To say they 'avoid' is to say they do something. The images' quality that I am implying through that phrase is their performativity. Beyond their artistic work of portraiture alone, beyond their theatrical play, they do something; they act. Like words. One of the many things they do is to take advantage of the ambiguity of images as such, in order to critique a tradition without dismissing it off-hand. For, living in the present and travelling to the past and back again, cultural tourists can no more avoid dirty hands than any other tourists can.

'Dirty' is the word that characterizes both this tradition and its disingenuous disavowal. It is a word that might at some point emerge as a concept. I think it would be a useful addition to the conceptual toolbox of cultural analysis. For, theoretically, it denotes the complicity that inhabiting a cultural situation inevitably entails. It is a gentle rebuttal of both false innocence and hasty distancing. Unlike words such as 'contamination,' which inspire fear of otherness, 'dirt' is not frightening. Dirt sticks to you but can be washed off, although after that washing you get dirty again.[37] It is inevitable, embarrassing too, but not deadly; as long as you take good care of yourself, you can continuously negotiate how dirty your environment can make you.

Fox has played with dirt by selecting a tradition that, by materially playing with dirt, is also ideologically dirty; working with it as an impossible ethnographic project that renounces the illusory pretension that you can 'come clean.' Too close to home – within Europe – but not really home – not in Britain – the Zwarte Piet tradition enables Fox to probe the ambiguities of our, and specifically her, relationship to the traditions that have comfortably shaped us, and that continue to shape us while negatively shaping others. She was also able to establish a connection between the cosy home and festive but dirty street, and 'high art.' The mediating objects are visual images.

Images are readable, but what they say exactly remains subject to debate. In our case – the Zwarte Piet tradition and Fox's photographs of it – this is all to the good. The ambiguities here are indispensable, for, as I have suggested, moralism is part of both the racism and the anti-racism that have coloured Dutch culture in the wake of post-colonial migration. Together with the taxonomies of race, gender, and class, which provide the grids through which children learn to bring order into the chaos of the world, moralism itself is tabled here. For it is moralism that attempts to channel children's affective lives and fill them with ideological interests. Disturbingly – but offering food for thought – moralism also underlies the wish to do away with this tradition.

The tool Fox uses to break this moralism open, while avoiding traps of any simple representation of the tradition, is to appeal to the identif-icatory trajectories that powerful images are able to propose. These allow viewers to travel backwards in time, not on the national but on the personal level, to relive their own childhood, and perhaps to exor-cize the fear that came with the fascination. The bed of the artificial ideological river that channelled childish anxiety through the special-ization of racial othering can be enlarged. Enlarged photographs of today's images infused with pastness as if they were the products of double exposures may, I would like to suggest, serve to trigger, by way of the allegorical exploitation of their medium, an intensification of the reflection on where we can go from here. The emphatic effect of a mas-querade that persuades us there is no real identity to be seen yet no fic-tional mask to hide behind in the face of a disturbing, yet, for the time being, ineradicable tradition: this is simultaneously the photographs' performance, the viewer's liberation, Fox's teaching, and Zwarte Piet's *démasqué*. And, as the next chapter will continue to suggest, teaching as the primary tool of the cultural analyst can only work if it, too, changes, through its 'travelling' practice.

Tradition's Last Word

Tradition, Edward Saïd recently reiterated, is not only a weapon in the service of the state-directed manipulation of cultural memories. It can also, precisely because of the power to empower the people that cultural memory possesses, be turned into a means of communicating and furthering understanding. But only if tradition is de-naturalized and thereby pluralized. With the impressive example of Israeli and Palestinian memories converging around the same symbols – prickly-pear cactus, orange groves, forests – he alleges Carol Bardenstein's sensitive analyses of the tensions, convergences, differences, and above all, conflicting usages of such symbols of 'the land.'[38]

Saïd urges each community to recognize the other's memories, fixed in tradition. But he also points out the different position of each tradition in relation to power inequalities in the present. In the face of the political urgency of these reflections, the playful theatricality of the Zwarte Piet tradition, as Fox's photographs probe it, may appear frivolous. It is not. The presence of a deeply racist tradition in one of the 'postcolonial' societies most proud of its liberal tradition cannot be called frivolous, especially not in confrontation with Bardenstein's examples. Its very playfulness, its theatricality, constitutes its appeal to the children it shapes.

Tradition, as a word we tend to take for granted as expressing a cultural value to be endorsed or rejected, is complicated by *tradition* as a concept, thus serving as a searchlight to illuminate the process, performance, and performativity whose subjects are seduced into realizing that they are doing the acting. No longer tourists, the Dutch and any other people addressed by this series are burdened with the ethnographer's duty to do fieldwork. Travelling to the past and making it a familiar country – one for which one is responsible – and to the foreign country within one's own, in which being coloured is not a theatrical festivity, the spectators of Sinterklaas' entrance fully participate in the tradition, as agents, and are thus themselves framed by that tradition but not passively subjected to it.

Where does that leave the object of analysis here, tradition, and specifically, the two kinds of tradition – the sustaining, identity-shaping ones, and the invented tools of state power that sustain the nation at the expense of others and of its own historical awareness – that I have distinguished for the sake of this discussion? Artistic traditions (the portrait) and 'popular' cultural traditions (Zwarte Piet) have been maintained and subverted here at the same time. The concrete analytical means was theatricality. Thanks to the wedge that theatricality inserts between these two traditions, they were not handled in the same way. Artistic traditions here served as markers of recognizable

forms, through which new perspectives, critical ideas, might be figured. The beauty of the images, their aesthetic quality, was used as a
tool, in the same way as the mobilization of tradition was used to
increase the affective quality of the images, which is a precondition of
their performative effectivity.

The cultural tradition has been transformed only slightly. Art cannot
simply change society, and believing that it can is an act of elitist
hubris. But, like that smudge of black paint on the lip of that woman
whose racial identity remains stubbornly ambiguous, the mirror of
self-reflection held up by her photograph helps, ever so slightly, to
enhance the painfulness of tradition. Until, that is, one day, the culture
concerned wakes up sick of the pain. Only then – perhaps – can this
tradition be relinquished, wholeheartedly; not suppressed by moralism, but rejected for the pain it causes to all its members. By that time,
another tradition will have been invented, one that fits the culture better – and that hurts less. Until it, too, becomes the culture's backlog,
dragging behind the times.

NOTES

This chapter was originally published as 'Tradition' in *Travelling Concepts in the Humanities: A Rough Guide* by Mieke Bal (Toronto, 2002), 213–52.

1 For commentary on an earlier – and radically different – kind of 'ethno-graphic' art, see Foster (1995). For a critical assessment and analysis of the work by an artist closer to Fox, see van Alphen (2001).

2 See Langeler (1994) for a historical study of the Zwarte Piet tradition.

3 See Eliot (1975 [1919]).

4 On the ideological aspect of concepts, see Donald Davidson's 'On the Very Idea of a Conceptual Schema' (1984).

5 See Hobsbawm and Ranger (1993).

6 This would be analogous to the function attributed to fairy-tales by Bruno Bettelheim in a well-known argument of the Freudian kind (1976). Here, I would like to be both more specific than Bettelheim and more critical of his one-sided interpretation of the ongoing use of cultural traditions in educa-tion.

7 This Dutch tradition is here analysed in its specific idiosyncrasies; that is not to say, however, that it is the only tradition of black-facing. For an alto-gether different tradition of this kind, see Rogin (1996).

8 See, again, Hobsbawm and Ranger (1983).

9 Fox's work can be seen within the British tradition of critiquing tradition, including that of black modernism, of which she may well have been aware when undertaking this project. For an excellent commentary on such issues, including that of different conceptions of time and 'time travel' in black modernisms and postmodernisms, see Paul Gilroy (1993). Given my project in this essay, to perform a cultural analysis focused explicitly on my own culture, I refrain from addressing this context.

10 I thank Darby English for this and other comments on an earlier draft. He commented that no culture would invent such a blatantly *typological* tradition of racism; the racism would be different in form only.

11 The Dutch don't deal easily with racism in their own culture. In 1990 an exhibition of racist imagery was mounted in the Tropenmuseum in Amsterdam. Black people hated it: why did they again have to be confronted with this offensive stuff? White people hated it too: a girl in a banana skirt, is that racism? See Nederveen Pieterse (1990).

12 The politics of 'we' is a problem that remains tenaciously difficult to resolve (Torgovnick, 1994). Here, I use 'we' to mark my position of inevitable collusion, which I hope, inevitably, leads to the kind of productive complicity that Spivak advocates throughout her work (e.g., 1999).

13 Incidentally, this is also largely how I see US culture as far as I know it. But there are differences, which I will not address here – particularly in the degree of explicitness with which such issues as I am discussing here can be raised.

14 Needless to say, the use of the term 'aboriginal' in this paragraph is meant ironically, but, like all irony, it also has a 'serious' meaning. I object to current usages of the binary 'allochthonic' versus 'autochthonic,' to keep distinguishing recent migrants from all others in European countries. In light of that use, it seems helpful to critically appropriate a term that keeps 'real' aboriginals in subordinate or at least exceptional positions.

15 Fox thus connects with the 'frog's perspective' inherent in much black British art, a perspective advocated by Gilroy in his essay 'Cruciality and the Frog's Perspective,' in his book *Small Acts* (1993). It is especially the impossibility of appealing to 'authenticity' discussed by Gilroy (also in his book *Black Atlantic*) that is important to me here. The position I am trying to stake out is not based on my 'authentic' Dutchness, but on the ambiguity of any person who is both Dutch and something else (critical, anti-racist, feminist, and a frequent traveller, to mention only those elements of my 'identity' that are relevant for this chapter).

16 The forms of identification I have in mind are varieties of what Kaja Silverman has called 'heteropathic identification,' based on a movement outside

of oneself, risking who one is, and 'autopathic identification,' of the canni-
balistic sort, where the other is reduced to a simulacrum of the self (1996).

17 See ch. 1 of *Double Exposures*, in contrast to ch. 5 of that book, where I probe
the problems of repeating the past under the pretext of critique.

18 This last sentence was suggested to me by Darby English, who said he was
one of those kids. His response, which I gratefully acknowledge, is here
coming from a position in relation to the AMNH that is symmetrical to my
relationship to the Zwarte Piet tradition.

19 For an illuminating review of positions and strategies pertaining to this
issue, see van Alphen (1997).

20 On the cultural function of memory seen as activity, see Bal, Crewe, and
Spitzer, eds. (1999).

21 Tom Verheul's sensitive documentary film *Tabee Tuan* (1995), but importantly, also his earlier *Denial* (1993), bear testimony to the ongoing suffering
that results from such massive repression.

22 See, on this issue of double ambivalence, Bhabha (1986).

23 I am very grateful to Darby English for insisting on this point.

24 See, on portraiture and its meanings today, van Alphen (1996).

25 A new centre for the study of the 'Golden Age' was recently created at the
University of Amsterdam. On some of the ironies of the idea of a Golden
Age, see Roxann Wheeler's essay 'New Golden Age' in *The Complexion of
Race* (2000).

26 The date, not the signature, has been contested. It is also not certain
whether both heads were painted from life. See Schwartz (1985: 315).

27 Lecture by Victor Stoichita at the University of Michigan, Ann Arbor,
24 February 1999.

28 This paragraph engages a more negative argument offered by Darby
English, who usefully cautioned me against idealizing Velázquez here.

29 The following remarks on Aptekar's two paintings are based on my earlier
article on his Corcoran project (Aptekar 1997).

30 I cannot do justice to the extremely thick concept 'invisibility blues' here.
Briefly rendered, it refers to the varied forms of cultural politics rendering
black people and black culture invisible. But a full account of this concept is
keenly relevant for this essay. See Wallace (1991).

31 I am alluding to my position as having been raised, *schooled*, in this tradition. Schools are productive fields for critical fieldwork. For the example of
geography, see Ineke Mok's detailed analysis of the racism underlying
geography textbooks in the Netherlands (1999). This study provides
extremely useful insights into geography's mapping of racial differences

and the drill with which an entirely white-invented race-consciousness is instilled in Dutch children.

32 I took this phrase from Ernst van Alphen's relevant analysis of cross-gender transvestitism, so far, unfortunately, unavailable in English (1998).

33 For the conception of gender that underlies this viewing of the photograph, see Butler (1993).

34 Nostalgia in relation to racism became painfully apparent in the wake of the release of Nelson Mandela and the turn to the rainbow regime in South Africa. At the time, Dutch television showed yesterday's anti-racist artists, such as Adriaan van Dis, dressed up as a pioneer Boer in sporting boots and a hat and singing 'Sari Mareis,' the white South African song best known in Holland.

35 Fred Wilson's successful exhibition at the Contemporary in Baltimore in 1996 offers one of many examples of how to deal with that pictorial past in and for the present. For a recent collection of essays on the problems of representation in a context that tries to define itself as post-racist – South Africa by way of the 1998 Johannesburg Biennial – see Atkinson and Breitz (1999).

36 See chs. 6 and 8 of *Double Exposures*.

37 On the fear of contamination, see Stallybrass and White (1986).

38 The examples from popular culture such as posters and shop windows, juxtaposed to poetry and diaries, demonstrate a continuity between tradition and (cultural) memory. The most recent version of Bardenstein's analysis focuses explicitly on the memory aspect of these symbols (1999).

BIBLIOGRAPHY

Aptekar, Ken. 1997. *Ken Aptekar: Talking to Pictures.* Washington, DC: Corcoran Gallery of Art (exhibition catalogue)

Atkinson, Brenda, and Candice Breitz, eds. 1999. *Grey Areas: Representation, Identity and Politics in Contemporary South African Art.* Johannesburg: Chalkham Hill Press

Bal, Mieke. 1996. *Double Exposures: The Subject of Cultural Analysis.* New York: Routledge

Bal, Mieke, Jonathan Crewe, and Leo Spitzer, eds. 1999. *Acts of Memory: Cultural Recall in the Present.* Hanover, NH: University Press of New England

Bardenstein, Carol. 1999. 'Trees, Forests, and the Shaping of Palestinian and Israeli Collective Memory.' In *Acts of Memory: Cultural Recall in the Present,*

ed. Mieke Bal, Jonathan Crewe, and Leo Spitzer, 148–68. Hanover and
London: University Press of New England

Bettelheim, Bruno. 1976. *The Uses of Enchantment: The Meaning and Importance of
Fairy Tales*. New York: Knopf

Bhabha, Homi K. 1986. 'The Other Question: Difference, Discrimination and
the Discourse of Colonialism.' In *Literature, Politics and Theory*, ed. Francis
Barker et al. New York: Methuen

Butler, Judith. 1993. *Bodies That Matter: On the Discursive Limits of 'Sex.'* New
York: Routledge

Davidson, Dónald. 1984. 'On the Very Idea of a Conceptual Schema.' In *Inquiries into Truth and Interpretation*, 183–98. Oxford: Clarendon Press

Eliot, T.S. 1975. 'Tradition and the Individual Talent.' In *Selected Prose of T.S.
Eliot*, ed. and with an introduction by Frank Kermode, 37–44. London: Faber
and Faber (first published in *Egoist*, September and December 1919)

Foster, Hal. 1995. 'The Artist as Ethnographer?' In *The Traffic in Culture: Refiguring Art and Anthropology*, ed. George E. Marcus and Fred R. Myers, 302–9.
Berkeley: University of California Press

Gilroy, Paul. 1993. *Small Acts: Thoughts on the Politics of Black Cultures*. London:
Serpent's Tail

– 1995. *The Black Atlantic: Modernity and Double Consciousness*. Cambridge:
Harvard University Press

Hobsbawm, Eric, and Terence Ranger, eds. 1983. *The Invention of Traditions*.
Cambridge: Cambridge University Press

Langeler, Arno. 1994. *Zwarte Piet: een Moor in dienst van Venetië*. Amsterdam:
Jan Mets

Lowenthal, David. 1985. *The Past Is a Foreign Country*. Cambridge: Cambridge
University Press

Mok, Ineke. 1999. *In de ban van het ras. Aardrijkskunde tussen wetenschap en
samenleving, 1876–1992 (Under the Spell of Race: Geography between Science and
Society, 1876–1992)*. Amsterdam: ASCA Press (PhD dissertation)

Nederveen Pieterse, J. 1990. *Wit over zwart: beelden van Afrika en zwarten in de
westerse populaire cultuur*. Amsterdam: Koninklijk Instituut voor de Tropen/
Stichting Cosmic Illusion Productions; The Hague: Novib

Rogin, Michael. 1996. *Blackface, White Noise: Jewish Immigrants in the Hollywood
Melting Pot*. Berkeley: University of California Press

Schwartz, Gary. 1985. *Rembrandt: His Life, His Paintings*. Harmondsworth:
Penguin

Silverman, Kaja. 1996. *The Threshold of the Visible World*. New York: Routledge

– 1999. *A Critique of Postcolonial Reason: Toward a History of the Vanishing
Present*. Cambridge: Harvard University Press

Stallybrass, Peter, and Allon White. 1986. *The Politics and Poetics of Transgression*. Ithaca: Cornell University Press

Torgovnick, Marianna. 1994. 'The Politics of "We."' In *Eloquent Obsessions: Writing Cultural Criticism*, ed. Marianna Torgovnick, 260–78. Durham, NC: Duke University Press

van Alphen, Ernst. 1996. 'The Portrait's Dispersal: Concepts of Representation and Subjectivity in Contemporary Portraiture.' In *Portraiture: Facing the Subject*, ed. Joanna Woodall, 239–56. Manchester: Manchester University Press

– 1997. *Caught by History: Holocaust Effects in Contemporary Art, Literature, and Theory*. Stanford: Stanford University Press

– 1998. 'Duchamp in travestie.' *De Witte Raaf* 76 (Nov.–Dec.): 14–15

– 2001. 'Imagined Homelands: Remapping Cultural Identity.' Lecture, ASCA soirées on the Politics of Place (org. Ginette Verstraete). Amsterdam: ASCA

Wallace, Michele. 1991. *Invisibility Blues: From Pop to Theory*. London and New York: Verso

Wheeler, Roxann. 2000. 'New Golden Age.' In *The Complexion of Race: Categories of Difference in Eighteenth-Century British Culture*. Philadelphia: University of Pennsylvania Press

ILLUSTRATIONS AND CREDITS

Chapter Five

Traditional Futures

JAMES CLIFFORD

In his introduction to this volume, Mark Phillips proposes an 'enlarged conversation about tradition' that could 'dissolve the simple binary of tradition and modernity.' He argues that once we stop defining tradition as resistance to modernity, the term 'becomes again a means of raising essential questions about the ways in which we pass on the life of cultures – questions that necessarily include issues of authority as well as invention, practice as well as interpretation.' Tradition becomes a newly complex, open-ended subject.

The Western idea of tradition, at least since the early modern period, has typically been opposed to notions like progress, science, rationality, modernization, development, and now globalization – all terms associated with a dynamic future. Tradition is bound up in the past, the repetitive (Lévi-Strauss's 'cold' societies), the conservative, the religious, the native, the local, the nonrational, the non-Western. Always a foil to the modern, tradition cannot be transformative or forward-looking. Mark Phillips does the critical work, within Western intellectual history, of bringing into view understandings of tradition which question this constitutive opposition. He reminds us that a sense of dynamic process can be derived from Christian and Jewish sources: Newman's recognition that 'variation and development are part of any great idea' and Scholem's vision of productive 'commentary' and 'contradiction.' Gadamer's sense of a shared, inventive 'language' – rather than a Burkian 'inheritance,' or a nationalist quest for 'origin' – points in the same direction. And, finally, Kuhn's account of social, communal processes such as education and authority at the core of tradition's archetypal 'modern' opposite, the natural sciences, completes the deconstruction.

Newman, Scholem, and Gadamer, though rooted in the West, help us see every 'traditional' culture as potentially changing and dialectical. Moreover, Kuhn shows how abrupt, even revolutionary, shifts of consensus can signal not necessarily a loss of tradition, but a community's ability to confront anomaly and fashion new configurations of knowledge. Communal transmission, in this view, works through breaks, translating and overcoming contradictions. Of course any community's ability to persist, to innovate, to change on its own terms, is relative to its structural power. There are material, historical reasons why some societies have been relatively immobile, others more dynamic. But these are matters of politics, not of essence, and thus subject to contestation and change. In what follows I will be exploring some of the contemporary historical changes, open-ended futures, that must affect any 'enlarged conversation about tradition.'

Released from its binary fix, tradition is recast by Mark Phillips as 'the complex problem of cultural transmission.' The move is persuasive and indeed urgent. But why now? What historical developments make 'tradition' today a genuine problematic, a site for social negotiations, political claims, and fraught conversations? A newly complex view of 'tradition' is inseparable from the decentring, the wavering, of its binary term 'modernity.' Over the past half-century, diffusionist visions of progress have been challenged by two interrelated but distinct shifts: decolonization and globalization. Both unfinished changes, in different, interconnected ways, displace the coherent subject of a singular modernity.

The anti-colonial struggles of the 'long sixties'[1] loosened the West from its self-appointed location at the progressive end and cutting edge of history. In this period, many so-called backward, traditional, or underdeveloped societies made strong claims to historical agency and a distinctive modern destiny. Of course it was not simply a matter of peripheral peoples suddenly emerging from repetitive traditions and finally, irreversibly, entering the modern world. Rather the whole 'allochronic' arrangement which had sorted the world's peoples into fundamentally different times was thrown into question.[2] People from the margins – ex-'primitives,' women, racialized minorities – made claims for equality, for a public voice, for room to manoeuvre in contemporary settings. In response to these pressures, theorists have begun to recognize different inflections, articulations of a modernity fracturing into 'modernities.'[3]

J.M. Blaut has trenchantly argued that progressive, Eurocentric world-views are based on a diffusionist myth.[4] According to this 'colonizers' model of the world' only a very limited number of communities are inventive, and over the past millennium, the inventions that have counted historically have originated from Europe: medieval technologies, the state, capitalism, world discovery, the first industrial revolution. In this 'tunnel history,' everything dynamic comes from 'inside' Europe and the West. The 'outside' is passive and inert – traditional. Blaut challenges this world history, both conceptually and empirically, drawing on a growing body of scholarship. The myth is, of course, still very much with us: in post–Second World War 'development' or 'modernization' thinking. It also persists in (both utopic and dystopic) projections of the homogenizing juggernaut of Westernization – a process reductively condensed in symbols such as Coke, McDonald's, the Internet, the free market, or simply 'America.' In this view, modernity is still a one-way street, or perhaps better, a multi-lane superhighway with only entry ramps. Critiques such as Blaut's project a modernity that is contradictory, layered, and multidirectional.

Decolonization, always shadowed by neocolonization, is a catch-all term for many incomplete, diverse and uneven, processes. Continuously embattled, stymied, deflected, decolonization nonetheless names persistent, cumulative challenges to the political and ideological hegemony of the West. The end of Europe's high colonial period after the Second World War has been marked by wars of national liberation and the significant entry of non-Western and subaltern peoples into a range of public spheres and institutions. There have been surprises (from the standpoint of both the 'progressive' Left and 'liberal' Right). Perhaps most striking, in recent decades, has been the widespread resurgence of 'indigenous' movements (Hawaiian, Maori, Pan-Indian, African, Arctic, etc.). I will focus below on a few of these contemporary mobilizations of 'tradition' as seen in the present volume's chapters by Andrea Laforet, Ruth Phillips, and Christopher Steiner – as well as in the complex 'indigenous' meditation offered by Mieke Bal.

A second set of historic changes needs to be tracked alongside, and intertwined with, movements of decolonization: the post-sixties recomposition of modernization as globalization. Globalization, as I understand it, is not simply another word for imperialism, neocolonialism, or Americanization. One can plausibly say 'globalization from below,'[5] but not 'imperialism from below.' Unlike those who see a new 'stage' of capitalist modernity, I invoke 'globalization' as a stopgap label for unfinished processes which are profoundly ambiguous, both system-

atic and anarchic. What John Tomlinson calls the 'complex connec-
tivities' gathered up in the term exceed any top-down, systemic
projection.[6] When seen as an essentially economic phenomenon, globalization readily falls into the old diffusionism – albeit now sometimes
spatialized in multiple, networked centres, for example, the ' global cities' analysed by Saskia Sassen.[7] But it is increasingly evident that
mobile capitalism exists concretely only as it is articulated locally, at
political, social, and cultural levels. Moreover, any account of the contemporary world must include a broad range of emergent social and
cultural movements which mobilize discrepant 'traditions' in struggles
around identity and place. These unstable movements disrupt the bina-
ries of any simply progressive, 'Westernizing,' world map. We cannot
therefore conclude, with optimists on the Right and pessimists on the
Left, that postwar decolonization movements have now been defeated
or absorbed by a neoliberal hegemony. The contemporary world economic system, centred in North America, Europe, and parts of Asia,
does have enormous power to coerce and stimulate. But its effects
remain very unevenly distributed, its 'triumph' insecure. Contradictory processes of decolonizing/neocolonizing, contestation/co-opta-
tion exist in dialectical tension and sometimes open struggle.

Globalization thus cannot be merely a more flexible form of Westernization. Cultural hegemony, the imperial 'civilizing mission,' is no
longer an essential goal. Non-Western traditions like Confucianism or
Islam can, with appropriate modifications, be articulated with capitalism or modern media – as can a wide range of local customs. It is now
abundantly clear that transnational contacts differentiate as much as
they homogenize, producing composite forms, 'aposteriori differences,' in Daniel Miller's phrase, created through inventive interaction.[8] Thus the cultures and identities that have both resisted and been
created by ongoing local/global contacts hold the seeds of distinct, if
entangled, futures. These historical vectors cannot be mapped from a
single 'advanced' point of historical prophecy or objective overview.
Diverse forms of cultural transmission (Newman's variations,
Scholem's reinterpretations, Gadamer's translations) that have been
historically immobilized, and distanced, as local 'traditions' can be recognized as conservative/inventive ingredients of what might be called
an 'aprogressive modernity.'

One post-1960s sign that peripheral 'traditions' were not going to stay
put was the moment when the widely accepted notion of 'invented' traditions began to run afoul of contemporary indigenous politics. Even as

anthropologists spoke of invented traditions or cultures in nonjudg-
mental ways,[9] the taint of inauthenticity (explicit in Hobsbawm and
Ranger's influential definition) clung to the term.[10] Indigenous intellectuals rejected the implication that dynamic traditions were merely political, contrived for current purposes. There was residual imperialism in
the outside expert's claim to distinguish between invented tradition and
organic custom, between conscious fabrication and the constant recom-
bination or bricolage of any society in transition. Definitions of 'traditional' authenticity became sites of struggle.[11]

Indigenous authorities, speaking out of distinct community attachments, have worked to both loosen and reclaim the notion of authenticity. When attributed to colonial 'natives,' or romantic 'primitives,'
authenticity could be a straitjacket, making every engagement with
modernity (religions, technologies, knowledges, markets, or media) a
contamination, a 'loss' of true selfhood.[12] Post-1960s indigenous movements – reoccupying lands, asserting and updating old ways, relearn-
ing languages, articulating larger tribal coalitions, rewriting colonial
histories and ethnographies, filing legal briefs, making films – have
pragmatically asserted a wide freedom of manoeuvre. Authenticity
thus becomes a process – the open-ended work of preservation and
transformation. Living traditions must be selectively pure: mixing,
matching, remembering, forgetting, sustaining, transforming their
senses of communal continuity. The sharp antinomies of progress –
before/after histories of colonial impact, acculturation, commodification – are frequently blurred, their vectors reversed. Moreover, in a
context of decolonizing tribal activism, it becomes easier to recognize
that native societies have always been both backward and forward
looking. Loyalty to a traditional past is, in practice, a way ahead, a distinct path in the present.

The Hawaiian historian Lilikala Kame'eleihiwa evokes this indigenous temporality:

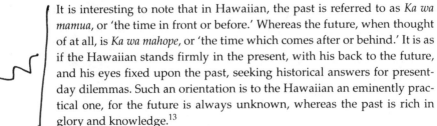

It is interesting to note that in Hawaiian, the past is referred to as *Ka wa
mamua*, or 'the time in front or before.' Whereas the future, when thought
of at all, is *Ka wa mahope*, or 'the time which comes after or behind.' It is as
if the Hawaiian stands firmly in the present, with his back to the future,
and his eyes fixed upon the past, seeking historical answers for present-
day dilemmas. Such an orientation is to the Hawaiian an eminently practical one, for the future is always unknown, whereas the past is rich in
glory and knowledge.[13]

The image of going backwards into the future recalls Walter Benjamin's famous 'Angel of History.'[14] But the differences are telling. Kame'eleihiwa's Hawaiian does not, like Benjamin's angel, confront the past as a ruin. Rather, she engages a generative, socio-mythic tradition, 'rich in glory and knowledge.' Most significantly, perhaps, there is no relentless 'wind' of Progress blowing the angel backwards. Time has no single, violent direction, but loops resourcefully between present dilemmas and remembered answers: a pragmatic, not a messianic orientation.

For the modern Hawaiian movement, a dynamic tradition includes many diverse activities: intensifying taro cultivation in rural enclaves, reviving and adapting hula, renewing native knowledge and language in charter schools (which also teach math and chemistry), mobilizing media for political actions, asserting a space for 'indigenous epistemologies' in the secular University, and connecting reggae rhythms with sovereignty lyrics. Tradition is not a wholesale return to past ways, but a practical selection and critical reweaving of roots. Changing gender roles show this clearly, as do engagements with Christianity, with national politics, with transnational indigenous coalitions. These and many other strategies are aligned through appeals to genealogy and grounded by attachment to land. In today's indigenous movements, some essentialisms are embraced while others are rejected. Practices of cultural/political struggle mediate differences of region, generation, gender, urban/rural location, and strategy. What is at stake is the power to define tradition and authenticity, to determine the relationships through which native identity is negotiated in a changing world.

Contemporary indigenous movements have dramatically reversed the modernist binary, giving new dynamism to its 'backward' part. Ultimately, perhaps the two terms modernity and tradition can be left behind. But for such a transcendence to be more than theoretical would require a real alteration in the material power relations which sustain the dominant, globalizing, 'modern' pole. People think and act in ambiguous post/neocolonial situations, in the tension – both contradiction and synergy – of decolonization and globalization. Reopening the lived problematic of tradition is crucial to understanding this predicament: a messy world in which fundamentalisms, ethnic chauvinisms, and tourist displays flourish alongside First Nations revivals and the mobilization of local communities against environmental devastation or invasive development.

As the history of social movements shows, people are generally

more ready to organize in defence of customary rights and local traditions than they are on behalf of more universal class solidarities or
human rights. At another scale, national ideologies express a sense of
loyalty to a wider community. The articulation of local attachments
with national mobilizations is, of course, complex and always, to a
degree, unstable. While prophecies of the nation-state's demise in the
face of globalization are clearly premature, there has been a wavering
of the assumed hierarchies of the 'nation-building' period: nationalism
vs. tribalism, large-scale 'invented' traditions vs. local, supposedly
repetitive, custom. The making, contesting, unmaking, and remaking
of traditions now appear as a permanent source of innovation and
instability at all political levels and spatial scales. This volume's
reopening of 'the problem of tradition' responds to the partial dis-artic-
ulating (not the disappearance) of modernizing nation-state projects at
global, regional, and local scales.

   The language of 'articulation,' I have argued elsewhere, gets at the
practical deconstructive, *and* reconstructive, activities of indigenous
traditionalisms better than the demystifying discourse of 'invention.'[15]
Indigenous movements cannot be reduced to just another (micro)
nationalism. Put another way, as nationalisms proliferate, within and
across state boundaries, the term 'nation' slips from its European
moorings. This is apparent in the many, and diverse, current invoca-
tions of the Western term 'sovereignty' by tribal and First Nations
groups. 'Applied sovereignty'[16] – for an Australian Aboriginal group's
'country,' for a California tribe's casino, for a vast new territory such as
Nunavut – involves pragmatic control over key elements of culture
and economy, not the establishment of a state on the model of
Bonaparte's France. Articulated sites of indigeneity form a continuum,
from declarations of 'national' independence (always a relative term)
to control over reservations, to negotiated regional autonomies, to
forms of 'cultural citizenship' within pluralist polities.[17]

   Articulated indigenous traditions include institutions like the innovative North American 'pow wow,' a pan-Indian circuit that reworks
and hybridizes Plains dances and regalia in a variety of local contexts:
tribal reservations, rodeos, college campuses. Differently positioned
participants and audiences are brought together in such performances,
and it is important to distinguish among the various levels, relative
'insides' and 'outsides,' that are at play. The same can be said for the
new tribal museums and cultural centres flourishing throughout the
world today, simultaneously expressions of local pride and heritage,

sites for oral history and language-reclamation projects, and destina-
tions in a spreading cultural tourism network. Revived, adapted forms
of indigenous art show the same multidimensional complexities.
Indeed the term 'art' is a site of ongoing translations and articulations
(including dis-articulations, as we shall see in a moment; for not every
tribal mask or image can now be freely promoted in this aesthetic context). Native artists exploit, and are exploited by, new markets, while
also creating works for family and ceremonial contexts. And given the
value increasingly accorded to their cultural productions in national
and international contexts, tribal authorities find themselves struggling against misappropriations, asserting 'sovereignty' over elements
of their heritage held by others. Often this involves a process of forcefully detaching and reattaching artifacts and their meanings: projects
of a dynamic tradition critically reworking its colonial history.

Andrea Laforet, in chapter 1 of this volume, focuses on current negotiations between Canadian First Nations and museums over the proper
ownership, preservation, and display of tribal artifacts. She shows how
indigenous understandings of the relation between stories and things
differ from the conceptions governing Western scientific collecting,
curating, and interpreting. It is not so much that stories are told about
artifacts as that artifacts are performative instances of stories. In this
ontology, stories (reframed and retold) are permanent, objects transient. Thus for people like the Nisga'a of northern British Columbia the
idea that a collection of things could represent, in any fixed or permanent way, a past culture or its tradition, makes little sense. Objects have
meaning for living, changing societies.

Tradition, in Laforet's terms, is redefined as 'historical practice.' The
word 'historical' as she uses it frees Nisga'a tradition from its association with a mythic and ritualized past, bringing it into the ontological
frame of 'what really happened and is happening' – what Westerners
call 'historical reality.' But, as she acutely shows, the translation in
question is itself historical, a matter of practical, cross-cultural negotiation and struggle. Whether in the land claims courtroom, in repatriation negotiations, or in collaborative discussions about the ways
objects in museum collections can be interpreted, a process of learning
and unlearning is underway. Words like tradition and history lose their
accepted meanings and function as 'translation terms.'[18] The crucial
Delgamuukw decision by the Supreme Court of Canada, giving indigenous oral histories equal footing with other documentary evidence, is

paradigmatic. In Australia and Aotearoa/New Zealand, similar developments make courtrooms into sites of practical translation. Fundamental Western notions of objectivity, fact, property, and linear time begin to make room for, to overlap and coexist with, understandings of a different, but equivalent, epistemological validity.[19]

In the process of translation and negotiation, both indigenous and Western traditions articulate new domains of practice. And while there is a real sense in which the return of tribal lands or repatriation of human remains and cultural artifacts is a reversal of the linear, progressive/destructive history of colonialism and modernization, these 'historical practices' do not turn back the clock. They revisit and retell traumatic pasts to (partly) make them right. Reburials heal the survivors, who must get on with their version of a modern life. Likewise, bringing distant clan and tribal artifacts 'home' marks a way forward. The planned construction of a 'Nisga'a common bowl,' a cultural centre in the Nass Valley to 'create a permanent public repository for what has been traditionally mandated to be known and handled by individuals or within lineages' shows the selective rearticuation of tradition in new 'tribal' forms which function within changing regional and national pubic spheres. Laforet's essay glimpses a post-assimilationist modus vivendi: practices of translation, live and let live, linked and separate traditions. The fact that Native societies in Canada are exerting real pressure in the courts, the national museums, and other public arenas clearly signals the dynamism of discrepant 'historical practices' in a complex modernity. This is not a return to atavistic 'tribalism,' nor is it a matter of acculturation or, as critical analysts of postmodernity tend to argue, of tribal societies getting with the neoliberal, multicultural, ethnic program. Both views gloss over the dynamic politics of contestation, translation, and articulation that Laforet describes – historical practices that reconnect the very new with the very old.

In her contribution to this volume – as in her seminal work, *Trading Identities* – Ruth Phillips gives temporal depth to messy and unfinished contact relations.[20] Like Laforet, she writes from within contemporary struggles over cross-cultural collecting, display, and possession. Museums have long been machines for producing the tradition/modernity opposition, as (particular) artifacts are recontextualized in terms of (universal) taxonomies and aesthetic principles. But when 'episodes of museum contestation are examined in detail, the cases, the labels, the lights, the taxonomies, and the security systems of museums come to be seen as integral to traditions as culturally specific as are those of the

Iroquois.' The colonial West and its universalizing, scientific/aesthetic institutions appear, in this contact perspective, as specific traditions. As Dipesh Chakrabarty puts it, they are 'provincialized.'[21] This recognition does not entail, I would insist, their refutation or degradation – though it may seem that way to people used to occupying the universal end of the tradition/modern binary. Seeing museums as 'contact zones,' sites where different historical practices clash and collaborate, merely specifies knowledges, always open to revision since history itself is open ended.[22]

Ruth Phillips shows how the changing meanings of Iroquois False Face masks (*Ga:goh:sah*) are part of an ongoing colonial/postcolonial contact relationship. And her history firmly locates museums within a broader popular culture of exoticism, surrealism, and commodification. She focuses on a critical moment of indigenous articulation-politics: acts of dis-connection and de-linking, and the maintenance of domains of secrecy, sacredness, and sociocultural knowledge which must not be universally shared. These are acts of power which refute museum and popular-cultural representations, whether they be primitivist stereotypes or modernist views of *Ga:goh:sah* as surrealist 'art.' As a consequence of legal and informal pressure during the past decade, the withdrawal of once highly popular False Face masks from North American public display has been virtually complete. And while, as Phillips makes clear, there is disagreement among Iroquois about the status of replicas and versions made for commercial purposes, the possibility of a complete 'disappearing act' from non-Iroquois public arenas (including the intertribal American Museum of the American Indian on the Mall in Washington) has been established. By calling this removal an 'act' Ruth Phillips signals its performative nature, a relational gesture and moment of empowerment in the current politics of tribal sovereignty and re-traditionalization.

To speak in this way of acts, gestures, or moments should not (in an articulation perspective) imply superficiality or a narrowly political agency. Repatriation claims, particularly when they assume an assertive, across-the-board nature, are manifestly claims to power – acts of reappropriation. But the empowerment goes much deeper than Western notions of ownership imply. For the emotional impact of return and reconnection – the healing and renewal felt by people repossessing traditional things and reburying lost ancestors – is profound. Iroquois *Ga:goh:sah* have strong tribal meanings today, both because they are used in traditional, secret ways by qualified individuals and because they can no longer be freely used by others, especially the non-Indians who have so long stereotyped and translated them. Removal of certain objects and images from intertribal, national, and international public spheres is critical to the maintenance of a 'we,' with significant degrees of 'sovereign' control over the interactions and interdependencies that are part of contemporary life everywhere. While Iroquois, as Phillips shows, may dis-articulate their tribal identity from larger contexts of representation in the case of the *Ga:goh:sah*, in other contexts they find ways to connect with the profitable Indian art market, or the multi-audienced 'appearing-acts' (if I may put it thus) of pow wows, cultural festivals, and other sites of tribal self-representation. Thus traditional-ism, even in its moments of disengagement and secrecy, is part of a complexly articulated, changing relationship of inside and outside, past and future.

Christopher Steiner's discussion of the Kalabari of Nigeria provides another example of tradition as dis- and re-articulation. The customiz-ing of imported cloth according to firm aesthetic rules shows a his-torical practice of conservative traditionalism resisting national and transnational norms of acculturation and commodification. Steiner writes of a 'calculated lack of innovation,' and sees the Kalabari's intriguing practice of 'subtractively' altering cloth made in India as a 'currency of cultural autonomy in defiance of outside pressures.' 'Con-servatism and restraint,' he argues, act as 'signs' of 'social identity.' Steiner does not discuss other historical practices of the Kalabari, which no doubt are less immobile. One assumes that they, like other local and tribal people under pressure to change and adapt, are inno-vating and preserving their identities in constrained ways. Custom-izing imported cloth functions, then, as a relatively 'cold' area of Kalabari culture, actively sustained in relation to other 'hot' domains of change. Moreover, this work with an *imported* commodity is, by def-inition, a traditionalism operating within relations of commercial and cultural contact. One is left with crucial questions about the nature of its 'conservatism.' Is this activity primarily a (relatively recent) ethnic boundary marker of the sort Fredrik Barth so lucidly analysed, or is it a transformational practice continuous with older Kalabari ideological/ social forms – the sort of dynamic structures Sahlins has theorized for the Pacific?[23] The two functions are, of course, not mutually exclusive, and indeed are both necessary for sociocultural survival. But weighing their relative importance at specific moments, in the continuum of articulations covered by an elastic term like 'tradition,' is critical for grasping the ongoing negotiation of collective insides and outsides, pasts and futures.[24]

Steiner is certainly right to reject all-or-nothing norms that pit tradition against change. Criticizing an academic 'postmodern' sensibility that, he argues, 'disparages tradition in favour of anything new or different,' he supplies a cogent baby/bathwater correction. The sensibility he questions has a specific history, however, which only partially overlaps with 'postmodernism.' The suspicion of any linking of 'tradition,' 'conservatism,' or 'immobility' with non-Western peoples is rooted in the current of 'colonial discourse critique' which flourished in the 1980s.[25] Colonial assumptions and institutions, Arjun Appadurai dramatically observed, 'imprisoned' subaltern natives, keeping them 'in their place.' Indeed, as Mani showed, purportedly ancient traditions were, in fact, inscribed and reified in the interests of imperial rule. A recognition of cultural dynamism was the antidote, signalled by titles such as Appadurai's *Modernity at Large*, Susan Vogel's *Africa Explores*, or Steiner's *African Art in Transit*.[26] In tandem with this trend, 'postcolonial theory' probed the transgressive and resistant possibilities of syncretic or hybrid cultural strategies, the unexpected ways 'newness enters the world.'[27] Many hierarchical, binary structures supporting colonial projections of progress and modernization were destabilized, at least conceptually.

However, to the extent that postcolonial theory's mixed and entangled tactics became identified with 'postmodern' visions of nomadism, flexibility, mix-and-match, a certain normativity took shape favouring mobility and innovation. The apogee of academic anti-traditionalism is perhaps visible in Steiner's opening anecdote about his difficulty getting a scholarly audience to take seriously 'conservative' African practices. The reverse trend is now well underway as cultural theorists register the return of the 'native,' the baby thrown out with the 'post' bathwaters.[28] Steiner's corrective essay is a sign of these times. But of course all returns mark a difference: contemporary indigenous subjects are no longer simply localized natives, the archaic homebodies of colonial discourses. Steiner's 'conservative' Kalabari – like the artists 'in transit' of his earlier work – are struggling for identity and control in historical import/export relations. As we have seen, diverse traditionalists today search for ways to move ahead, or sideways, in a discrepantly rooted/routed modernity.

Connections with tradition are seldom uncritical. Mieke Bal, writing as an 'indigenous' intellectual, provides a poignant example of ambivalent loyalty to a Dutch tradition which touches her deeply. Bal writes of Zwarte Piets – blackface, devilish clowns that frighten children – as someone who has herself been in their power. An adult, she finds herself repelled by the racist and colonialist legacies of the black/white imagery with its invocation of savagery. Class connotations, and the gender-transgressive possibilities of the performances, complicate her attitude. Is this a tradition that can be reformed? Simply re-colouring the faces blue, red, or green, in an effort to purge Zwarte Piet's racism for a progressive multiculturalism, will not do, she says, unless the changes reflect a kind of organic decision by the society. An imposed, politically correct moralism would merely evade the deep historical problem. Bal suggests that living traditions cannot, indeed should not, be cleansed of their dissonant, painful elements. The questioning they persistently evoke is an element in the critical, hermeneutic process of cultural transformation. Drawing an analogy with current contestations of revered museum displays (one thinks of the work of Fred Wilson, for example, introducing artifacts of slavery into a sanitized historical exhibit),[29] she argues that while 'the Dutch don't like to be confronted with their inner contradictions ... they must be, forced by social reality and intellectual and moral debate.' Such processes of difficult self-examination can contribute to a genuine 'working through' of a past, 'bringing that work to bear on today's ambivalences.'

Mieke Bal's reckoning with these darkened Dutch faces is subtle and multidimensional in ways I cannot adequately summarize here. It includes a 'native's' self-conscious engagement with an outside 'ethnographic' gaze: the provocative mirror provided by British photographer Anna Fox's photographic series on Zwarte Piet. We see the critical performativity of Bal's self-construction through engagement with a defamiliarizing 'outside.' The often overgeneralized 'indigenous' position is specified by gender, race, and class – salient points of tension and struggle in the process of displacing and remaking any tradition. Her work of 'insider' cultural critique is relevant to that of women in particular contexts of sociocultural change around the world – simultaneously invoking and criticizing tradition, *kastom*, *coutume*, *costumbre*, and so on.[30] In engagements with local, ethnic, religious, and national identifications women selectively rearticulate (in Bal's terms 'work through') past elements, actively forgetting those most hostile, emphasizing sites of female power and agency. This may involve creative engagements with world religions, new nationalist projects, migration, feminism, and other 'modernizing' ideologies. Struggles over tradition, by differently empowered insiders and outsiders, are integral to a relational politics of identity.

Such struggles can be bitter and prolonged. Mieke Bal ends with a hopeful vision of a 'culture' (rather like a self-reflective, therapeutic individual) letting go of a negative pattern of behaviour. Critical attention keeps the wound (in this case Zwarte Piet's racism) open

> until ... one day, the culture concerned wakes up sick of the pain. Only then – perhaps – can this tradition be relinquished, wholeheartedly; not suppressed by moralism, but rejected for the pain it causes to all its members. By that time, another tradition will have been invented, one that fits the culture better – and that hurts less. Until it, too, becomes the culture's backlog, dragging behind the times.

While recognizing this open-ended process of transformation, I find myself returning to Bal's 'perhaps,' wondering about the healing process of change. The vision of tradition-as-process I have been sketching is more political than hermeneutic/therapeutic. Structured antagonisms, and successive realignments of self and other, play a greater role. Thus, moralistic suppressions, hostile disarticulations, will always be necessary parts of a process which produces cultural solutions that are less 'reasonable' than the one Bal projects. Of course she knows this very well and is writing primarily as a participant/reformer, expressing hope for the transformation of a specific Dutch legacy to which she remains complexly loyal.

For her connection to Zware Piet is not simply that of a (frightened) Dutch child or a champion of cultural distinction. It is also a commitment to grappling with negativity, a dedication to the principle of collectivities confronting and understanding the dark legacies of their pasts. This too is part of tradition, seen as critical 'historical practice' – whether the reckoning takes the form of truth and reconciliation commissions, the repatriation of bones and artifacts, or arguments over female circumcision. Mieke Bal leaves us, as do all the essays I have discussed, with a vision of traditions as unresolved and productive – ways into our different, interconnected futures.

NOTES

1 Fredric Jameson, 'Periodizing the Sixties,' in Sohnya Sayres et al., eds, *The 60s without Apology* (Minneapolis, 1984), 178–209.

2 Fabian, Johannes, *Time and the Other: How Anthropology Makes its Object* (New York, 1983).
3 For example: Mike Featherstone, *Undoing Culture* (London, 1995); Jonathan Friedman and James Carrier, eds, *Melanesian Modernities* (Lund, 1996); Lisa Rofel, *Other Modernities: Gendered Yearnings in China after Socialism* (Berkeley, 1999); Charles Taylor, 'Modernity and Difference,' in Paul Gilroy, Lawrence Grossberg, and Angela McRobbie, eds, *Without Guarantees: In Honour of Stuart Hall* (London, 2000), 364–74.
4 J.M. Blaut, *The Colonizer's View of the World: Geographical Diffusionism and Eurocentric History* (New York, 1993).
5 Jeremy Brecher, Tim Costello, and Brendan Smith, *Globalization from Below: The Power of Solidarity* (Boston, 2000).
6 John Tomlinson, *Globalization and Culture* (Chicago 1999), 1.
7 Saskia Sassen, *The Global City: New York, London, Tokyo*, rev. ed. (Princeton, 2000).
8 Daniel Miller, 'Introduction: Anthropology, Modernity and Consumption,' in Daniel Miller, ed., *Worlds Apart: Modernity through the Prism of the Local* (London 1995), 1–23.
9 Allan Hanson, 'The Making of the Maori: Cultural Invention and Its Logic,' *American Anthropologist*, 91 (Fall 1989): 890–902; Roy Wagner, *The Invention of Culture* (Chicago, 1980).
10 Eric Hobsbawm and Terence Ranger, eds, *The Invention of Tradition* (Cambridge, 1983).
11 For influential 'indigenist' interventions see: Haunani-Kay Trask, 'Natives and Anthropologists: The Colonial Struggle,' *The Contemporary Pacific* (Spring 1991): 159–77; M. Annette Jaimes and George Noriega, 'History in the Making: How Academia Manufactures the "Truth" about Native American Traditions,' *Bloomsbury Review*, 4, no. 5 (1988): 24–6. For critical analysis of the confrontation see: Margaret Jolly, 'Specters of Inauthenticity,' *The Contemporary Pacific*, 4 (Winter 1992): 49–72; Charles Briggs, 'The Politics of Discursive Authority in Research on the "Invention of Tradition,"' *Cultural Anthropology*, 11, no. 4 (1996): 435–69.
12 A pointed critique is offered by Frank Ettawageshik, 'My Father's Business,' in Ruth Phillips and Christopher Steiner, eds, *Unpacking Culture: Art and Commodity in Colonial and Postcolonial Worlds* (Berkeley, 1999), 20–32.
13 Lilikala Kame'eleihiwa, *Native Land and Foreign Desires* (Honolulu, 1992), 22–3.
14 Walter Benjamin, 'Theses on the Philosophy of History,' in Hannah Arendt, ed., *Illuminations* (New York, 1969), 253–65.

15 James Clifford, 'Indigenous Articulations,' *The Contemporary Pacific*, 13, no. 2 (Fall 2001): 468–90.

16 Mark Maccaro, 'Applied Sovereignty,' conference paper at 'Sovereignty 2000: Locations of Contestation and Possibility,' Native American Studies Research Cluster, University of California at Santa Cruz, 19 May 2000.

17 William Flores and Rina Benmayor, eds, *Latino Cultural Citizenship: Claiming Identity, Space, and Rights* (Boston, 1997).

18 James Clifford, *Routes: Travel and Translation in the Late Twentieth Century* (Cambridge, 1997), 39.

19 Robert Layton explores these issues in an Aboriginal context: 'Representing and Translating People's Place in the Landscape of Northern Australia,' in Alison James, Jenny Hockey, and Andrew Dawson, eds, *After Writing Culture* (London, 1997), 122–43.

20 Ruth Phillips, *Trading Identities: The Souvenir in Native North American Art from the Northeast, 1700–1900* (Seattle, 1998).

21 Dipesh Chakrabarty, 'Postcoloniality and the Artifice of History: Who Speaks for the "Indian" Pasts?' *Representations*, 37, no. 1 (1992): 1–26.

22 Clifford, *Routes*, 188–219.

23 Fredrik Barth, *Ethnic Groups and Boundaries: The Social Organization of Cultural Difference* (Boston, 1969); Marshall Sahlins, *Islands of History* (Chicago, 1985).

24 Charles Piot's recent ethnography of West African 'village modernity' engages these issues with considerable subtlety: *Remotely Global: Village Modernity in West Africa* (Chicago, 1999).

25 For example: Edward Said, *Orientalism* (New York, 1978); Fabian, *Time and the Other*; Arjun Appadurai, 'Putting Hierarchy in Its Place,' *Cultural Anthropology*, 3, no. 1 (1988): 36–49; Ella Shohat and Robert Stam, *Unthinking Eurocentrism: Multiculturalism and the Media* (London, 1994); Lata Mani, *Contentious Traditions: The Debate on Sati in Colonial India* (Berkeley, 1998).

26 Arjun Appadurai, *Modernity at Large* (Minneapolis, 1996); Susan Vogel, *Africa Explores: Twentieth Century African Art* (New York, 1991); Christopher Steiner, *African Art in Transit* (Cambridge, 1994).

27 Homi K. Bhabha, 'How Newness Enters the World,' in *The Location of Culture* (London, 1994), 212–35.

28 For example: Jonathan Friedman's 'The Hybridization of Roots and the Abhorrence of the Bush,' in Mike Featherstone and Scott Lasch, eds, *Spaces of Culture: City, Nation, World* (London, 1999). For a complex 'Native' perspective, see Teresia Teaiwa, 'L(o)osing the Edge,' *The Contemporary Pacific*, 13, no. 2 (Fall 2001): 343–57, and 'Militarism, Tourism and the Native: Artic-

ulations in Oceania' (PhD dissertation, History of Consciousness Department, University of California, Santa Cruz, 2001).

29 Fred Wilson, *Mining the Museum: An Installation by Fred Wilson* (New York, 1994).

30 For example, Margaret Jolly explores women's critical engagements with tradition in Melanesia in *Women of the Place:* Kastom, *Colonialism and Gender in Vanuatu* (Chur, Switzerland, 1994); and Aniuar Majid highlights the work of Muslim feminists in forging a progressive Islam in *Unveiling Traditions: Postcolonial Islam in a Polycentric World* (Durham, 2000).

Part II

Chapter Six

Tacit Knowledge: Tradition and Its Aftermath

MICHAEL MCKEON

The following essay is an effort to explore the meaning of 'tradition' from the perspective of English Enlightenment culture. The perspective seems promising because we commonly see Enlightenment thought as predicated on a more-or-less absolute repudiation of tradition. My inquiry is motivated by two basic questions. First, how might the idea of tradition coalesce under the powerful pressure of its whole-sale critique? My second question grows out of the notion that once-valued ideas and institutions do not simply disappear when their force has been undermined. What 'does the work' of tradition after it has lost its authority in modern culture? The short answer to my first question is that tradition fails because it is seen to be a mode of 'tacit'[1] knowledge. The short answer to my second question is that in the modern world, the tacit knowledge embodied in 'tradition' is replaced by the tacit knowledge embodied, in different ways, in 'ideology' and 'the aesthetic.' Throughout this essay, when I speak of 'modernity' as the opposite number of 'tradition,' I mean to refer to both the chronological and the anthropological – both the diachronic and the synchronic – senses of those terms. My argument will be broadly temporal in focus; but I think the general idea of tacit knowledge is relevant also to our spatial sense of the difference between tradition and our own cultural 'modernity.'[2]

Tradition

I will begin with four quotations that span the English Revolution of 1642–60.

In 1628, Parliament petitioned Charles I to affirm his support of what it argued were the English people's accustomed freedoms from arbitrary governmental demands. In the debate that followed it was suggested that the Petition of Right also affirm the customary locus of 'sovereign power' in the monarchy. Sir Henry Marten argued strenuously against such an affirmation, however, because it would invite controversy too explicitly. '[T]his petition will run through many hands,' he pointed out, and people will 'presently fall to arguing and descanting what sovereign power is – what is the latitude? whence the original? where the bounds? etc. – with many such curious and captious questions ... [S]overeign power is then best worth when it is held in tacit veneration, not when it is profaned by vulgar hearings or examinations.'[3] Fourteen years after the Petition of Right, on the eve of civil war, Charles himself made a similar prediction about the consequences of disturbing the constitutional balance:

> [S]o new a power will undoubtedly intoxicate persons who were not born to it, and beget not only divisions among them as equals, but in them contempt of us, as become an equal to them ... [A]ll great changes are extremely inconvenient, and almost infallibly beget yet greater changes, which beget yet greater inconveniences ... till ... at last the common people ... discover this *arcanum imperii,* that all this was done by them, but not for them, and grow weary of journey-work, and set up for themselves, [and] call parity and independence liberty.[4]

Although Charles's prophecy came strikingly to pass, in the end 'the common people' grew weary of the commonwealth as well, and Charles's son was restored to the throne in 1660. On the eve of the Restoration, however, George Monck, its chief military engineer, claimed that the anti-monarchical consequences of the civil war were probably irreversible: 'Before these unhappy Wars the Government of these Nations was Monarchical in Church and State: these wars have given birth and growth to several Interests both in Church and State heretofore not known; though now upon many accounts very considerable ... *That Government then that is most able to comprehend and protect all Interests as aforesaid must needs be Republique.*'[5] Of course, Monck was wrong. But if the most immediate political consequences of the civil war could thus be reversed by military and legal means, its more long-term implications could not. Five years after the Restoration, Edward Waterhouse, bemused by England's changing social landscape, ruefully reflected in similar terms on the limits of legal authority. Our ancestors, he observed, distinguished between their social stations by tacit social practice, by their 'Garb, Equipage, Dyet, Housholdstuff, Clothes, [and] Education of Children ... not by sumptuary Laws, or Magistratique sanction, but by common agreement, and general understanding.'[6]

What interests me about these four passages is how they articulate the discovery of what might be called 'tradition,' which paradoxically is found in and through the very process of realizing that it has been lost. 'Tradition' owes its force to what Marten calls the 'tacit' veneration by which it goes without saying: its taken-for-granted-ness, its deep embeddedness within customary social practice. To 'discover' tradition is to abstract it and throw it into relief, literally to remove the cover afforded by its customary embeddedness. Thus Charles predicts the common people will discover the *arcana imperii*, which, no longer woven invisibly and mysteriously into the fabric of collective necessity, now appear nakedly before them, one interest among many. It is in this sense that Monck sees the civil war as having 'given birth' to the present multiplicity of interests, which did not exist previously in that they were 'heretofore not known' or acknowledged as such.[7] The metaphor of tradition as a kind of invisible clothing is also pertinent to Waterhouse's insight into the way dress and other kinds of customary behaviour enforce a rule of tradition that is very different from the rule of law. Sumptuary legislation announces not tradition but its decay, the point at which the law discloses the social symbolism of clothing for what it is, obviating its tacit authority in the very act of proclaiming and exploiting it explicitly.

In speaking this way I am of course pursuing a special understanding of the concept. By this understanding, a 'modern tradition' is, strictly speaking, a contradiction in terms, in that it posits a tacit knowledge under cultural conditions – especially, the condition of explicit enunciation – that prohibit it. Although I will soon be moved to modify the strictness of this understanding, it has some advantages over other ways of conceiving the relationship between tradition and modernity. In the fruitful hypothesis of the modern 'invention' of traditions, the tacitness of tradition, although acknowledged, plays a less prominent role in defining the nature of tradition. As a result, the problem central to my inquiry – how the tacitness of tradition can survive the self-consciousness of invention – is not fully pursued there.[8] One aim of the present argument is to pose the problem of tradition in modernity in terms of the persistence or invention not of tradition as such, but of the tacitness that 'traditionally' distinguishes tradition as a mode of knowledge.

The most concrete and powerful model for what happens to tradition when knowledge becomes explicit involves an epochal change in the material technology of knowledge production and consumption: the long-term 'replacement' of orality by literacy and of script by print. (Needless to say, the impression of irreversibility and permanence associated with change in the technology of knowledge when conceived as an epochal 'discovery' is belied by the temporal and regional multiplicity of such changes.) When knowledge is rendered relatively ostensive, objective, and permanent by such technologies, it undergoes a transformation that is akin to less material processes of rationalization which also concentrate attention on knowledge that previously had been customary and 'taken for granted.'[9]

In early modern England, this insight proved most immediately useful, perhaps, in the context of religious dispute, where the self-consciously 'objective' religion of the Book was understood to improve upon the defects and corruptions attendant on the tacitness of the Roman Catholic 'tradition.' Justifying his Protestantism against the scepticism of Father Richard Simon in 1682, John Dryden was quick to make the crucial point:

> If *written words* from time are not secur'd,
> How can we think have *oral Sounds* endur'd?
> Which *thus* transmitted, if *one* Mouth has fail'd,
> Immortal Lyes on *Ages* are intail'd:
> And that some such have been, is prov'd too plain;
> If we consider *Interest*, *Church*, and *Gain*.

In fact, Dryden is content to use the term 'tradition' to refer to the legitimation mechanisms of both Christian churches, so long as the superiority of the Protestant version is clear:

> Must *all Tradition* then be set aside?
> This to affirm were Ignorance, or Pride.
> ...
> *Tradition written* therefore more commends
> *Authority*, than what from *Voice* descends:
> And this, as perfect as its kind can be,
> Rouls down to us the Sacred History ...

Before Gutenberg and Luther, priests could be infallible with impunity:

> In those dark times they learn'd their knack so well,
> That by long use they grew *Infallible*:
> At last, a knowing Age began t'enquire
> If *they* the *Book*, or *That* did *them* inspire ...

Dryden's confidence makes clear that contemporaries of this 'knowing age' were ambivalent about the discovery of tradition, which could mean by turns a debilitating loss of social cohesion and a liberating gain in enlightenment. Indeed, it could mean both to the same person. Having defended himself against the demands of the priest, the Anglican Dryden now joins forces with Charles I in defence against the demanding common people:

> The Book thus put in every vulgar hand,
> Which each presum'd he best cou'd understand,
> The *Common Rule* was made the *Common Prey*;
> And at the mercy of the *Rabble* lay.[10]

Where the context of debate was not religious, Protestant English people found it even harder to dispense with the doctrinal authority of tradition. Largely in relation to the developing conflict between king and Parliament, seventeenth-century common lawyers had propounded a theory of English history that explained and legitimated present practice by reference to 'fundamental law,' to the traditionality of unwritten, indeed immemorial, custom. According to Sir John Davies, 'the *Common Law of England* is nothing else but the *Common Custome* of the Realm: and a Custome which hath obtained the force of a Law is always said to be *Jus non scriptum*: for it cannot be made or created either by Charter, or by Parliament, which are Acts reduced to writing, and are alwaies matter of Record; but being onely matter of fact, and consisting in use and practice, it can be recorded and registered no-where but in the memory of the people.'[11]

According to Sir William Blackstone, 'Aulus Gellius defines the *jus non scriptum* to be that which is "*tacito et illiterato hominum consensu et moribus expressum.*"'[12] The 'common-law interpretation of English history' is one of the most radical, and paradoxical, attempts to sustain the credibility of tradition under conditions of its increasingly epidemic disclosure, a subservience to the notion of historical precedent so absolute as to seem, with hindsight, a counterintuitive 'stop in the mind' vainly postponing the modern recognition of historical change and difference. Already in 1649 John Warr was writing: 'The notion of fundamental law is no such idol as men make it ... For what, I pray you, is fundamental law but such customs as are of the eldest date and longest continuance? ... The more fundamental a law is, the more difficult, not the less necessary, to be reformed.'[13]

Francis Bacon was conventional in grounding his account of 'tradition' etymologically in the process of transfer: '[T]he expressing or transferring our knowledge to others ... I will term by the general name of Tradition or Delivery.' But the very effort to enunciate the tacit nature of such a transfer leads Bacon to remark on its epistemological undependability – on the conflict, that is, between belief and knowledge: 'For as knowledges are now delivered, there is a kind of contract of error between the deliverer and the receiver: for he that delivereth knowledge desireth to deliver it in such form as may be best believed, and not as may be best examined; and he that receiveth knowledge desireth rather present satisfaction than expectant inquiry and so rather not to doubt than not to err ... [I]n this same anticipated and prevented [i.e., anticipated] knowledge, no man knoweth how he came to the knowledge which he hath obtained.' Like Dryden, moreover, Bacon associates the fallibility of tradition with that of orality: 'The most ancient times ... are buried in oblivion and silence: to that silence succeeded the fables of the poets: to those fables the written records which have come down to us. Thus between the hidden depths of antiquity and the days of tradition and evidence that followe there is drawn a veil, as it were, of fables, which come in and occupy the middle region that separates what has perished from what survives.'[14] Thomas Hobbes made a similar point about the opacity of the fabulous, but his emphasis was political not epistemological and his judgment was positive not negative. In the year of the regicide Hobbes observed there was no shortage of rationales for rebellion.

> I think that those ancients foresaw this who preferred that the knowledge of Justice be wrapped up in fables rather than exposed to discussion. Before questions of that kind began to be debated, Princes did not lay claim to sovereign power, they simply exercised it. They did not defend their power by arguments but by punishing the wicked and defending the good. In return the citizens did not measure Justice by the comments

of private men but by the laws of the commonwealth; and were kept at
Peace not by discussions but by the power of Government. In fact, they
revered sovereign power, whether it resided in a man or in an Assembly,
as a kind of visible divinity ... The simplicity of those time evidently could
not understand such sophisticated stupidity. It was peace therefore and a
golden age.[15]

For Hobbes, tradition is to be valued as a guarantor of political
peace. But for Bacon, tradition is problematic as a mode of knowledge
because it precludes the detachment necessary for 'examination' and
'inquiry,' the separation of the 'what' from the 'how' ('No man
knoweth how he came to the knowledge which he hath obtained') that
is encouraged by literacy and especially by print. The idea that knowledge presupposes detachment itself may be seen as a modern development, in that it entails the fundamental principle of empirical
epistemology. To know something requires that it be constituted, over
against the knowing subject, as an object of knowledge. In Robert
Boyle's formulation, this condition is met in the separability of 'opinion' from 'experiment': let the experimenter's 'opinions be never so
false, his experiments being true, I am not obliged to believe the
former, and am left at liberty to benefit myself of the latter; and though
he have erroneously superstructed upon his experiments, yet the foundation being solid, a more wary builder may be very much furthered
by it in the erection of more judicious and consistent fabrics.'[16] John
Locke articulates the same principle when he denies the authority of
religious enthusiasm as a ground of assent: 'Every Conceit that thoroughly warms our Fancies must pass for an Inspiration, if there be
nothing but the Strength of our Perswasions, whereby to judge of our
Perswasions: If *Reason* must not examine their Truth by something
extrinsical to the Perswasions themselves; Inspirations and Delusions,
Truth and Falshood will have the same Measure, and will not be possible to be distinguished.' In Locke's formulation, the problem with
tradition is that it confuses chronological with epistemological detachment, antiquity with truth; whereas in fact, *'in traditional Truths, each
remove weakens the force of the proof.'*[17]

The critique of religious knowledge – the cornerstone of Enlightenment thought and here exemplified in Locke – provided contemporaries with their first and easiest access to a more comprehensive
formulation and critique of traditional knowledge as such. In his most
notorious work, Bernard Mandeville followed the deist lead in con-

ceiving the system of moral virtue as a plot of 'moralists' and 'politicians' to govern the multitudes. John Toland had lately argued that 'the *natural Man* ... counts Divine Things mere Folly, calls *Religion* a feverish Dream of superstitious Heads, or a politick Trick invented by States-men to aw the credulous Vulgar.' Later in his career, however, Mandeville explicated this argument as a kind of shorthand for describing a social process that is really neither so intentional, so personalizable, nor so punctual in its effects as this account suggests. He gives the names of 'Moralists and Politicians,' Mandeville writes, 'promiscuously to All that, having studied Human Nature, have endeavour'd to civilize Men, and render them more and more tractable, either for the Ease of Governours and Magistrates, or else for the Temporal Happiness of Society in general. I think of all Inventions of this Sort [as] the joint Labour of Many. Human Wisdom is the Child of Time. It was not the Contrivance of one Man, nor could it have been the Business of a few Years, to establish a Notion, by which a rational Creature is kept in Awe for Fear of it Self, and an Idol is set up, that shall be its own Worshiper.'[18] Retaining as metaphor the religious language of idol worship already familiar from Bacon's four 'idols' 'which by tradition, credulity, and negligence have come to be received,' Mandeville's crucial qualification affords us the germ of social theory.[19] The calculating corruption of governing personages and institutions provides a means of conceiving the process of socialization itself – of conceiving the 'institution' of society as having a trans-personal, supra-intentional agency. But this is also to describe the production of tacit knowledge: tacit not only for the recipients of moral doctrine (as in the relatively crude model of politico-religious conspiracy), but also for its promulgators.

If the critique of religious knowledge gives Enlightenment writers their first access to the critique of tradition as tacit knowledge, religion retains a special status thereafter as the one branch of knowledge for which the emergent norm of epistemological explicitness, of sceptical detachment, may yet be questionable. Locke distinguished between the credibility of religious 'faith' or 'revelation,' which are confirmed by 'reason,' and the credulity of religious 'enthusiasm,' which is not. And of enthusiastic modes of knowledge he wrote: 'If such groundless thoughts as these concerne ordinary matters and not religion and possesse the minde strongly we call it raveing and every one thinkes it a degree of madnesse, but in religion men accustomed to the thoughts of revelation make a greater allowance to it.'[20] Jonathan Swift alters

Locke's terminology by using 'enthusiasm' as the general category for all religious belief, whether credible or credulous; but the division of knowledge he proposes is nonetheless similar. With respect to the other two realms of knowledge, Swift's attack on false knowledge is unqualified. With religion alone he is willing to affirm the existence of a realm of faith or 'inspiration' in which knowledge is properly tacit.[21] Except in the extreme and relatively uncommon case of agnosticism, religion remained the one category in the ongoing disclosure of 'tradition' for which a tacit dependence on authority – that is, for which 'faith' – was deemed not only proper but requisite.

For this reason alone, my opening account of tradition's 'discovery' by modernity – the doubleness whereby what is found is also lost in the very same movement – stands in need of revision. For under the aegis of empirical epistemology, tradition is not so much obliterated in the modern experience as vastly discredited – or consigned, where still acceptable, to the narrow and increasingly besieged enclosure of religious faith. In the modern world, 'religion' explicitly defines the territory of normative tacit knowing once tacitly encompassed by the vast domain of 'tradition.' When tacit knowledge is acknowledged to be inescapable in emergent 'political' theory as well it can only cause problems. A case in point is the contractarian refutation of patriarchalism. Sir Robert Filmer began his famous treatise by assuring the reader that 'I have nothing to meddle with mysteries of the present state. Such arcana imperii, or cabinet councils, the vulgar may not pry into. An implicit faith is given to the meanest artificer in his own craft; how much more is it, then, due to a Prince in the profoundest secrets of government[?]' Algernon Sidney's reply was acerbic: Filmer 'renounces these inquiries through an implicit faith, which never enter'd into the head of any but fools ... Such as have reason, understanding, or common sense, will and ought to ... suspect the words of such as are interested in deceiving or persuading them not to see with their own eyes, that they may be more easily deceived.'[22] But how does the contractarian justify the notion of a consensual 'original' compact that can bind later generations? Distinguishing between 'an express [i.e., a verbal] and a tacit consent' to 'the Laws of any Government,' Locke remarks that '[t]he difficulty is, what ought to be look'd upon as a *tacit Consent*, and how far it binds, *i.e.* how far any one shall be looked on to have consented, and thereby submitted to any Government, where he has made no Expressions of it at all.' Locke's solution to the problem is that tacit consent to the laws of a government is given by anyone who owns land and/or resides 'within the Territories of that Government,' a solution that, by shifting the burden of binding obligation from a temporal to a spatial register, detaches the notion of tacit consent from its problematic proximity to the idea of tradition.[23]

So Enlightenment 'politics' was weaned of its dependence on the tacit knowledge of tradition as 'religion' was consecrated its last bastion. These observations may help clarify the paradoxical logic of our premise that the coalescence of 'tradition' as a category occurs in the early modern period through its abstraction from the ground of social practice in which it is 'traditionally' embedded. Another way to say this is that 'tradition' coheres as a category when it is judged not by the standards that pertain to a comprehensive and manifold social practice that is more or less coextensive with experience itself but by the more acute and concentrated standards of empirical epistemology. In emphasizing 'political' over epistemological considerations in the evaluation of tacit knowledge (and hence in defending the *arcana imperii* against the open discussion of public policy), Hobbes evinces a view of tradition as social practice, for which the maintenance of peace and communal collectivity subsumes all considerations of accuracy and precision of judgment. In the writings of Bacon, Boyle, and Locke, the division of knowledge that elevates epistemology to its modern position of dominance is already evident: not simply in their preoccupation with questions of epistemology, but also in the conviction – less explicit in Bacon and Boyle than in Locke – that like all things, social practice is subject to epistemological scrutiny. This rigorous process of definition and delimitation both brings 'tradition' (and 'religion') into categorial being and, by plucking them from the ample ground of experience, radically diminishes their being. In calling the tacit knowledge of which tradition partakes 'the science of the concrete,' Claude Lévi-Strauss claims for it the status of a rigorous method of knowing that avoids the abstraction characteristic of epistemology and thereby has the efficacy of (not a material but) a social practice.[24]

But this formulation is still too crude, relying as it does on a reductively partial view of Enlightenment thought. For the discovery of tacit knowledge that gains momentum during the early modern period does not simply demystify the credulity of tradition so as to underscore (although it surely does this too) the benightedness of the European past and the non-European present. Once set in motion, the engine of empirical epistemology and its servant social theory also turns upon modernity itself, discovering within enlightenment a systematic structure of tacit knowledge so deeply implicated in the material fabric of everyday life as to be well-nigh ineradicable.

The early modern effort to throw into relief this invisible but palpable force had frequent recourse to the available categories of 'custom' and 'education.' Mounting a wholesale critique of customary bans on divorce in England, John Milton observed that 'Custome still is silently receiv'd for the best instructer ... because her method is so glib and easie, in some manner like to that vision of *Ezekiel* [2:8–3:3], rowling up her sudden book of implicit knowledge, for him that will, to take and swallow down at pleasure.'[25] The insensibility with which custom instructs us Milton compares to the prophet's physical ingestion of the divine book that tastes as sweet as honey. I have already alluded to the Mandevillian inquiry into the process of socialization as a discovery of tacit knowledge in our most familiar and domestic precincts. Female chastity is a case in point. 'The Lessons of it,' writes Mandeville,' like those of *Grammar*, are taught us long before we have occasion for, or understand the Usefulness of them ... A Girl who is modestly educated, may, before she is two Years old, begin to observe how careful the Women, she converses with, are of covering themselves before Men; and the same Caution being inculcated to her by Precept, as well as Example, it is very probable that at Six she'll be ashamed of shewing her Leg, without knowing any Reason why such an Act is blameable, or what the Tendency of it is.'[26]

Mary Astell similarly stresses the tacitness (the 'ignorant,' 'irrational,' 'customary,' and 'habitual inadvertancy') of women's socialization as crucial to its force: 'Thus Ignorance and a narrow Education lay the Foundation of Vice, and Imitation and Custom rear it up ... 'Tis Custom therefore, that Tyrant Custom, which is the grand motive to all those irrational choices which we daily see made in the World ... having inur'd our selves to Folly, we know not how to quit it ... we have little time and less inclination to stand still and reflect on our own Minds ... By an habitual inadvertency we render ourselves incapable of any serious and improveing thought.'[27]

In these authors, 'education' may be felt to stand in relation to socialization as, more generally in Enlightenment thought, 'religion' does to tradition. Mandeville's analogy with the teaching of grammar is particularly telling here, since it evokes both a pedagogic scene of explicit instruction and a habituation in tacitly but rigorously rule-bound behaviour. Like 'religion,' 'education' suggests the concrete specificity of an institutional and personalized agency, and feminist authors of the period (rightly) return again and again to the deficiencies of a 'narrow education' to explain why the status of women is a matter of nurture rather than nature. Ultimately, however, the explanatory force of 'education' is most powerful as it leads these authors to the more encompassing notion of socialization, in which the intentional promulgation of educational programs plays only one part. Of course, not all tacit knowledge is traditional knowledge, at least in the commonly accepted sense of that term. But the association of 'education' with 'custom' suggests a close connection between tradition and even the more limited and intentional idea of pedagogic practice, which can be felt to operate, at the micro-level of individual formation, as tradition does at the macro-level of cultural formation.[28]

In other words, the Enlightenment that gave us the empirical critique of tacit knowledge also gave us the critique of enlightenment and of empirical knowledge itself. Thomas Kuhn's famous figure for the social (or 'community') constitution of 'normal' science, the figure of the 'paradigm,' recalls not only Mandeville's comparison of tacit social knowledge to the rules of grammar, but also David Hume's insistence that what we experience as the immediate perception of a causal relationship is really nothing but 'custom.' For 'we call every thing CUSTOM, which proceeds from a past repetition, without any new reasoning or conclusion ... Objects have no discoverable connexion together; nor is it from any other principle but custom operating upon the imagination, that we can draw any inference from the appearance of one to the existence of another.'[29] Kuhn's work is indebted to that of Michael Polanyi, who has argued that although

> [t]he declared aim of modern science is to establish a strictly detached, objective knowledge[,] ... tacit thought forms an indispensable part of all knowledge ... Since a problem can be known only tacitly, our knowledge of it can be recognized as valid only by accepting the validity of tacit knowing ... It appears then that traditionalism, which requires us to believe before we know, and in order that we may know, is based on a deeper insight into the nature of knowledge than is a scientific rationalism that would permit us to believe only explicit statements based on tangible data and derived from these by a formal inference, open to repeated testing.[30]

In this sense, then, the modern critique of tradition as tacit knowledge is inseparable from the modern recognition that the 'traditionalism' of tacit knowledge is inescapable.[31] And of course common usage, less invested than I either in the distinction between tacit and explicit knowledge or in that between tradition and modernity, is content to accord modernity its own traditions. The interest of these distinctions, however, lies in their historical status, their powerful and pervasive plausibility to early modern commentators. For them, in fact, false dichotomy is a necessary precondition for the rapid, revisionist insight that opposition is also interconnection. I have already observed contemporaries' ambivalence toward the 'discovery' of tradition, which seemed to entail both a gain in the power of knowledge and a loss in the experience of community. In the second half of this essay I will argue that the Enlightenment articulated this ambivalence by elaborating two innovative kinds of discourse. One of these discourses enabled the confident and ongoing critique of tacit knowledge despite the apparent decay of its traditional medium, tradition itself. The other promised a way of continuing to experience the affective and communitarian rewards of tacit knowledge without suffering its epistemological consequences.

Ideology

When Dryden remarks, in *Religio Laici*, that the fallibility of Roman Catholic tradition is 'prov'd too plain; / If we consider *Interest*, *Church*, and *Gain*' (ll. 274–5), he departs momentarily from his primary concern, which is soteriological and epistemological, to pursue what appears a related, material, view of tradition's tenacity. The critique of tradition can be made not only on epistemological, but also on material grounds – on the grounds not of 'custom' but of 'interest.' I have already suggested how Mandeville's emergent theory of socialization sophisticates Dryden's claim by implying that society may exercise a trans-personal, supra-intentional agency which is yet 'political' in its effects. In other words, Mandeville discovers a kind of knowledge that is at once tacit and 'interested.' The disclosure of tradition as a customary formation is close here to the disclosure of tradition as an interested formation: that is, as an 'ideology.' If the Enlightenment 'theory' of tradition disempowers it by disembedding knowledge from customary social practice, the Enlightenment theory of ideology finds a related power of knowledge in its embeddedness in material interest. 'Ideology' is the category the Enlightenment elaborated to acknowledge and to understand the ongoingness of tacit knowledge despite modernity's apparent triumph over the tacitness of tradition. 'Material interest' is a modern elaboration of 'custom's' invisible efficacy, now operative even in a setting of explicit rationalization, of 'enlightenment.' 'Material interest' substantializes the force of the customary so as to account for a condition of motivation so deeply rooted that it flies under the radar of conscious motive.

However, the 'theory of ideology' as it has become familiar to us is not the same as the theory of 'ideology' from which it was derived. In fact, the term was first used, at the end of the eighteenth century, to name the new, rational and explicit, science of ideas by which the tacitness of tradition might be criticized and replaced. 'It is in this way that ideologies in the restricted sense first came into being. They replace traditional legitimations of power by appearing in the mantle of modern science.'[32] 'Ideology thus entailed the emergence of a new mode of political discourse ... [It] separated itself from the mythical and religious consciousness; it justified the course of action it proposed, by the logic and evidence it summoned on behalf of its views of the social world, rather than by invoking faith, tradition, revelation or the authority of the speaker.' But it was also 'one of ideology's essential social functions ... to stand outside of science itself, and to reject the idea of science as *self*-sufficient or *self*-grounded.'[33]

Thus in its original, late-Enlightenment meaning, 'ideology,' so far from being the mode of knowledge that extends tradition's tacitness in other terms, instead articulates the commitment of empirical rationality to the explicitness that derives from epistemological detachment. This earliest sense of 'ideology' as nothing but the rational 'discovery' of tradition fed, as I have already observed, the experience of both gain and loss. If 'ideology' in this sense of the term plausibly liberates us from the prisonhouse of tradition, by the conservative understanding its explicitness could rather be felt as a deforming reduction, an 'abridgment' of the knowledge bound up within traditional implication: 'The ideological style of politics ... is a traditional manner of attending to the arrangements of a society which has been abridged into a doctrine of ends to be pursued ... The complexities of the tradition which have been squeezed out in the process of abridgment are taken to be unimportant.'[34]

The speed with which the term 'ideology' came, in the early nineteenth century, to mean not an explicating technique for disclosing tacit tradition but a category of tacit knowing itself in need of disclosure, is testimony to the fact that empirical epistemology could not long rest without turning its weapons on itself. In this way, the theory of 'ideology' was quickly supplanted by 'the theory of ideology,' which conceived ideology to be an idealism, in its stealthy tacitness as vulnerable to criticism as tradition itself. Henceforth ideology could be seen as a 'replacement' of tradition in the sense not of a correction but of a modernization. 'It is, in fact, precisely at the point at which a political system begins to free itself from the immediate governance of received tradition ... that formal ideologies tend first to emerge and take hold ... That such ideologies may call ... for the reinvigoration of custom or the reimposition of religious hegemony is, of course, no contradiction. One constructs arguments for tradition only when its credentials have been questioned. To the degree that such appeals are successful they bring, not a return to naive traditionalism, but ideological retraditionalization – an altogether different matter.'[35]

But if retraditionalization is an ideological process, so is tradition itself. 'For tradition is in practice the most evident expression of the dominant and hegemonic pressures and limits ... What we have to see is not just "a tradition" but a *selective tradition*: an intentionally selective version of a shaping past and a pre-shaped present, which is then powerfully operative in the process of social and cultural definition and identification ... What has then to be said about any tradition is that it is in this sense an aspect of *contemporary* social and cultural organization, in the interest of the dominance of a specific class. It is a version of the past which is intended to connect with and ratify the present.'[36] So the distinction between custom and material interest is not a simple one. Just as it has proved possible to descry 'tradition' operating in the modern world in much the same way as we might expect of a comparably tacit 'ideology,' so 'ideology,' now generalized beyond its Enlightenment moment of identification, could be discovered within pre-modernity, uncertainly related there to 'tradition,' but most often helping to redirect the epistemological critique of tradition in a sociopolitical direction.[37]

The influence of an emergent 'ideology theory' on the critique of tradition (or, to put it differently, the sociopolitical expansion of 'tradition theory' itself) can be felt even in authors to whom the term 'ideology' was not yet available. The Enlightenment demystification of aristocratic status provides an example. Daniel Defoe knew the fragility of this perhaps necessary fiction: '[A]ll Great things begin in Small, the highest Families begun low, and therefore to examine it too nicely, is to overthrow it all.'[38] Tom Paine's repudiation of titles of rank carries the

argument further: 'Imagination has given figure and character to cen-
taurs, satyrs, and down to all the fairy tribe, but titles baffle even the
powers of fancy and are a chimerical nondescript.' 'The romantic and
barbarous distinction of men into kings and subjects,' he continues,
'though it may suit the condition of courtiers, cannot that of citizens,
and is exploded by the principle upon which governments are now
founded.' But Paine also saw that the logic of his argument implied a
systematic correspondence between knowledge and its material conditions that took in both traditional and modern cultures: 'Whether the
forms and maxims of governments which are still in practice were
adapted to the condition of the world at the period they were established is not in this case the question. The older they are, the less correspondence can they have with the present state of things. Time and
change of circumstances and opinions have the same progressive effect
in rendering modes of government obsolete as they have upon customs and manners.'[39] From here it is a relatively short distance to
Marx's rhetorical question: 'Is the view of nature and of social relations
on which the Greek imagination and hence Greek [mythology] is based
possible with self-acting mule spindles and railways and locomotives
and electrical telegraphs?'[40]

   Broadly speaking, the critique of tradition learns from the critique of
ideology the explanatory utility of having recourse to material interest
as the grounds of knowledge; the critique of ideology learns from that
of tradition an epistemological emphasis on illusion. They have in
common a concern with the tacitness of knowledge, its inseparability
from and determinate dependence upon its customary or interested
conditions of existence. Ideology theory soon learns to complicate the
relatively simple model of intentional motivation that first colours the
notion of 'interest' with which it is bound up. Indeed, '[i]t is essential
to the concept of interest that it is ambiguous as to whether the gratifi-
cation it entails for persons is "known" to them.' Ideology therefore 'is
pushed toward rationality by the interest on which it is grounded, but
is limited in this rationality by that same interest.' Ideologies 'are not
simply a mask for self-interest: they are also a tacit and a genuine offer
of support for different groups.'[41] This trans-intentional feature of ideologies is supported not only by the view that they are, like traditions,
collective and shared ('class') beliefs, but also by the analogy between
ideological and specifically religious belief, the way in which a subject
is insensibly 'called' to acknowledge and inhabit its ideological identification.[42]

In its most sophisticated development, the theory of ideology deepens the theory of tradition as tacit knowledge by specifying more concretely, but also by opening out, the conditions under which tradition loses its tacitness. In the theory of tradition, the more-or-less monolithic loss of tradition is ultimately grounded in the advent of innovative technologies – literacy, print – for the production, objectification, and disembedding of knowledge. In their classic account of 'the German ideology,' Marx and Engels describe history itself as though it were the limit case of tradition, a more continuous and ongoing generation, corruption, and re-generation of knowledge whose material explanation requires a more densely articulated field of productive determinacy. This is a general 'correspondence theory' of ideology of the sort already exemplified by Paine, which binds together the 'external' explanation of how tacit belief is materially determined and re-determined with an account of what this feels like 'from the inside.'

To speak in the abstract of the determinate relation between 'infrastructure' and 'superstructure' – between 'forces of production,' 'relations of production,' and 'ideology' – is to describe a dialectical relationship which is experienced as a tacit correspondence: that is, as an internal and necessary condition of existence. But the relationship is unstable because it is historical. Its component parts change at different rates, so that their abstract 'correspondence' at different moments becomes more or less 'contradictory': the relationship comes to feel not necessary and internal but 'accidental' and 'external':

> The difference between the individual as a person and what is accidental to him, is not a conceptual difference but an historical fact ... What appears accidental ... is a form of intercourse which corresponded to a definite stage of development of the productive forces ... The conditions under which individuals have intercourse with each other, so long as the above-mentioned contradiction is absent, are conditions appertaining to their individuality, in no way external to them ... The definite condition under which they produce, thus corresponds, as long as the contradiction has not yet appeared, to the reality of their conditioned nature, their one-sided existence, the one-sidedness of which only becomes evident when the contradiction enters on the scene and thus exists for the later individuals. Then this condition appears as an accidental fetter ... These various conditions, which appear first as conditions of self-activity, later as fetters upon it, form in the whole evolution of history a coherent series of forms of intercourse, the coherence of which consists in this: in the place of an

earlier form of intercourse, which has become a fetter, a new one is put, corresponding to the more developed productive forces and, hence, to the advanced mode of self-activity of individuals – a form which in its turn becomes a fetter and is then replaced by another.[43]

In this fashion, the theory of ideology takes over from the theory of tradition, explaining the discovery and rediscovery of tacit knowledge as a perpetual historical process because it is grounded in the complex multiplicity of material history. The argument can be made, at least in part, in non-Marxist terms:

> If it is an established fact for the enlightenment that all tradition that rea-
> son shows to be impossible, i.e. nonsense, can only be understood histori-
> cally, i.e. by going back to the past's way of looking at things, then the
> historical consciousness that emerges in romanticism involves a radical-
> ization of the enlightenment. For the exceptional case of nonsensical tra-
> dition has become the general rule for historical consciousness. Meaning
> that is generally accessible through reason is so little believed that the
> whole of the past, even, ultimately, all the thinking of one's contemporar-
> ies, is seen only 'historically.' Thus the romantic critique of the enlighten-
> ment ends itself in enlightenment, in that it evolves as historical science
> and draws everything into the orbit of historicism.[44]

The theory of ideology may therefore be said, in its strongest articulation, to sustain the theory of tradition even as it goes beyond it.

The Aesthetic

In that articulation, the theory of ideology has the neutrality of an objective method for disclosing the material conditions by virtue of which knowledge comes into being. In its historical development, however, the 'discovery' of ideology has been coloured most commonly by the triumphalism of a demystifying and liberatory enlight-
enment. And this in turn supports the plausibility of seeing the growth of ideology theory as only a partial accounting for the persistence of tacit knowledge in the modern world. True, the discovery of tradition, and the resulting insight into the customary embeddedness of knowledge, often met with a comparably optimistic response. But as I have already observed, the discovery of tradition also evoked the apprehen-
sion that an inestimably valuable condition of social coherence was

being sacrificed in the process. How does modernity extend not only the former, but also the latter, experience of the loss of tacit knowledge? How do we perpetuate, in a culture 'beyond' tradition, the nostalgic recognition of a normative coherence lost – but also, in that very recognition, vicariously repossessed for a moment?

In the book that provoked Paine's experiment in ideology theory, Edmund Burke had accepted the challenge of defending tradition from an (inevitably) enlightened perspective. To this end he exploited the capacity of empirical epistemology to turn its weapons on itself. For Paine, the tradition of inherited nobility is 'chimerical' because it is tacit, unrationalizable apart from its own antiquated belief system. For Burke, the modern doctrine of 'the rights of men' is 'metaphysical' so long as it remains untested against its moral, political, and historical context. The putative rationality of the doctrine hides the unreflectiveness with which it is espoused: 'What is the use of discussing a man's abstract right to food or medicine? The question is upon the method of procuring and administering them. In that deliberation I shall always advise to call in the aid of the farmer and the physician rather than the professor of metaphysics.'[45]

Burke's and Paine's mutual recriminations, if not quite the same, nonetheless sustain an analogy. In Burke's analysis, abstraction is no safeguard against the stealthy tacitness of knowledge.The abstract detachment of enlightened reason generates the tacit knowledge of reason itself. If all ages are ruled by their illusions, should we not most suspect those rational beliefs that most closely 'correspond' to our modern enlightenment? Indeed, in the very antiquity of tradition may be found a principle of historical detachment that crucially supplements, and thereby corrects, the epistemological detachment whose formidable powers are nonetheless vulnerable to its own metaphysics. 'Aristocracy' is preferable to 'the rights of men' because our historical detachment from it ensures our epistemological detachment from it. Locke had rejected the historical detachment of tradition on empirical grounds.[46] One hundred years later, Burke can embrace it on similar grounds. In fact, we can believe in aristocracy despite our epistemological detachment from it, precisely because of our historical detachment from it. This is the perspective from which 'tradition' may be cherished, startlingly enough, as 'prejudice': 'You see, Sir, that in this enlightened age I am bold enough to confess that we are generally men of untaught feelings, that, instead of casting away all our old prejudices, we cherish them to a very considerable degree, and, to take more shame to ourselves, we cherish them because they are prejudices; and the longer they have lasted and the more generally they have prevailed, the more we cherish them.'[47] To be sure, Burke can sound very much like Sir Henry Marten, in an earlier age of revolution, on the dangers of explicitly 'arguing and descanting what sovereign power is': 'It has been the misfortune ... of this age that everything is to be discussed as if the constitution of our country were to be always a subject rather of altercation than enjoyment.'[48] Burke's genius, however, is to turn this problem into its own solution.

To return to my opening figure for cultural embeddedness as a kind of invisible clothing, in his most famous passage Burke makes a virtue of tradition's disclosure – of the clothing's visibility – by deploring not the clothing itself but the logic whereby its visibility dictates its removal. Rather than strip it off, he would seize the occasion to admire its pleasantly and self-consciously artful properties:

> But now all is to be changed. All the pleasing illusions which made power gentle and obedience liberal, which harmonized the different shades of life, and which, by a bland assimilation, incorporated into politics the sentiments which beautify and soften private society, are to be dissolved by this new-conquering empire of light and reason. All the decent drapery of life is to be rudely torn off. All the superadded ideas, furnished from the wardrobe of a moral imagination, which the heart owns and the understanding ratifies as necessary to cover the defects of our naked, shivering nature, and to raise it to dignity in our own estimation, are to be exploded as ridiculous, absurd, and antiquated fashion.[49]

Although Burke shares the epistemological detachment of ideology theory, the idea that tradition loses its efficacy when it becomes explicit plays no part in his argument. On the contrary, he employs the language of aesthetic response to suggest that for us there is a middle way between the unavailable tacitness of traditionality and the crude ostensiveness (or, the undetectable tacitness) of modernity. By this middle way, pragmatic social efficacy becomes available to belief at the moment it loses its tacit social efficacy. In fact, our historical distance from the antiquated politics of the ancien régime – from the tradition – gives them an imaginative power over us that fuels their pragmatic efficacy. We cherish tradition not because of its essential value, but because it gives us pleasure to do so, and in our affective response to tradition lies the ground of its social utility: not the immediate coherence of cultural embeddedness, but the mediated pleasure of self-conscious reenactment. This sort of scepticism lies at the heart of the modern strain of conservative political philosophy that emerged toward the end of the eighteenth century. Contemptuous of the notion that traditional social hierarchy bears any but an 'accidental' relation to virtue, Johnson nonetheless told Boswell that 'I would no more deprive a nobleman of his respect, than of his money. I consider myself as acting a part in the great system of society ... I would behave to a nobleman as I should expect he would behave to me, were I a nobleman and he Sam. Johnson ... Sir, there would be a perpetual struggle for precedence, were there no fixed invariable rules for the distinction of rank, which creates no jealousy, as it is allowed to be accidental.'[50] Once ideologized and aestheticized, we might say, tradition becomes traditionalism.

But what is 'the language of aesthetic response'? How is it related to tacit knowledge? Like 'ideology,' the term 'aesthetics' was coined in the latter half of the eighteenth century. As the word itself suggests, the aesthetic is that subcategory of empirical epistemology which involves strictly sensible – as disinct from rational – knowledge; it was soon narrowed to refer more specifically to our knowledge of the beautiful and the sublime. In this more limited sense of the term, the aesthetic, rooted like empirical reason in sense impressions, provides a different avenue of detachment from them: not rational abstraction but imaginative distance. Its conceptual formulation precedes the term itself, especially in English Enlightenment thought.[51]

In one of his celebrated papers on the pleasures of the imagination, Joseph Addison wrote that they 'are not so gross as those of Sense ... A Man of a Polite Imagination ... meets with a secret Refreshment in a Description, and often feels a greater Satisfaction in the Prospect of Fields and Meadows, than another does in the Possession. It gives him, indeed, a kind of Property in every thing he sees, and makes the most rude uncultivated Parts of Nature administer to his Pleasures ... A Man should endeavour ... to make the Sphere of his innocent Pleasures as wide as possible, that he may retire into them with Safety, and find in them such a Satisfaction as a wise Man would not blush to take.' In this view, the pleasures of the imagination are 'innocent' of the corruptions to which merely physical pleasures are vulnerable. They are also innocent of the dangers of empirical reality, so much so that aesthetic pleasure requires – even, consists in – the consciousness that it is not empirical. 'How comes it to pass,' asks Addison, that we should take delight in being terrified or dejected by a Description, when we find so much Uneasiness in the Fear or Grief which we receive from any other Occasion? ... The Nature of this Pleasure ... does not arise so properly from the Description of what is Terrible, as from the Reflection we make on our Selves at the time of reading it. When we look on such hideous Objects, we are not a little pleased to think we are in no Danger of them. We consider them at the same time as Dreadful and Harmless; so that the more frightful Appearance they make, the greater is the Pleasure we receive from the Sense of our own Safety ... This is, however, such a kind of Pleasure as we are not capable of receiving, when we see a Person actually lying under the Tortures that we meet with in a Description; because in this Case, the Object presses too close upon our Senses, and bears so hard upon us, that it does not give us time or leisure to reflect on our selves.[52]

Addison's pleasures of the imagination obviate by their very immateriality the prudential critique of physical pain and corruption. They are akin to the pleasures of sense experience yet detached from their material implications. They mimetically capitalize on the empirical powers of sense perception while avoiding their physical consequences. Through the replacement of physical and sensible activity by a representation or imaginative enactment, the pleasures of the imagination escape both the crude literalism of empirical epistemology and the risks attendant on physical experience. What Addison calls 'the leisure to reflect on our selves' is a special version of the epistemological detachment Locke had identified at the heart of empirical epistemology. In the aesthetic attitude, merely sensible knowledge finds the detachment characteristic of rational knowledge.

The insight that the pleasure derived from artistic imitation is predicated on an emotional state that is both immediate and mediated is as old as the Aristotelian doctrine of *catharsis*. However, it finds new life in Enlightenment thought and becomes canonical in Coleridge's account of 'that willing suspension of disbelief for the moment, which constitutes poetic faith.'[53] To willingly suspend disbelief is to authorize belief within a sceptical framework. It is also to revive the social coherence and solidarity of 'traditional' cultures, but now at the level of, not physical presence, but imaginative identification. 'The illusion is lasting and complete,' wrote an enthusiastic novel reader. 'I interrupt the unhappy Clarissa, in order to mix my tears with hers: I accost her, as if she was present with me. No Author, I believe, ever metamorphosed himself into his characters so perfectly as Richardson.'[54] Clara Reeve thought that the perfection of the 'novel is to represent every scene, in so easy and natural a manner, and to make them appear so probable, as to deceive us into a persuasion (at least while we are reading) that all is real, until we are affected by the joys or distresses, of the persons in the story, as if they were our own.'[55]

Coleridge's famous words remind us that even at its historical emergence, the aesthetic attitude was being associated with religious (and by that association, I would suggest, with traditional) 'faith.' It is a commonplace that one end of art in the modern world is to secularize religion, to replace its traditional functions and responsibilities by a thoroughly humanized mode of spirituality. In the context of my present argument, art can be seen to secularize religion by purifying it of tacit knowledge. Hedged about as it is by empiricist scepticism, aesthetic belief is a curiously guarded and notional belief. The aesthetic substitutes for the powers of divinity and spirituality an internalized and humanized replacement that evades the demystifying strictures of empirical epistemology by avoiding the metaphysical claims of religious spirituality – at least in principle. In practice, the scepticism that framed the aesthetic pleasure experienced by readers of the novel was also capable of obstructing it. At such times, the definitive gap between the aesthetic and the religious could be felt to dissolve. Not only the special authority exercised by aesthetic belief, but also the social solidarity putatively encouraged by it, could seem as illusory as those associated with a discredited religious enthusiasm. 'In the enthusiasm of sentiment,' wrote one reader, 'there is much the same danger as in the enthusiasm of religion, of substituting certain impulses and feelings of what may be called a visionary kind, in the place of real practical duties, which, in morals, as in theology, we might not improperly denominate good works.' Another reader was 'afraid lest the same eye which is so prone to give its tributary tear to the well-told history of fancied woe, should be able to look upon real misery without emotion, because its tale is told without plot, incident, or ornament.'[56]

This soon became a minority response. And in the more general confidence that in these respects the aesthetic 'improves on' the religious, we can detect a tendency to make 'religion' bear some of the weight of 'tradition' itself. This is suggested, at least, by the historicizing language writers use to describe the peculiar sort of detachment afforded by aesthetic experience. The madness of Don Quixote is first of all epistemological, consisting in the confusion of romance illusions with reality. But throughout *Don Quixote* (1605, 1615) this epistemological error is hard to separate from the historical error of confusing chivalric tradition with contemporary social practice. From the old romances Don Quixote has extracted what may justly be called the 'tradition' of chivalry, the complex body of semiotic codes and rituals of a bygone culture. To be thus embedded in tradition is to experience madness – the loss of reason – in two forms that are distinguishable but coextensive: the inability to detach illusion from reality and the inability to detach the past from the present. For European culture, the ultimate solution to Don Quixote's madness required that the state of mind capable of entertaining the empirical reality of illusion be reconceived not as madness, but as aesthetic response. This demanded an appreciation of the aesthetic attitude as a special mode of epistemological detachment, to which the posture of historical detachment was quite closely tied.

The process by which 'romance' error had, by the end of the eighteenth century, been positively revalued as 'romantic' truth was bound up with the emergence of the cult of the medieval and the gothic during the same period. At first demystified and repudiated by empirical epistemology, in time these barbaric archetypes of 'the traditional' had become sufficiently distanced from enlightened modernity to afford it the pleasure of aesthetic enjoyment. Ann Radcliffe was supreme among gothic novelists at facilitating this pleasure, in part because her insistence on 'explaining' her supernatural effects ensured that the reader's disbelief would be willingly suspended. As one reviewer wrote of *The Mysteries of Udolpho* (1794), 'the reader experiences in perfection the strange luxury of artificial terror, without being obliged for a moment to hoodwink his reason, or to yield to the weakness of superstitious credulity.'[57]

Once subjected to the transformative machinery of the aesthetic, moreover, the pleasures of tradition and its tacit knowledge could even yield a genuine species of truth, rightly conceived. In 'An Ode on the Popular Superstitions' (written 1750), William Collins urged his friend John Home to exploit the traditionality of his homeland for its poetic yield. The key to this process is a detachment at once historical and aesthetic:

There must thou wake perforce thy Doric quill,
'Tis Fancy's land to which thou sett'st thy feet;

Where still, 'tis said, the fairy people meet
Beneath each birken shade on mead or hill.
...
Let thy sweet muse the rural faith sustain:
These are the themes of simple, sure effect,
That add new conquests to her boundless reign,
And fill with double force her heart-commanding strain.
...
Nor need'st thou blush that such false themes engage
Thy gentle mind, of fairer stores possessed;
...
Proceed, in forceful sounds and colours bold
The native legends of thy land rehearse:
To such adapt thy lyre and suit thy powerful verse.

In scenes like these, which, daring to depart
From sober Truth, are still to Nature true,
And call forth fresh delights to Fancy's view,
The heroic Muse employed her Tasso's art![58]

Like Burke, Collins reverses the Lockeian critique of tradition as historical detachment by reconceiving sensible as aesthetic judgment.
Collins argues the value for poetry of what he frankly calls the 'false
themes' of archaic Scottish culture – fairies, wizard seers, runic bards,
the little people – a value that depends entirely on the fact that they are
articles not of credulous belief but of fanciful 'superstition.' No longer
either commanding religious faith or eliciting enlightened incredulity,
such themes are resonant with the secularized spirituality of the poetic
passions. No longer tacitly embraced as tradition, they may now be
self-consciously embraced as 'tradition.' Collins urges Home to recover the 'naive' poetry of the ancient Celts as Schiller soon would do
with respect to that of the ancient Greeks. To be a naive poet today,
however, requires the double consciousness of the aesthetic attitude,
which re-creates the naive immediacy of tradition within the 'sentimental' framework of an inevitable (indeed, constitutive) mediation.[59]
Only because they are historically outmoded may Scottish superstitions be taken up aesthetically as articles of poetic 'faith.' Collins's
poem was composed five years after the last military gasp of archaic
Jacobite politics, the '45, whose romance aura reinforced (as it later
would for Walter Scott) the sense of a landscape that is the last refuge

of the spirit in the modern world. By conflating the melancholy anachronisms of religion and politics – of Celtic myth, aristocratic honour, and the 'feudal' Highlands – Collins's poem participates in an emergent reconceptualization of tradition as, like the aesthetic, a mode of tacit knowledge that may be pleasingly evoked at will.

To conclude: if the Enlightenment is responsible for our most intense and implacable 'discovery' of tradition, by that very same movement it is also responsible for elaborating those categories, ideology and the aesthetic, by which modernity has most successfully theorized and extended the idea of tradition in other terms.

NOTES

1 I use the term throughout not in the literal and restricted sense of 'silent' but in the more general sense of 'implicit' or 'inferred.'

2 The distinction between tradition and modernity is most persuasively seen as methodological – that is, as a differential ratio that can be applied usefully to a variety of diachronic and synchronic fields. In this essay I treat the Enlightenment as the watershed between tradition and modernity not to make a positive claim for the authority of this application over all others, but because I think that the (modern) idea of tradition depends most crucially on conceptual developments that occurred during this period.

3 *Commons Debates 1628*, III: *21 April–27 May 1628*, ed. Robert C. Johnson et al. (New Haven, 1977), 578–9.

4 'The king's answer to the Nineteen Propositions,' 18 June 1642, in *The Stuart Constitution 1603–1688: Documents and Commentary*, ed. J.P. Kenyon (Cambridge, 1966), 22–3. Charles here invokes his father's precepts, whose very explicitness, belying the tacitness they demand, itself conveys a crisis in tacit knowledge: 'That which concerns the mystery of the King's power is not lawful to be disputed; for that is to wade into the weakness of Princes, and to take away the mystical reverence that belongs unto them that sit in the throne of God ... [I]t is presumption and high contempt in a subject to dispute what a King can do, or say that a King cannot do this or that.' James I, *Political Works of James I*, ed. C.H. McIlwain (London, 1918), 333, quoted in J.R. Tanner, *English Constitutional Conflicts of the Seventeenth Century 1603–1689* (Cambridge, [1928] 1961), 20.

5 George Monck, 'A Letter of General George Moncks ... directed unto Mr. Rolle ... [and] the rest of the Gentry of Devon,' 23 Jan. 1660, in *A Collection*

of *Several Letters and Declarations sent by General Monck* ... (1660), 19. George
Savile, Marquess of Halifax's related observation emphasizes the epistemological more than the political effects of the civil war. '[T]he liberty of
the late times gave men so much light, and diffused it so universally
amongst the people, that they are not now to be dealt with, as they might
have been in an age of less inquiry.' Quoted in Derek Hirst, *England in
Conflict 1603–1660: Kingdom, Community, Commonwealth* (Oxford, 1999),
328.

6 *The Gentleman's Monitor: or, A Sober Inspection into the Vertues, Vices, and
Ordinary Means, Of the Rise and Decay of Men and Families* (1665), 261–2.
Compare Sir William Davenant in 1654: 'And subjects should receive good
education from the State, as from vertuous Philosophers, who did anciently
with excellent success correct the peoples manners, not by penall Statutes
and Prisons, but by Moral Schooles and Heroick Representations at the
publick charge ... *Armies* ... are improper to command belief and conformity,
because they do it by compulsion; for the minde ... should be govern'd by
the insinuations of perswasion.' [Sir William Davenant], *A Proposition for
Advancement of Moralitie, By a new way of Entertainment of the People* (1654), 2,
5, reprinted in James R. Jacob and Timothy Raylor, 'Opera and Obedience:
Thomas Hobbes and *A Proposition for Advancement of Moralitie* by Sir William Davenant,' *The Seventeenth Century,* 6 (1991): 243. Davenant's proposal
is to revive ancient methods of obtaining 'a quick and implicit obedience' to
state authority by 'civiliz[ing] the people' through theatrical and operatic
productions. But he is also mindful that now 'Perswasion must be joyn'd to
Force' (5, 11; 242–3, 244). Foucault's followers sometimes take him to be
arguing that Enlightenment discipline 'dissociates power from the body' in
the sense of elaborating methods of 'discursive' persuasion to achieve the
ends of social control that traditionally had been undertaken by physical
force alone (Michel Foucault, *Discipline and Punish: The Birth of the Prison,*
trans. Alan Sheridan [New York, 1979], 138). The testimony of Waterhouse
and Davenant suggests that what is new is not 'disciplinary' persuasion,
but the recognition that persuasion and force are distinct components of
domination which can be exploited in distinct ways.

7 The 'traditional' idea of the public interest assumed its coextension with the
royal interest. 'Significant discussion about the public interest begins with
the Civil War': J.A.W. Gunn, *Politics and the Public Interest in the Seventeenth
Century* (London, 1969), 1.

8 See Eric Hobsbawm, 'Introduction: Inventing Traditions,' in Eric
Hobsbawm and Terence Ranger, eds, *The Invention of Tradition* (Cambridge,1984), 1–14.

9 See in general Jack Goody and Ian Watt, 'The Consequences of Literacy,' in Jack Goody, ed., *Literacy in Traditional Societies* (Cambridge, 1968), 27–68.

10 *Religio Laici or A Laymans Faith* (1682), ll. 270–5, 305–6, 350–3, 386–9, 400–3, in H.T. Swedenberg, Jr, and Vinton A. Dearing, eds, *The Works of John Dryden*, II: *Poems 1681–1684* (Berkeley and Los Angeles, 1972). That Dryden misrepresents Roman Catholic 'tradition' as exclusively oral does not compromise the force of his argument for present purposes.

11 Davies, *Irish Reports* (1612), quoted in J.G.A. Pocock, *The Ancient Constitution and the Feudal Law: English Historical Thought in the Seventeenth Century* (New York, 1967), 32–3.

12 *Commentaries on the Laws of England*, 4 bks. in 2 vols., ed. Thomas M. Cooley (Chicago, 1871), I: 63.

13 The first phrase is Pocock's: see 46; the second is Christopher Hill's: see *The Century of Revolution, 1603–1714*, 2nd ed. (New York, 1980), 54. Warr, *The Corruption and Deficiency of the Laws of England* (1649), in *Harleian Miscellany* (1744-6), III: 240, quoted in Christopher Hill, *The World Turned Upside Down: Radical Ideas during the English Revolution* (New York, 1973), 219. It is in this sense that Ellen Meiksins Wood can speak of 'the British ideology of tradition': *The Pristine Culture of Capitalism: A Historical Essay on Old Regimes and Modern States* (London, 1991), 76. As I argue below, however, 'tradition' and 'ideology' may usefully be seen to have a special relationship that complicates this sort of usage.

14 14 Bacon, *The Proficiencie and Advancement of Learning, Divine and Human* (1605); 'Author's Preface,' *Of the Wisdom of the Ancients* (Lat. original 1609), in Robert L. Ellis and James Spedding, eds, *The Philosophical Works of Francis Bacon*, rev. John M. Robertson (London, 1905), 121, 124, 822. Bacon's scepticism in the latter work justifies the cheerful negligence of his own rereadings of the ancient fables: 'The wisdom of the primitive ages was either great or lucky ... My own pains, if there be any help in them, I shall think well bestowed either way: I shall be throwing light either upon antiquity or upon nature itself' (824).

15 Hobbes, *De Cive* (1642), 1649 'Preface to the Readers,' trans. and ed. by Richard Tuck and Michael Silverthorne as *The Citizen* (Cambridge, 1998), 9.

16 *The Works of the Hon. Robert Boyle*, 3rd ed., ed. Thomas Birch (1772), I: 304.

17 *An Essay concerning Human Understanding* (1690), ed. Peter H. Nidditch (Oxford, 1975), IV, xvi, xix, secs. 10, 14 (664, 704). Although the 'discovery' of tradition, especially through technological innovation, is most powerfully conceived as a once-and-for-all revolution in consciousness, its multiple and overlapping nature can be seen in the plausible argument that the epistemological separation of the subject and object of knowledge was

achieved first of all by Plato, under the more-or-less direct influence of the literacy revolution: see Eric A. Havelock, *Preface to Plato* (Cambridge, 1963), chaps 11–12.

18 *Christianity Not Mysterious*, 2nd ed. (1696), 58; Mandeville, *Origin of Honour* (1732), 40–1: both quoted by the editor in Mandeville, *The Fable of the Bees* (1705, 1714), ed. F.B. Kaye (Oxford, 1924), I, 46–7n.1. For Mandeville's earlier usage, see 'An Enquiry into the Origin of Moral Virtue,' in *Fable of the Bees*, I, 41–57.

19 Bacon, *Novum Organum* (1620), in *Philosophical Works*, 265, in specific reference to the Idols of the Theater.

20 *Essay concerning Human Understanding*, IV, xix (697–706); Locke to Damaris Cudworth, later Lady Masham, 6 Apr. 1682?, in *Correspondence of John Locke*, ed. E.S. de Beer (Oxford, 1976), II, 500.

21 Swift's other two realms are variously 'empire' and 'knowledge,' 'empire' and 'philosophy,' and 'faction' and what we might call 'popular culture': see Swift, 'A Discourse Concerning the Mechanical Operation of the Spirit'(1704) and 'A Tale of a Tub' (1704, 1710) in A.C. Guthkelch and D. Nichol Smith, eds, *A Tale of a Tub To which is added The Battle of the Books and the Mechanical Operation of the Spirit*, 2nd ed. (Oxford, 1958), 266–7, 162, 62–3.

22 Filmer, *Patriarcha* (written c. 1640, printed 1680), in *Patriarcha and Other Political Works*, ed. Peter Laslett (Oxford, 1949), 54; Sidney, *Discourses concerning Government* (written 1680–3, printed 1696), I, iii, ed. Thomas G. West (Indianapolis, 1996), 12–13.

23 Locke, *An Essay Concerning the True Original, Extent, and End of Civil Government* (*The Second Treatise of Government*) (1690), Bk. II, ch. 8, sec. 119, in *Two Treatises of Government*, ed. Peter Laslett, 2nd ed. (Cambridge, 1967), 365–6. The problem of tacit consent provided Dryden the opportunity for a *reductio ad absurdum* that implied an anti-Christian tendency in contractarian thinking: 'If those who gave the Scepter, could not tye / By their own deed their own Posterity, / How then coud *Adam* bind his future Race? / How coud his forfeit on mankind take place? / Or how coud heavenly Justice damn us all, / Who nere consented to our Fathers fall?': *Absalon and Achitophel* (1681), ll. 769–74, in *Works*, II, 28. Cf. Sir John Vanbrugh's Lady Brute, whom the playwright economically employs to satirize in the same breath contractarianism, tacit consent, and patriarchalism: 'Why, what did I vow? I think I promised to be true to my husband. Well; and he promised to be kind to me. But he hasn't kept his word. Why then I'm absolved from mine. Aye, that seems clear to me. The argument's good between the King and the people, why not between the husband and the wife? Oh, but that condi-

tion was not expressed. No matter, 'twas understood': Sir John Vanbrugh, *The Provok'd Wife* (1697), I, i, 69–76, ed. Anthony Coleman (Manchester, 1982), 59–60.

24 See Lévi-Strauss, *The Savage Mind* (Chicago, 1966), chap. 1.

25 *The Doctrine & Discipline of Divorce Restor'd to the good of both Sexes ...* (1644), in *Complete Prose Works of John Milton*, II: *1643–8*, ed. Don M. Wolfe et al. (New Haven, 1959), 222–3.

26 Mandeville, 'Remark (C.),' *Fable of the Bees*, I, 69.

27 Astell, *A Serious Proposal to the Ladies for the Advancement of their True and Greatest Interest*, Part I, 3rd ed. (1696), in *The First English Feminist: Reflections Upon Marriage and Other Writings by Mary Astell*, ed. Bridget Hill (Aldershot, Hants, 1986), 147–8.

28 Enlightenment educational theory sought to acknowledge the role of implication in the pedagogic process: compare Fenelon's 'indirect instructions' and Locke's idea of inculcation by 'insensible degrees.' See generally Richard A. Barney, *Plots of Enlightenment: Education and the Novel in Eighteenth-Century England* (Stanford, 1999), chap. 1.

29 Hume, *A Treatise of Human Nature* (1739–40), I, iii, sec. 8, 2nd ed., ed. L.A. Selby-Bigge and P.H. Nidditch (Oxford, 1978), 102–3. For relevant reflections on the paradigm figure, see Thomas S. Kuhn, *The Structure of Scientific Revolutions*, 2nd ed. (Chicago, 1970), 23–5, 176–9.

30 Polanyi, *The Tacit Dimension* (Gloucester,1983), 20, 87, 61–2. For his acknowledgment of earlier work by Polanyi, see Kuhn, *Structure*, 44, 191.

31 The recognition has been had in other areas as well: e.g., compare the notion of 'implication' in hermeneutics, 'latent content' and 'the unconscious' in psychoanalysis, etc. Issues of tacit knowledge also may (although they need not) be pertinent to contemporary second-order, methodological debates about whether the social sciences should 'interpret' or 'explain' their objects of study: whether they should understand their objects from the 'inside' or from the 'outside,' according to concepts 'internal' or 'external' to them, by reference to 'motives' or by reference to 'causes.' For an illuminating discussion see Alasdair MacIntyre, 'The Idea of a Social Science,' in *Against the Self-Images of the Age: Essays on Ideology and Philosophy* (Notre Dame, 1978), 211–29.

32 Jürgen Habermas, *Toward a Rational Society: Student Protest, Science, and Politics*, trans. Jeremy I. Shapiro (Boston, 1970), 99.

33 33 Alvin W. Gouldner, *The Dialectic of Ideology and Technology: The Origins, Grammar, and Future of Ideology* (New York, 1976), 30, 36.

34 Michael Oakeshott, *Rationalism in Politics and Other Essays* (London, 1974), 122–3.

35 Clifford Geertz, 'Ideology as a Cultural System,' in *The Interpretation of Cultures: Selected Essays* (New York, 1973), 219 and n. 42.
36 Raymond Williams, *Marxism and Literature* (New York, 1977), 115–16.
37 The uncertain relationship of tradition and ideology as modes of tacit knowledge is expressed by John Plamenatz in *Ideology* (London, 1970), 21: 'Though the term ideology is by no means confined to explicit beliefs it is in practice seldom used to refer to the beliefs of primitive peoples. I do not know why this should be so.'
38 Defoe, *The Compleat English Gentleman* (written 1728–9), ed. Karl D. Bülbring (London, 1890), 13.
39 Paine, *Rights of Man*, Part I (1791), in Nelson F. Adkins, ed., *Common Sense and Other Political Writings* (Indianapolis,1953), 89, 108, 111.
40 Marx, *Grundrisse: Foundations of the Critique of Political Economy,* trans. and ed. Martin Nicolaus (Harmondsworth, 1973), 110.
41 Gouldner, *Dialectic*, 211, 214, 222.
42 See Louis Althusser's pursuit of the analogy through the idea of 'interpellation': 'Ideology and Ideological State Apparatuses,' in *Lenin and Philosophy and Other Essays*, trans. Ben Brewster (London, 1971), 162–70. The relationship between ideology and tradition can also be felt in Althusser's emphasis on 'education' at the root of 'ideological state apparatuses': see 144–5.
43 Marx and Engels, *The German Ideology, Part One, with Selections from Parts Two and Three*, ed. C.J. Arthur (New York, 1970), 86–7. They go on (87) to formulate the corollary principle of 'unequal development': '[T]he various stages and interests are never completely overcome, but only subordinated to the prevailing interest and trail along beside the latter for centuries afterwards.'
44 Han-Georg Gadamer, *Truth and Method*, trans. William Glen-Doepel (London, 1979), 244.
45 Burke, *Reflections on the Revolution in France* (1790), ed. Thomas H.D. Mahoney (Indianapolis, 1955), 69; cf. 70–1.
46 See above, n.17.
47 Burke, *Reflections*, 98–9.
48 Burke, *Reflections*, 104; for Marten see above, n. 3.
49 *Reflections*, 87.
50 James Boswell, *Life of Johnson*, ed. R.W. Chapman (Oxford, 1980), 316, 317. To perceive the 'accidental' nature of social forms is therefore not necessarily (as in Marx's ideology theory) to experience them as 'fetters.' Rather, it confirms the impersonal and rule-bound nature of 'the great system of society': that is, its systematicity.

51　The following three paragraphs draw on my essay 'The Origins of Interdisciplinary Studies,' *Eighteenth-Century Studies*, 28, no. 1 (Fall, 1994): 22–3.

52　Addison, *Spectator*, nos. 411, 418 (21, 30 June 1712), in Donald F. Bond, ed., *The Spectator* (Oxford, 1965), III, 537–9, 568–9.

53　See Aristotle, *Poetics*, 1449b; Coleridge, *Biographia Literaria* (1817), ed. George Watson (London, 1965), II, xiv (169). Cf. Dryden, *Of Dramatic Poesy: An Essay* (1668), in *Of Dramatic Poesy and Other Critical Essays*, ed. George Watson (London, 1964), 50–2, 62; Burke, *A Philosophical Inquiry into the Origin of our Ideas of the Sublime and the Beautiful* (1757), ed. J.T. Boulton (London, 1958), 44–51, 91; Johnson, 'Preface' to *The Works of William Shakespeare* (1765), in Arthur Sherbo, ed., *The Yale Edition of the Works of Samuel Johnson* (New Haven, 1968), 76, 78. Coleridge had earlier described this effect with regard to the reading not of poetry but of the novel: see *Critical Review*, 2nd ser., 19 (Feb. 1797), 195, quoted in Joseph F. Bartolomeo, *A New Species of Criticism: Eighteenth-Century Discourse on the Novel* (Newark, 1994), 140.

54　Anon., *The Gentleman's Magazine*, 40 (Oct. 1770), in Ioan Williams, ed., *Novel and Romance 1700–1800: A Documentary Record* (New York, 1970), 274–5.

55　Reeve, *The Progress of Romance* (1785), I, 111.

56　Henry Mackenzie, *The Lounger*, 20 (18 June 1785); Thomas Monroe, *Olla Podrida*, 15 (23 June1787): in Williams, ed., *Novel and Romance*, 330, 350. Cf. Davenant's proposal to revive 'heroick representations,' above, n. 6. On the evidence of these passages, contemporaries simultaneously recovered the Aristotelian doctrine of *catharsis* and attained the Brechtian insight that *catharsis* militates against, by substituting for, moral behaviour.

57　William Enfield, *The Monthly Review*, ser. 2, 15 (Nov. 1794), in Williams, ed., *Novel and Romance*, 393.

58　Collins, 'An Ode on the Popular Superstitions of the Highlands of Scotland, Considered as the Subject of Poetry,' ll. 18–21, 32–5, 172–3, 185–91, in Roger Lonsdale, ed., *The Poems of Thomas Gray, William Collins, and Oliver Goldsmith* (London, 1976), 503–16.

59　Schiller's distinction between the 'childish' and the 'childlike' elements of the naive parallels my argument concerning the ambivalence with which Enlightenment thought 'discovered' tradition: see Friedrich Schiller, 'Naïve and Sentimental Poetry,' in Julius A. Elias, trans. and ed., *Naïve and Sentimental Poetry and On the Sublime* (New York, 1966), 87–90.

Chapter Seven

The Traditions of Liberalism

DANIEL T. RODGERS

'There are always two parties,' Ralph Waldo Emerson wrote in an aphoristic mood in the 1860s: 'the party of the Past and the party of the Future; the Establishment and the Movement.'[1] By those lights, nineteenth-century liberalism was the party of the future. It was the party of emancipation from the iron cage of predetermined rank and status, from the overbearing claims of states and monarchs, from the relics of social custom, from the dead hand of the past itself. Liberalism was an ideological movement couched in the present and future tense, whose pride was to have swept away 'traditional' society and given humankind modernity. All this it claimed in the name of values that were in themselves timeless and universal, unshackled from context and custom. On the face of it, it would be hard to imagine a more unlikely focal point for an inquiry into the relationship between ideology, social practice, and tradition.

And yet despite the formidable energy devoted to its study, nineteenth-century liberalism remains a phenomenon full of vexatious questions. In the Anglo-American world, liberalism is counted as one of the century's prime ideological movers, a powerful mobilizer of institutions and opinions. Yet inquiries into its content return over and again to a handful of classic texts, whose historical relationship to the popular social movement they are said to have empowered is rarely subject to close examination. From John Locke's writings in the seventeenth century to John Rawls's in the twentieth, textbook liberalism marches with giant's strides across eras and lifetimes. But the mechanisms by which liberal ideology reproduced and perpetuated itself, by which its distinctive imaginative construction of experience was transmitted across the entropic effects of time from one generation to another, are barely acknowledged to form a serious point of inquiry.

In contemporary scholarship, in consequence, nineteenth-century liberalism lives a strangely disembodied life. It possesses texts but not schoolrooms, extraordinary historical force with barely any corporeal historical presence. In Britain after 1868, William Gladstone's Liberal Party gave liberalism's partisans a political rallying point, a social identity, and a set of defining issues. In the United States, by contrast, liberalism's axioms are said to have simply swept through the century's social and ideational air. Liberalism in America passes as a historical anomaly: an ideology without institutional substance, a creed without a church. In this manner liberalism's universalistic individualism, its evasion of time and context, tacitly work their way into the study of liberalism itself.

But no strong ideational system exists in an institutional vacuum. That system's ways of understanding experience must be learned and disseminated. Its axioms must not only be popularized in the printed or spoken word. They must be crystallized in actions repeated so often as to constitute the tacit relationship of things. What historians call gender systems, for example, are sustained not by ideas of masculinity and femininity in themselves, not by rereadings of Sigmund Freud or Carol Gilligan. They are sustained in childrearing expectations, courtship rituals, and marriage roles – practices so intensely ideational, so overflowing with ideas and assumptions, that the common-sense line between intellect and behaviour disappears altogether. Ideas of citizenship are learned in a similar way: through the ritual exercise of standing in line at a voting booth, or by serving in or not serving in the armed forces, by declaring one's rights, or by talking back to the talking political heads on television.

Ideologies need arenas of practice in which their core assumptions are acted and reenacted, learned and internalized. They need places and occasions for the repeating of their key verities, their already scripted slogans, their creeds and catechisms. They need rituals and institutions. They need all this not only for the purposes of social mobilization. They need this, no less critically, to reproduce themselves over time, so that the young not only know how to speak the symbolic language of their parents but they actually see the world of experience in their elders' way.

This is tradition's work. Transmission through time, Edward Shils reminds us, is tradition's defining function. 'The decisive criterion' of tradition, he writes, is that its content, 'having been created through human actions, through thought and imagination ... is handed down from one generation to the next.'[2] Infusing the past into the present, traditions ensure that social practices persist and ideational systems endure – that the mass will be said week in and week out in the same way, that the family stories will be told as we remember them, or, at least, appear so. No powerful ideational system can endure without traditions – not even those, like liberalism, that celebrate their emancipation from the past and their victory over time.

What follows, then, is a historical inquiry into an apparent oxymoron: the traditions of liberalism. Mediating between the work of intellectual and social historians, its aim is a reassessment of the historical force of nineteenth-century liberalism by inquiring into the social practices that embodied and sustained it, vested its abstractions with powerful experiential force, and transmitted its modal experiences across generations. Its aim is explorative and synthetic, not definitive. Our destination is not liberalism's timeless essence; it is to ask, rather, through what historically grounded practices and traditions did nineteenth-century Americans learn to think in terms distinctive to liberalism, to experience the world in recognizably liberal terms?

Classical liberalism has had many definitions, but as a first approximation it is fair to say that it entailed a mental revolution along three different but complementary axes: of society, time, and self.[3] The first of these, sometimes called 'sociological individualism,' took the many forms of human solidarity and reconfigured them in the mind as complicated aggregations of individuals. Family, kin group, nation, tribe, community, class, church, and sect: all these mattered to the liberal philosophers. But within the liberal frame, none of them could legitimately claim primordial status vis-à-vis the human self, or overriding interests of their own, or authority that could legitimately transcend the welfare of the individuals who constituted them. 'The public happiness is ... the aggregate of the happiness of individuals,' Daniel Webster put the commonplace assertion. 'Society is a joint-stock company,' Emerson put the point more radically. Liberalism denaturalized and desacralized society. However inescapable or advantageous social institutions might be, they were never as real in the liberal world-view as the individual self.[4]

With the same stroke with which the publicists of classical liberalism desacralized society, they also desacralized time. Liberalism celebrated human emancipation from entrenched institutions and ancient statuses – from tradition, custom, even memory itself. It was characteristic of those who wrote within classical liberalism's circle of assumptions that they could leap imaginatively forward to a progressive future (as conservatives temperamentally could not); they could leap back, like Locke, to the beginnings of time; but wherever they sprang, they found the essentials the same. The truths of liberalism were timeless and self-evident; once human beings grasped them, there was no going back, no need to undergird them with the customs and rituals that lesser, frailer truths relied on. As for liberalism's practice, it was always under improvement. Governments, society, even the merit-accumulating self were deliberate constructions that functioned best when their undertaking was most deliberate.

Finally, liberalism reordered the needs of the human self so that liberty and autonomy came out on top. The publicists of classical liberalism were too close to older traditions of mind to imagine that liberty was all that humans needed, that they could get along without love, or faith, or bonds of affection, or even obedience – all that messy, emotion-laden, intersubjective stuff that human beings construct vis-à-vis others. Still, the autonomously acting self came first in the liberal imagination: the self surrounded by a clear circle of rights and immunities, as John Stuart Mill put it: the self broken free from dependency, from the prying gaze and preemptory commands and sweaty emotional demands of others, pursuing, without harm to others, its own happiness and its own interests.

The liberal self was, in this sense, self-interested; it possessed a kind of property right in itself. Liberalism was never simply another name for self-aggrandizement or property consciousness, both of which long antedated the intellectual construction of liberalism and which had no shortage of other ideological props and legitimations. What liberalism provided, instead, was a distinctively benign justification of self-interested behaviour through the 'natural' adjustments of a self-balancing system of exchange. Classical liberalism, as Sheldon Wolin pointed out acutely long ago, was not a creed for hermits.[5] When liberal publicists imagined social relations, however, their imaginations were drawn to those that seemed to impinge least on the individual actors, that left them least marked and least transformed by that relationship. That is why contract loomed so large in liberal thinking as the domain of voluntary freedom. That is why contractual metaphors played so vital a part in liberal political theory, why classical liberals could entertain the idea that even society itself might have been created by a variant of the same transaction by which two farmers might bargain over the price of a horse or a hogshead of tobacco.

Not all of those who wrote within the tradition of classical liberalism imagined that free, rational action of this sort came naturally to human beings. Their celebration of a modern age of liberty was laced with fears that individuals might mistake their interests, misperceive their true advantages, and abuse their freedom. Nineteenth-century liberals poured a great deal of energy into educational projects aimed at constructing human characters capable of standing the pace of the good society they envisioned. Discipline was central to the liberal self.[6] And yet compared with those around them, compared with those who talked of innate human sinfulness, or of grades of human beings possessed of such radically different capacities that they deserved radically different rights and freedoms, classical liberals were markedly optimistic about human capacities. Less reverent than others with regard to custom, they were more tolerant than others of competition and dissension – whether in the marketplace, in partisan political division and parliamentary debate, in the clash of courtroom lawyers, or in the heresies of religious pluralism and dissent. The liberal society did not make individuals uniform. It strove toward a different goal: to regularize individual action and disagreement within systems of fair rules and procedures.

Liberalism, in brief, is our shorthand term for the enterprise by which the essentially and inescapably situated character of human beings in history, in institutions, and in thick relationships to each other was challenged by a radically different vision of a world of free, self-acting, contract-making, difference-tolerating, rights-possessing individuals.

Whether the classical liberal project strikes one as premised on a thin and meagre account of human experience or, conversely, on a crystallization of humankind's very essence, it would be difficult to exaggerate the fundamental role it plays in contemporary writing in politics and history. Among English-language political theorists no other problem has been more central in the last thirty years than that of probing the possibilities that lie within liberalism's frame. The cascade, the veritable Niagara, of debates set off by John Rawls's revival of social contract theory in 1971 still goes on. Neoliberal theorists push hard at the edges of the formulations of Locke, Mill, or Rawls to argue that there is far more to liberalism's understanding of the good society than simply a regime of individually held rights and overall procedural fairness. Liberalism's critics counter that if we want societies of purposive and substantive justice we cannot fashion them of liberal principles alone.[7]

In this thrust and counterthrust of political theory, it is taken for granted that the principles of classical liberalism once saturated political culture in the United States. 'It has long been a truism,' Stephen Macedo writes, that 'the "basis of [American] national identity" is the liberal tradition ... the tradition of John Locke, John Stuart Mill, and John Rawls.' American history, Louis Hartz wrote in the book that still casts a powerful spell over the field, reflects 'a remarkable collusion between Locke and the New World.' To fathom the limits, the flexibilities, and the capacities of the liberalism of Locke, Adam Smith, and Mill is not an abstract exercise; among political theorists, it gets straight to the foundational values of contemporary America.[8]

Historians, more sensitive to the nuances of time (if not always to the nuances of ideas) express the point of liberal origins with much more qualification. No historians now believe, as Hartz did, that the tenets of classical liberalism came to British North America in the first emigrants' boats. Most, though not all, historians agree that even the American Revolution was not waged in the pure terms of classical liberalism that seemed plain to Hartz and the historians of his generation. The patriots, it is now recognized, drew on all sorts of other traditions: on the language of dissenting Protestantism, on dreams of secular millennialism, and above all on that pervasive sense of imperilled liberty that historians now call revolutionary 'republicanism.' For most of the Revolution's publicists, liberty was not timeless but fragile, historically situated, contingent on the material circumstances of the people and, still more, on their ability to set their individual interests aside when the good of the whole demanded it. Public virtue, vigorously enough practised and widely enough disseminated, was the preserver of the republic. How all this mixed with the liberal assumptions of natural rights and social contract that are so familiar from the Declaration of Independence is a matter that historians are still struggling to sort out. But certainly the free-standing self, intent on the pursuit of its own interests, was a monster the Revolutionists distrusted.[9]

Yet if liberalism has all but disappeared from the first century and a half of American history, it is virtually impossible to write about the following two centuries without invoking its massive, transformative presence. The timing of the 'Great Transition' from republican to liberal culture varies considerably from interpreter to interpreter. T.H.

Breen and Timothy Hall write of the construction of a recognizably 'liberal self' in the mid-eighteenth century. In her Phelps lectures, Joyce Appleby put the transitional moment in the 1790s. Most historians now favour a turning point sometime between 1815 and 1840. By the former date, Gordon Wood writes, 'Americans had become, almost overnight, the most liberal, the most democratic, the most commercially minded, and the most modern people in the world.' The politics of virtue were supplanted by interest-group competition and individual ambition; distrust of the corrupting power of wealth and commerce gave way to an explosion of capitalist ambitions. Individualism was named and normalized. The routine competition of interests was legitimated in politics and party organization. New havens of domestic privacy were constructed. Contract and commerce now saturated the language and ideological productions of the age.[10]

All this, historians make clear, was deeply and vigorously contested, but the direction of change in these accounts is certain. The victors in these battles were 'the liberal commitments to possessive individualism, a competitive ethos, and economically self-interested politics,' Robert Shalhope concluded. 'A new conception of politics converged with a new appreciation of enterprise, and a new character ideal was created,' Appleby writes, as Americans 'became the self-conscious shapers of a liberal society.'[11] Not all historians use the term 'liberalism' to mark the emergent social pattern. But in their Weberian sense of 'transition' – not merely a shift in one or another key historical institution but a general social and cultural displacement that quickly reconstituted them all – and in their bundling together of the century's dominant traits, confident in the logical entailments between them, the historians' debt to the constructions of political theory is close and undisguised.

Now there are many ways in which these claims are true. But there is a great deal that is clearly wrong with this story as well. Most Americans in the early nineteenth century did not occupy a world of experience that can be conceivably characterized as liberal. Nor did most Americans in 1900, for that matter. Women, to start with, hardly had access at any time during the century to the kind of free-standing, contract-making, autonomous selfhood that liberalism entails. They were not altogether without rights and certainly not without selves. But the selves they fashioned were negotiated within constraints and contexts that were radically different from those of most men. As long as marriage was the expected lot and economic necessity for the vast majority of women, and as long as the structures of marriage allotted them a social part different from and subordinate to their husbands, they can hardly be said to have lived themselves, unmediatedly, within the world of liberal individualism. The selves women fictionalists and diary writers constructed were rarely the unitary, self-possessed selves of male liberal publicists; for most women to entertain for themselves the possibility of the freely contracting self, independent of relations, needs, and dependencies, was, as Elizabeth Cady Stanton demonstrated so eloquently, an act of rebellion.[12] The social transformations of the nineteenth century had a profound impact on women. Their very distance from the arenas of liberal action helped etch liberal privileges still more strongly on the mind. But none of this made women's world of experience itself liberal.

For that matter, most men did not live in a liberally constituted world of experience either. Slaves, dispossessed of the most basic rights of self-ownership, were clearly beyond liberalism's bounds. And so, in a no less important way, were the ante-bellum South's slave masters. Slavery injected into Southern life a template of social relationship utterly foreign to the contract ideal. Mastership was a hierarchical not a horizontal relationship, an institution of custom not of contract, a thick and emotion-laden relationship that left both parties scarred and changed, not a contingently contractual one that left the autonomy of the parties intact. However aggressively Southern slaveholding men might watch out for their interests in the market or in politics, however hard they worked during the crisis over slavery and section to develop a contractual understanding of nationhood, their world-view was at best liberal only in certain of its phases, and their everyday experience barely liberal at all.[13]

Even the formal abolition of slavery did not radically alter the distance of American Southerners, both black and white, from a world shaped on classical liberal principles. Fragile, second-class rights, on the one hand, and investment in a system of domination, on the other, gave the late nineteenth-century South a racial culture in which relationships were constituted not of contracts but of subordinations, patronages, coercions, nightmares, and terror.[14]

The list of exceptions continues. Liberalism fails as a description of the culture of the nineteenth century's emerging industrial, male working class, torn as labour historians have repeatedly shown between private dreams of success, rituals of masculine authority, and powerful visions of class and craft solidarity.[15] For the Catholic immigrant working class – Irish, German, Polish, or Italian – liberalism fails almost entirely as a descriptor altogether.[16] Even now, as Herbert Gans has contended, the 'individualism' of contemporary working-class and lower-middle-class Americans differs sharply from the classical liberal individualism of the textbooks. The majority of wage-earning Americans value economic security more than economic competition; they value home ownership and family solidarity more than individual autonomy; about open, unrestrained competition between ideas and cultures they harbour profound uneasiness.[17]

All this is not to deny that liberal assumptions were an exceptionally powerful engine of social and political transformation in nineteenth-century America. The notion of sorting out those who stood inside the sphere of liberal experience from those who stood outside it is obviously too binary, and far too static, to do much more than raise an initial vein of doubt. Hegemonic ideas may dominate economic and social structures without saturating all the relationships constitutive of them. They may control without commanding general assent. They may frame and limit the conditions of everyday life without themselves being directly experienced. But the concept of a liberal transition claims more than this. It portrays a shift not only in power but in legitimacy: a deep-seated rearrangement of norms, expectations, and feelings. It portrays a people learning to think in new terms.

But how did nineteenth-century Americans (some of them, at any rate, some of the time) learn to think within the system of liberal assumptions? In what arenas of daily life and practice were its foundational ideas crystallized, imbued, reproduced, and reinforced (arenas of daily life, we must insist, not in daily life itself)? Even in small-scale societies the arenas of practice are always multiple. People act multiple parts, carrying both their selves and their sense of the scenery, as it were, from stage to stage. Thus in the space of a day a nineteenth-century American might be an independent farmer, the sovereign head of a family, and a sinner asking for restoration in grace. One might be a dutiful wife, an imperious mistress, a redeemed saint, and a woman of sentiment. Nineteenth-century Americans walked in and out of arenas in which liberalism's distinctly contractual, autonomous idea of self and society was set into custom and ritual, and other arenas that constituted selves and society on quite different lines.

These arenas of experience were not stable, of course, and they were not independent of each other. It was in the nature of things that clusters of idea-laden practice should slip over from one stage and setting to another. The truly momentous events in the social history of ideas occur when one arena of experience comes finally to stand as a synecdoche for all the others – so that all the world suddenly looks like a market, for example, or a family, or a state of war, or a valley of the shadow of death. But those moments are rare.

In looking for liberalism's traditions, we are not looking for the string of great books that political theorists knot together (with a confidence that Quentin Skinner exploded long ago) as the 'liberal tradition.'[18] We are not looking for the birth of the liberal era, nor for the emergence of a new social character responsive to the incentives that the liberal view of self and society offered. We are looking, more modestly, for the customs and practices that crystallized liberal assumptions into everyday experience.

The axes along which these questions might be pursued are too numerous to exhaust here. But let us try four in which the historical literature is particularly well developed: the customs of the economy, law and litigation, religion, and family life.

Trade, it scarcely needs to be emphasized, occupied a centrally important place in liberal ideology. Classical liberalism not only idealized and normalized the early modern marketplace, that site of fearful liminality, as Jean-Christophe Agnew put it.[19] Liberalism put its idealized conception of market exchange at the very centre of the social imagination. Through the magic of prices and exchange, private, self-regarding actions were transformed into an engine of social progress. Even the rights of free expression were eventually reformulated as a kind of market right – the right to put up for trade what stock of notions one might have in a great Hyde Park of competing idea vendors.

But how did men and women actually trade in the nineteenth century? What customs of commerce did they sustain? The great historiographical discovery here has been the unearthing of two profound, interrelated events: the 'consumer revolution' of the late eighteenth century and the 'market revolution' of the nineteenth. The first of these refers to the dramatic rise in British-exported goods into the American colonies. This new flood of goods worked a marked change in material circumstances; it also meant that the purchasing of goods began for the first time to be not an occasional and special activity but a central activity, perhaps even self-defining one.[20] What historians call the market revolution runs deeper still, grounded not in consumption but in labour and production. Over the course of the early nineteenth century, as historians have now shown in detail, rural households moved more and more deeply into the production of market goods; they sold more of the things they raised and more of their labour time, began to reorient more of what they produced around a cash crop, began, in short, to live more and more of their lives within a world of price and commerce.[21] In the towns, servant and apprenticeship systems gave way to wage-labour markets. Women developed discrete networks of exchange.[22] Even slaves – commodities themselves – found a small but vital place as market actors, trading garden produce in the towns, sometimes even contracting sales with their owners.[23] Along every dimension, experience in trade underwent a dramatic increase in the first half of the nineteenth century.

But trading is far older than liberalism's particular rendering of it, and it carries a very wide range of potentially invested meanings. Exchange may be priced or unpriced; routine or fraught with resentments and distrust; gift-based or profit-driven; organized horizontally as a momentary and convenient transaction between autonomous actors or stacked in tight, vertical structures of patronage and prestige. In the late eighteenth century, as T.H. Breen has shown, Southern tobacco planters traded as much on their honour as on the condition of their hogsheads, and they could not understand, in their anguished pleadings to their creditors, why the value of the one should not outweigh the defects of the other.[24] In the early nineteenth-century countryside men and women sold goods and labour to each other continually, but these neighbourhood transactions rarely involved exchanges of cash; nor were they, indeed, quite exchanges as liberal theory imagines them. 'Book' transactions, historians call them, after the ledger books in which they were noted down, each sale and purchase carefully accompanied by a price but a price that was half 'notional' because such accounts were almost never formally balanced out but maintained, rather, as a running expression of a relationship of reciprocal obligation that was as much personal as commercial. In time, these book transactions gave way to exchange transactions much more closely matched to the liberal-contractual model of the market: written contracts of loan or sale, specifying interest and conditions, much more straightforwardly enforceable in the courts. In Connecticut, most court actions for debt involved contracts of one sort or another by the middle of the eighteenth century. In western Massachusetts, book transactions remained the primary mode of local exchange into the 1830s.[25]

The record of legal action for debt, however, captures only a fraction of the story. In day-to-day economic action, liberal and 'preliberal' modes of exchange persisted in competing and intermingled forms all through the nineteenth century. Early analytical attempts to distinguish sharply between stages of rural economic organization – between subsistence-first and market agriculture, between household and commercial modes of production, between production of use values and production of money values – have given way to an understanding of rural households as enmeshed, by the very necessities of the rural economy, in all of these at once.[26] Into the twentieth century, informal systems of local exchange persisted in the northern countryside along with highly organized staple crop production and wage-labor employment.[27] In the post–Civil War South, market production of cotton went hand in hand with systems of tenancy heavily overlaid with custom, patriarchy, and racial subordination.

Like their rural counterparts, nineteenth-century urban Americans lived in an economic world that was deeply commodified and yet intractably personalized. Even in 1900, only a fraction of wage-earning jobs were covered by formal labour contracts, and even those were fraught with tension.[28] Working-class Americans got their jobs through connections of kin and neighbour; they paid over a portion of their wages to their husbands or fathers or wives, all according to customs that lay far beyond the individuals themselves; they dickered over their book debts at the butcher and grocery store in a transaction that was anything but formal and impersonal. Even for men of the emerging commercial bourgeoisie, constructors of the new regime of contract, market relations remained freighted with nightmares of failure, affairs of honour, and tests of masculinity.[29]

Within these complex, personalized patterns of exchange it is possible, nonetheless, to see the emergence of forms of contract making that much more closely mirrored the imagined world of liberal, contractual exchange: precise and impersonal, undertaken by parties equal and independent enough in the exchange for both to imagine advantage from it. As the markets expanded, how many Americans participated regularly in this sort of exchange, reenacting day by day the contractual individualism that both constituted liberal ideology and was an essential engine in its perpetuation? How wide an arena did it form in their lives? How did this arena of action, once confined to a few, slowly become a public stage, a set of parts that enough others began to act that its particular behaviours would seem to characterize all exchange – indeed, to characterize society itself?

The history of exchange in this regard is still in its infancy. But clearly the 'market' acted as a school in ideology and customs, not simply as an arena for the expression of desires and interests already formed elsewhere. The reductive equation of liberalism with the bourgeoisie or 'the philosophy of a business civilization' (as Harold Laski put it in 1936) was never more than a crude approximation.[30] A more qualified formulation, however, may hold the deeper kernel of truth: as the mechanisms of nineteenth-century exchange slowly became more formal and impersonal, shedding some of the extra cultural freight they had carried, the market became a site within an illiberal world of experience where some of liberalism's key abstractions were given social text, accustomed actions, and potential experiential credence – where one of liberalism's constituent traditions was formed.

A second formative arena for the traditions of liberalism lay in the courts of law. Nineteenth-century Americans went to the courts far less often than to market, but it was often enough to leave a deep impress on their polity. In the lawyer-dominated American legislatures, experience at law formed the primary training for the arts of politics and governance. Like the market, moreover, the courts of law occupy a key place in a liberally imagined society. Liberal justice does not descend from on high through the commandments of God, the wisdom of kings, or the reason of enlightened bureaucrats; neither is it latent in the very texture of things, as natural law philosophers imagine it. Liberal justice emerges, like a fair price, from collisions of interests, the vigorous clash of argument and evidence, the strivings of competing rights and selves. If we are to ask where nineteenth-century Americans learned to see the world in terms of autonomous selves, meeting in an arena of neutral rules, alchemizing competing private interests into collective justice, the rituals of action at law form a second clear candidate.

Readiness to engage in legal contest is not in itself the meaningful factor. Seventeenth-century New England Puritans took each other to court with an astonishing frequency; in colonial Virginia, the personalized and elaborately coded rituals of court day were pivotal social events. Even in Quaker Pennsylvania and West Jersey, almost half the adult males who possessed enough status to be tapped as jurors or witnesses in the thirty-year period 1680–1710 had been embroiled in at least one legal action themselves during the period.[31] But none of these were remotely liberal societies with competition, contract, and rights as their core organizing principles. The defining mark of a liberal legal culture is not quarrelsomeness; nor is it quickness to translate the everyday tangle of private disputes into the language and practice of the law. The defining mark of a liberal legal culture lies in its expectations about how those disputes will be played out in the law's arena: argued afresh by openly competing, individual parties, in a language of freely acting wills, neutral rules, and tangibly possessable rights.

It was in the direction of these liberal expectations, as a generation of legal historians have now made clear, that the transformation of nineteenth-century legal culture indeed moved. The elaborate pleading rules of the eighteenth-century common law, which privileged not the lawyers' or lay plaintiffs' abilities to argue a case but their ability to fit it into an extremely complicated and arcane sorting box of legal categories – a 'fumbling and raking amidst the rubbish of writs, indictments, pleas, ejectments, enfiefed, illatebration and one thousand other *lignum vitae* words which have neither harmony nor meaning,' as John Adams complained in 1756 – were radically simplified in the early nineteenth century. The personalized rituals of debt and honour played out in colonial Virginia's courthouses were increasingly brought to rule. Juries ceased to behave as republican organs of the local will and moral justice. As their competence on matters of law was trimmed back by judicial instruction and published legal precedent, they began to behave more often, instead, as detached, delocalized, neutral arbiters of logic and evidence. Into this transformed context moved new sorts of professional legal pleaders – their skills of debate and manoeuvre, extemporized principles and extemporaneous oratory, all let out for hire and sharpened in day-to-day courtroom contest.[32] The lawyer folk-heroes made in this system, like Daniel Webster in the nineteenth century or Clarence Darrow in the twentieth, became actors in a new, popular theatre of liberal experience, as accessible as the nearest courthouse.

The revolution in courtroom practice was joined by an equally wide-ranging transformation in legal doctrine and categories. Property was edged out of the law's centre in favour of more mobile constructions of contract. The law's new emphases fell on will and action rather than place and permanence, on economically dynamic uses of property rather than static ones, on 'intention rather than possession' (as John Orth sums up this literature), on 'voluntarism rather than vestedness.' Accelerated ideologically by the legal destruction of slavery and materially by the newly mobile forms of capital, the result was to intrude liberal contractualism into the rhetorical and doctrinal heart of the law.

By the last third of the nineteenth century, Robert Gordon argues, legal thought and practice not only had become saturated with the tenets of the new 'liberal legal science' but had turned into a powerful engine for the ideological reproduction of liberalism itself. Purging the law of its older claims to equity or virtue, judges and law writers recast the law as a set of formal rights, theoretically equitable contracts, and sharply etched domains of autonomous action – 'combat zones of free conduct' Gordon calls them – in which domination was not adjudicated or legitimized but, rather, made to seem altogether to disappear.[33]

Like the transformations in economic culture, the transformation in legal culture in the nineteenth century was never complete. The leaders of the bar may have reconstructed the law in liberal terms, but the lawyers' new norms of amoralized, adversarial practice rarely were publicly defended. In the middle of the nineteenth century, Lord Brougham's suggestion that a lawyer forget everything else upon entering a courtroom except his client's interest was roundly condemned in the United States as perjuring the law's true dignity and promoting mere argument for hire. Fifty years later, the giants of the bar were still insisting to the world at large on the timeless principles intrinsic to the law in itself. In the law schools, the old lecture system of education was on the eve of serious challenge from the case method of legal instruction. Training in 'legal thinking,' it would be called: an education in legal process rather than the law lecturers' bootless search for the foundations of the law itself. To the very end of the century, however, the case method's inventors thought themselves in modern, scientific search of principles of precisely that sort.[34]

Where the culture of professional lawyers was torn between its publicly professed structural-idealist understandings of the law and its privately acknowledged liberal-procedural ones, the general population never succeeded in keeping the terms of liberal justice distinct from the disputations of everyday life. The repertoire of extra-legal actions – brawling, feuding, bickering, slandering, mobbing, lynching – was immense in nineteenth-century America. Even now the core conversation in lawyers' offices, as legal anthropologists have shown, entails sorting out the narrowly defined rights and procedural claims that the law will actually admit from the emotion-laden and philosophically complicated messiness that brings clients to resort to the law to begin with – to make proper liberal subjects, that is to say, out of ordinary litigants.[35]

Exactly how the transformation of the law impinged on everyday consciousness and experience in nineteenth-century America, in short, is far from clear. But at some level adeptness at the law's new forms of action must surely have become not only practical but ideological knowledge. The courts never overtly claimed to mirror the world at large; their wigs and robes, their formalities and arcane linguistic remnants were all designed to make clear the courts' distinctive, theatrical nature. But it was theatre of a compelling sort, its boundaries porous, easy to conflate with society itself. As long as we are careful not to foreshorten the process by which the rituals of liberal justice were constructed out of much older scripts and materials, not to anticipate the legal profession's own acknowledgment of what it had wrought, not to mistake the sharply defined liberal legal science of the late nineteenth century for the much broader, free-wheeling rights consciousness of the late twentieth century, we are safe in looking to the new habits of legal action as a second, key strand in liberalism's traditions.

From courts and markets, nineteenth-century Americans moved through other, equally central, arenas of experience, however, in which liberalism's distinctive view of the world was not only much more weakly felt but sharply contradicted. Over time, day-to-day experiences at law and in commercial exchange must have formed a tense, imperfect, but increasingly effective representation of liberal ideology. But that was hardly the case in two other key arenas of social thought and practice: the church and the family.

The great nineteenth-century age of markets was also the great American age of Protestantism. Paved from beginning to end with souls stricken by conversion, it was the century in which evangelical revivalism became a permanent fixture of American life. This eruption of religious experience, played out in individual hearts and consciences, where conversions had been played out in the English-speaking world since the sixteenth century, has too often been bundled together with the century's other manifestations of 'individualism.' The nineteenth-century Protestant revival, one of its best recent interpreters writes, 'reflected and accelerated forces that were shaping an open society of free individualism: in its marketing of faith through innovative mass communications, in its radical and competitive pluralism, and in its focus on conversion and individual choice – the elevation of volitional conscience.' In structure and message, the revivals' most successful product, Methodism, 'embodied a liberal conception of reality.'[36]

Between evangelical and liberal individualism, however, the rift was much sharper than such a formulation would make it appear. Evangelical Protestants played a transformative role in breaking down the monopolies of faith on which so much of the cultural authority of the colonial and early nineteenth-century elites had rested. The modern world of competitive religious pluralism was, almost single-handedly, their construction.[37] But the liberal's ease with competitive pluralism was not theirs. The issues that brought the evangelical churches into politics – temperance, Sabbatarianism, sexual purity, slavery – turned, as Lewis Perry, Richard Carwardine, and others have shown, as much on obedience as on freedom. Their imagined Christian America did not march to the beat of a thousand different drummers, but in voluntary, consensual harmony to the will of God.[38] Choice and chosenness saturated the evangelical world. But it would radically mistake the political imagination of nineteenth-century evangelical Protestants to suppose that, in a world as starkly divided between sin and righteousness as theirs, these choices, even in the formally Arminian denominations, were, in the liberal meaning of the term, free.

From within the circles of community and self, the distinctions between Protestant and liberal individualism were more striking still. Nineteenth-century evangelical communities were knit not by the impersonal ties of contract but by bonds of discipline and affection. Seeking to bring men and women out from their slumbering churches, evangelical preachers pleaded with the unconverted to 'dare to think, and speak, and act for yourselves'; they kept nineteenth-century Protestantism in continual centrifugal motion. But Protestant self-emancipation could not be unlinked from intense forms of voluntary self-suppression. Baptists, Methodists, and Mormons made a name for themselves in their disciplinary strictness; even nineteenth-century Quakers, among the most 'liberal' of the Protestant offshoots, put the marriage choices of their children up for adjudication by their Monthly Meetings, and lost thousands of members by the strictness of their decisions. Children's wills were deliberately 'broken' at an early age in evangelical families, long after the practice had faded elsewhere. (The Baptist moral philosopher and free trade economist Francis Wayland was still giving instruction in how to accomplish it in 1831.) Adult converts were enveloped in love feasts of collective religious expression and washed over by pieties that were often profoundly at odds with marketplace truisms. And all this was because in Protestant circles the 'self' was, at every level, so acutely problematic. Evangelical selves

were saved one by one, but only – in the rhetoric of evangelical conversion – through the 'death' of self-will and selfishness, indeed through
the death of the very self.[39]

Evangelical individuation, in short, worked in sharply different
terms than the competing, contracting, rights-bearing, immunity-
surrounded selves of the liberal imagination. That is not to suggest that
the customs of the one did not invade the other; that the churches did
not, over time, cede territory to the customs of the market or the law
(refraining, more and more often, from criticizing the economic actions
of their members, for example, or from trying to interpose their own
mechanisms of dispute mediation in place of the law); or that there did
not arise a wide variety of translation mechanisms to help ease the
strains of emotional and ideological inconsistency between arenas of
daily practice. The range of religious associations in nineteenth-
century America was very large. From the small body of religious
liberals associated with New England Unitarianism to the huge camps
of Methodists and Baptists, to Catholics (with their own, quite differently pitched quarrel with liberal individualism) no easy generaliza-
tion about nineteenth-century religious experience will stretch. But for
the vast majority of nineteenth-century Americans, it seems evident,
the world of faith neither clearly reflected nor taught the outlines of a
liberally constructed universe. That left the burdens of liberalism's
ideological construction all the heavier elsewhere.

If the historians of nineteenth-century American religion have sometimes been tempted into overdetermined readings of the 'great transition,' historians of nineteenth-century family life have too often rushed
to embrace them. In a desire to yoke the history of the family to
material forces of the age, there has been a tendency to simplify and
foreshorten. 'The emergence of the freely contracting, autonomous
individual as the ideal actor ... permeated all domestic relations,'
Michael Grossberg wrote in the standard 1980s history of nineteenth-
century American family law. Other historians write of the family reor-
ganized on a 'voluntaristic, equalitarian' basis; of the 'evolution of the
contractual family'; of 'the egalitarian, fluid, privatized, calculating
style emerging in the homes of the northern well-to-do.' Locke replaces
Filmer; the family that steps out of patriarchy's broken shell is the
modern, liberal one, reconstructed to mirror the individualizing,
rights-holding, contractual, ideational forces around it.[40]

The American revolution against patriarchal authority, as Jay
Fliegelman calls it, did, indeed, cut a vivid swath through political and

domestic life, as the rich and detailed work of historians of gender and the family has made clear. Late eighteenth-century diaries show a dramatic rise in child-centred affections. Husbands' claims to stand in relation to their wives and children as dictators of their domestic kingdoms came under attack as an abuse of power. Parents' manuals began to appear in which the old, will-breaking regimes of Protestant child-rearing were replaced by more tenderly and rationalistically constructed systems of family governance. In the new discourse of the family, paternal authority and filial obedience gave way to an emphasis on shared affections, reciprocal sympathies, and mutual comforts.[41]

In several important regards the material props of family life bent to the same individuating tendencies. By the early nineteenth century, New England male family heads had begun to leave their property to their children in simple, equal proportions, rather than the complex arrays of bequests and obligations that had been common before – though this was in part a function of the shift from land to commercial wealth. Married women slowly won a degree of control over property they might bring into marriage and, more slowly still, over property they might earn there. Urban middle-class families pioneered in the invention of new forms of domestic privacy, constructing more individuated spaces within the household and clearing out more and more of its commercial productive enterprises – all, it is said, to give 'market-ravaged men' a haven from which to venture, restored and reinvigorated, out into the competitive, calculating markets of liberal capitalism.[42]

But for all its strengths, this is a partial view of the transformation of the nineteenth-century family. In the world of day-to-day experience, patriarchy was never so quickly defeated. There is little evidence that the word of the family advice writers greatly diminished the experience of corporal punishment in most children's lives in the nineteenth century or eliminated those moments of angry confrontation between fathers and sons that marked a young man's passage to adulthood. The married women's property acts of the mid-nineteenth century made barely a dent in the modal forms of family economic organization. In the countryside, as fathers found themselves less and less able to set up their adult children on nearby land, their ability to manage family property across the generations decayed. But in other respects the 'household' mode of production, the concentrated deployment of the family's economic resources as a single unit under the father's management, continued unchanged by farm households' deeper and deeper immersion in market production. In working-class families, the earnings of individual family members and decisions about their labour belonged, by the same token, to the household. From the extra portions of meat on fathers' plates to the universally gendered wage differentials at work, patriarchy was not only sustained in nineteenth-century America but continuously reproduced.[43]

The point of change, as historians have long recognized, was in the families of the middle class. But here, as in the churches, liberal individuation was only one of the post-patriarchal family's possible forms – and for the nineteenth century the least common. Whatever signs there were of the development of a middle-class domestic egalitarianism in the years immediately following the Revolution, those tendencies were not sustained.[44] The new-model families of the nineteenth century were to be held together not by mutual rights but by manners and sentiments, not by interests but by the veiling of interests, not by egalitarian premises but by sharply divided gender differentiations that made the terms of liberal selfhood (self-possession, autonomy, enforceable rights) all but inaccessible to women. The affectionate family individuated; children were seen more strongly than before as fundamentally different from adults, the rearing of sons as fundamentally different from the rearing of daughters, and women as radically different from men. The affectionate family devolved many of the powers formerly monopolized by men; legal child custody decisions, for example, now began to balance off men's claims of patriarchal primacy with women's special maternal sentiments and abilities.[45] But for the women whose 'sphere' the family was now said to be, almost nothing in this reconstructed domestic experience ratified the premises of liberal individualism.

To the extent that Filmer was dethroned, it was not by Locke's rational contractualism but by the sentimentality of Harriet Beecher Stowe. Most telling was the obvious: women's marginality to the liberal world of contract. At marriage, young men and women in the nineteenth century chose their partners with an increasingly free hand. But unlike other contracts, the marriage 'contract' was voluntary only on entrance, not on exit. Once entered into, marriage was an obligation that could be broken only with great difficulty, freighted for both men and women with custom, feelings, inequalities, and obligations. Early in the century, the courts had allowed women who had been deceived by false promises of marriage to bring suit for the damages of their broken marriage contract. By the end of the century, the practice had all but fallen away – to the satisfaction of the law review commentators who heralded the recognition that marriage was too sacred and its feelings too tender to be reduced to the barbaric materialism of a mere contract.[46]

The gendered inequalities and incommensurabilities within the new-model, affectionate family did not bar women from resources of the self. Many of these were constructed in conscious distance from liberal selfhood, in interiorities of sentiment and identity that, being more elusive than the selves of men, might better resist their possession. On these premises, a broad, distinctive, women-generated political theory had begun to emerge by the middle of the nineteenth century, pitched in terms of duties and bonds of feeling rather than (male) rights and autonomies.[47]

No matter how hard they tried to keep the spheres of gendered action distinct, middle-class families were never able to hold the claims of liberalism, even symbolically, at bay. Back and forth across the thresholds of these complex and tension-filled households, men moved as transient actors. By the middle of the nineteenth century, fiction writers were already offering boys fantasies of escape from the family claim (a possibility nineteenth-century fiction writers never offered girls) as the new mark of masculinity. But in real life the experience of middle-class men seems rather less one of escape than of continuous disjunctures in rules and arenas, practices and gendered spaces, personas and presumptions, whose invigorating effects on nineteenth-century capitalism have been assumed far more often than they have been demonstrated. For women, the everyday passage of sons and husbands across the family threshold kept the terms of liberal selfhood, whether disdained or envied, continuously visible and just out of reach.

Experience within the arena of nineteenth-century families was, in short, ideologically complex, fractured, and messy. Hardly immune to the material transformations of the age, domestic experience hardly mirrored them either. Full of sharp distinctions, its bright lines were not those of liberalism. As institutional sites for the production and reproduction of liberal ideology, nineteenth-century families seem at best confused and inefficient.

Returning to textbook liberalism in the wake of these probes into the social history of liberalism's traditions, one cannot but be struck by its peculiarly weightless obesity. It sprawls across the interpretive landscape without itself acquiring tangible form. These efforts to simultaneously cut nineteenth-century liberalism down to size and to give it foundation could obviously be carried further. The sites of everyday experience were multiple; markets, law courts, churches, and families do not begin to exhaust the list. Nineteenth-century schools were a conscious factory of ideational production. So was politics in an age marked simultaneously by sharply rising liberal, anti-statist sentiment, by aliberal, intensely collective modes of party mobilization, and by illiberal racism.

Print-media dissemination of liberalism's classic texts and core ideas forms another, obvious, but understudied site of inquiry. Texts created circles of texts and communities of readers, both informally constituted (as in the lists Thomas Jefferson circulated of books for young republicans) and formally constituted (as in the circulation of E.L. Godkin's late nineteenth-century *Nation*). The realm of letters was also, in its own way, a site for the formation of custom. The dream of the self-acting universe, more perfect even than Adam Smith's 'system of natural liberty,' was one of the nineteenth century's prime literary productions. 'The *voluntary principle*,' John L. O'Sullivan called it in 1837 in one of its most striking early formulations: 'the beautiful natural process of crystallization' through which the 'floating atoms will distribute and combine themselves' as God intended, without government's bungling hand.[48] Over the course of the century, this was to become less a controlling idea than a moving trope – a polemical and literary tradition – that passed through many hands and purposes in nineteenth-century America, from Jacksonian Democrats like O'Sullivan, labour radicals, and Transcendentalists in the early part of the century to the late nineteenth century's most strenuous labour antagonists.

What the concept of liberalism's traditions might help us do is take more seriously the links between scene and ideology, the site-specific nature of ideas, even of those ideas that masquerade as universal in time and space. Ideational life in nineteenth-century American life was formed in a complicated array of differentiated arenas. Its characteristic productions were scripts for place-specific social theatres. Keeping the arenas of social action distinct, the prescribed parts straight, the implied world-views clearly and firmly attached to their appropriate settings, was not simple work. Conflations of spheres and transgressions of roles were a constant of ideational life.

But thinking about liberalism in terms of its social texts and experienced traditions may offer a way past both the historically thin and excessively bookish character of the political theorists' concept of liberalism and the social historians' excessively dichotomous rendering of the great liberal transition. The one dissolves at the extreme into a complex acrostic puzzle of context-free texts; the other dissolves at the extreme into a Rip Van Winkle story in which everything changes in the wink of history's eye. We might more fruitfully come to think, rather, of differently constituted and differently timed transformations in different fields of experience. Some of these distinctions would in time erode, and the language of rights or market exchange bleed over into new terrains, but not until much later than conventional historical accounts have it. The world of contractual families, supermarket churches, unapologetically adversarial justice, and pervasive commodity exchange – which hovers so patently behind so many accounts of nineteenth-century liberalism – is the late twentieth century, not the nineteenth.

In tracing out those sites where liberalism's key abstractions were given experiential credence, we might, finally, rediscover the critical role in ideational life not only of the production but of the reproduction of ideas; the ongoing work of transmitting ideas across time and generations; the necessity of custom and ritual to ideology; in short, all that is imbedded in the concept of tradition. We might discover that even liberalism, by necessity, had traditions.

NOTES

1   Ralph Waldo Emerson, 'Historic Notes of Life and Letters in New England,' in Mark Van Doren, ed., *The Portable Emerson* (New York, 1946), 514.

2   Edward Shils, *Tradition* (Chicago, 1981), 12.

3   Classical liberalism is a distinctly different construct than what came to be called 'liberalism' in twentieth-century American politics. For two quite differently formulated treatments of the latter see: Gary Gerstle, 'The Protean Character of American Liberalism,' *American Historical Review*, 99 (October 1994): 1043–73, and Wilson Carey McWilliams, 'Ambiguities and Ironies: Conservatism and Liberalism in the American Political Tradition,' in W. Lawson Taitte, ed., *Moral Values in Liberalism and Conservatism* (Dallas, 1995).

4   Thus David Johnston, at pains to imagine more generous possibilities for liberal theory than a narrow, brittle libertarianism, still formulates liberalism's first axiom: 'Only individuals count.' David Johnston, *The Idea of a Lib-*

eral Theory: A Critique and Reconstruction (Princeton, 1994), 18. Webster is quoted in Gordon S. Wood, *The Radicalism of the American Revolution* (New York, 1992), 359; Emerson is quoted in Louis P. Masur, '"Age of the First Person Singular": The Vocabulary of the Self in New England, 1780–1850,' *Journal of American Studies*, 25 (August 1991): 207.

5 Sheldon S. Wolin, *Politics and Vision: Continuity and Innovation in Western Political Thought* (Boston, 1960), chap. 9.

6 Richard Bellamy, *Liberalism and Modern Society: An Historical Argument* (Cambridge, England, 1992), chap. 1; Stefan Collini, 'The Idea of "Character" in Victorian Political Thought,' *Transactions of the Royal Historical Society*, 35 (1985): 29–50.

7 John Rawls, *A Theory of Justice* (Cambridge, MA, 1971). Among the important contributions to the cascade: Bruce A. Ackerman, *Social Justice in the Liberal State* (New Haven, 1980); Alasdair C. MacIntyre, *After Virtue* (Notre Dame, 1980); Michael J. Sandel, *Liberalism and the Limits of Justice* (Cambridge, England, 1982); Michael Walzer, 'Liberalism and the Art of Separation,' *Political Theory*, 12 (August 1984): 315–30; Judith N. Sklar, 'The Liberalism of Fear,' in Nancy L Rosenblum, ed., *Liberalism and the Moral Life* (Cambridge, MA, 1989); William A. Galston, *Liberal Purposes: Goods, Virtues, and Diversity in the Liberal State* (Cambridge, England, 1991); Stephen Holmes, *Passions and Constraint: On the Theory of Liberal Democracy* (Chicago, 1995); Patrick Neal and David Paris, 'Liberalism and the Communitarian Critique: A Guide for the Perplexed,' *Canadian Journal of Political Science*, 23 (September 1990): 419–39.

8 Stephen Macedo, *Liberal Virtues: Citizenship, Virtue, and Community in Liberal Constitutionalism* (Oxford, 1990), 5–6, 4; Louis Hartz, *The Liberal Tradition in America* (New York, 1955), 17.

9 Daniel T. Rodgers, 'Republicanism: The Career of a Concept,' *Journal of American History*, 79 (June 1992): 11–38.

10 T.H. Breen and Timothy Hall, 'Structuring Provincial Imagination: The Rhetoric and Experience of Social Change in Eighteenth-Century New England,' *American Historical Review*, 103 (December 1998): 1411–38; Joyce Appleby, *Capitalism and a New Social Order: The Republican Vision of the 1790s* (New York, 1984); Wood, *Radicalism of the American Revolution*, 336. On the great 'transition' generally: John M. Murrin, 'Self-Interest Conquers Patriotism: Republicans, Liberals, and Indians Reshape the Nation,' in Jack P. Greene, ed., *The American Revolution: Its Character and Limits* (New York, 1987); Sean Wilentz, 'Society, Politics, and the Market Revolution, 1815–1848,' in Eric Foner, ed., *The New American History* (Philadelphia, 1990); Charles Sellers, *The Market Revolution: Jacksonian America,*

1815–1846 (New York, 1991); Melvyn Stokes and Stephen Conway, eds, *The Market Revolution in America: Social, Political, and Religious Expressions, 1800–1880* (Charlottesville, 1996); Paul A. Gilje, ed., *Wages of Independence: Capitalism in the Early American Republic* (Madison, WI, 1997). For especially subtle readings of the ideology of contract and commerce see: Amy Dru Stanley, *From Bondage to Contract: Wage Labor, Marriage, and the Market in the Age of Slave Emancipation* (Cambridge, England, 1998); Richard F. Teichgraeber III, '"A Yankee Diogenes": Thoreau and the Market,' in Thomas L. Haskell and Richard F. Teichgraeber III, eds, *The Culture of the Market: Historical Essays* (Cambridge, England, 1993); and Masur, 'Age of the First Person Singular.'

11 Robert E. Shalhope, 'Individualism in the Early Republic,' in Richard O. Curry and Lawrence B. Goodheart, eds, *American Chameleon: Individualism in Trans-National Context* (Kent, OH, 1991), 84; Joyce Appleby, *Inheriting the Revolution: The First Generation of Americans* (Cambridge, MA, 2000), 11.

12 Gillian Brown, *Domestic Individualism: Imagining Self in Nineteenth-Century America* (Berkeley, 1990); Catherine E. Kelly, *In the New England Fashion: Reshaping Women's Lives in the Nineteenth Century* (Ithaca, 1999). On Stanton: Elizabeth B. Clark, 'Matrimonial Bonds: Slavery and Divorce in Nineteenth-Century America,' *Law and History Review*, 8 (Spring 1990): 25–54.

13 Douglas R. Egerton, 'Markets without a Market Revolution: Southern Planters and Capitalism,' in Gilje, *Wages of Independence*; Elizabeth Fox-Genovese, *Within the Plantation Household: Black and White Women of the Old South* (Chapel Hill, 1988).

14 Grace Elizabeth Hale, *Making Whiteness: The Culture of Segregation in the South, 1890–1940* (New York, 1998).

15 Herbert G. Gutman, *Work, Culture, and Society in Industrializing America* (New York, 1976); Sean Wilentz, 'Against Exceptionalism: Class Consciousness and the American Labor Movement, 1790–1920,' *International Labor and Working Class History*, 26 (Fall 1984): 1–24.

16 Robert A. Orsi, *The Madonna of 115th Street: Faith and Community in Italian Harlem, 1880–1950* (New Haven, 1985); Robert A. Orsi, *Thank You, St Jude: Women's Devotion to the Patron Saint of Hopeless Causes* (New Haven, 1996).

17 Herbert J. Gans, *Middle-American Individualism: The Future of Liberal Democracy* (New York, 1988). Christopher Clark puts the contextual point succinctly: 'Individualism, inventiveness, mobility, freedom, and entrepreneurialism were not the conditions under which most nineteenth-century people lived.' Christopher Clark, 'The Consequences of the Market Revolution in the American North,' in Stokes and Conway, *Market Revolution*, 38.

18 Quentin Skinner, 'Meaning and Understanding in the History of Ideas,'
    History and Theory, 8 (1969): 3–53.
19 Jean-Christophe Agnew, *Worlds Apart: The Market and the Theater in Anglo-
    American Thought, 1550–1750* (Cambridge, England, 1986).
20 T.H. Breen, 'An Empire of Goods: The Anglicization of Colonial America,
    1690–1776,' *Journal of British Studies*, 25 (October 1986): 467–99; T.H. Breen,
    '"Baubles of Britain": The American and Consumer Revolutions of the
    Eighteenth Century,' *Past and Present*, 119 (May 1988): 73–104; John
    Brewer and Roy Porter, eds, *Consumption and the World of Goods* (New
    York, 1993).
21 Alan Kulikoff, 'Households and Markets: Toward a New Synthesis of
    American Agrarian History,' *William and Mary Quarterly*, 50 (April 1993):
    342–55; Christopher Clark, 'Economics and Culture: Opening Up the Rural
    History of the Early American Northeast,' *American Quarterly*, 43 (June
    1991): 279–301; Christopher Clark, *The Roots of Rural Capitalism: Western
    Massachusetts, 1780–1860* (Ithaca, 1990); Robert A. Gross, 'Culture and Cul-
    tivation: Agriculture and Society in Thoreau's Concord,' *Journal of American
    History*, 69 (June 1982): 42–61; Lacy K. Ford, Jr, *Origins of Southern Radical-
    ism: The South Carolina Upcountry, 1800–1860* (New York, 1988); Stephanie
    McCurry, *Masters of Small Worlds: Yeoman Households, Gender Relations, and
    the Political Culture of the Antebellum South Carolina Low Country* (New York,
    1995).
22 Laurel Thatcher Ulrich, 'Martha Ballard and Her Girls: Women's Work in
    Eighteenth-Century Maine,' in Stephen Innes, ed., *Work and Labor in Early
    America* (Chapel Hill, 1988); Jeanne Boydston, 'The Woman Who Wasn't
    There: Women's Market Labor and the Transition to Capitalism in the
    United States,' in Gilje, *Wages of Independence*; Nancy Grey Osterud, 'Gen-
    der and the Transition to Capitalism in Rural America,' *Agricultural History*,
    67 (Spring 1993): 14–29.
23 Dylan Penningroth, 'Slavery, Freedom, and Social Claims to Property
    among African Americans in Liberty County, Georgia, 1850–1880,' *Journal
    of American History*, 84 (September 1997): 405–35; Betty Wood, *Women's
    Work, Men's Work: The Informal Slave Economies of Lowcountry Georgia* (Ath-
    ens, GA, 1995); John Campbell, 'As "A Kind of Freeman"?: Slaves' Market-
    Related Activities in the South Carolina Upcountry, 1800–1860,' in Ira Berlin
    and Philip D. Morgan, eds, *The Slaves' Economy: Independent Production by
    Slaves in the Americas* (London, 1991); Harry L. Watson, 'Slavery and Devel-
    opment in a Dual Economy,' in Stokes and Conway, *Market Revolution*,
    40–54.
24 T.H. Breen, *Tobacco Culture: The Mentality of the Great Tidewater Planters on*

the Eve of Revolution (Princeton, 1985); more generally, John Davis, *Exchange* (Buckingham, England, 1992).

25 Bruce H. Mann, *Neighbors and Strangers: Law and Community in Early Connecticut* (Chapel Hill, 1987), chaps 1–2; Allan Kulikoff, *From British Peasants to Colonial American Farmers* (Chapel Hill, 2000), chap. 5; Thomas S. Wermuth, 'New York Farmers and the Market Revolution: Economic Behavior in the Mid-Hudson Valley, 1780–1830,' *Journal of Social History,* 32 (Fall 1998): 179–96; Clark, *Roots of Rural Capitalism.*

26 Bettye Hobbs Pruitt, 'Self Sufficiency and the Agricultural Economy of Eighteenth-Century Massachusetts,' *William and Mary Quarterly,* 41 (July 1984): 333–64; Stephen Innes, 'Fulfilling John Smith's Vision: Work and Labor in Early America,' in Innes, *Work and Labor in Early America;* Daniel Vickers, 'Competency and Competition: Economic Culture in Early America,' *William and Mary Quarterly,* 47 (January 1990): 3–29; Richard Lyman Bushman, 'Markets and Composite Farms in Early America,' *William and Mary Quarterly,* 55 (July 1998): 351–74. For the sharp, early formulations: Michael Merrill, 'Cash Is Good to Eat: Self-Sufficiency in the Rural Economy of the United States,' *Radical History Review,* 4 (Winter 1977): 42–71; James A. Henretta, 'Families and Farms: *Mentalité* in Pre-Industrial America' (1978), reprinted in his *The Origins of American Capitalism: Selected Essays* (Boston, 1991); Winifred Rothenberg, 'The Market and Massachusetts Farmers, 1750–1855,' *Journal of Economic History,* 41 (June 1981): 283–314; Winifred Rothenberg, 'Markets, Values, and Capitalism: A Discourse on Method,' *Journal of Economic History,* 44 (March 1984): 174–8.

27 Mary Neth, *Preserving the Family Farm: Women, Community, and the Foundations of Agribusiness in the Midwest, 1900–1940* (Baltimore, 1995), chaps 1–2.

28 Stanley, *From Bondage to Contract,* chap. 2; David Montgomery, *Citizen Worker: The Experience of Workers in the United States with Democracy and the Free Market during the Nineteenth Century* (Cambridge, England, 1993); Karen Orren, *Belated Feudalism: Labor, the Law, and Liberal Development in the United States* (Cambridge, England, 1991).

29 Toby L. Ditz, 'Shipwrecked; or, Masculinity Imperiled: Mercantile Representations of Failure and the Gendered Self in Eighteenth-Century Philadelphia,' *Journal of American History,* 81 (June 1994): 51–80.

30 Harold J. Laski, *The Rise of Liberalism: The Philosophy of a Business Civilization* (New York, 1936).

31 John M. Murrin, 'Review Essay,' *History and Theory,* 11 (1972): 250–1; Jonathan M. Chu, 'Nursing a Poisonous Tree: Litigation and Property Law in Seventeenth-Century Essex County, Massachusetts: The Case of Bishop's Farm,' *American Journal of Legal History,* 31 (July 1987): 221–52;

A.G. Roeber, 'Authority, Law, and Custom: The Rituals of Court Day in Tidewater Virginia, 1720 to 1750,' *William and Mary Quarterly,* 37 (January 1980): 29–52; Rhys Isaac, *The Transformation of Virginia, 1740–1790* (Chapel Hill, 1982), 88–94; William M. Offutt, Jr, *Of 'Good Laws' and 'Good Men': Law and Society in the Delaware Valley, 1680–1710* (Urbana, 1995), chap. 2.

32 Mann, *Neighbors and Strangers*; William E. Nelson, *Americanization of the Common Law: The Impact of Legal Change on Massachusetts Society, 1760–1830* (Cambridge, MA, 1975); John M. Murrin, 'The Legal Transformation: The Bench and Bar of Eighteenth-Century Massachusetts,' in Stanley N. Katz, ed., *Colonial America: Essays in Politics and Social Development* (Boston, 1974); A.G. Roeber, *Faithful Magistrates and Republican Lawyers: Creators of Virginia Legal Culture, 1680–1810* (Chapel Hill, 1981); Michael Grossberg, 'Institutionalizing Masculinity: The Law as a Masculine Profession,' in Mark C. Carnes and Clyde Griffen, eds, *Meanings for Manhood: Constructions of Masculinity in Victorian America* (Chicago, 1990). Adams is quoted in Murrin, 'Legal Transformation,' 433.

33 John V. Orth, 'Contract and the Common Law,' in Harry N. Scheiber, ed., *The State and Freedom of Contract* (Stanford, 1998), 49; Robert W. Gordon, 'Legal Thought and Legal Practice in the Age of American Enterprise, 1870–1920,' in Gerald L. Geison, ed., *Professions and Professional Ideologies in America* (Chapel Hill, 1983), esp. 88–93.

34 Charles M. Haar, ed., *The Golden Age of American Law* (New York, 1965), 33; Robert W. Gordon, '"The Ideal and the Actual in the Law": Fantasies and Practices of New York City Lawyers, 1870–1910,' in Gerard W. Gewalt, ed., *The New High Priests: Lawyers in Post-Civil War America* (Westport, CT, 1984); Robert Stevens, *Law School: Legal Education in America from the 1850s to the 1980s* (Chapel Hill, 1983); Julius Goebel, Jr, *A History of the School of Law, Columbia University* (New York, 1955), esp. 154–5.

35 Sally Engle Merry, *Getting Justice and Getting Even: Legal Consciousness among Working-Class Americans* (Chicago, 1990); Austin Sarat and William L.F. Felstiner, 'Lawyers and Legal Consciousness: Law Talk in the Divorce Lawyer's Office,' *Yale Law Journal*, 98 (June 1989): 1663–88.

36 Nathan O. Hatch, 'The Second Great Awakening and the Market Revolution,' in David Thomas Konig, ed., *Devising Liberty: Preserving and Creating Freedom in the New American Republic* (Stanford, 1995), 245, 264. See also Richard Carwardine, '"Antinomians" and "Arminians": Methodists and the Market Revolution,' in Stokes and Conway, *Market Revolution*. As Hatch and Carwardine demonstrate, the reverse claim, advanced in Sellers, *Market Revolution*, that the early nineteenth-century Protestant revival was fun-

damentally a revolt against market values, oversimplifies in precisely the opposite direction.

37 Isaac, *Transformation of Virginia*; Nathan O. Hatch, *The Democratization of American Christianity* (New Haven, 1989).

38 Lewis Perry, *Radical Abolitionism: Anarchy and the Government of God in Antislavery Thought* (Ithaca, 1973); Richard J. Carwardine, *Evangelicals and Politics in Antebellum America* (New Haven, 1993); Mark A. Noll, ed., *Religion and American Politics: From the Colonial Period to the 1980s* (New York, 1990).

39 Gregory A. Wills, *Democratic Religion: Freedom, Authority, and Church Discipline in the Baptist South, 1785–1900* (New York, 1997); Barry Levy, *Quakers and the American Family: British Settlement in the Delaware Valley* (New York, 1988); Philip Greven, *The Protestant Temperament: Patterns of Child-Rearing, Religious Experience, and the Self in Early America* (New York, 1977); William G. McLoughlin, 'Evangelical Childrearing in the Age of Jackson: Francis Wayland's Views on When and How to Subdue the Willfulness of Children,' *Journal of Social History*, 9 (Fall 1975): 20–39; Christine Leigh Heyrman, *Southern Cross: The Beginnings of the Bible Belt* (New York, 1997); Kenneth Moore Startup, *The Root of All Evil: The Protestant Clergy and the Economic Mind of the South* (Athens, GA, 1997); J.E. Crowley, *This Sheba, Self: The Conceptualization of Economic Life in Eighteenth-Century America* (Baltimore, 1974); Barry Alan Shain, *The Myth of American Individualism: The Protestant Origins of American Political Thought* (Princeton, 1994). The quoted passage is from Hatch, *Democratization of American Christianity*, 136.

40 Michael Grossberg, *Governing the Hearth: Law and the Family in Nineteenth-Century America* (Chapel Hill, 1985), 24; Jay Fliegelman, *Prodigals and Pilgrims: The American Revolution against Patriarchal Authority, 1750–1800* (Cambridge, England, 1982), 53; Peter W. Bardaglio, *Reconstructing the Household: Families, Sex, and the Law in the Nineteenth-Century South* (Chapel Hill, 1995), chap. 5; Steven M. Stowe, *Intimacy and Power in the Old South: Ritual in the Lives of the Planters* (Baltimore, 1987), 258. The Filmer to Locke formulation is Mary Beth Norton's in her *Founding Mothers and Fathers: Gendered Power and the Forming of American Society* (New York, 1996).

41 Fliegelman, *Prodigals and Pilgrims*; Jan Lewis, *The Pursuit of Happiness: Family and Values in Jefferson's Virginia* (Cambridge, England, 1983); Daniel Blake Smith, *Inside the Great House: Planter Family Life in Eighteenth-Century Chesapeake Society* (Ithaca, 1980).

42 Toby L. Ditz, 'Ownership and Obligation: Inheritance and Patriarchal Households in Connecticut, 1750–1820,' *William and Mary Quarterly*, 47 (April 1990): 235–65; Norma Basch, *In the Eyes of the Law: Women, Marriage, and Property in Nineteenth-Century New York* (Ithaca, 1982); Mary P. Ryan,

The Cradle of the Middle Class: The Family in Oneida County, New York, 1790–1865 (Cambridge, England, 1981). The 'market-ravaged' phrase is from Melvyn Stokes, 'Introduction' to Stokes and Conway, *Market Revolution*, 6.

43 Jon Gjerde, *The Minds of the West: Ethnocultural Evolution in the Rural Middle West, 1830–1917* (Chapel Hill, 1997); Susan Porter Benson, 'Living on the Margin: Working-Class Marriages and Family Survival Strategies in the United States, 1919–1941,' in Victoria de Grazia and Ellen Furlough, eds, *The Sex of Things: Gender and Consumption in Historical Perspective* (Berkeley, 1996).

44 Jan Lewis, 'The Republican Wife: Virtue and Seduction in the Early Republic,' *William and Mary Quarterly,* 44 (October 1987): 689–721; Norma Basch, 'From the Bonds of Empire to the Bonds of Matrimony,' in Konig, *Devising Liberty.*

45 Michael Grossberg, *A Judgment for Solomon: The d'Hauteville Case and Legal Experience in Antebellum America* (Cambridge, England, 1996).

46 Stanley, *From Bondage to Contract*; Amy Dru Stanley, 'Home Life and the Morality of the Market,' in Stokes and Conway, *Market Revolution*; Sarah Barringer Gordon, '"The Liberty of Self-Degradation": Polygamy, Woman Suffrage, and Consent in Nineteenth-Century America,' *Journal of American History,* 83 (December 1996): 815–47; Grossberg, *Governing the Hearth,* chap. 2.

47 Elizabeth B. Clark, '"The Sacred Rights of the Weak": Pain, Sympathy, and the Culture of Individual Rights in Antebellum America,' *Journal of American History,* 82 (September 1995), 463–93; Elizabeth B. Clark, 'The Politics of God and the Woman's Vote: Religion in the American Suffrage Movement,' PhD dissertation, Princeton University, 1989.

48 Joseph L. Blau, ed., *Social Theories of Jacksonian Democracy: Representative Writings of the Period, 1825–1850* (Indianapolis, 1954), 28.

Chapter Eight

Law/Custom/Tradition: Perspectives from the Common Law

DAVID LIEBERMAN

The pairing of 'law' and 'tradition' appears with sufficient frequency in legal scholarship, and for such a variety of purposes, that no discussion of the topic can proceed without some ruthlessly imposed boundaries and principles of selection. In what follows here, I shall draw on materials from the history of English legal thought and practice in order to explore some of the ways in which the idea of tradition has been understood and valued in the arena of jurisprudence.

My starting point concerns an influential account of England's system of customary or common law, which received its classic formulation in the seventeenth and eighteenth centuries in the writings of such jurists as Edward Coke, John Selden, Matthew Hale, and William Blackstone.[1] Their claims about the nature and historical identity of English law figured critically and, at times, authoritatively in a host of fierce political controversies over the structures and operation of government authority in England.[2] And their works attempted to fashion order and system out of the complex, heterogeneous, and arcane materials of England's early modern legal practices. This latter enterprise in legal rationalization achieved its most celebrated expression in the form of William Blackstone's mid-eighteenth-century, four-volume *Commentaries on the Laws of England*, 'the most influential law book in Anglo-American history,' according to a recent and enthusiastic estimate.[3]

To turn to these particular legal texts in the setting of this volume of essays, moreover, is not to engage in a narrowly antiquarian or parochial inquiry. In terms of contemporary jurisprudence, these seventeenth- and eighteenth-century materials continue to be invoked and recruited, most typically by self-consciously *dissident* voices raised in opposition to the less historically framed and historically respectful conventions of modern legal thought.[4] And in terms of modern Western intellectual history, these materials are credited as one major source for the formation of historically based and historically oriented approaches to human society, particularly as these developed in self-consciously conservative responses to French revolutionary fervour and the host of intellectual monstrosities and more material horrors it was taken to exemplify.[5]

What features of the early modern account of English common law have been thought to provide such a fruitful rehearsal of the case for traditionalism in law? First, and perhaps most obviously, was a set of claims regarding the appropriate presence of the legal past (whether real or imagined) in the operations of present-day law. The routine practice of the common law in the here-and-now operated as it did because of the manner in which the process of historical development pervasively shaped its doctrines, rules, and procedures. For this reason, a comprehension of the law inevitably required an understanding of the legal past. 'An infinite number of questions receive the only light they are capable of,' as the commonplace was formulated in 1774, 'from the reflection of history.'[6] Of course, the common lawyers' past was a whiggish, *juridical* past, in which modern practice determined what of the *historical* past was relevant for historical examination and excavation. And, of course, the widely acknowledged institutional fact that present-day law stood as it did because of its history need not, of itself, generate that sort of respectful response which distinguishes common law traditionalism. The historical reality might just as readily elicit a Benthamite denunciation of 'ancestor-wisdom.'[7] 'It is revolting,' as Oliver Wendell Holmes lectured a Boston University Law School audience in 1897, 'to have no better reason for a rule of law than that so it was laid down in the time of Henry IV. It is still more revolting if the grounds upon which it was laid down have vanished long since, and the rule simply persists from blind imitation of the past.'[8]

Deference to the past accordingly involved more than an attitude of 'blind imitation.' For the common law, 'the past' was 'a repository not just of information but of value, with the power to confer legitimacy on actions in the present.'[9] This claim that the past not only did, but also should, remain a part of the legal present received considerable amplification, often in terms of the unique benefits of incremental legal change and the unique achievements of cumulative legal development. Matthew Hale's writings (composed in the middle decades of the seventeenth century, but frequently appearing in posthumous eighteenth-century editions) supplied long-influential rehearsals of these themes. 'Ancient laws,' he maintained, were 'not the issues of the prudence of this or that council or senate,' but rather 'the production of the various experiences and applications of the wisest thing in the inferior world; to wit, time.' In such a process of historical formation, 'day after day new inconveniences' were discovered, and these in turn stimulated 'new remedies,' so that in time the legal order came to embody 'a kind of aggregation of the discoveries, results and applications of ages and events.'[10] Or, as Hale pointedly explained in response to Thomas Hobbes's strictures against common law, given the amassed judgment embodied in long-surviving systems of customary law, 'I have reason to assure myself that Long Experience makes more discoveries touching conveniences or Inconveniences of Laws than is possible for the wisest Council of Men at first to foresee.'[11]

Hale's understanding of a law which had been continually corrected by many hands over the centuries can, in principle, be contrasted with an alternative and more static version of common law's historical nature, frequently associated with Edward Coke, which emphasized the law's antiquity, permanence, and immemorial identity: law – in the formal legal phrase – 'whereof the memory of man runneth not to the contrary.' But, most often, the claim for common law's antiquity was a point about the *continuity* of the law's history; and the emphasis remained, as in Hale's seminal *History of the Common Law of England*, on the benefits of gradual and cumulative legal change.[12] 'Traditional laws in general,' Blackstone maintained, 'suffer by degrees insensible variations in practice,' and although it was 'impossible to define the precise period in which [a particular] alteration accrued,' nevertheless 'we plainly discern the alteration of the law from what it was five hundred years ago.'[13]

If the process of incremental legal development produced law, in Blackstone's phrase, 'fraught with the accumulated wisdom of ages,'[14] it additionally created a law which was uniquely well suited to the community whose legal rights and obligations it maintained. The English jurist Sir John Davies prefaced his 1612 collection of Irish *Reports* by identifying the historical origins of England's common law in the 'honest and good Customes' which had been 'delivered over from age to age by Tradition.' With the passage of time, this law had been rendered 'so framed and fitted to the nature and disposition of this people' that it became 'connatural to the Nation' and impossible to imagine this community 'ruled by any other Law.'[15] Matthew Hale in his *History of the Common Law of England* echoed the theme, emphasizing how the processes of 'long experience and use' produced not only a law 'very just and excellent ... in it self,' but also an 'administration of common justice' 'singularly accommodated' to the 'disposition of the English nation.' Common law had become 'incorporated' into the 'very temperament' of the people, and 'in a manner [became] the complection and constitution of the English commonwealth.'[16]

Finally, the processes of 'long experience and use' gave the law a kind of specificity and detail that served as a guard against 'arbitrary and uncertain law.' Again, this degree of admirable certainty in law was beyond what the 'wit of Man' – lacking the benefit of gradual refinement and development – 'could either at once foresee or aptly remedy.'[17] Moreover, the same dynamic 'of long and iterated experience' not only perfected the law, but also served to stabilize professional legal judgment. 'It appears that men are not born common lawyers,' Hale explained; and the kinds of practical and technical knowledge which properly regulated and coordinated the professions' judgment were 'gained by the habituating, and accustoming, and exercising' of reason in the dense texture of this finely wrought historical artifact.[18] Common law decision making, as Edward Coke notoriously instructed his sovereign, was a matter of 'artificial reason and judgment of law,' requiring 'long study and experience before that a man can attain to the cognisance of it.'[19]

It is tempting to identify this common law valorization of the legal past under the convenient shorthand label of 'Burkean.' Edmund Burke, himself, of course, was trained and steeped in these legal materials. Among his early writings was an unfinished 'Essay towards an History of the Laws of England'; and his mature political theory drew extensively on the categories and vocabulary of jurisprudence.[20] Certainly, like Burke, the common lawyers frequently approached the English past with that spirit of reverence and humility later championed in the *Reflections on the Revolution in France*. 'We are but of yesterday,' explained Edward Coke, 'and our days upon earth are but as a shadow.' 'The laws,' in contrast, had been 'by the wisdom of the most excellent men, in many successions of ages, by long and continual experience ... fined and refined,' and thus conveyed 'the wisdom of those that went before us' and the requisite 'light and knowledge from our forefathers.'[21] Given the continuity of England's customary law – 'this Body [that] never dies' – maintained the later law writer Robert

Atkyns, 'we lived in Our Ancestors a Thousand years ago, and those Ancestors are still living in us.'[22]

But equally and more typically, the common law case for deference to past authority was advanced with greater caution and restraint. A historical approach to law did not generate only Burkean conclusions. Reforming critics of the law, for example, embraced legal history in order to reveal the antiquated and anachronistic nature of inherited legal rules and practices.[23] And the defenders of legal custom found it prudent to speak in more pragmatic and qualified terms than those on occasion deployed by Coke and Burke. 'The particular reason of every rule in the law,' Blackstone explained, could not 'at this distance of time be always precisely assigned' or understood. Nevertheless, 'the law will presume it to be well founded,' which meant that the modern improver properly proceeded with appropriate caution in attempting to revise any particular piece of this legal inheritance.[24]

Common law jurisprudence thus articulated a robust case for 'traditionalism' in the sense of its explicit commitment to 'the authority of the past.'[25] But what, more precisely, was it that was being preserved in this valued institutionalized mediation between legal past and legal present?

For the modern common lawyer, the answer centres on the 'rule' of *stare decisis*, 'the practice of (courts') deciding disputes on the basis of earlier decisions: the practice of following precedent.'[26] Decision making based on precedent is standardly taken to be 'perhaps the most characteristic mode of reasoning in the common law';[27] and the 'practice of following precedent' may very well comprise the present-day common law's most visible manifestation of the law's concern with its institutional inheritance. Nevertheless, the modern common law doctrine of binding precedent offers a poor and misleading entry point into the common law traditionalism of an earlier era. In much of the contemporary jurisprudence of common law, the justification for judicial adherence to precedent turns on arguments having little to do with any direct valuing of the legal past as such.[28] And the now-familiar rule of *stare decisis* is a relatively modern, nineteenth-century conceptualization of common law decision making, which involved a major revision of earlier understandings of the relationship between decided cases and the common law.[29]

These earlier accounts readily acknowledged that common law judges followed precedents. What was famously denied was the idea that these judicial precedents constituted the common law itself. 'The law and the opinion of the judge are not always convertible terms or one and the same thing,' Blackstone maintained; instead, 'these judicial decisions are the principal and most authoritative evidence, that can be given, of the existence of such a custom as shall form part of the common law.'[30] Precedents supplied 'authoritative evidence' of common law, but law itself was a certain type of custom.[31] It is in terms of this understanding of law and custom that the practices of common law traditionalism are best explored.[32]

According to Blackstone, England's 'lex non scripta,' or common law, comprised 'general customs,' 'particular customs of certain parts of the kingdom,' and 'those particular laws that are by custom observed only in certain courts and jurisdictions.'[33] To identify this common law as 'lex non scripta' was in part to distinguish it from the other principal branch of English law: parliamentary statute (the lex scripta). But the term also disclosed something of what was customary and traditional about the common law. Although materials of common law were in no sense 'at present merely oral,' common law itself still displayed 'a great affinity and resemblance' to those purer examples 'of an oral unwritten law, delivered down from age to age, by custom and tradition merely.'[34]

There was nothing novel in the claim that England's common law was chiefly 'custom'; nor was there anything particularly English about a jurisprudence of customary law. Seventeenth- and eighteenth-century jurists frequently chose to celebrate English common law by emphasizing its insularity and isolation from the pattern of continental legal development, whereby native custom was observed to fall victim to the importation of Roman and canon law rules and procedures. Yet, ironically, much of the conceptual apparatus of customary jurisprudence was itself a product of the learned juristic debate within classical and medieval Roman law scholarship; and English law drew readily, if often without acknowledgment, from these large and complex materials.[35] One important result of this protracted process was the highly technical meaning the term 'custom' frequently enjoyed in legal settings. As the common law's most ambitious eighteenth-century critic, Jeremy Bentham, carefully warned, 'The word Custom in Law has a peculiar sense, very different from the common one, and yet not so different as not to be liable to be confounded with it.'[36]

One favoured 'sense' given to the idea of custom was the idea of social usage and practice: custom as the stable, recognized, and normatively valued social practices and communal traditions of a given community, which functioned as a principal source of law. This approach now is perhaps most familiar from those classic legal anthropologies of the nineteenth and early twentieth centuries that sharply contrasted the pervasiveness of custom-based law in primitive societies to the self-consciously innovative legislation of the modern world.[37] Modern anthropology has dismissed much of this once-favoured image of customary law as 'just popular practice' and 'jolly folk custom.'[38] But the earlier approach still echoes in contemporary jurisprudence, where 'the role of custom in rule-making' remains best exemplified in 'pre-state' communities 'lacking formalized institutions for enacting and enforcing the law.'[39]

In the early modern common law theory under examination here, the treatment of custom likewise often began with settled social usage, not yet touched by the institutions of law and government. Thus, John Davies traced the origins of England's law to those 'reasonable act(s)' and 'practice(s)' which, through 'often iteration and multiplication,' became settled as 'custome' and finally endowed with 'the force of a Law.'[40] On this understanding, the typical function of the institutions of the common law was to settle precisely and authoritatively which of the customary practices of the community enjoyed or deserved legal validity. This institutional functioning helped account for that enveloping connectedness between law and community that the jurists praised as a distinctive merit and achievement of the common law. And it also helped explain the nature of the processes of gradual alteration and refinement that comprised common law development: as the usages and practices of the community altered through time, so too did the law change in response to these altered social conditions.[41]

Finally and most momentously, the identification of legal custom and communal practice served to sustain the political value in terms of which common lawyers most ardently celebrated their legal order: English liberty. Since legal authority followed previously established social practice, the law embodied the independently adopted usages of the community itself. 'And indeed,' enthused Blackstone, 'it is one of the characteristic marks of English liberty that our common law depends upon custom, which carries this internal evidence of freedom along with it, that it probably was introduced by the voluntary consent of the people.'[42]

In treating custom in these terms, early modern jurists rationalized some of the basic properties of medieval customary law as well as the early institutional history of the common law. At the point of its origins under Angevin kingship, the common law referred to a structure of centralized royal courts and local officials, whose eventual impact was to wrest cases from the jurisdiction of rival courts and tribunals. What distinguished these royal courts were their procedural forms and requirements, rather than the norms and practices they enforced. In deciding causes between litigants, the courts generally adhered to the rules and customs that already governed such issues – hence, the variety of forms and devices in early common law (as in European customary law more generally) for 'finding' and 'proving' local custom.[43]

Well before the seventeenth century, of course, common law in key areas was as much about settled rules and arcane doctrines as about procedures for law-finding, but not in a manner that obliterated the perceived connections between legal custom and the customary practices of the community. The 'law-finding' function of the common law jury had been extensively tamed and restricted by the eighteenth century. Nonetheless, this heralded feature of English law remained valued for its role in mediating between local practices and centralized courts of justice.[44] The legal category of 'particular customs' continued as a principal branch of common law, denoting the plethora of situations in which the general law of the realm was abandoned in deference to the settled usages of a particular local or a particular group of subjects. Thus, according to the standard stock of illustrative examples, by common law estates in land descended to the eldest male heir; but in Kent, according to the local custom of gavelkind, all the sons enjoyed the inheritance. According to common law, the widow's dower constituted one-third of her husband's lands; but under the local customs of many boroughs, the proportion differed.

However, what requires most emphasis and clarification is the extent to which this rendering of custom as community usage captured only a limited part of the larger jurisprudential picture. Legal 'custom,' even in its avowed and praised connections with settled social practice, was a pervasively shaped and constituted juridical construction, where customs and traditions were those of courts and lawyers, not localities or folkways. 'The starting-point,' observes English law's modern historian, 'is in customs, not the customs of individuals but the customs of courts governing communities.'[45] And on this rendering, what gave the law its distinctive excellencies and achievements as a historical artifact was the continuous refinements over time of the usages of the courts, their officials, and professional practitioners.

This idea of custom as the practices 'of courts governing communities' can be explicated by returning to the categorization of common law, adopted by Blackstone, into the three main component parts of 'general customs,' 'particular customs,' and 'particular laws.' The third category – particular laws – provides the most striking example of the juridically constituted nature of common law custom. Here custom referred to specific bodies of foreign and international law and procedure adopted into the practice of specific English courts of justice, as in the case of the utilization of Roman and canon law in England's courts of admiralty, court martial, and ecclesiastical tribunals.[46] Such law, of course, was neither social usage nor even unwritten; nor, of course, was it English. Nonetheless, it formed part of England's customary law on account of its having been adopted 'by custom' into the practice of those particular courts – just as in other courts of justice, alternative rules of procedure were adopted 'by custom' for legal decision making.

This category, admittedly, offered what the jurists themselves recognized to be a strained example. But similar complexities apply in the cases of the other two branches as well. General customs, the first and largest branch of the common law, covered the general law of property, exchange, civil rights, and obligations – areas of law for which social practice and usage supplied important source materials. But 'general customs' no less described customary materials specific to the law itself, such as 'the rules for expounding wills, deeds, and acts of parliament,' or the institutional arrangement 'that there shall be four superior courts of record,' or the procedural requirement 'that money lent upon bond is recoverable by action of debt.'[47]

Even the remaining branch of common law – the 'particular customs' applying in specific places, where it seems most appropriate to think of the law's operation as the provision of legal force in support of previously developed local usages – is not without its clear trace of legal construction. For here we need recall that in 'receiving' such particular custom, the action of the courts of common law historically was not simply to validate raw social practice, but rather to acknowledge and confirm those customs and usages which had been previously settled and defined in the practices of local courts and tribunals. Local custom thus was still juristically shaped custom. And common law practice still needed carefully to distinguish those particular 'customs which really form a part of the common law of the land' from the 'many other customs or usages' which could be readily seen to exist as social 'facts,' but which had not been received by the relevant judicial bodies as common law.[48]

The notion that 'custom' referred to the customs and usages of courts enjoyed an equally distinguished historical pedigree as the understanding of custom as social practice. And likewise, it involved a rationalization that drew on extensive historical and institutional practice. Indeed, that there was such a legal category of 'general customs' of the realm at all testified to the long-term successes of the centralized royal courts in wresting jurisdiction from rival tribunals and forging a unified legal practice over the discrete and once-separate territorial units over which the royal writ extended.[49] And that the common law came to emerge as a mass of intricate rules and distinctions which needed systematic exposition and ordering testified to the long-term successes of common law judges and elite practitioners in generating doctrine out of procedural routines.

The pattern reached its most fabulous and luxuriant extent in the common law of tenures and estates (or what came to be called the law of real property). By the early modern period, following several centuries of adaptation and revision, this law had become a monstrously and notoriously technical mass of jurisprudence, containing rules to distinguish legal interests from equitable interests; to distinguish words of purchase from words of conveyance; to differentiate estates in possession from estates in remainder, and estates in remainder from estates in reversion; rules to discourage uses but to facilitate entails; rules to facilitate fees, but to limit fees upon a fee; and rules to identify perpetuities and then to bar them. The ironic overall result of such incremental growth and adaptation was a labyrinthine body of customary law which could scarcely be understood by most of the community over which it operated, let alone thought simply to embody its customary practices, norms, and traditions. As the Lord Chief Justice of King's Bench, in a 1775 ruling, bluntly noted of the most basic common law distinction between real and chattel property, 'Generally speaking, no common person has the smallest idea of any difference between giving a person a horse and a quantity of land. Common sense alone would never teach a man the difference.'[50]

Common law jurisprudence thus wove together two distinct referents for custom and legal development: social custom and usage as well as legal custom and usage. The theory of the common law served to unify the two kinds of custom, and indeed all the disparate materials that comprised England's common law. What made all these customs *law* in England was the practice of relevant courts and legal officials to receive them as law; and its being the practice to receive them as such, in turn, depended upon claims concerning the historical origins and continuity of this institutional treatment.

At the same time, however, less sympathetic jurists found it easy work to unravel this supposed unity of legalized customs. Bentham, in his critique of common law, developed a distinction between what he termed 'customs *in pays*' and 'customs *in foro*' – the former referring (roughly) to the customs prevailing among members of the community, and the latter referring (roughly) to the customs among judges concerning the legal sanctioning of certain forms of social conduct.[51] In the twentieth century, C.K. Allen found it more useful to appropriate the terminology of German law to clarify much the same point: 'it is ... well known,' he explained, that 'the "custom of the realm" was in a very large measure the custom of the courts, not of the people – *Gerichtsrecht* rather than *Volksrecht*.'[52]

My aim in this final section is to further pursue several aspects of the common law's distinctive negotiation of the relationship between legal past and legal present. Once more, much of the discussion centres on the specifically legal treatment of the idea of custom. But here my hope is to move somewhat beyond these legal materials themselves and to consider how the juridical case for legal custom might bear on any more general and less institutionally specific defence of custom and tradition.

The first such exploration involves a shift from the more technical jurisprudence of legal custom towards what might loosely be described as the politics of English custom. In recent decades, early modern social historians have emphasized the power and pervasiveness of custom as an idiom of expectation and of legitimation during this period. Appeals to custom framed daily routines in trades and agrarian labour, accompanied the operation of political power, and furnished the normative vocabulary of social protest and popular resistance. 'Customary consciousness and usages were especially robust in the eighteenth-century,' maintained E.P. Thompson, the historian who has done the most to advance this line of study.[53]

This social history has been especially concerned to chart the prominence of custom in so 'many of the classic struggles at the entry to the industrial revolution.'[54] Over the period from very roughly 1750 to 1820, the dynamics of commercial innovation and market exchange, politically furthered through the instruments of parliamentary statute and judicially crafted legal doctrine, led to the displacement and expropriation of customary entitlements and practices across a wide number of contested areas of economic life. Manorial custom and common use-rights in agriculture withered under the force of parliamentary enclosure and the common law's increasing commitment to clearly individuated property rights. Established production routines and settled artisan privileges were eroded by laws banning workers' combination and wage-setting. Paternalist restraints on market practices and prices in staples fell to a new regime of the unfettered exchange of absolute private properties.[55]

This scholarship usefully reminds us of the wider and contested social contexts that accompanied the jurisprudence of custom. Custom was never solely a matter of abstruse juridical theory, and the common law defence of custom was itself an expression of a more generalized pattern of social norms and orientations. No less forcefully it reminds us that issues of social and political power are ever-present in the processes of legal ordering, even in a legal order that extolled its basis in custom and usage.

But this same scholarship also warns us not to conflate (as previous commentators have done) the popular mobilization of 'custom' and the distinguishable idea of a fixed order of traditional community and customary folkways falling before forces of industrialization and commercialization.[56] Against such an interpretation, it is important to note, once again, how frequently 'custom' in this context was 'rooted in law' and comprised a set of routines and orientations extensively shaped and permeated by legal materials.[57] Not only was the appeal to custom itself often understood as a specifically legal claim of right and property, but the content of the custom no less revealed the impacts of the law. Thus, in the case of the 'custom' of markets and the 'custom' of trades, the popular customs invoked against market innovation appear as much the product of earlier Tudor legislation and earlier common law doctrine as they do the expression of traditional social usage. As Thompson emphasized in his deservedly influential study of the customary 'moral economy' of the eighteenth-century grain riot, this form of popular resistance reproduced 'sometimes with great precision' the specific procedures for magistrates codified in the Elizabethan *Book of Orders* and related legal mandates.[58] 'Customary culture,' one distinguished historian of eighteenth-century labour concludes, was 'not the simple antithesis of "market culture,"' and the claims to 'custom' and 'tradition' could as readily denote demands for fair treatment under novel conditions as describe 'forms of working that were of actual longevity.'[59] In these settings, we observe less a dynamic of legal and market modernization overwhelming a traditional society than a process in which one legally shaped order of 'custom' was displaced by a succeeding regime of parliamentary enactment and judicial doctrine.

The explicit insistence on moral norms and just entitlements in the popular mobilization of custom provides an opportunity to consider further the common law jurists' own account of the moral dimensions of England's customary law. According to settled doctrine, historical pedigree and historical continuity were not in themselves sufficient to establish which customs formed part of the common law. In addition, customs had to conform to 'reason,' or (as it was more typically presented) customs 'must not be unreasonable.' No practice or usage, whatever its antiquity, that was found contrary to 'reason' would be accepted in law as an 'established custom of the realm'; and hence, in Blackstone's fulsome expression, 'our lawyers are with justice so copious in their encomiums on the reason of the common law; that they tell us that the law is the perfection of reason, that it always intends to conform thereto, and that what is not reason is not law.'[60]

It is evident that English jurists of the early modern period embraced a range of particular, and even contrasting, positions in their attempts to link custom and reason. But the association itself formed a fundamental and prominent element of common law theory.[61] Blackstone was especially forthright in connecting the established rule that customs must not be 'unreasonable' to the more general argument in support of the morality and justice of England's law. The validity of all human law was dependent on its conformity to the divinely ordained 'law of nature' (or, 'what we call ethics'); and therefore 'the rational science' of English law required explicit demonstration of common law's 'foundation in nature or in natural law.'[62]

Obviously, the linking of custom and reason, and of common law and natural law, did not mean that the content of the common law could be regarded as a body of logical deductions from some set of axioms of reason. England's law was emphatically a historical artifact, and many of its rules and doctrines concerned 'things in themselves indifferent' to any foundational scheme of rational moral norms.[63] Nonetheless, as a historical artifact, the common law embodied the cumulative and tested applications of human reason to the changing circumstances and social conditions of the particular community it served. In this way, the law's customary character and survival over the centuries testified to its rationality no less than it displayed its superiority and singular appropriateness for the English people.

The idea that custom was both reasonable as well as historical attracted considerable controversy; and later jurists frequently judged the notion a crude conflation of categories of justification (reason and history) that needed to be kept separate and even juxtaposed. Henry Maine, in the mid-nineteenth century, thus protested such 'mixed modes of thought' that 'characterized all but the highest minds during the infancy of speculation' and which continued to infest jurisprudence through the eighteenth century.[64] And like-minded commentators tended to restrict the doctrine by giving the formula a largely narrow, technical meaning: by 'reasonable' custom little more was intended than that the custom in question needed to be sufficiently precise and clear for the purposes of guiding conduct, or that the custom could be shown to advance some genuine public good.[65]

However, it is by no means plain that the original doctrine required such drastic revision, especially in light of the elegant restatements of the common law orthodoxy that have appeared in modern jurisprudence.[66] The common law effort to combine 'reason, custom and experience,' Philip Selznick maintains, provides valuable insight and instruction concerning modern law's 'continuing quest' for a form of 'legal decision-making that is at once rational and traditional' and that appropriately acknowledges 'the interplay of critical and conventional morality.'[67] More broadly, the common law doctrine can be viewed as a juridical rendering of the (contested) points emphasized by the modern defenders of tradition, such as MacIntyre, that 'all reasoning takes place within the context of some traditional mode of thought'; and that a tradition, when 'in good order,' is itself 'always partially constituted by an argument about the goods' the tradition is taken to embody and promote.[68] As in these endorsements of tradition, the common law commitment to custom was not taken to mean an undifferentiated surrender to inherited ways or an inability to treat critically the manner in which this inheritance had been previously conceived.

The common law linkage of custom and reason has thus come to receive more robust and sympathetic philosophical consideration than the jurists of Maine's generation were prepared to render it. At the same time, the critical dismissal of the legal doctrine enjoys something of its own important historical pedigree. In the early modern period, the common law's most ambitious critics eagerly seized on the claim as especially vulnerable to attack. The common lawyers' arguments on behalf of the reason of custom supplied an inviting setting for the elaboration of now-familiar oppositions between reason and authority and between tradition and critical morality.

Thomas Hobbes in the posthumous 1681 *Dialogue between a Philosopher and a Student of the Common Laws of England*, which scrutinized the writings of Edward Coke, found in the doctrine suitable materials for challenging the professional jurists' standard presumption to speak authoritatively over matters of law. If, as maintained by Coke, common law comprised 'Laws of Reason,' then it obviously followed that any private individual might readily invade the profession's monopoly of presumed expertise. 'Upon this ground,' insisted the *Dialogue's* Philosopher, 'you are not to think it Arrogance' if 'I pretend ... to make myself able to perform the Office of a Judge'; 'for you are to allow to me, as well as to other Men, my pretence to Reason, which is the Common Law.'[69]

Bentham, in his unfinished polemic against Blackstone's *Commentaries* of the mid-1770s, also focused on the same doctrine. Once it was acknowledged that only those customs and usages of suitable moral merit were to be allowed as law, then one inevitably had to consider whether the favoured formula of 'reasonable' or 'not unreasonable' customs could possibly perform the critical task to which it was assigned. 'What,' Bentham charged, precisely did it mean for a judgment of law 'to be most evidently contrary to reason?' And precisely 'whose reason' did Blackstone mean 'to propose for the standard' of critical evaluation? 'Had our Author,' Bentham promptly countered, 'instead of reason said utility, he would have said something ... He would have referred us to calculation founded upon matter of fact: future contingent utility founded upon past utility experienced.'[70]

In these polemics, Hobbes and Bentham (notwithstanding their own legal learning and erudition) presented themselves as iconoclastic outsiders to the legal establishment Bentham later derided as 'judge and company.'[71] The very capacity to situate themselves in this rhetorical fashion reflected features of common law practice that are frequently identified as critical supports for the maintenance and preservation of any tradition: clear lines of collective identity for the participants in and bearers of the tradition; established methods for the determination of authoritative texts and canons of interpretation; processes for inculcating forms of 'tacit knowledge' and for the stable transmission of inherited learning and values across generations.[72] Viewed from this perspective, it becomes plain that common law was served by a dense fabric of institutional structures and routines which facilitated the law's survival as a customary artifact. Many of these features are familiar points of emphasis in the comparative scholarship on the contrasting lines of historical development between England's legal order and the civil law systems of continental Europe. But these features equally serve to disclose those institutional routines that sustained English customary jurisprudence.[73]

Legal custom was sustained, in part, by an elaborate process of recruitment and education, which simultaneously functioned to equip practitioners with forms of expertise of scant use outside the law and to exclude those outside professional practice from access to this knowledge. Unlike the Continent, England maintained an institutional separation between the learned law (Roman law and canon law) taught at the universities and the training in English law based at the Inns of Court. It was not until the mid-eighteenth century that English law became an academic subject at an English university, and plans of that era to establish a university education as a basic or required part of professional training bore no immediate fruit.[74]

English legal training, instead, remained principally a matter of mastering the intricate techniques for handling legal cases, or what Thomas Littleton in the fifteenth century described as 'the science of pleading well.'[75] Common lawyers obtained command of the technical forms for the initiation and processing of cases (writs, forms of actions, special pleadings); of a legal literature dominated by learning about cases and methods of processing cases (yearbooks, reports, formularies of writs); and of a pedagogy focused especially on pleadings and responses in hypothetical legal contests. English law utilized its own private and professional language, Law French. (English did not become the official language of the law until the early eighteenth century.) [76] And well after the first impacts of print and print culture, major parts of the materials of English legal education and practice remained in private manuscript collections and professional copybooks.[77]

English law isolated and advanced its practitioners, moreover, in a manner that tightly bound elite bar and bench. The Inns of Court, even after they ceased to be important pedagogic centres, preserved the separation of the upper division of the profession from the lower ranks of law workers (notaries, scriveners, conveyancers). The formally identified upper rank of the Inns governed the profession, and the judiciary (again unlike the situation on the Continent) was recruited from elite professional practice. And, perhaps most critically, common law at this elevated level remained a very small and close professional world. As the enforcement of English law involved considerable numbers of unpaid, part-time, and local officials (justices of the peace, constables, sheriffs), and as the process of trial gave important responsibility to untrained laymen (grand and petty jurors), the number of actual elite judges, who so shaped the common law world, could remain remarkably small. The highest royal court in eighteenth-century France, the Parlement of Paris, contained up to 240 judges, and this body was itself supplemented by the twelve other regional Parlements. From 1200 to 1800, the number of permanent judges of the central royal courts in England of Westminster Hall at any one time rarely exceeded fifteen. And the two superior courts of the common law, the Court of Common Pleas and the Court of King's Bench, combined to number eight judges.[78]

All of this bespoke an institutional order of shared training and experience, common outlooks and technical proficiency, direct and ready transmission of privileged learning. This professional infrastructure receives relatively little attention in the recent scholarship devoted to the *theory* of early modern common law. But among the jurists themselves there was evident appreciation of the more practical arrangements helping to sustain a jurisprudence of custom. Thus, Matthew Hale immediately invoked this institutional reality in seeking to explain what he took to be the remarkable lack of uncertainty and disagreement in the processes of England's unwritten law. The 'Justices,' Hale explained, all received 'a common education in the study of the Law,' and daily would 'converse and consult with one another' and 'sit near one and another in Westminster Hall,' so that their 'Judgments and Decisions' were 'necessarily communicated to one another.' Given this proximity and routine contact, their 'Administrations of Common Justice' readily achieved 'a Consonancy, Congruity and Uniormity' that could never be secured where the administration of justice was left to 'several incommunicating Hands' or separate 'provincial Establishments.'[79]

Hale's unselfconscious report of how much this form of law owed to the structured and coordinated conversation among a select number of like-minded professionals supplies a broader message for the modern treatments of tradition. In later centuries, when a jurisprudence of custom came to be advanced in repudiation of the projects of legislative rationalization associated with Enlightenment reform, there was a marked tendency to associate the power of tradition and legal custom with highly generalized and generic features of collective life: tradition and language; tradition and myth; tradition and folkways; tradition and culture. (And this approach has been sustained in modern philosophical explorations of the nature of tradition, such as Gadamer's hermeneutics, which also turn to law as manifesting universal features of tradition's pervasiveness and shaping authority.)[80] Thus, Burke, in the *Reflections*, notwithstanding all his emphasis on the properly revered historical particularity of the English political experience, still characterized this traditionalist orientation as operating 'in a just correspondence and symmetry with the order of the world' and realizing 'a constitutional policy working after the pattern of nature.'[81] And Friedrich Karl von Savigny, in his famous polemic against eighteenth-century codification and in support of the alternative 'strict historical method of jurisprudence,' located the ultimate source of law in 'the common consciousness of the people,' where law proved inseparable from 'their language, manners and constitution.'[82]

Of course, as we have seen, there was much in the writings of the early modern common law jurists that supported this more universalistic approach to the nature of custom. But Hale's account made clear that a system of customary law, which prized the past achievements and continuity of cumulative legal development, was no less a product of professional structures, trainings, and procedures. His customary jurisprudence was appropriately *The History of the Common Law of England*, and not a sermon on humanity and the nature of its social condition.

NOTES

I am greatly indebted to several friends and colleagues for their comments and criticisms of earlier drafts of this essay: James Gordley, Laurent Mayali, Gordon Schochet, and especially Martin Krygier and Mark Phillips.

  1 My approach to these materials is heavily indebted to the following important treatments: A.W.B. Simpson, 'The Common Law and Legal Theory,' in A.W.B. Simpson, ed., *Oxford Essays in Jurisprudence*, 2nd series (Oxford, 1973); Gerald J. Postema, *Bentham and the Common Law Tradition* (Oxford, 1986), chaps 1–4; and Martin Krygier, 'Law as Tradition,' *Law and Philosophy*, 5 (1986): 237–62; 'Traditionality of Statutes,' *Ratio Juris*, 1 (1988): 20–39; and

'Common Law,' in *Routledge Encyclopedia of Philosophy*, 10 vols, ed. Edward Craig (London, 1998), 1: 440–6.

2 J.G.A. Pocock's *The Ancient Constitution and the Feudal Law* (Cambridge, 1957) established in modern scholarship the importance of these legal writings for the study of English political thought and culture. More recent contributions since the work's first appearance are considered by Pocock himself in his extended 'Retrospect' to the second edition (Cambridge, 1987), and in Glenn Burgess, *The Politics of the Ancient Constitution* (University Park, PA, 1993).

3 Albert W. Alschuler, 'Rediscovering Blackstone,' *University of Pennsylvania Law Review*, 145 (1996): 2. On the general genre of early modern legal literature to which Blackstone's *Commentaries* contributed, see J.W. Cairns, 'Blackstone, An English Institutionist: Legal Literature and the Rise of the Nation State,' *Oxford Journal of Legal Studies*, 4 (1984): 318–60, and S.F.C. Milsom, 'The Nature of Blackstone's Achievement,' *Oxford Journal of Legal Studies*, 1 (1981): 1–12.

4 For illustrative examples, see the use of Burke in Anthony T. Kronman, 'Precedent and Tradition,' *Yale Law Journal*, 99 (1990): 1029–68; the use of Hale in David A. Strauss, 'Common Law Constitutional Interpretation,' *University of Chicago Law Review*, 63 (1996): 877–935; and the survey presented by Harold J. Berman, 'Origins of Historical Jurisprudence: Coke, Selden, Hale,' *Yale Law Journal*, 103 (1994): 1651–1738. For a critical response to the revival of these materials offered by Kronman, see David Lubban, 'Legal Traditionalism,' *Stanford Law Review*, 43 (1991): 1035–60.

5 Burke, as ever, remains the central figure for this particular line of intellectual lineage; see, for example, J.G.A. Pocock, 'Burke and the Ancient Constitution,' *Historical Journal*, 3 (1960): 125–43, and Paul Lucas, 'On Edmund Burke's Doctrine of Prescription,' *Historical Journal*, 11 (1968): 35–63.

6 Edward Wynne, *Eunomus: Or, Dialogues concerning the Law and Constitution of England*, 4 vols (London, 1774), 1: 59.

7 Jeremy Bentham, *Fragment on Government*, in *A Comment on the Commentaries and A Fragment on Government* (1776), ed. J.H. Burns and H.L.A. Hart (London 1977), 424n.

8 Holmes, 'The Path of the Law' (1897), reprinted in *Harvard Law Review*, 110 (1997): 1001.

9 Kronman, 'Precedent and Tradition,' 1032–3.

10 Hale, 'Considerations touching the Amendment or Alteration of Laws,' in Francis Hargrave, ed., *A Collection of Tracts, Relative to the Law of England* (London, 1787), 254.

11 Hale, 'Reflections by the Lord Chief Justice Hale on Mr. Hobbes, His Dia-

logue of the Law,' in William Holdsworth, *A History of English Law*, 16 vols (London, 1922–66), 5: 504.

12 These rival conceptions of the historical nature of common law are treated in Pocock, *Ancient Constitution and the Feudal Law*, chap. 2, and in Burgess, *Politics of the Ancient Constitution*, 20–37.

13 William Blackstone, *Commentaries on the Laws of England* (1765–69), 4 vols, ed. Joseph Chitty (London, 1826), 4: 409 (hereafter cited as: 4 *Comm* 409).

14 4 *Comm* 442.

15 Sir John Davies, *Reports of Cases and Matters in Law* (Dublin, 1762), Preface, 5–6. Davies here uses 'Tradition' in the root sense of a custom handed down from ancestors to posterity.

16 Hale, *History of the Common Law of England*, ed. Charles M. Gray (Chicago, 1971), 30. The date of the composition of Hale's *History* is not known; it was first published posthumously in 1713.

17 Hale, 'Reflections on Hobbes,' in Holdsworth, *History of English Law*, 5: 504–5.

18 Ibid., 505.

19 'Prohibitions del Roy' (1607), *Reports of Sir Edward*, reprinted in J.P. Kenyon, ed., *The Stuart Constitution*, 2nd ed. (Cambridge, 1986), 80–1; and see Coke, *First Part of the Institutes of the Laws of England* (London, 1670): fol. 97, cited in Burgess, *Politics of the Ancient Constitution*, 45–6. For a recent rendering of this theme, see Charles Fried, 'Artificial Reason of the Law or What Lawyers Know,' *Texas Law Review*, 60 (1982): 35–58.

20 See *Works of Edmund Burke*, 12 vols, 8th ed. (Boston, MA, 1884), 7: 475–88.

21 7 Coke *Reports*, 3a–4a.

22 Robert Atkyns, *Parliamentary and Political Tracts* (London, 1734), 190.

23 I explore several leading examples of the attempts to link legal history and law reform in *The Province of Legislation Determined: Legal Theory in Eighteenth-Century Britain* (Cambridge, 1989), chap. 7, and in 'Property, Commerce, and the Common Law,' in John Brewer and Susan Staves, eds, *Early Modern Conceptions of Property* (London, 1995), 144–58.

24 1 *Comm* 70. Blackstone continued with the established explanation: 'And it hath been an ancient observation in the laws of England that whenever a standing rule of law, of which the reason perhaps could not be remembered or discerned, hath been wantonly broken in upon by statutes or new resolutions, the wisdom of the rule hath in the end appeared from the inconveniences that have followed the innovation.'

25 Kronman, 'Precedent and Tradition,' 1044.

26 Ibid., 1031.

27 Melvin Aron Eisenberg, *The Nature of the Common Law* (Cambridge, MA, 1988), 50.

28 Kronman, 'Precedent and Tradition,' 1036. For important examples of such modern treatments, see Martin Shapiro, 'Stability and Change in Judicial Decision-Making: Incrementalism or Stare Decisis?' *Law in Transition Quarterly*, 2 (1965): 134–57; Frederick Schauer, 'Precedent,' *Stanford Law Review*, 39 (1987): 571–605; Lewis Kornhauser, 'An Economic Perspective on Stare Decisis,' *Chicago-Kent Law Review*, 65 (1989): 63–92; and Eisenberg, *Nature of the Common Law*, 50–76.

29 See Rupert Cross, *Precedent in English Law*, 2nd ed. (Oxford, 1968), and A.W.B. Simpson, 'The Ratio Decidendi of a Case and the Doctrine of Binding Precedent,' in A.G. Guest, ed., *Oxford Essays in Jurisprudence* (Oxford, 1961).

30 1 *Comm* 68–71.

31 See the important explication of this point in Simpson, 'The Common Law and Legal Theory.'

32 In the section which follows I attempt to highlight some selective features of 'customary law' as it developed in medieval England and Europe, and particularly as it came to be understood by later English jurists, such as Hale and Blackstone. My understanding of these themes is heavily indebted to several important comparative discussions: John P. Dawson, *The Oracles of Law* (Ann Arbor, MI, 1968); Fredric Cheyette, 'Custom, Case Law and Medieval "Constitutionalism,"' *Political Science Quarterly*, 78 (1963): 363–90; Donald R. Kelley, '"Second Nature": The Idea of Custom in European Law, Society and Culture,' in Anthony Grafton and Ann Blair, eds, *Transmission of Culture in Early Modern Europe* (Philadelphia, 1990), 131–72; Donald R. Kelley, *The Human Measure: Social Thought in the Western Legal Tradition* (Cambridge, MA, 1990), chaps 6 and 10; James Q. Whitman, 'Why Did the Revolutionary Lawyers Confuse Custom and Reason?' *University of Chicago Law Review*, 58 (1991): 1321–68.

33 1 *Comm* 63.

34 4 *Comm* 408. For Blackstone, the 'ancient Druids in Gaul' best exemplified the practice of purely oral law.

35 The Roman and canon law treatments of legal custom and their extensive impacts are surveyed in Dawson, *Oracles of Law*, and Kelley, '"Second Nature."' See also Laurent Mayali, 'La Coutume dans La Doctrine Romaniste au Moyen Age,' *Recueils de la Société Jean Bodin*, 1 (1989).

36 Bentham, *Comment on the Commentaries*, 180–1.

37 See, as leading examples, William Graham Sumner, *Folkways: A Study of the Sociological Importance of Usages, Manners, Customs, Mores and Morals* (1906)

(Boston, 1940), 53–7, and Paul Vinogradoff, *Custom and Right* (Cambridge, MA, 1925), chap. 2.

38 Sally Falk Moore, *Law as Process* (London, 1978), 16; and see E. Adamson Hoebel, *The Law of Primitive Man* (New York, 1979), 18–28.

39 Leon Sheleff, *The Future of Tradition. Customary Law, Common Law and Legal Pluralism* (London, 1999), 4–5; see also the more careful formulation in H.L.A. Hart, *The Concept of Law* (Oxford, 1961), 89–90.

40 Davies, *Reports*, 3.

41 See my 'Property, Commerce, and the Common Law,' 144–60.

42 1 *Comm* 74. Somewhat ironically, this understanding of the links between custom and freedom (as Blackstone recognized) was Roman in origin; see Kelley, ' "Second Nature," ' 133–7.

43 For a recent survey of these legal forms, see Whitman, 'Custom and Reason,' 1331–40.

44 Hale praised trial by jury as 'the best Trial in the World,' *History of the Common Law*, 160; and Blackstone celebrated it as 'the glory of the English law,' 3 *Comm* 350. The transformation of the medieval jury from a 'law-finding' to a 'fact-finding' institution is explored in contrasting ways in Thomas A. Green, *Verdict According to Conscience* (Chicago, 1985), and Marianne Constable, *The Law of the Other* (Chicago, 1994). See also J.H. Baker, *An Introduction to English Legal History*, 2nd ed. (London, 1979), chap. 5.

45 S.F.C. Milsom, *Historical Foundations of the Common Law*, 2nd ed. (London, 1981), 1; and see Albert Kiralfy, 'Custom in Medieval English Law,' *Journal of Legal History*, 9 (1988): 26–39.

46 See Blackstone, 1 *Comm* 79–84, and the corresponding discussion in Hale, *History of the Common Law*, 18–20.

47 1 *Comm* 67–8.

48 See J.H. Balfour Browne, *The Law of Usages and Customs* (London, 1875), 27–8.

49 The critical innovations for law that attended the juridical construction of 'general customs' and their systematic rationalization in the early modern period are emphasized in Whitman, 'Custom and Reason,' 1340–52, and in Klaus Luig, 'The Institutes of National Law in the Seventeenth and Eighteenth Centuries,' *Juridical Review*, 17 (1972): 193–226.

50 *Hogan v Jackson* (1775), in Henry Cowper, *Reports of Cases adjudged in the Court of King's Bench* (London 1783), 299, 306.

51 *Comment on the Commentaries*, 180–5; and see the discussion in Jeremy Waldron, 'Custom Redeemed by Statute,' *Current Legal Problems*, 51 (1998): 93–114.

52 C.K. Allen, *Law in the Making* (1927), 7th ed. (Oxford, 1964), 124.

53 E.P. Thompson, *Customs in Common: Studies in Traditional Popular Culture*
    (New York, 1993), 1.
54 Thompson, *Customs in Common*, 4–5.
55 A valuable synthetic statement of this historical interpretation is found
    in Douglas Hay and Nicholas Rogers, *Eighteenth-Century English Society*
    (Oxford, 1997), chaps 6–7. Thompson explores the cases of manorial custom
    and grain markets in *Customs in Common*, chaps 3–5. See also the further
    treatments of this theme in John Rule, *The Experience of Labour in Eighteenth-
    Century Industry* (London, 1981); Robert W. Malcolmson, *Popular Recreations
    in English Society 1700–1850* (Cambridge, 1973); and Bob Bushaway, *By Rite:
    Custom, Ceremony and Community in England 1700–1880* (London, 1982). My
    discussion here ignores the important criticisms that have been advanced
    against this account of eighteenth-century social history and legal develop-
    ment. Thompson briefly considers some of these criticisms in *Customs in
    Common*, chap. 5. See also the ambitious alternative account offered in Paul
    Langford, *Public Life and the Propertied Englishman* (Oxford, 1991), and my
    more modest undertaking in 'Contract before "Freedom of Contract,"' in
    Harry N. Scheiber, ed., *The State and Freedom of Contract* (Stanford, 1998),
    89–121.
56 This familiar image was frequently suggested in much of the classic histori-
    ography of the Industrial Revolution; see, for example, the preface to the
    1925 second edition of J.L. Hammond and Barbara Hammond, *The Town
    Labourer*, intro. John Lovell (London, 1978), xliv. It figured even more
    emphatically in less historically specific critiques of industrialization and
    mass consumerism; see, for example the treatment of 'the loss of the
    organic community' in F.R. Leavis and Denys Thompson, *Culture and Envi-
    ronment* (London, 1950), 1–4, 87–98.
57 Hay and Rogers, *Eighteenth-Century English Society,* 94 (here considering the
    'custom of markets'). For similar emphasis, see their discussion of manorial
    custom and custom of trades, *Eighteenth-Century English Society*, 86, 92, and
    Thompson, *Customs in Common*, 97–100.
58 Thompson, *Customs in Common*, 224.
59 John Rule, 'Against Innovation? Custom and Resistance in the Workplace,
    1700–1850,' in Tim Harris, ed., *Popular Culture in England* (New York, 1995),
    185, 187.
60 1 *Comm* 70; and see 1 *Comm* 77–8, on the rule 'customs must be reasonable.'
61 The point receives proper emphasis in Burgess, *Politics of the Ancient Consti-
    tution*, chap. 2; but see the somewhat contrasting formulation of the com-
    mon law position in Alan Cromartie, *Sir Matthew Hale* (Cambridge, 1995),
    11–41. The insistence that only customs conforming to reason were good

law had been an important feature of canonist jurisprudence; for a summary, see Dawson, *Oracles of the Law*, 128–34. (I am indebted to my Berkeley colleagues, James Gordley and Laurent Mayali, for explaining to me the importance of these canon law sources.)

62 See 1 *Comm* 38–44 and 2 *Comm* 2. For a fuller account of Blackstone's theory, see the discussion in my *Province of Legislation Determined*, 36–8, 42–7.

63 See 1 *Comm* 55, and the discussion in Burgess, *Politics of the Ancient Constitution*, 30–7.

64 Henry Sumner Maine, *Ancient Law* (1861) (New York, 1864), 70; see also his comments on common law at 29–32.

65 See, for example, Browne, *Law of Usages and Customs*, 19–24; and Allen, *Law in the Making*, 140–6.

66 See, especially, Postema, *Bentham and the Common Law Tradition*, 4–13, 30–8.

67 Philip Selznick, *The Moral Commonwealth* (Berkeley, CA, 1992), 450–2.

68 Alasdair MacIntyre, *After Virtue*, 2nd ed. (Notre Dame, IN, 1984), 222 (where MacIntyre advances these points in repudiation of the 'Burkean' juxtaposing of reason and tradition). See also the like-spirited positions presented in Carl J. Friedrich, *Tradition and Authority* (London, 1972), 45–56; and Michael Walzer, *Interpretation and Social Criticism* (Cambridge, MA, 1987), 21–32.

69 Thomas Hobbes, *A Dialogue between a Philosopher and a Student of the Common Laws of England Dialogue* (1681), ed. Joseph Cropsey (Chicago, 1971), 56.

70 Bentham, *Comment on the Commentaries*, 199.

71 Bentham explained his meaning of the often-used phrase in his 1825 *Indications Respecting Lord Eldon*; see Jeremy Bentham, *Official Aptitude Maximized; Expense Minimized*, ed. Philip Schofield (Oxford, 1993), 254.

72 These features receive emphasis and explication in Edward Shils's account of the 'endurance of past objects' and the 'bearers of tradition' in his *Tradition* (Chicago, 1981), especially chaps 2 and 7, and in Krygier, 'Law as Tradition,' 240–51.

73 See the important contributions in Dawson, *Oracles of the Law*; R.C. van Caenegem, *Judges, Legislators and Professors* (Cambridge, 1987); Peter Stein, *Legal Institutions: The Development of Dispute Settlement* (London, 1984); and Peter G. Stein, 'Judge and Jurist in the Civil Law: An Historical Interpretation,' *Louisiana Law Review*, 46 (1985): 241–57.

74 See H.G. Hanbury, *The Vinerian Chair and Legal Education* (Oxford, 1958), and Paul Lucas, 'Blackstone and the Reform of the Legal Profession,' *English Historical Review*, 77 (1962): 456–89.

75 Thomas Littleton, *New Tenures* (printed 1481), cited in Baker, *Introduction to English Legal History*, 62.

76 The fact that the language of the law was not English caused obvious embarrassment in those settings where common law was celebrated for its singular fit with 'the nature and disposition' of the English people; see, for example, Davies, *Reports*, 7–9.

77 For the long survival of the 'memorial culture' of English law, see Richard Ross, 'The Memorial Culture of Early Modern English Lawyers: Memory as Keyword, Shelter, and Identity, 1560–1640,' *Yale Journal of Law and the Humanities*, 10 (1998): 229–326.

78 Dawson, *Oracles of the Law*, 2–3.

79 *History of the Common Law*, 162.

80 This, at least, is how I understand Gadamer's treatment of the 'exemplary significance of legal hermeneutics'; see Hans-Georg Gadamer, *Truth and Method*, 2nd rev. ed., trans. Joel Weinsheimer and Donald G. Marshall (New York, 1989), 324–41.

81 Edmund Burke, *Reflections on the Revolution in France* (1790), ed. Conor Cruise O'Brien (Harmondsworth, 1969), 120.

82 Friedrich Karl von Savigny, *Of the Vocation of Our Age for Legislation and Jurisprudence* (1814), trans. Abraham Hayward (London, 1931), 137, 28, 24.

Chapter Nine

Tradition, Ethical Knowledge, and Multicultural Societies

GEORGIA WARNKE

My concern in this paper is the relation between ethical knowledge and tradition in contemporary multicultural societies. Such societies are characterized by the recognition on the part of their members that their own cultures and traditions, including their ethical traditions, are not unique. My question, then, is how our ethical knowledge can orient our actions once we recognize the existence of diverse traditions, all with action-orienting conceptions of their own. I elucidate the link between tradition and ethical knowledge by looking at the work of Jane Austen. I then explore the problem with this link by looking at Bernard Williams's *Ethics and the Limits of Knowledge*.

Austen's Use of Tradition

Austen's *Pride and Prejudice* contains a puzzle: namely how is it possible for Elizabeth Bennet to shed as quickly as she does her initial prejudices against Mr Darcy, the man she eventually marries, and in favour of Mr Wickham, the man who eventually runs off with her sister? In the first part of the book, Elizabeth holds two firm prejudices about Darcy. First, she thinks that he has deprived Wickham of the living his father left to him, believing Wickham's own suggestions that Darcy must be either jealous or spiteful. Second, she thinks that Darcy has separated his friend Bingley from her sister, Jane Bennet, because he is overly concerned with issues of wealth and social standing, in both of which the Bennets are somewhat lacking. For these reasons, when Darcy first asks Elizabeth to marry him, she replies that:

From the beginning, from the first moment, I may almost say, of my acquaintance with you, your manners impressing me with the fullest belief of your arrogance, your conceit and your selfish disdain for the feelings of others, were such as to form that ground of disapprobation on which succeeding events have built so immovable a dislike; and I had not known you a month before I felt that you were the last man in the world whom I could ever be prevailed upon to marry.[1]

Still, a day later, so immovable a dislike begins to remove itself. Darcy gives Elizabeth a letter which she begins to read, Austen writes, 'with a strong prejudice against everything he might say.'[2] A minute later she is less convinced of her assumptions and two hours later she has 'reconciled herself' to a total reversal not only of her beliefs about Darcy, but about Wickham, the consequences of her mother's moral emptiness, and the proper measure of misplaced pride to be parcelled out to Darcy and herself. 'Pleased with the preference of one, and offended by the neglect of the other, on the very beginning of our acquaintance I have courted prepossession and ignorance, and driven reason away, where either were concerned.'[3]

How is this swift reversal to be explained?[4] It cannot be explained by recourse to Enlightenment conceptions of the eventual force of reason in overcoming the strength of a prejudice rooted in pride and hasty judgment for, given the strength of Elizabeth's prejudices against Darcy, it is not clear how she can even begin to think rationally about his claims. Darcy's letter states that his actions in separating Bingley and Jane Bennet were motivated by a concern with the general vulgarity and materialism of the Bennet family rather than a concern with wealth or social standing. Moreover, he claims that he acceded to Wickham's own desire to exchange the living for money and chose not to give Wickham more money or the living when he later asked for it. In addition, he notes the 'general profligacy' and 'extravagance' of Wickham's nature, which led him to be unsuited for a life in the church and eager for money to support his lifestyle. Still, if Elizabeth is as prejudiced in her perception of the world as Austen suggests she is, how does she ever start to replace her 'prepossession' and 'ignorance' with understanding?

To be sure, Elizabeth acknowledges that she can find no proof of the injustice of the claims Darcy makes. She acknowledges, for example, that she cannot recall observing one act of goodness, integrity, or benevolence on Wickham's part. Still, since she is prejudiced in favour of Wickham and against Darcy, why does she suddenly think she needs proof of the injustice of Darcy's claims instead of their justice?

Austen's account relies on a connection between understanding and what might be called the productive or enabling prejudices of a tradition, upon traditional standards of virtue and propriety which can provide a reliable backdrop for interpreting action and behaviour. In this regard, the impact of Darcy's letter on Elizabeth has less to do with its actual explanation of his actions than with the reminder it offers Elizabeth of the 'impropriety' and 'indelicacy' of certain aspects of Wickham's behaviour. Although she was originally too inclined to think well of him to notice, she now sees he should not have put himself forward on the first evening he and Elizabeth spent together at her aunt's house. Nor, since she was almost a complete stranger at the time, should he have told her of Darcy's supposed misconduct towards him. To these failings in proper behaviour, Elizabeth adds her recollection that Wickham had eagerly spread his story of Darcy's misconduct after Darcy and the Bingley party had left the area and despite his professed regard for Darcy's father and therefore for the family's name. Because Wickham does so, Elizabeth now knows how to understand his character and virtue. She is able to do so because she can question her first impressions of him by relying upon the authority of a tradition that contains assumptions about appropriate forms of action and behaviour and the meaning of deviations from them.

The ethical knowledge that Elizabeth acquires by belonging to a coherent tradition of action and behaviour is clearest in her response to Lady Catherine de Bourgh. Lady Catherine confronts her with the rumour that she is to marry Darcy, who is Lady Catherine's nephew, and asks her to declare that she will never marry him. For her to do so would, in Lady Catherine's eyes, 'pollute the shades of Pemberley' since Elizabeth, she thinks, can bring neither honour nor credit to the marriage. Not only is she inferior in wealth and social status, but her family has had to arrange a hasty marriage to cover up her sister's shame in running away with Wickham. But Elizabeth replies with unwavering conviction with regard to the criteria appropriate to her own actions. Lady Catherine insists that marriage to Darcy is a selfish, unfeeling act on Elizabeth's part that will disgrace him 'in the eyes of everybody' and she asks whether Elizabeth is really resolved 'to have him' under these circumstances. Elizabeth responds: 'I am only resolved to act in that manner which will, in my own opinion, constitute my happiness, without reference to you, or to any person so wholly unconnected with me.' When Lady Catherine claims that she thereby violates 'the claims of duty, honour, and gratitude,' she is even firmer in her conviction. 'Neither duty, nor honour, nor gratitude have any possible claim on me in the present instance,' she replies. 'No principle of either would be violated.'[5]

Elizabeth's ethical standards are secure. Lady Catherine insists that honour, decorum, and prudence require her to give Darcy up, that her connection to his family can only disgrace it, and even that proper gratitude and deference to Lady Catherine herself forbid the marriage. But Elizabeth knows what she owes to whom, who is entitled to what from her, and what Darcy or anyone really owes his or her family. She knows that one need not be imposed upon by the desires of those 'wholly unconnected' to one by family or friendship. Moreover, she knows that duty requires deference to her own silly mother rather than to Lady Catherine, that honour is a question not just of social station but actions in accord with it, and that, if gratitude is due anyone, it is due Darcy for his attentions to her in spite of her behaviour towards him. She knows that she need not be grateful to Lady Catherine for her condescension to her, nor need she pretend that Lady Catherine's snobbery is a form of propriety. Whereas Lady Catherine's appeal to a tradition of action and behaviour refers only to the most superficial conventions of status and privilege, Elizabeth is able to focus on the substance of the concepts of her tradition, concepts that include norms of honour, duty, deference, and social disgrace as well as ideas about what it is and is not to be a gentleman.

But Elizabeth's certainty and security raise two problems. First, as significant as what her tradition allows her to recognize is what it does not. It allows her to revise her original understanding of both Wickham and Darcy, to see through Lady Catherine's standards, and to come to a better understanding of herself and her happiness. Yet, it does not allow her to question the justice of the social hierarchy she takes for granted or why her own life options should be limited to the choices contained in various proposals of marriage. The form of life to which Elizabeth is bound is one that provides a framework within which she can develop sound interpretations of the meaning of the actions and behaviour she encounters. But this framework also excludes what seem to be significant issues.

Second, Elizabeth's certainty seems obsolete. If the strength of her tradition and the unquestioned character of its assumptions allow her to overcome misleading prejudices, it is not clear what lesson we might draw from this accomplishment. While Lady Catherine's appeal to tradition is simply an appeal to a superficial version of the same tradition to which Elizabeth appeals, the problem with certainty and ethical knowledge in contemporary society seems, at least in part, to involve the encounter with different traditions in which different groups appeal to equally substantive assumptions about action and behaviour. Elizabeth's poise in countering insult is the result of the sure ethical knowledge that comes of participating in a tradition that has no doubts about itself. But what happens to the possibility of such knowledge and of sure action in a multicultural society in which individual traditions can no longer assume the unique legitimacy of their own assumptions and in which they must acknowledge the presence of different traditions with substantive assumptions of their own? How are we to respond to the issues that divide us if these issues can be understood under different assumptions and in different ways depending upon the traditions to which we appeal?

Consider surrogate mothering. Do duty, honour, and gratitude require a surrogate mother to surrender custody of her child to the biological father, for example? Certainly some insist that she has at least a contractual duty to do so.[6] If, in addition, honour involves keeping the promises and contracts one has made and if gratitude is due sponsoring parents because of the financial and emotional support they typically give the surrogate mother, then one might well decide that all three concepts of duty, honour, and gratitude do require a surrogate mother to surrender custody of her child. If we introduce a concept of selfishness that renders it part of a mother's duty and honour to sacrifice her good for the good of her child, then relinquishing a child to a father who is typically wealthier than the surrogate seems perhaps even more appropriate.

Yet, we also have recourse to alternative traditions with different values, ones that speak to the value and duties of motherhood and to the sanctity of the family as a sphere of life inaccessible to the demands of contracts and economics.[7] According to this tradition, duty, honour, and gratitude are defined in terms of family bonds, and if selfishness is an issue at all it pertains to those who would uphold a contract over a mother's love for her child. It seems that as members of contemporary societies, we might appeal equally easily to either tradition in trying to resolve the issue. Moreover, whichever ideas about surrogate motherhood we do adopt, it seems impossible to convince either ourselves or others of their exclusive validity or therefore to act on the certainty of our ethical knowledge. We can understand the issues surrounding surrogacy and motherhood under at least two sets of premises and assumptions, and the same would seem to hold of other issues currently confronting society. What are the conceptions in terms of which we need or ought to understand the issues of abortion, affirmative action, or pornography, for example? If we know we can understand these issues and practices in different, legitimate ways, how are we to argue for our views with regard to them or take any action at all? What does it mean to overcome our possibly unproductive or misleading prejudices with regard to these issues in a context in which they are possibly unproductive or misleading only from one among a number of possible points of view? What does it mean to overcome them under circumstances in which our traditions no longer orient us in only one way but have become porous enough to include different sets of assumptions and orientations that make claims on different groups?

The Limits of Ethical Knowledge and Reflection

Bernard Williams employs a notion of thick concepts to make the point I have been trying to draw from *Pride and Prejudice* that our understanding at least of our human and social world is bound up with the orientations provided by our traditions. Thick concepts, such as cowardice, brutality, and gratitude, combine fact and value by providing for both the accurate description of an action or character and the proper evaluation of it.[8] Description and evaluation cannot be pulled apart in thick concepts; their evaluative aspect cannot be stripped off the description to leave a simply neutral way of depicting facts of the social world. Rather, one understands the meaning of the concept by taking up the evaluative stance contained in it and understanding how it is differentiated from the other possible evaluative stances characteristic of the particular tradition to which the thick concepts belong. Thick concepts thus form parts of traditions with other assumptions and evaluations. One can be a coward in different ways in different cultures, and the particular way in which one is a coward in a particular culture will depend upon both the concepts to which cowardice is related – for instance, fear of battle in one and fear of intimacy in another – as well as the other concepts from which cowardice is distinguished. One can have the sort of proper pride that Darcy has only in cultures where pride can be proper and improper, and where it is not automatically a vice signalling a hubris unbecoming to God, for example. The proper pride that Darcy has is intimately connected to other thick concepts of the culture, to the duties and obligations of gentlemen, for instance, as well as to the deference due them by others simply for who they are.

Thick concepts have two additional features as Williams conceives of them. First, they are action-motivating. When we know the concept in terms of which to understand someone or something, we also know how to act with regard to that person or thing. The difference between a person with improper pride and one with proper pride in cultures where that distinction makes sense will affect the way the members of the culture relate to him or her. Second, thick concepts admit of right and wrong applications and are thus world-guided, as Williams puts the point.[9] Knowing what it means to attribute cowardice to someone and how cowardice is to be distinguished from diffidence and timidity depend upon the features of the social world to which these concepts belong. Similarly, knowing how pride is to be distinguished from both arrogance and disdain for the feelings of others 'tracks the truth' in the sense that it adequately comprehends actual features of the tradition or social world to which the thick concepts belong.

Still, what happens to the possibility that thick concepts can orient action and track truth if our social world contains multiple traditions and competing sets or understandings of thick concepts? Williams suggests a notion of confidence, looking to institutions, upbringing, and public discourse in general and concluding that 'One question we have to answer is how people, or enough people, can come to possess a practical confidence that, particularly granted both the need for reflection and its pervasive presence in our world, will come from strength and not from the weakness of self-deception and dogmatism.'[10]

Williams does not try to answer this question or indicate how confidence might help resolve such ethical issues within single societies as that of surrogate mothering. Indeed, he sees confidence primarily as the appropriate attitude that a democratic culture might take towards cultures alien to it. Nonetheless, I want to apply his idea of confidence to the appropriate attitude that members of the diverse traditions within a pluralistic and multicultural society might take towards each other's orientations and understandings. Moreover, I want to suggest that one way to instil confidence might be to recognize the place it already has in our discussions of art and literature. For one way to characterize these understandings and discussions is to show that they already replace rational conviction with confidence and knowledge with understanding. To this extent, they might form part of the answer to the question of how members of multicultural societies can acquire the practical or ethical confidence Williams proposes.

Confidence and Interpretation

The account of Austen's *Pride and Prejudice* that I have offered attends to issues of prejudice, knowledge, and self-knowledge. It does so because it addresses the text with a specific question, namely, how is Elizabeth Bennet's progression from blind prejudice to knowledge and self-knowledge possible? This question leads to further questions about the limits of a tradition-bound knowledge and the possibility of ethical knowledge in a society with competing traditions. To this extent, the question emerges from a particular context of expectations and assumptions that involves late twentieth-century suspicions about the force and limits of reason as well as late twentieth-century issues about pluralism and multiculturalism.

That *Pride and Prejudice* offers an answer to the question of overcoming blind prejudices, however, does not mean that this question is one that Austen intended to answer. To the contrary, to suppose that Austen's questions and our own converge is to assume that what a person intends to do or say is always transparent in his or her speech act, text, or action or that one's plans always coincide with the actual course of events. But if it is only by examining the resulting text, speech act, or action as we find it that we can reconstruct the question, then the question we reconstruct is one to which the text or action actually provides an answer, at least for us. It is not necessarily the question the author or agent may have initially intended to answer.[11]

But who is the *we* here? If the meaning of a text can be disassociated from its author's intentions and if questions about knowledge and prejudice lead to one way of understanding Austen's *Pride and Prejudice*, they are clearly not the only questions one might address to the novel. Nor are they the only ones that can arise for late twentieth-century readers. Others might attend to the ways in which Austen undermines a particular patriarchal form of the novel[12] or to issues concerning the ethics of laughter.[13] Such attention will emphasize different aspects of the novel and reveal different dimensions of it. What the novel means to some of us because of the questions and interests we bring to it and the hermeneutic context into which we place it will differ from the hermeneutic context and questions others bring. The meaning we understand does not conform to the objective meaning of the text, then, but to the meaning of the text for us, given the interpretive context within which we find ourselves.

Still, if objectivism is ruled out in the literary domain, so is a relativism that would argue that because meaning is dependent on the questions we ask, any questions and therefore any meaning must be legitimate. Rather, our understanding of texts and works of art remains work-guided in the way in which an appropriate use of thick concepts is world-guided for Williams. Just as thick concepts of propriety and impropriety lead Elizabeth to a deeper understanding of Wickham, Darcy, and herself, the prejudices from which we proceed and the questions we ask of a text are validated to the extent that they help to reveal dimensions of the meaning of the text. One way to specify the content of this revelation is to employ the hermeneutic concept of a unity of whole and part. The claim here is that only the premise that a text as a whole forms a coherent, unified meaning allows the sort of investigation into it and revision of initial inadequate interpretations that can illuminate it for us. Furthermore, despite theories such as deconstruction, even the claim that a text subverts its meaning presupposes an understanding of what that meaning, in its unity, could be.[14] Still, the argument against relativism in our understanding of texts is simply that we can distinguish between the various legitimate understandings of a text and those that fail to make sense of it at all.

Indeed, we can even distinguish between understandings of its unity that allow us to learn from a text and those that do not. Elizabeth's understanding of the thick concepts of duty, honour, gratitude, and the like is more adequate, in this sense, than Lady Catherine's, for example, because it not only gives a coherent sense to the thick concepts of her tradition but because it grasps their point and is not attentive only to their surface appearance. Similarly, the more illuminating understandings of a text will be those that allow it to speak to concerns that are or can be shown by the interpretation to be real concerns for us. Of course, a given text may not have a point, and attempts to show that it does will often possess a forced character, usually betrayed in the necessity the interpretation confronts of giving up some portion of the unity of part and whole.[15] Showing the point of a text does not require conscious efforts to modernize it or show its relevance. In the main, however, the understandings of a text that are most productive or helpful are those that succeed in showing that the meaning it has provides answers or provokes new questions about issues with which we are or can learn to be concerned. Texts that cannot ask or answer questions for us are thus dead in the sense that we can no longer find or inhabit the hermeneutic horizon that might awaken their meaning for us.

Both nonobjectivist and nonrelativist sides of this analysis of the understanding of textual meaning help, I think, to elucidate Williams's account of the possibility of confidence in our ethical understanding. On the one hand, in interpreting texts, we are already aware of what Williams calls nonobjectivity. We are aware that our interpretations are not the only possible ones, that interpreters with different concerns, different theoretical and practical commitments, and different historical and hermeneutic contexts can find very different meanings in the same text. On the other hand, we are also aware of the adequacy of our own interpretations as interpretations that awaken meaning, that allow perhaps new or different dimensions of the meaning of a text to emerge. Our textual interpretations are not ones about which we can have conviction as long as the concept of conviction implies an absolute trust in the exclusive correctness of our own views; nor are our interpretations ones that we think others could reject only on pain of irrationality. Rather, our textual interpretations are ones in which we appropriately have confidence as adequate, revealing, and illuminating interpretations insofar as they can tell us something about a text and, perhaps, even about ourselves. Our understanding of texts as well as works of art are ones in which we can have confidence, then, rather than conviction because we recognize that the understanding we have is both disclosive of meaning and nonexclusive.

The other side of this confidence in our own interpretations is an acknowledgment of the confidence others have in their interpretations. If we recognize the nonexclusive character of our understanding of meaning, then we must also recognize that other interpretations are capable of delivering important, nonexclusive insights of their own in which their proponents can appropriately have confidence. In the literary domain we offer our interpretations as ones that illuminate the text in a way that we are confident others might appreciate. But we also assume that we can appreciate and even learn from their interpretations as well. Indeed, this assumption seems crucial to our interest in engaging in discussions of texts and works of art in the first place. We are not concerned to show the mistake in every possible interpretation other than our own; nor are we interested in ending discussion of specific texts and works of art once and for all. Rather, we assume that different vantage points, different connections, and different interests will continue to reveal new dimensions of a text or work of art in a never-ending way. Moreover, we assume that the strength of our own interpretation depends upon its openness to others, upon its ability to incorporate the insights it may have that are relevant to our own understanding, and upon its ability to situate these insights in relation to our own.

The idea of a confidence in our interpretations of texts and works of art transfers easily to the ethical confidence on which Williams focuses. In both cases, first of all, we can distinguish between legitimate and illegitimate interpretations of meaning without insisting that our legitimate interpretations are canonically correct. Second, in both cases we can allow for the possibility of other thick concepts and legitimate interpretations. Thus we recognize that Jane Austen's novels admit of different illuminating interpretations and that we can have confidence in our own understanding even as we appreciate that of others. Similarly, a principle linking pride not to social standing but to achievement is a principle in which we can have confidence even if we recognize alternative thick concepts in terms of which the idea of pride can be constructed. We can recognize that a principle respecting the sanctity of human life can be understood in at least two different ways, in terms that speak either to the creativity of nature in creating biological life or to the investment of human beings in their own lives and the lives of those close to them.[16] A principle of liberty can be understood to involve both the capacity for the autonomous decisions of individuals and the rights of self-determination of communities in establishing what they understand as the conditions for flourishing lives.

Third, we recognize that the strength of our interpretations depends upon their capacity to participate in an ongoing discussion and elaboration of meaning. In the case of diverging interpretations of a literary text, we acknowledge, appreciate, and even try to learn from the interpretation that differs from our own. We try to understand what it understands of the text that we may have missed and we try to incorporate some of its insights into our own account. Were each side to proceed in this way in the case of interpreting our principles and practices, we might acknowledge that different sides can understand them in ways from which we all might learn.

If we add to these three similarities a commitment to avoid those interpretations that suppress the interpretive voices of others, then I think we can appropriately have a nondogmatic confidence in our ethical understanding as we do in our understanding of texts. Interpretations that suppress the interpretive voices of others violate the conditions of the sort of interpretive or hermeneutic conversation I am suggesting. They limit the number of possibly legitimate interpretations from which our own interpretations might learn and hence undermine their own strength. If we are aware of nonobjectivity, dogmatically trying to impose our own particular interpretation as ethical truth not only seems 'remarkably inadequate' as Williams writes; it also reflects a move we have productively done without in the domain of art and literature.

To this extent, the discussions of art and literature in which we already commonly participate seem to provide a kind of quasi-institutional setting and a part of our common upbringing that lend themselves to answering the question Williams raises, as to 'how people, or enough people, can come to possess a practical confidence that, particularly granted both the need for reflection and its pervasive presence in our world, will come from strength and not from the weakness of self-deception and dogmatism.'[17] How might such confidence in our ethical understanding help resolve the ethical differences we confront as members of multicultural societies? Discussions of how we might resolve our ethical differences typically look to the means for legitimately imposing or establishing one understanding of the issues under consideration as the proper one. If we take our discussions of art and literature as our guide, however, we might work to remain open to the ethical understandings of others and try to incorporate what we can of each other's understandings into our own. Moreover, we might compromise on what we cannot incorporate, in the recognition that what is at stake is what we can accept of each other's interpretations as ones in which they and we might have confidence, and we might compromise on what we cannot incorporate, on the recognition that what is at stake is not knowledge but understanding, not conviction but confidence.

Two different traditions of thought compete in their understanding of the practice of abortion, the principles it involves, and the issues of sex, reproduction, and motherhood surrounding it.[18] Pro-life groups understand abortion as murder and, hence, as a violation of the principles of respect for the sanctity of life. Further, they understand sex as a sacred act, reproduction as the most basic point of human life, and motherhood as that place in any culture which speaks to its regard for the virtues of care and concern for others. Conversely, pro-choice groups understand abortion as a personal procreative decision based on a family's particular understanding of respect for the sanctity of life. In addition, they see sex as either sacred or not sacred depending upon its connection to intimacy, reproduction as a life option, and mother-hood as a grave responsibility to be entered into, at best, under condi-tions that allow families to flourish. But it is unclear how either side can maintain the conviction that its interpretation of this complex of principles, values, and meanings is the only possible one. How might one say definitively what motherhood, for example, is once one is aware of the different forms it has historically taken and the different forms it may take in the future? And while we might say that, at least for us, the ideal of motherhood speaks to a kind of selfless love and generosity, it also may legitimately seem to include the idea of a responsibility taken up freely and consciously. But why should we have to choose between one concept of motherhood and the other? Rather, each set of interpretations is one in which its proponents can have confidence as a legitimate understanding that illuminates some part of what abortion, respect for the sanctity of life, sex, reproduction, and motherhood mean even if it cannot illuminate all of what any mean and, indeed, even if no interpretation can illuminate all of what any mean. But if each set of interpretations is one in which its advo-cates can have confidence as opposed to conviction, then might we not look for a solution to the controversy over abortion that tries to accom-modate both? Might we not look for solutions that reduce the inci-dences of abortion while creating the social and economic conditions under which women can make autonomous and responsible choices as well as good lives for their children?

Our different understandings of surrogate mothering seem to admit of a similar confidence. Carmel Shalev argues that if we conceive of surrogate mothering in terms of norms involving the freedom of con-tract, we are led to demand specific compliance of surrogacy contracts even in cases in which the surrogate mother finds it difficult to relin-quish the child she has conceived and to whom she has given birth.[19] To allow surrogate mothers to change their minds and renege on the contracts they have made freely and consciously is, according to Sha-lev, to deny women both autonomy and rationality. The policy assumes that women cannot be trusted to act responsibly, to under-stand the consequences of their actions, or to think clearly and with foresight. Hence, it revokes any thought of women's equality with men

and associates women with the age-old stereotype of emotional imma-
turity.

But this interpretation of surrogate mothering is not the only one
that makes sense to us. We can also understand surrogacy as an exploitation of poor women for the benefit of economically better-off
couples. In this case, we will understand the demand for specific compliance as further exploitation. Poorer women sell their procreative
capacities in relatively selfless attempts to help their own families and
infertile couples. When they cannot help but treat the babies to which
they give birth as family, they are required to sacrifice their own happiness and what they conceive of as their own babies' well-being in order
to satisfy the demands of an economic marketplace that has intruded
into all spheres of life, even those of love and intimacy. On this interpretation of surrogacy, either the practice is inhumane and ought to be
prohibited or, at the very least, its norms should mirror those of adoption rather than commerce.

Given these different rubrics and traditions in terms of which we
might confidently understand surrogate mothering – those of family
versus marketplace and love versus commerce – how can we come to
any conclusion as to whether it amounts to an extension of contract
law or an extension of adoption law? If we combine Williams's suggestions with the form our literary discussions already take, then we
might say that while we maintain our commitment to our own understanding of the practice, we recognize the nonobjective or nonexclusive character of that understanding and refuse to rule out the
possible legitimacy of other interpretations. Hence we might acknowledge that both sides in the debate understand the practice of surrogacy as a coherent whole and that neither tries to minimize the
significance of the issues involved, those of autonomy, rationality,
equality, love, and family. But this circumstance seems to indicate that
we might try to accommodate both interpretations of the practice.
Hence we might develop a policy on surrogate mothering that accords
women autonomy and rationality in their decisions to try to become
surrogate mothers and yet allows them to decide not to relinquish custody of their babies once they have given birth and as long as they
make their decision within a short period of time. On the other side,
our policy might take seriously the contract into which the surrogate
and sponsoring couple have entered and allow for the father's custody rights as well as those of the mother. The answer to the issue of
surrogate mothering might then be a flexible policy that leads to joint

custody in cases in which the birth mother cannot give up all custody of her child.

Compromises of this sort stem from the recognition that in multicultural and pluralistic societies our ethical knowledge warrants confidence rather than conviction and thus has more in common with our interpretations of texts and works of art than it does with a moral absolutism. At stake is neither scientific knowledge nor unjustified opinion but, instead, differences in legitimate understandings of the meaning of our principles and ideals. While not every interpretation of their meaning will be legitimate, more than one may be. Our confidence in our own interpretations comes from our ability to show their legitimacy as productive illuminations of the issues at stake. At the same time, this confidence is one that can admit and even learn from the possible illumination that other approaches offer as well. This sort of confidence leads away from dogmatism and to an openness that is willing to try to accommodate all legitimate voices in our discussions of meaning.

NOTES

This paper was originally given at *The Journal of the History of Ideas* conference in New Brunswick, New Jersey, in 1997. I subsequently developed it into chapter 7 of *Legitimate Differences: Interpretation in the Abortion Controversy and Other Public Debates* (Berkeley, 1999). This initial version is published here with the permission of the University of California Press. I would like to thank the participants in the conference for their criticism and comments.

1 Jane Austen, *Pride and Prejudice* (New York: Bantam Classic Edition, 1981), 145.
2 Ibid., 153.
3 Ibid., 156.
4 Since Austen's ability to describe such processes seems fairly well established by her other work, I assume the swift reversal cannot be attributed to any failure on Austen's part. See George Haggerty's account of her attempts to find a suitable language for the expression of thought processes in 'The Sacrifice of Privacy in *Sense and Sensibility*' in *Tulsa Studies in Women's Literature*, 7 (1988), esp. 230–3.
5 *Pride and Prejudice*, 268.
6 See Carmel Shalev, *Birth Power: The Case for Surrogacy* (New Haven, 1989).

7 See, for example, Elizabeth Anderson, *Value in Ethics and Economics* (Cambridge, 1993), 168–89.
8 Bernard Williams, *Ethics and the Limits of Philosophy* (Cambridge, MA, 1985), 140.
9 Ibid., 141.
10 Ibid., 171.
11 See Hans-Georg Gadamer, *Truth and Method*, 2nd rev. ed., trans. Joel Weinsheimer and Donald G. Marshall (New York, 1994), 373.
12 See George Haggerty, *Unnatural Affections: Women and Fiction in the Later Eighteenth Century* (Bloomington, 1998).
13 See Edward Copeland and Juliet McMaster, eds, *The Cambridge Companion to Jane Austen* (Cambridge, 1997).
14 See Diane P. Michelfelder and Richard E. Palmer, *Dialogue and Deconstruction: The Gadamer-Derrida Debate* (Albany, 1989).
15 Dworkin thus insists that his criteria of fit and best light stand and fall together. See 'How Law Is Like Literature' in *A Matter of Principle* (Cambridge, MA, 1985).
16 See Ronald Dworkin, *Life's Dominion: An Argument about Abortion, Euthanasia, and Individual Freedom* (New York, 1993), 30–101.
17 Williams, *Ethics and the Limits of Philosophy*, 171.
18 See, for example, Kristin Luker, *Abortion and the Politics of Motherhood* (Berkeley, 1984).
19 See Shalev, *Birth Power*.

Chapter Ten

Ideas about Tradition in the Life and Work of Philippe Ariès

PATRICK H. HUTTON

On Inheritance and Invention: A Context for Discussing Tradition

Current thinking about the relationship between tradition and history owes much to the anthology edited by Eric Hobsbawm and Terence Ranger entitled *The Invention of Tradition*.[1] Published in 1983, it was widely read and is the basis for a good deal of the recent scholarly interest in the topic. Hobsbawm and Ranger emphasize the way politicians used factitious images of a traditional past to further their projects for building the nation-state in the late nineteenth century. Ironically, these authors conclude, the traditions the state-builders 'invented' crowded out the customary past they professed to honour. Some of their contributors link the invention of tradition to European imperialism in the non-Western world. All of them underscore the constructed nature of tradition as an instrument of political power. Since its publication, this anthology has been cited by almost everyone engaged in research on tradition and more generally on memory and identity.[2]

But now, some twenty years after this heuristic study's first appearance, we might ask whether the concept of invented traditions has not come to restrict the conceptual possibilities of the topic it explores. Hobsbawm and Ranger, after all, were dealing with a particular way of understanding tradition at a specific time in modern history. The late nineteenth century witnessed the triumph of the nation-state's efforts to fashion a culture in its own image, and the historians of invented traditions have rightly pointed out the degree to which that image was contrived. But what then are the authentic foundations of tradition?

In the search for an answer, much depends upon the perspective from which we approach the topic. There is a way of understanding tradition in terms of uses of the past that serve present ends, as Hobsbawm and Ranger have shown us. Tradition invokes the authority of past practices and beliefs as a basis for action in the present. All traditions are constructed, in the sense that they are products of human ingenuity. But there is also a way of understanding tradition as it is carried forward out of the depths of the past. Reiteration is a distinguishing feature of tradition's power, building on its connections with sustaining foundations. It is here that the interest in tradition beyond invention lies.[3]

One can see this difference in the historical perspective on tradition offered only a generation ago. If scholars have been preoccupied with the political uses of tradition since the 1980s, they were in the 1960s more concerned with the continuities that tradition perpetuates. The history of mentalities was then the historiographical focus of the famous French Annales school of historical scholarship, and its take on tradition was one that put a decided accent on the inertial power of long-established mores and practices. The early studies, notably those by Lucien Febvre and Robert Mandrou, defined tradition in terms of habits of mind, inveterate beliefs, and conventions of thought that persisted despite changing realities. Tradition in this view was about the enduring influence of the customary past on present thinking.[4]

In this essay I would like to consider the concept of tradition caught between these two perspectives in the historiography of our time – in the move from the history of mentalities, which stressed the residual power of the past as it inheres in popular mores, to the history of constructed identity, which imposes a politics of present memory from above. To do so I want to look at the ideas about tradition of the French cultural historian Philippe Ariès (1914–84). Ariès is well known as an original, somewhat idiosyncratic pioneer in the history of mentalities. He was deeply influenced by Annales historiography but even more so by the royalist tradition into which he was born and to which he maintained a lifelong attachment.

The problem of the relationship between tradition and history is a running theme in Ariès's life work, and his progress as a scholar is marked by a deepening critical perspective on it. In his own broad outline, he presented the dynamics of modern history as an interplay between two types of culture: an older one based on popular traditions and a newer one based upon the scientific, rationalizing techniques promoted by the modern state. He argued that they openly rivalled each other through the eighteenth and nineteenth centuries. By the beginning of the twentieth century, however, the culture of techniques was demonstrably placing its stamp upon modern civilization. Here Ariès would have agreed with Hobsbawm and Ranger that the late nineteenth century was prime time for inventing traditions. Ironically, he once observed, even the royalist-inspired Action française reconstructed its own tradition to respond to the trend toward the centralization of the political process. Political nationalism underpinned its activities both before and after the Second World War and prepared the way for the political regime ushered in by Charles de Gaulle.[5]

But as a royalist who harked back to more ancient traditions, Ariès was unwilling to consign them to a vanishing world. As the popular traditions of old France were crowded out of public life, he contended, they found refuge in the private sphere. Far from disappearing, they came to be lodged in those institutions that sustained the mores of everyday life, notably in the family. This was the hidden history that Ariès wished to expose.[6] Political parties may rise and fall, he argued, but popular traditions survive by adapting to new realities. Tracing their historical retreat into the private sphere was to be his major contribution to the newly emerging history of mentalities.

Ariès's historical writings span the period from the early 1940s to the early 1980s and in a way mediate these two notions of tradition, one that endures and one that is invented. Though he came to understand tradition from a critical historical perspective, he never abandoned his love of the particular tradition that had nurtured his own imagination, nor his early insight into tradition's formative role in human experience. As a young man he had been a traditionalist, in the sense that he was committed to advancing a politics that favoured the restoration of the French monarchy and even some of the cultural trappings of the ancien régime. In his youthful writings he sought to show how the political traditions of old France continued to exercise their influence in compelling ways. But in his more mature writings, he displayed greater sensitivity to the way traditions are continually remodelled. Though the phrase 'invented tradition' was one that acquired currency only after his death, he might have acknowledged its utility during his later years. By then he conceded that the architects of the modern state had succeeded in imposing a national identity upon French culture through their influential powers of representation and publicity. But to the end of his life he retained a faith in the capacity of the traditional values of old France to survive as long as they continued to serve the needs of families and other small communities. The local traditions through which such values were transmitted had once been a mainstay of diversity in a society since given to standardization and conformity under the aegis of centralized government. In advancing his tradition-alist view, he wished to distinguish his position from that of the Gaullist right, which in the mid-twentieth century had inherited the mantle of conservative politics and invented a tradition of old France based upon the nationalist ideal.[7]

For this reason, Ariès's work stands as a counterpoint to the scholar-ship inspired by the Hobsbawm/Ranger study. I shall analyse his developing ideas about the nature of tradition as he presented them in stages along his life's way: as a traditionalist interested in preserving the memory of the particular traditions of old France, as a historiogra-pher interested in the interaction between tradition and history, and finally as a historian of the fate of ancient traditions in the modern world.

Ariès is best known for his *L'Enfant et la vie familiale sous l'ancien régime* (1960), his widely read work on childhood and family, and his *L'Homme devant la mort* (1977), on attitudes toward death and mourn-ing.[8] While these studies implicitly convey many of his ideas about tra-dition, two of his earlier works do so more explicitly and are essential reading for our understanding of his views on the topic. The first of these, *Les Traditions sociales dans les pays de France* (1943), composed during the Second World War, was inspired by his search for a new conception of community under the Vichy regime. The second, *Le Temps de l'histoire* (1954), was a series of essays on the relationship between history and tradition, culled from his experience of the war. Ancient traditions, he would argue, nurtured the milieux of social memory out of which our modern ideas about community emerged, and the perspectives on the past that they embody continue to inform our tacit understanding of our everyday lives. In the first study he still sensed himself to be immersed in the social traditions of old France that he believed could reinvigorate public life in the contemporary age. By the time he wrote the second, he was no longer so confident and looked at his own tradition as but one among many that had been overshadowed by the rising power and influence of modern culture.

An ardent spokesman for royalism before the war, Ariès in the post-war era played as gracefully as he could a losing political game. He continued to write for royalist newspapers, but his articles became more reflective, placing present-day cultural problems in historical perspective.[9] His turn from political journalism to cultural history during the 1950s and 1960s signalled his acknowledgment that the traditions of old France could have little place in contemporary public life. Though he held fast to social values that he associated with them, he came as their historian to concede first their legends, then their politics. His consolation was the hope that reflection on the nature of tradition might help us to rethink and enlarge our conception of history. Such was his essential project as a historian.

His work takes on added importance, moreover, when one considers that it is situated at the end of a historiographical tradition that had sustained modern scholarship since the Enlightenment. In the parlance of our times, his writings about tradition and history are situated on the boundary between modern and postmodern historiographical conceptions. The former might be characterized as history conceived as a grand narrative tending toward some projected human destiny, the latter as the dissolution of that narrative in the historians' recourse to the milieux of memory from which modern history had originally sprung. With the demise of the grand narrative in contemporary historical writing, however, history lost its once transparent meaning. Historians began to look for alternative sources for comprehending the past, sometimes finding them embedded in traditions lost or obscured by dominant historical interpretations. Ariès was one of the first historians to sense the change and to suggest some of the implications involved in crossing that historiographical divide. In this respect, *Le Temps de l'histoire* is prophetic in its anticipation of the memory/history issues of our times.

Old France in the Enchanted Childhood of Philippe Ariès

My first perspective concerns Ariès's idealized vision of old France. In his autobiographical reminiscences, he describes a childhood enchanted by its legends.[10] His family honoured royalism as much for its old-fashioned culture as for its politics. In its lore, he lived in the presence of kings and their courtiers, the gentry on their landed estates, and the rural communities that lived close to the land and cherished their local traditions. His childhood image of old France, he later admitted, was derived largely from nineteenth-century conceptions. By then royalism had come to be closely identified with the notables of provincial France, who still exercised considerable influence at the local and regional level. A new France, fashioned by republican politicians and administrators of the nation-state, was all the while intruding more deeply into local affairs. The rivalry of royalists and republicans was as much about idealized conceptions of community as about political institutions. In its way, the rivalry reinforced the confidence of the royalist faithful in their old-fashioned ways. Though their influence was waning by the time Ariès was born, their legends were part of his living memory from childhood and drew him into a love of the history of this ancient heritage.[11]

Ariès's reverence for that tradition-bound world took on a more erudite cast during his days as a student at the University of Paris in the 1930s. He wrote his master's thesis (*diplôme d'études supérieures*, 1936) on the judicial lords of Paris in the sixteenth century, one of the professional communities that made the old regime work. He admired them for their solidarity, their sense of civic duty, and their loyalty to the traditions of their profession. Simultaneously, he joined the Action française, an influential movement of intellectuals on the extreme right that extolled a classical literary tradition to the exclusion of modern intellectual fashions. Writing for its student newspaper, he confidently defended its political cause and paid homage to its leader, Charles Maurras. Mostly, though, his traditionalist views were reinforced by friendships formed among students within this group, whose sociability seemed akin to that he ascribed to the fraternal societies of old France. For Ariès, the loyalties of tradition and of friendship were always closely intertwined.[12]

But Ariès's efforts to invest royalist politics with such attractive qualities came to ruin in the shame of Vichy France during the Second World War. Upon the fall of France in 1940, he had some hope that Vichy head of state Philippe Pétain and his government might adapt the traditions of old France to the realities of the contemporary age. He taught a course for a while in a Vichy-sponsored school in which he developed some of his ideas about history and regional identities. But the school brought its own disappointments and he soon left.[13] Disillusioned with Vichyssois policies and chastened by the presence of Nazi censors, he and a few trusted friends turned from the politics of the present to the culture of the past as a more circumspect way of exposing the traditionalist perspective.[14] They sponsored publication of a series of books concerning 'national restoration,' the first being Ariès's *Les Traditions sociales dans les pays de France* (1943), his understated thesis about the historical groundwork involved in any such project.

Herein Ariès was looking for a principle of decentralization that might serve as an alternative to the republican-inspired, centralized nation-state. He found it in the social networks that had sustained traditional ways. He focused on the *pays*, an ancient unit of regional organization, as a favourable basis for rethinking an ideal of community that was large enough to transcend the networks of the extended family, yet small enough to retain personalism in social relationships. The social traditions of the geographically and culturally diverse *pays* of France, he argued, had once given rural people a deep sense of communal identity. Concrete and practical, their time-honoured customs, mores, and folklore carried the authority of the past but were continually adapted to serve present needs. Conveying the presence of a past that had emerged from immemorial beginnings, they provided an uninterrupted continuum between past and future.[15]

The social traditions of the *pays*, Ariès argued, had once contributed to the cultural and political diversity of France as a nation. Much of his text is devoted to inventorying the geographical, economic, and cultural differences among several of the regions of old France: Normandy, Brittany, Champagne, Burgundy, the Languedoc, and the Île de France. Here he drew upon the scholarship in regional geography that had proliferated in the 1930s and then acquired a particular relevance under the political conditions of Vichy.[16] He analysed the varying ways in which urbanization had penetrated the different regions of France, with attention to the integration of such changes into their local economies and traditional cultures. With an eye to the success of practical solutions in the past, he argued that even the proliferating 'zones' of industrialization might be integrated into the framework of the ancient *pays*.[17] The challenge, he contended, was to envision a new kind of regionalism, sensitive to the historical diversity of the ancient *pays*, that might blend the new urban culture into preexisting rural ways.

In their ensemble, Ariès suggested, these regional entities provided a prototype for a federalist alternative to the homogenizing and centralizing nation-state. Federalism as a political option had been suppressed since the founding of the First Republic in 1792 and its possibilities further obscured by the rationalizing tendencies of modern administrative organization. He extolled the role that the notables, the landed gentry with deep historical roots in the *pays*, had played in local governance before their power had been eclipsed by a prefectoral administration and a legislative system imposed by the central government. The administrative redesign of France into departments during the French Revolution may have obscured the political identity of the *pays*, he explained. But their social traditions continued to thrive, and Vichy, whatever the unfortunate conditions of its emergence, provided an opportunity for resuscitating them as the foundation of a restored French nation.[18]

Such a notion was never tested. Weighed down in defeatist attitudes, Vichyssois collaboration fatally compromised royalism as a political cause. With it vanished Ariès's dream of a royalist federalism, grounded in the social traditions of the ancient *pays*. In fact, Ariès's experience of the war wrested him from his naive commitment to traditionalism. He had become poignantly aware of the parochialism of such views.[19] But to abandon traditionalism was not to repudiate his conviction about the essential social role that tradition plays, and he conjured up spectral images of what a society that had abandoned its traditions might look like. He was especially bothered by the memoirs of erstwhile fascist intellectuals which began to appear in the aftermath of the war. The restoration of the Republic provided them with an easy opportunity to disown earlier allegiances while currying popular sympathy for their openness and vulnerability. They claimed that their confessional candour was a mark of their honesty. Yet Ariès found it difficult to take them at face value. With no anchor in tradition, their opinions changed with reversals in their fortune. Their memoirs augured the coming of a new style of political rhetoric distinguished by its pliability. Herein he began to formulate his notions about the coming of a mass society. This new type of rootless intellectual was conspicuous for the ease with which he repudiated his earlier convictions. He might shed the rhetorical garb of yesterday's ideology. But in doing so he was assuming the cloak of tomorrow's terrorist.[20]

History's Existential Grounding in Tradition

If he could no longer promote his own tradition in the present age, Ariès decided, he could at least reaffirm its values by placing it in historical perspective. In the immediate aftermath of the war, therefore, he sought to relate his understanding of tradition to the emergence of modern historical thinking. The youthful traditionalist who had turned to history to confirm the validity of the tradition in which he had been raised now became the middle-aged historian who used his skills to understand the role that tradition had played in modern society. *Le Temps de l'histoire*, published in 1954 but composed of essays written in the late 1940s, marks the beginning of that inquiry. A history of French history, it is also a meditation on the nature of historical time and documents his growing awareness of the inadequacy of his youthful conception of a transparent connection between his own tradition and a more cosmopolitan historiography.

Ariès came away from his experiences of the war with the understanding that History, conceived as the existential human past, is a larger force than the histories that we have written to encompass it. He had come to recognize, moreover, that the histories we write are nested within historiographical traditions that develop within specific historical circumstances. For Ariès, reckoning with the far-reaching effects of the war, the authority of the modern French historiographical tradition, based on a political framework conceived in light of the rise of France as a nation-state, had come to display its limitations. As a conceptual framework, it was too narrow to make adequate sense of the tide of human experience that overwhelms our efforts as historians to grasp the past.[21] Given its scope and complexity, he argued, History cannot be reduced to the interpretations that we impose upon it. Even in their most capacious expressions, the histories that we write are thin accounts of the reality of the past. The realities of the war had shaken Ariès's confidence in the conceptual frameworks that modern historians had discerned in their histories of the French nation and set him thinking about the myriad alternatives that they had overlooked. Beneath the surface of their notions about a collective national destiny, he suggested, lies an unfathomed depth of alternative meanings the past might hold, some derived from ancient traditions long since forgotten.[22] The war had uprooted Ariès from his traditionalist world. Now as a historian he wanted to go in search of France's multiple historical roots buried deep in the many traditions that issue from its past.

Ariès was a historian, not a philosopher. But his *Le Temps de l'histoire* has some deep philosophical implications for understanding the relationship between tradition and history. Although his argument is implicit rather than explicit, he considers the past in terms of an interplay between two ways of understanding historical time – one as it flows through living tradition, the other as it punctuates historical reconstruction. The time of tradition is existential: it embodies lived experience as it emerges out of the past and so confirms our sense of continuity with it. The time of history is hermeneutical: it interprets the meaning of the past by breaking it up into discrete units and so makes us aware of the differences between past and present. Historians interpret particular traditions in terms of their specific characteristics. One of their tasks is to show the diversity of human experience in the variety of its traditions. But the meaning of tradition for those immersed in each of them, he argued, is incommensurable with such particularities, for it conveys contact with a unifying, ontological ground of human experience. That is why tradition appears to embody the presence of the past.

The ambiguity of the historians' enterprise, Ariès also suggested, is that historians, too, are immersed in their own traditions of historical writing. They may differentiate past from present in the infinite variety of their historical interpretations. But the act of writing history is itself a lived experience that they share with their colleagues and predecessors and tends to reinforce their sense of participation in a common search for the meaning of the human predicament.

To adduce his argument, Ariès traced the particular traditions out of which modern French history had been constructed. These, he argued, provide the matrices from which historical writing proceeds. In the making of modern history, historians composed their narratives out of the materials of ancient traditions. Modern French history, he explained, had been cobbled together in the seventeenth century out of the fragments of medieval chronicles, which in turn drew upon the collective memories of scattered oral legends. In the making of history in early modern France, these elements had been assimilated into a common narrative about the rise of the modern French state. It conflated the times of particular traditions into a single chronology, demarcated by highlights in the lives of the French kings.[23] Ariès suggested that this grand narrative imposed a new temporal framework, one that defined the time of history more abstractly and consigned to oblivion the sense of time as repetition that had informed the local traditions from which it was derived. Modern history was more than an aggregation of narratives derived from local traditions. It imposed its own sense of time upon tradition, and with it the way the idea of tradition itself was understood. The notion of the presence of the past within immemorial tradition was recontextualized within a history informed by a sense of direction between a formative beginning and a projected end. In the process, he proposed, the modern understanding of tradition took on the shape of historical time.[24]

French history, Ariès maintained, has since the Revolution been interpreted in light of opposing conceptions of what France's destiny might be. Historians sympathetic to the revolutionary tradition viewed the Revolution as a series of formative events setting the direction of moral intention the nation would seek to further; those who favoured

the counterrevolutionary alternative construed the same events as har-
bingers of the collapse of an ill-conceived experiment in modern government that would eventually lead to the restoration of the political
ideals of old France. But in a way, Ariès contended, these views of history are mirror images of one another. With variations of emphasis and
sympathy, each contributed to an emerging national tradition of historiography. In that sense, historians loyal to royalism and those inspired
by the Revolution have been tethered together in their efforts to reckon
with France's past. The irony for Ariès was that royalist historiogra-
phers had as a consequence lost sight of the cultural substance of the
royalist heritage – the local traditions of old France – in favour of a conception of a national tradition that reduced that heritage to political
abstractions.[25]

That is why Ariès turned from epic to ordinary lives in his own historical investigations. Here, he believed, local traditions provide subject matter ignored by political historians that is essential to our
understanding of the past. It may be that we can no longer naively promote particular traditions, he conceded. But as a historian, he called for
an examination of the sustaining role that tradition itself has played in
human culture, given that the present age is one in which the pluralism
that tradition promotes is in danger of being lost in a conformist and
easily manipulated mass society. Though he was historicizing the
problem of tradition, Ariès continued to underscore its existential con-
solations, as if the surviving traditions of old France had come to serve
as salvage ships in the turbulent sea of History. If the social traditions
of the ancient *pays* were no longer places where his political hopes
might be invested, then he would look for cultural settings in which
they have retained their value. It was in his musings on the family as
an asylum for the traditional values of old France that he formulated
his earliest notions about the history of mentalities.[26]

The Domestication of Traditional Values in the History
of Mentalities

Ariès's work on the history of mentalities encompassed two major
projects, the first dealing with family, the second with death and
mourning. In the former he stressed how popular mores retain their
vitality by accommodating, even encouraging change. In the latter he
considered how such mores are perpetuated, even as they are transformed over long periods of time.

Ariès found his way to the history of the family through his research on demography, which began even before the war was over and which culminated in his *Histoire des populations françaises* (1948). His research was inspired by a desire to rebut the Vichyssois claim that the fall of France was a product of the biological degeneration of the French people, made manifest in France's declining birth rate since the seventeenth century. The decline of the French population, he countered, reflected a changing mentality among the aristocracy and the middle class about life's prospects, and so signified cultural, not biological issues.

Ariès attributed the levelling of the French population in the modern age to a revolution in mores – the adoption of practices of birth control by married couples beginning in the seventeenth century. It was a revolution whose significance was not immediately appreciated because it was carried out through decisions made in privacy, and so went unperceived in public life. It was in such secret agreements, Ariès contends, that the modern mentality emerged among ordinary people, who decided to take control of their own private destinies by limiting the size of their families in order to provide better lives for themselves and their progeny.[27]

This was his first insight into the emergence of a private sphere of life as a refuge apart from the public one, and so a place where old traditions might be perpetuated. The key to understanding the place of tradition in the modern world, he therefore concluded, was not in regionalism but in families.[28] This led him to his most original observations on the way traditions formed in the public life of old France had been domesticated in the private spaces of modern culture. Their qualities were twofold:

(1) *Mentalities as a vehicle for traditional values.* For Ariès, traditional values in our times are sustained by fundamental attitudes toward life as they are understood by ordinary people. Lodged between instinct and tacit understanding, such attitudes become habits of mind, close in conception to what the Annales historians Febvre and Mandrou had called 'mentalities' and which he himself called a 'collective unconscious.' What Ariès had in mind were attitudes inspired by the practical realities of coping with life's everyday problems: growing up, falling in love, raising children, practising religious piety, growing old, mourning the dead. In a history of mentalities, he hoped to provide an appreciation of the human predicament as it is lived every day, a saga punctuated by the ritual passages of marriage, birth, and death.[29] Fam-

ily traditions are the vehicles by which such mentalities are conveyed from generation to generation.

In their early studies of mentalities, Febvre and Mandrou had put their emphasis on traditions as centres of resistance to change. Ariès rather put his accent on mentalities as a mode of adaptation. The social traditions of old France changed, he explained, but at a pace too slow to be perceived by those who lived within them, bound as they were by the span of living memory – roughly the continuum of recollection communicated across three generations. Living memory, therefore, conveyed the illusion of immobility in the presence of the past, and hence the perception of continuity in tradition. While traditions value the practical wisdom inherited from the past, they update it continually to suit changing realities. All the while, modern culture, with its imperative for punctuality, has remodelled tradition to conform to its quickening pace and so conveys an impression of time accelerating toward a destiny before which tradition must yield. Ariès wanted to show how that too is an illusion.

(2) *Modern tradition between nostalgia and invention.* The mentality that sustains popular traditions in modern France, Ariès argued, is caught between the appeals of repetition and change, and so brings into being notions of an informing heritage and a beckoning destiny. The traditional society of old France honoured the past as a fated world to be accepted. Modern society, born of the Enlightenment, exalted in a world of opportunity in which people might fashion their own future. As historians of mentalities, Ariès argued, we study traditions in order to understand how the relationship between the value accorded continuity and that accorded change is reconfigured over time. Such was his interest in the transmission of the mores of old France into the modern era, which he set out to trace in his study of attitudes toward childhood and family. In his way, he was suggesting that modern traditions accommodate the notion of invention without ascribing everything to it. They continue to serve as agencies calculated to transmit the wisdom of the past.

This remodelling of the traditions of old France to favour the modern mentality provides the basis of Ariès's narrative of the changing nature of the family in modern French cultural history. To put it another way, his argument is based less on a lament for the passing of traditional French society, more on a critique of the rise of its modern counterpart, whose conception of human destiny would transform cultural attitudes about the purposes of family life. The reconfiguration of the family from a mutually dependent kin network into a nuclear core prepared to advance the interests of its individual children exemplifies Ariès's conception of the move from a culture beholden to custom to one eager to plan its own future. But a continuous tradition of family life sustained both in the transition.[30]

For Ariès, the values of old traditions came to be nested in this newly defined sphere of private life. The redefinition of the family as a private realm apart permitted the survival of the qualities that had been most esteemed in traditional society and that appeared to be losing their place in the public life of the modern world – personalism, sociability, loyalty, and civility.[31] For Ariès, private milieux, of which the modern family provided the prototype, permitted the survival of a sense of heritage that was in danger of being lost in the public sphere. But Ariès recognized that the concept of destiny, too, was vulnerable in the diminishing expectations of contemporary society. The search for destiny in our times, he argued, has increasingly been found in our private lives. It was a notion well suited to the temper of the 1960s and 1970s, which in the minds of many observers was coming to value private pursuits over public responsibilities.[32]

The Passing of Royalist Politics

Despite his optimism about the privatization of ancient traditions in the modern family, Ariès knew that the political cause to which he had given his youthful allegiance was passing. For nearly two decades after the war he had continued to write for royalist newspapers, searching for a way in which royalism might be reconceptualized to deal with present realities. Such efforts were finally bankrupted in the futile efforts of his old friends from his Action française days to stay the independence of Algeria during the early 1960s.[33] Despairing of any further political uses for his lingering royalist convictions, he turned more exclusively to his scholarship, this time to the history of attitudes toward death and mourning. By then it was becoming a hot topic in the history of mentalities, and Ariès had been thinking about its possibilities since his demographic research of the late 1940s on mortality rates. The topic also enabled him to address directly the problem of the relationship between tradition and notions of destiny. Death is about destiny, Ariès explained. It is there that we reckon with the meaning of endings. Not surprisingly, the sustaining thread of his argument concerned the decline of the medieval rituals of mourning that had comforted the dying in a way that nothing does today. He plotted stages spanning the history of Western civilization since the Middle Ages, from the 'tamed death' based on trust in an otherworldly destiny to the 'forbidden death' of the present age, based upon the diminishing expectations that the notion of destiny has come to convey.[34]

Interestingly, this project drew him into a long debate with Michel Vovelle, who had also turned to this topic, but who hailed from the Jacobin/Marxist tradition of historiography. Though they came from opposite ends of the political spectrum, both were deeply attached to their respective traditions – Ariès the royalist, Vovelle the revolutionary one – and they may have turned to the topic of death and mourning out of a sense that the force of the traditions to which they had given their youthful allegiances was waning. Both had written major studies of changes in attitudes toward death à la longue durée, and they agreed on the substance of these changes. Their disagreement turned on the conception of destiny these changes implied.

They played out their intellectual contest in professional conferences for nearly a decade (1974–82) in a courteous, even friendly way.[35] Ariès reaffirmed his interpretation of the role of a collective unconscious in the slow reformulation of traditional attitudes. Vovelle emphasized instead the historical rise of a more rational consciousness that dismissed traditional attitudes as superstitious. Ariès's conceded Vovelle's point that the notion of a 'collective unconscious' conveyed unfortunate spiritualist overtones and therefore substituted that of 'collective nonconscious' for it.[36] But in return Ariès obliged Vovelle to acknowledge that consciousness-raising does not lead to a dénouement in the way Marx had defined it. Like the traditions from which they are derived, our historical perspectives are continually changing.[37] What these scholars shared in this dialogue was a recognition of the loss of the vitality of the political traditions to which they had once been so fervently attached.[38]

Still, there is an epilogue to Ariès's reflections on the eclipse of the traditions of old France in public life. Ironically, the decline of his own political cause coincided with the rise of another that seemed closely attuned, as he found himself surprised by the student uprising of 1968 for its championing of a position not unlike the one he had espoused in the Vichy era. In the interest of this younger generation in ecology Ariès saw the rebirth of his ideal of regionalism, moribund since the end of the Second World War. This movement emerged on the political left rather than the right. But for Ariès, it evinced the same political concerns that had motivated him as a young man: the need to acknowledge the diversity of traditions menaced by the growing power of the omni-competent state. The welfare state was promoting a conformism that was alien to the human spirit, and in the views voiced by the student protesters of 1968 he saw the restatement of his own youthful critique of the culture of techniques. Their concern for the environment reaf-firmed his conviction that particular traditions may lose their influence, but the need that tradition fulfils varies hardly at all.[39]

In a series of late-life essays, Ariès reiterated his view first stated in *Le Temps de l'histoire* that a civilization is sustained by its traditions, not its politics. While political regimes may rise and fall, traditions are adapted to new circumstances in which they are modified, even meta-morphosed, but the stance on life that they embody ultimately en-dures. In a profound sense, the human recourse to tradition battens upon the existential permanence of certain basic human needs and so defies the apparent trend of modern politics toward abstract, often contrived conceptions of community.

Ariès at the Postmodern Crossing

I shall close with some remarks about the meaning of Ariès's line of inquiry considered at the crossing of the postmodern divide. The key to the postmodern stance is the repudiation of history conceived as a grand narrative moving toward a dénouement – history as a timeline with a beginning, a middle, and an end, the middle punctuated by memorable events that illustrate the movement of history. Ariès sensed that he lived at the edge of this breakup of the unity of modern histori-ography.[40] For him, history's meaning for the present age was to be found at the margins of civilization rather than its centre. His reinter-pretation of history from a present-minded perspective is evident even in his early study of historical time. What is interesting about the past, he argued ever more insistently, is its differences from, not its anticipa-tion of, the present. We invoke that past which speaks to our needs.[41] What began as his seemingly ingenuous inquiry into the history of popular traditions as a new domain for research, therefore, enabled him in the end to confirm his early insight into the way the fabric of modern historical writing had been knitted together out of the strands of many traditions.

The critical study of the traditions out of which modern history emerged has become a preoccupation of the generation of historians that followed Ariès. They have tended to focus on the contingency of tradition, its dependence on the political circumstances in which it emerges. Traditions operate within pluralistic milieux, and their appeal is relative to the power of the social groups that invent them. If Ariès tended to think of tradition as a source of an existential need to reaffirm an abiding truth about who we are, his successors were more likely to view it as a field of contention for explaining the relativism of history to the politics of its historians, as they did in the histories of tradition and public memory that Hobsbawm and Ranger inspired. That is why topics about tradition have today become the places of our disputes over the meaning of the past, and why commemorative ruins have come to interest us for what they reveal about negotiations over how the past ought to be remembered.[42]

Ariès had long since considered this perspective. It was part of his own reckoning with his traditionalist past in his essays in *Le Temps de l'histoire*. He had come to recognize that his tradition was but one among many, neither the most powerful nor the most important. Still, he continued to be drawn to the resources it offered him for maintaining a personal identity in a socially amorphous, increasingly anonymous mass culture. I would argue, therefore, that Ariès's history of mentalities remains on the earlier side of the postmodern divide because of his lingering identification with the traditions he interpreted. His history was designed to reaffirm the continuity of humankind's saga, though with ever more modest expectations about its dénouement. Indeed, his originality was in domesticating that notion – in redirecting attention from the politics of nations toward the culture of everyday life, from an epic destiny publicly understood toward ordinary destinies privately conceived. The history he wrote conveyed the tug of a culture that had passed from the public into the private sphere. There he sought to reaffirm the vitality of the mores of traditional society and so to underscore the mediating role of popular tradition in maintaining the continuity between past and present.[43] In his histories, he traced the flow of time forward, much as the tributaries of traditions flow into the river of history. For him, tradition moves within our lives. As participants in tradition we innovate continually, and only as historians can we appreciate the way in which traditions evolve over long periods of time. The history of mentalities documents that change, and in doing so reaffirms the vitality of the traditions on which our history is based.[44] With such insights Ariès encouraged his colleagues to take seriously the contribution of popular traditions to historical understanding. A subject that was largely the preserve of folklorists at the beginning of the twentieth century thus became one for reinvigorating historical scholarship at century's end.

In light of our consideration of Ariès, it is interesting to look at Terence Ranger's reconsideration of *The Invention of Tradition* twelve years after he edited it. Now at the end of the age of colonialism, he conceded, it has become possible to see how traditions are never simply imposed and always develop in ways their inventors could not have conceived. In fact, he suggested, the term 'imagined communities' (borrowed from the anthropologist Benedict Anderson) conveys more aptly the ongoing redescription of living tradition that he had in mind. Traditions are not simply forums for imperialism, but places of contest between those who invent them and those who inhabit them. Invented traditions are bent to popular need, just as the customary ones that are superseded often reinvent themselves in these new frameworks in order to survive. Ranger's argument is surprisingly similar to that formulated by Ariès fifty years before. From this perspective, Ariès shows how the traditions of old France survived 'colonization' by the modern French state, and how a world that some believed had been lost found the means to survive in the interstices of a new culture.[45]

Still, the tenor of today's discussion of tradition for the most part runs counter to that in which Ariès was engaged. He came out of, and in his way remained loyal to, a traditionalist world. His views on history now seem slightly dated, given our contemporary concerns. Indeed, the history of mentalities that he pioneered is increasingly interpreted as only a stage in the development of a new cultural history.[46] His enduring historiographical importance lies in his challenge to the uncritical acceptance of the postmodern notion of 'invention' that so pervades current thinking about the nature of tradition. That scholars in our time should have been drawn to so narrow a focus on the politics of tradition suggests the tenuousness of our present sense of identity in comparison with what seemed so certain to Philippe Ariès in his reflections on the tradition-bound world from which he came.

NOTES

Excerpts from this essay appear in different form in the author's *Philippe Ariès and the Politics of French Cultural History* (Amherst, 2004), and appear here by permission of the publisher.
 1 Eric Hobsbawm and Terence Ranger, eds, *The Invention of Tradition* (Cambridge, 1983).

2 Ten years after its publication, Ranger reported that the book had outsold all the other titles on the Cambridge University Press list for the Past and Present series, and that it was cited on nearly every social anthropology application to funding agencies in the United States. Terence Ranger, 'The Invention of Tradition Revisited: The Case of Colonial Africa,' in Terence Ranger and Megan Vaughan, eds, *Legitimacy and the State in Africa* (London, 1993), 62–3.

3 For an overview, see David Gross, *The Past in Ruins; Tradition and the Critique of Modernity* (Amherst, MA, 1992), 8–19. See also the philosophical meditation on tradition by George Allan, *The Importances of the Past* (Albany, NY, 1986), esp. 191–243.

4 Lucien Febvre, *A New Kind of History*, ed. Peter Burke (New York, 1973); Robert Mandrou, 'L'Histoire des mentalités,' *Encyclopédie universalis*, 8 (1968 ed.): 436–8.

5 Philippe Ariès, 'Confessions d'un anarchiste de droite,' *Contrepoint*, 16 (1974): 93–5.

6 See Ariès's inaugural lecture at the École des hautes études en sciences sociales, in which he explains the rise of privacy as a secret passage. 'Le Secret,' in *Essais de mémoire*, ed. Roger Chartier (Paris, 1993), 34–41.

7 'Entretien avec Philippe Ariès,' *Nouvelle Action française*, 144 (30 January 1974): 6–7; Alison Browning, 'Une Conversation avec Philippe Ariès,' *Cadmos*, 12 (Winter 1980): 4.

8 See the review essay by Richard T. Vann, 'The Youth of Centuries of Childhood,' *History and Theory*, 21 (1982): 279–97.

9 A complete run of these articles has been edited by Jeannine Verdès-Leroux, *Le Présent quotidien, 1966–96* (Paris, 1997). See my analysis of them in my 'The Postwar Politics of Philippe Ariès,' *Journal of Contemporary History*, 34 (1999): 365–81.

10 Philippe Ariès, *Le Temps de l'histoire* (Monaco, 1954), 9–21; see also his late-life autobiography, *Un Historien du dimanche* (Paris, 1982), 13–36.

11 Ariès, 'Confessions d'un anarchiste de droite,' 90.

12 Philippe Ariès, 'La Ressemblance,' in *Essais de mémoire*, 62–3; André Burguière, 'La Singulière Histoire de Philippe Ariès,' *Le Nouvel Observateur*, 20 February 1978, 81. See also the observations of his lifelong friend, François Leger, 'Les Fidélités de Philippe Ariès, *Aspects de la France*, 2 October 1980.

13 I discuss his role in the school in some detail in my 'The Politics of the Young Philippe Ariès,' *French Historical Studies*, 21 (1998): 475–95.

14 One of these was an anthology dealing with the relations between state and society in the sixteenth century. That too had been an era in which France was torn by civil strife and regional solutions to the problem of community

presented themselves. Ariès contributed an essay, 'Journal de l'Estoile,' in François Leger, ed., *La Fin de la ligue (1589–1593)* (Paris, 1944), 159–75.

15 Philippe Ariès, *Les Traditions sociales dans les pays de France* (Paris, 1943), 13–15, 38, 155–9.

16 As a student at the University of Paris, Ariès was inspired by his geography teacher, Emmanuel de Martonne. Regional geography was then much in vogue, and for his book Ariès drew upon studies by Georges Lizerand, Pierre Deffontaines, Marc Bloch, André Sigfried, and Yann Morvran Goblet. Goblet's *La Formation des régions; introduction à une géographie régionale de France* (Paris, 1942) is the source for Ariès's discussion of new industrial zones. See François Leger, 'Philippe Ariès: L'histoire d'un historien,' *Revue universelle des faits et des idées*, 65 (1986): 65.

17 Ariès, *Les Traditions sociales*, 109–23.

18 Ibid., 155–9.

19 Ariès, *Le Temps de l'histoire*, 9–12, 33–9, 45.

20 Ariès was not dismissive of all the intellectuals uprooted by the war. Among them, he singled out for sympathy an English resister named Hugh Dormer. Dormer witnessed the destruction of the traditional world from which he hailed, yet dedicated himself to reaffirming it in a different way in a postwar setting. For Ariès, his life was worthy of emulation. Ibid., 61–87.

21 In a late-life reflection, Ariès noted that his conception of History as an existential tide in *Le Temps de l'histoire* was quite similar to that of André Malraux. Ariès, 'Le Temps de l'Histoire' (1983), in *Essais de mémoire*, 45–58.

22 Ariès, *Le Temps de l'histoire*, 22–24, 313–18. See also Burguière, 'La Singulière Histoire,' 82.

23 Ariès, *Le Temps de l'histoire*, 140–53, 160–71.

24 Ibid., 45–59.

25 Ibid., 26–33, 271–2.

26 Philippe Ariès, 'Familles du demi-siècle,' in *Renouveau des idées sur la famille* (Paris, 1954), 162–70; 'La Famille d'Ancien Régime,' *Revue des travaux de l'académie des sciences morales et politiques*, 109, 4th series (1956): 46–55.

27 Philippe Ariès, *Histoire des populations françaises et de leurs attitudes devant la vie depuis le XVIIIe siècle* (1948; Paris, 1971), 344–72.

28 Philippe Ariès, 'Interprétation pour une histoire des mentalités,' in Hélène Bergues, ed., *La Prévention des naissances dans la famille* (Paris, 1960), 311–27.

29 Philippe Ariès, 'L'Histoire des mentalités,' in Jacques Le Goff, ed., *La Nouvelle Histoire* (1978; Paris, 1988), 187–8.

30 Philippe Ariès, 'Le XIXe Siècle et la révolution des moeurs familiales,' in *Renouveau des idées sur la famille*, 111–18; *L'Enfant et la vie familiale sous l'Ancien Régime* (1960; Paris, 1973), 266–7, 299, 308–10.

31 Philippe Ariès, 'Une Civilisation à construire,' in Pierre Andreu et al., eds, *Écrits pour une renaissance* (Paris, 1958), 207–9, 212, 215–20.

32 Philippe Ariès, 'La Famille hier et aujourd'hui,' *Contrepoint*, 11 (July 1973): 89–97. See also Christopher Lasch, *Haven in a Heartless World* (New York, 1977).

33 Jeannine Verdès-Leroux, 'La "Fidélité inventive" de Philippe Ariès,' in *Le Présent quotidien* by Philippe Ariès (Paris, 1997), 7–38.

34 Philippe Ariès, *Western Attitudes toward Death* (Baltimore, 1974).

35 Patrick Hutton, 'Of Death and Destiny: The Ariès/Vovelle Debate about the History of Mourning,' in Peter Homans, ed., *Mourning, Monuments, and the Experience of Loss: Coming to Terms with the Past at Century's End* (Charlottesville, VA, 2000).

36 One critic has pointed out the affinities between Ariès's notion of a 'collective unconscious' and that of Carl Jung. Gilles Ernst, 'Table ronde sur la communication de Roger Chartier,' in Roger Chartier, ed., *La Mort Aujourd'hui* (Les Cahiers de Saint-Maximin) (Marseille, 1982), 127. But Ariès did not know the depth psychology of Jung and it is more likely that his use of the concept is derived from his reading of Maurice Halbwachs, the sociologist who developed a theory of collective memory, or of some other savant of the school of sociology pioneered by Émile Durkheim.

37 For the proceedings of the debate between Ariès and Vovelle, see esp. the *Archives de sciences sociales des réligions*, 39 (1975): 7–29, and *La Mort aujourd'hui* (Les Cahiers de Saint-Maximin), ed. Roger Chartier (Marseille, 1982).

38 The historiographical implications of the waning of the Revolutionary tradition were first raised by François Furet in his provocative *Penser la Révolution française* (Paris, 1978). Furet is famous for having declared that the 'French Revolution is over,' by which he meant as a guide to envisioning changes for the future. For Ariès as for Furet, its waning influence liberated historians to consider older traditions. See Browning, 'Une Conversation avec Philippe Ariès,' 7–11.

39 Among Ariès's articles on the revival of regionalism, see esp. 'Une Interprétation tendancieuse de l'histoire des mentalités,' *Anthinéa*, 3, no. 2 (February 1973): 7–10; 'Culture orale et culture écrite,' in Bernard Plongeron and Robert Pannet, eds, *Le Christianisme populaire; les dossiers de l'histoire* (Paris, 1976), 234–5; 'Le Régionalisme, perspective historique,' *Critère*, 24 (Winter 1979): 41–50; Vie et mort des civilisations,' in Christian Chabanis, ed., *La Mort, un terme ou un commencement* (Paris, 1982), 103–18.

40 Ariès, 'Confessions d'un anarchiste de droite,' 96–9; 'Le Temps de l'Histoire,' 56–8; 'L'Histoire des mentalités,' 175–7.

41 Ariès, *Le Temps de l'histoire*, 322–5; 'La Ressemblance,' in *Essais de mémoire*, 64–6; 'Confessions d'un anarchiste de droite,' 91–2.

42 But in a history in which the present becomes the interpretative frame of reference, the historian's assessment of what is memorable in the past becomes less certain. Such a history is more open to the infinite ways in which the past might serve present needs. So conceived, history is more visibly shaped by the politics of tradition. See François Hartog, 'Time, History and the Writing of History: The *Order* of Time,' *KVHAA Konferenser*, 37 (1996): 95–113.

43 Philippe Ariès, 'La Sensibilité au changement dans la problématique de l'historiographie contemporaine,' in Gilbert Gadoffre, ed., *Certitudes et incertitudes de l'histoire* (Paris, 1987), 171, 174.

44 It is interesting to compare Ariès's *Le Temps de l'histoire*, composed in the late 1940s, with Pierre Nora's *Les Lieux de mémoire*, written in the 1980s and exemplary of the postmodern approach to tradition. There is a way in which they participate in a common endeavour – an exploration of the myriad of traditions that had contributed to the making of the modern French identity. What divides them are opposing ways of formulating the time of tradition. Nora traces historical time backward, as in the branching of a genealogical tree. He sets aside the notion of the time of tradition as a continuum between past and future, and locates it instead at places of memory, in surviving images of traditions that have otherwise ceased to inform tacit understandings. The interest of tradition is in its mementos. To put it another way, he reduces the vision of history that Ariès sought to portray on a grand scale to readings of memorable places in the past among which there are no necessary connections. In this world of time-travelling, tradition as a sustaining presence gives up the sense of continuity it once provided. Its potential meanings as sources of renewal for the present age are evoked severally at these multiple sites of memory. Pierre Nora, ed., *Les Lieux de mémoire*, 3 vols (Paris, 1984–92).

45 Ranger, 'The Invention of Tradition Revisited,' 62–111.

46 Roger Chartier, 'L'Histoire culturelle,' in Jacques Revel and Nathan Wachtel, eds, *Une École pour les sciences sociales* (Paris, 1996), 84–5.

Chapter Eleven

Tradition as Politics and the Politics of Tradition

GORDON SCHOCHET

A substantial part of the link tradition makes between past and present is irreducibly political, as all the essays in this volume, especially those in Part II, demonstrate. Etymologically, tradition is a 'handing down,' or over, from the past to the present, but it *functions* as a 'reaching back' from the present to the – perhaps better thought of as *a* – past. To identify something as a tradition, or traditional, is to assert and in some instances to establish that link and to embed a specific present in an equally specific (although not necessarily specified and however general) past. Placing a text, a practice, a rule, a fashion, or even a mode of understanding within – or declaring it to be part of – a tradition is interpretatively to constitute it and functionally to *police*[1] it: to establish backward-looking controls over what it is, what it requires, and what can be said about it. The invocation of tradition prescribes standards for behaviour and establishes the borders of permissibility against rival claimants; in short, it establishes what Friedrich Carl von Savigny, the founder of German historical jurisprudence, described as 'the vital connection that ties the present to the past.'[2]

Michael McKeon uses the perspective of the English Enlightenment to focus on the implicit, unstated, and tacit aspect of tradition. Part of his goal is to understand the differences between pre-Enlightenment cultures of tradition and what he calls 'our own cultural modernity,' which has replaced tradition with 'ideologies' and, following Clifford Geertz, 'belief systems.' In the end, however, the modern world is no freer because it does not overtly appeal to traditions. Tradition per se might be undermined when tacit knowledge is rendered explicit, but the formal ideologies into which tradition is transformed are no less constricting. All societies are partially constituted by the 'cultural embeddedness' of their unstated presumptions. In the eyes of Enlightenment rationalists, tradition and custom were the servants of religion, all of which were allied with ignorance. But even as it attacked the hold of religion and tradition, the Enlightenment replaced their hegemony with its own unquestioning faith in reason and its own 'tacit knowledge.' While it is correct to see traditions as incorporating tacit knowledge, it would be a serious error to reduce them to one another, and McKeon certainly does not suggest that we should. Traditions incorporate and depend on tacit knowledge, but the conscious invocation of tradition is exhortative and justificatory – to urge or defend actions or policies – and ultimately makes those tacit understandings explicit.

Daniel Rodgers's examination of the various strands of what is called the 'liberal tradition' presents it both as what numerous scholars have treated as a description of nineteenth-century American life and society and as an account of what is often taken to be the nation's dominant ideology. Again, the 'tradition' functions in part as a definer of permissibility, and Rodgers forcefully demonstrates that its power in this respect is barely diminished by the facts that much of what it claims is false and that it is in large part an 'invention' of its proclaimers. Even in the hands of their proponents 'liberalism' and the 'liberal tradition' are confusing and often confused labels, referring at once to what so-called liberals actually did or believed and to what is a retrospective imposition on the past. Accuracy emerges as less important than coherence, but it is to be hoped that the notion of a 'liberal tradition' will not be used so loosely after Rodgers's analysis.

Liberalism, with its emphasis on individual rights and liberties and its commitment to the rational solution of social and political problems, sees itself as the modern bearer of Enlightenment reason. In this respect, it is a peculiarly and, until recently, self-consciously Western and especially Anglo-American notion. In that period of which Rodgers writes, before the 'rugged individualism' of nineteenth-century liberalism branched out to comprehend the 'welfare liberalism' of the twentieth century, liberalism generally viewed the state with suspicion and looked to the private realm of economics to advance personal freedom. Its ideological enemies were romantic authoritarianism and various strands of socialism. The continuation of Rodgers's account would show that the direct heirs to the imagined liberalism he describes, now calling themselves 'classical liberals,' are vigorous in objecting to what they see as the 'statist' policies of modern 'welfare liberalism.' Thus, the tradition, whatever might be made of it, is certainly alive and continues to grow and change.

One of the hallmarks of the politics that was incorporated into the liberal, Enlightenment world-view is the 'rule of law,' the principle that government itself is limited, that it proceeds by and operates under the aegis of clear, public, and consistent rules rather than the edicts of officials. As David Leiberman shows, law is one of most conspicuously traditional institutions in modern society; the common law jurisprudence of England – and therefore of Canada and the United States – he argues, is inseparably tied to the 'authority of the past.' Law invariably and unavoidably draws upon, reflects, and carries on the past. The common law is often proclaimed to be the distillation of English legal custom, a record of its gradual and cumulative change, kept alive through the judicial practice of *stare decisis*, the doctrine of precedent that requires that contemporary cases generally be decided by like holdings from the past, which functions as tradition and establishes a jurisprudential *presumption* in favour of the past.[3]

Cultural traditions often contain complete world-views. There is, in consequence, a kind of dogmatic intolerance that frequently inheres in traditions, making it difficult for them to live at peace with their rivals, but the growing contacts among cultures – and their traditions – that characterize the modern world require precisely that they become tolerant. Georgia Warnke's examination of the relationships between traditions and ethical knowledge thus raises one of the central problems facing modern society: How can the varying traditions that give rise to and sustain the multiculturalism of diversity coexist? Warnke's solution is a 'confidence' in our own beliefs and interpretations of the world that renders traditions strong enough to survive these unavoidable confrontations without attempting to destroy their competitors. Somehow, people must learn that while not every interpretation of the world is correct, more than one may be. It is a suggestion that recognizes the ineliminability of tension and yet provides some measure of hope for the future. I will return to Warnke's discussion at the conclusion of the chapter.

In the last essay in this section, Patrick Hutton presents Philippe Ariès's view that writing history is something of an act of correctly understanding tradition. Ariès, who would have agreed with Warnke's concerns about pluralism and truth, saw history as a kind of mediation between tradition and the present and between invented, static traditions and those that are living and dynamic. Ariès sought to invigorate what he saw as the modern, revolutionary tradition of France with vital aspects of the royalist tradition he favoured and which had been retained in the family. He viewed modern historical writing as an amalgam of the strands of many traditions and, according to Hutton, stood in direct opposition to the scholarship of 'invented tradition.' Again, there are themes here that will be addressed later in this essay.

Tradition asserts the primacy of local conventions and practices over grander, universal schemes and, in that respect, is the opponent of cosmopolitanism.[4] Tradition thus stands for localism and univocality in contrast to the cosmopolitan heterogeneity that increasingly characterizes the modern world.[5] That modernity, at least in the West, dictates that we share a humanity – and little else, if that much, in the minds of many – with the utter strangers who are our fellow citizens. The assertion of tradition in the midst of all this, no less than the recently familiar call for the reestablishment of 'family values,' is a nostalgic yearning for the return of the simpler life in which we had more in common than in difference with our neighbours and when the bonds of kinship and friendship were closely intertwined. It is a response to the loneliness many feel in this world of strangers, a mark of frustration at the failure of institutional proceduralism to solve the problems of diversity, and a cry for the reinsertion of social affect into the rationality of public life.

'Tradition,' like so many of our stock social and political concepts, is rooted in the world-views of that older and presumably homogeneous order. In that rapidly disappearing universe, societies and states may have included several different 'cultures,' but it was possible to exist protected in one's own enclave without the need to have more than superficial dealings with the members of other similarly insulated groups.

Tradition was never meant to serve the ends of cultural pluralism; traditions belong to *cultures* and are among the ways they maintain their distinct identities. But even further back, societies and states were culturally unified; their members shared religions, heritages, and 'ethnicities,' and they were held together by common traditions – at least that is the story that is told.

Another part of that story – and until recently all but untold – has to do with the imposition or 'invention' of unity across the lines of class and gender.[6] Social and cultural historians have revealed the historical traditions that are peculiar to sexual and economic groups *within* cultures. Marx was one of the first to argue that these 'identities,' to use the contemporary terminology – specifically those of economic class membership – transcended geographic and cultural boundaries and were more important than the identities provided by territorial cultures. To Marx, the bonds of tradition were part of the romanticized 'superstructure' – ideology – that sustained the ruling classes. The same kind of reasoning has been used to much the same kind of end by feminists and queer theorists in our own day;[7] in all these cases it is held that overarching, society-wide traditions and practices have obscured the various diversities and 'identities' that societies contain.

In societies that include different and potentially conflicting cultures, the resort to tradition is inherently problematic. Traditions teach and then remind people that what they have in common is greater and more important than their differences, but when rival values, interests, and needs cannot be peacefully accommodated without some surrender of vital interests, the battles may have to be fought among traditions. The very consciousness and assertion of local traditions that multiculturalism legitimates as an antidote to suffocating universalism could destroy that multiculturalism itself.

In the attacks on 'foundations' and 'master narratives' and the unmasking of imposition that characterized much academic analysis of the late twentieth century, virtually all notions tied to conceivable pasts – 'tradition' not least among them – endured difficult times.[8] The postmodernism that underlay many of these assaults in its most overt forms is on the wane, but the sceptical, critical mood it fostered remains, a scepticism that is especially evident in historical analysis. In many respects, this mood suggests a return – so far unappreciated – to something like the logical positivism of the 1940s and 1950s, or even to the sentiment expressed in John Locke's *Two Treatises*, 'At best an Argument from what has been, to what should of right be has no great force.'[9]

Normative appeals to history continue to be effective and frequently use modes of explanation and justification in politics, however suspiciously they are regarded in academic circles. There are few defences of authority that work so well as the invocation of historical continuity.[10] The simple but generally unexamined claim that 'This is the way we have long done things' readily serves as a foundation for institutions and policies and effects the conversion of what appears to be mere 'history' into action-motivating legends and political mythology.[11]

This is notoriously so in the United States, where such nearly holy phrases as 'our way of life' and the 'American heritage' are regularly made to function as the bedrocks of the nation's values.[12] While these phrases are not exactly empty, they are sufficiently open-ended to permit the inclusion of varying practices, institutions, and rules, all drawn from romanticized and, as it were, 'traditionalized' conceptions of the American past.

It is almost trivial to remark that the institutions and practices that surround and help to construct our lives are products of history; we have 'inherited' them – which is really a question-begging phrase in this context – from the past. However much they seek to control future behaviour, politics and law are inevitably rooted in the past and its practices. States have long justified their existence and consequent power over their members by claiming temporal and, at least since the seventeenth century, territorial continuities, justifications that implicitly rest upon the unstated and more often unexamined premise that political legitimacy is as much a matter of endurance as it is of substance. To that extent, the modern state is dependent upon something very close to what is meant by 'tradition' even though neither the word nor the concept need necessarily be used.

Policies are often justified by appeals to what was done in the past, and the unstated implication is that standards of that past retain some measure of their vitality. It is occasionally contended that the present must conform to them. It is more often claimed, of course, that traditional standards may be modified or in some cases actually overthrown and replaced.[13] 'Modernization,' a one-time darling concept of the social sciences, is about the transformation of 'traditional societies,' which are often agrarian and/or tribal but conceivably in part urban, into those that are capable of sustaining industry and accumulating capital and seek to improve standards of living and to redistribute wealth.

While it is often the case that improvement of this sort will be of much greater benefit to the group or class that is already better off, the ideological or rhetorical aim is the improvement of the 'masses,' who are said to be caught in the deprivations that their tradition imposes. But members of these so-called traditional societies often perceive the result as the overthrow of their established ways of life, and they must somehow be persuaded to abandon their traditions. The costs can be greater than they are willing to bear, as witness Native American responses to the coming of white settlers to their home territories in the nineteenth century, even apart from issues of expropriation and displacement. Today, Native peoples the world over – but especially in North America – are struggling to revive the traditions that were ultimately taken from them as well as to recover their 'traditional' lands and entitlements.[14]

In sharp contrast is the lament of Tevye in the musical *Fiddler on the Roof*; he wanted nothing more than the abandonment of the tradition within and by which he and his family were trapped.[15] In both cases, tradition was crucial to identity. To the Natives, that identity was more important than material improvements. To Tevye, on the other hand, the tradition had become oppressive, and no one directly argued against him in favour of its preservation. But in a sadly ironic twist, as the story of *Fiddler on the Roof* unfolded and Tevye and his family and friends left their village, at least one part of the *shtetl* tradition was broken; its replacement, however, was something far worse than the original, which left the larger issue unresolved.[16] Nonetheless, Tevye can stand as the prototype of those who question tradition and groan under its weight.

In all these cases – Tevye, American political orators, members of traditional societies facing modernization – the notion is something like 'This is our tradition; it is what makes us a people.' 'Tradition' is thus a solution, for better or for worse, to the problem of social cohesion, an answer to the question, What holds society together? As important as they are, 'social bonds,' in the terminology of Werner Stark,[17] are deeply problematic. The existence and continuation of societies – as well as of the states that usually superintend them – seem largely to be matters of shared or at least compatible *dispositions* or wills to be members.

Whatever its source, this 'social cement' is finally more mysterious than rational and comes to rest on the joint willingness to believe and accept. Acceptance of this sort lends itself to the perpetration of conceptual frauds by those who are aware of its nonrational elements and intentionally manipulate public beliefs in order to create allegiances. The sloganeering uses of tradition (heritage, way of life) suggest the 'invented' traditions of Eric Hobsbawm and his colleagues, but they can also be used in a more positive way as the construction of 'social [or 'collective'] memories'[18] of people's genuine pasts and practices in ways that elicit feelings of pride and attachment, which always has contradictory aspects. In this sense, however, memory and tradition are not so much 'constructed' or 'invented' as they are 'discovered' and '*re*constructed.' But in either case, participation in one's tradition and traditional practices – as rituals, perhaps – can be satisfying sources or confirmations of 'identity.' The difficulty comes when we attempt to explain the ways in which such 'memories' or traditions are *shared* among various members of society. Even in a relatively homogeneous community, people will have varying outlooks, objectives, and understandings; it is therefore unlikely that everyone will have the same conception of their cultural memories and traditions.

Traditions can stand in the way of modernization because people (and/or their leaders) often fear change, preferring the familiar to the innovative. That, as it were, is something of a sociological or empirical truth. But as if to acknowledge the modern validity of Edmund Burke's objections to the French Revolution[19] while giving them a bit of a modern twist, tradition in various guises today plays a political role as well by providing the context within which virtually all intentional social and political changes are *required* to operate. Since the mid-twentieth century, in response to colonial incursions and intrusive attempts to 'modernize' and 'industrialize' what were called 'underdeveloped' or 'third world' nations, the preservation of cultural identities has competed with policies that purport to aim at economic improvements and extensions of human rights.

'Identity' has become a watchword; it is one of the components of individual as well as cultural existence that we are constrained to respect and preserve. In the form of cultural tradition, it sometimes becomes an anthropological plaything that functions as what could be termed a 'living museum.' Unqualified, cultural identity can stand in the way of all change, but especially that which is introduced from the outside.[20] Cultures themselves, acting through their spokespersons, sometimes insist upon their rights to be free of external influences, or, more often, that what remains of their traditions must be preserved. Thus, from the perspective of international political and economic policies, the competing demands of heritage and material need must be balanced. While it is often difficult to conceive of a serious and acceptable argument that favours the preservation of tradition over progress in ways that will perpetuate deprivation, this does mean that recourse to 'tradition' and tradition-based arguments is with increasing frequency a call for political solutions to what appear to be cultural problems.

Tradition is a form of cultural and societal continuity, for it is a retention of *some* version of the past as a guide to appropriate actions and policies in the present. Sometimes, however, the appeal to tradition is intended to repair what are perceived as ruptures or breaks and to restore traditional procedures and beliefs. But the memory concerned may be unconscious, and part of what is implicit in the character of 'traditional societies' is that their adherence to what is retained in and kept alive in their cultural (collective) memories is not necessarily at the level of articulation, at least not as tradition. But where they are articulated, even in the form of stories about, as Peter Laslett termed it, 'the world we have lost,'[21] such memories still convey a great deal to the members of society about who they are[22] as a consequence of who they have been. But this too is not a part of an active tradition that mandates and legitimates behaviour within a culture, unless the story-telling is itself constitutive of a tradition.

Tradition is one of a family of concepts with similar meanings or imports, all pointing to and suggesting things that are done regularly. Initially, these regularities are enforced very weakly, if at all, but that enforcement tends to grow stronger with the passage of time and the increase of consciousness. This conceptual family – going from what is presumably the weakest to the strongest – includes *habit, custom, folk-ways, ritual, convention, practice*, and finally *tradition* itself. Except in the case of religion, the behavioural standards or norms are rarely formal-ized; within religion, ritual has the force of law. In the eyes of highly self-conscious and rational critics, all the members of this family smack of ignorance. More charitably and from what can be called an 'exter-nal' perspective, they are, as I have already observed, features of cul-tural or societal memory and are among the constituents of 'social cement.'

The members of this 'family' can be further differentiated according to the levels of social organization to which they pertain. This differen-tiation is about the degree of official compulsion and the extensiveness of membership and liability to act in accord with the norm. Modern states, or political societies, and governments have *laws* that apply to everyone within their territorial boundaries. The requirement of obedi-ence is involuntary, as is, for people born within the territory, some form of membership.

Social groups – clubs, teams, schools, political parties and associa-tions, and a variety of partial and what are called 'voluntary associa-tions' that exist *within* society and the state – are structured by *rules*. For members, these rules may have the force of law, but in comparison with the state, obedience is obligatory only so long as one remains a member.[23] Unlike laws, however, these rules are not enforced by official governmental agencies. Externally, that is, from the perspective of the outsider (who may be an analyst), these rules might be recorded as 'practices' or 'rituals.' Internally, as experienced by the participant, they are rules.

This distinction between 'internal' and 'external' perspectives is central to understanding the nature of tradition and the family of concepts to which it belongs. *Internal* participants may act in conformity with traditions without being fully conscious of the constraints on their behaviour, but when asked to explain themselves, they might well reply, 'That's the way things are' or 'That's the way we do things here.' As a source of behaviour, tradition is most effective when it functions below the level of consciousness, but in cases of uncertainty or deviance, it is available to prescribe or justify. To say that, however, is to move from the internal perspective of participants to the *external* vantage of the onlooker or analyst for whom recourse to tradition is explanatory and descriptive.[24]

Despite the fact that the notion of tradition invokes accumulated and more or less coherent sets of practices and conventions that have persisted and perhaps evolved over time – people have to have been doing something in recognizably related if not identical ways for a relatively long period for it to be called 'traditional' – the actors need not recognize that their behaviour is 'traditional. In fact, it is often outsiders with 'external' or anthropological and *descriptive* perspectives who identify traditions in the first instances and point out their regulatory powers.

The internal invocation of tradition is almost always rhetorical and *prescriptive*; it calls attention to established and therefore controlling practices. When the aim is not, as it was for Tevye, to identify tradition in order to break free of it, the purpose is defensive or motivational, either to justify something that has been attacked or is presumed to be in danger of being undermined or to give people reasons to do things they might otherwise avoid or to accept what they might reject. In this form, the appeal to tradition is often presented as a descriptively true and correct statement of prevailing conventions and informal practices to which people should conform. As societies grow more complex – in consequence of the pluralism of their populations, of social, economic, and geographic mobility, of the division of labour, and of the general increase in available options – traditions are obscured, which, paradoxically, makes all the more urgent the need to resort to them to remind people of how they are expected to behave.

The once-popular social sciences distinction between 'traditional' and 'modern' societies[25] owed much to Max Weber's division of ideal types of authority into 'charismatic,' 'traditional,' and 'rational-legal.'[26] The social science version of the differentiation signalled a contrast between relatively uncomplicated, labour-intensive, and usually agrarian societies and those that are comparatively complex, usually industrial (and therefore relatively urban), and have division of labour. Traditional societies, in addition, are characterized by fairly rigid schemes of stratification and social status with minimal mobility, little or no economic growth, and the concentration of wealth in the hands of a small upper class. For present purposes, the most important difference is between the unarticulated and the unwitting as causes or sources of behaviour, on the one hand, and the conscious and presumably rational and understood as motives and justifications, on the other.

This distinction was not meant to suggest that reason-giving, justification, and conscious acceptance, and, therefore, *understanding*, are absent from traditional societies. But the reasons and justifications tend to consist in appeals to or articulations of customs or social habits of long-standing and of more or less sacrosanct status. It is difficult if not impossible to conceive of human communities whose members go about their routines wholly without the ability and inclination to have reasons and justifications. The powers of thought and communication virtually entail explanation, even if that explanation is a rote recitation of what one has been taught, a rationalization provided by others, or a simple statement of one's beliefs, shared with others in the community or altogether private.

It certainly cannot be claimed that the relationship between 'traditional societies' and their 'traditions' is such that people live solely by their traditions rather in accord with whatever circumscribes their societies. The designation 'traditional' in this context is intelligibly applied comparatively and in reference to a more 'developed' (and often 'later') society. So the determination that a society is 'traditional' is unavoidably an *external* judgment about other societies or about the past and is dependent upon a consciousness that is presumed not to have been available to members of the society so labelled. Thus, the recognition of the traditions, traditional institutions, and practices that obtain in traditional societies depends upon a perspective that is presumed not to have been (or be) characteristic of what must be regarded as 'less conscious' societies. Applied to one's own society, this capacity permits the identification of traditions that operate in the contempo-rary world, giving rise to that analytic, historical consciousness that has been seen as one of the markers of modern society.[27]

All this is related in ironic if not strange ways to the distrust of his-tory and sentimentality and the corresponding championing of reason that are ascribed to the Enlightenment, at least in its Continental incar-nations. With the recognition that human beings and their institutions are in important respects products of history came the belief that peo-ple could shape their worlds as well, that they could simultaneously stand inside and outside the historical forces they had discovered, a view that played out to very different ends in the engaged writings of Marx and Engels, on the one hand, and the theoretical analyses of Hob-sbawm, Ranger, and company, on the other. Among the lessons to be gleaned from an awareness of the political force of traditions in history is a realization that they exist in our own worlds as well, as extensions or continuations of the past and as signs of departures from or rup-tures in our histories. This historical awareness – that is, the sense that there *was* (or *is*, depending on one's metaphysical views) a past that can be differentiated from the present – is a precondition to the con-sciousness that is itself necessary to the identifying and naming of tra-dition. Specifically in the case of tradition, it carries with it a modern and in many respects Kantian[28] notion of cultural and ultimately moral freedom and the presumption that peoples are capable of overcoming their pasts and creating futures that are free from the constraints of tradition.

The transformation of tradition-based into 'rational' societies has something to do with the process of self-conscious and overt justifica-tion. But the origins of that process – if, indeed, it is a process that can be said to have identifiable *origins* – are covered over by impenetrable layers of cultural sediment. When people started questioning the prac-tices of their cultures and seeking foundations for them and when they were first given answers can never be known. Nonetheless, we can *hypothesize* that the process of seeking and receiving justifications started at some point, however indeterminate, and that at some subse-quent point, versions of 'We have always done things this way' and/or 'This is the way we do things' became the standard responses. There are several important and almost teleological consequences that follow from the initiation of public reason-giving and the establishment of justification as a regular societal practice, as it were.[29] The reasons and traditions thus invoked become stabilized (in the sense that amorphous, ill-defined 'moving targets' have been rendered more or less 'stationary') and therefore subject to scrutiny and criticism. In addition, there *appears* to be a movement away from 'tradition' and toward reason and rationality. And there is what could be termed a 'Pandora effect' to the entire process of justification, analysis, and criticism: once begun, it is difficult to halt if it is not, in fact, irresistible.[30]

But this is not a matter of 'tradition' inevitably giving way to 'reason' so much as it is of 'reason' assuming a role in the justificatory process, partially supplanting 'tradition' and partially joining it. What is implicitly omitted from this conceptualization is the fact that even in 'modern,' 'reason-based,' 'complex' societies, traditions continue to function in the justificatory process and to serve as societal and political bonds. Thus, while the distinction between 'traditional' and 'modern' societies retains some utility, the contrast is not nearly so extreme as might first be presumed, and one of the pressing analytic issues is the determination of the place of tradition in the complex world of modernity.

The codification or formalization of tradition – usually into law – is often a response to a challenge, real or simply perceived; the intention is to attach costs to departures, but one of the consequences is to make the tradition and the behaviour in question more conscious. Among the justifications for the codification is the somewhat circular claim that the rule is already sanctioned by tradition, but from the analytic perspective of a legal system, what counts is the *transformation* of traditions into laws. Of course, people who accepted the tradition and were already inclined to act in accord with it would obey the new law virtually without further thought.[31]

Politics involves public authority, which is, *inter alia*, a matter of control through domination and imposition. Authority certainly need not be malevolent, and its harsher aspects may be disguised and even accepted as necessary consequences of social living. The domination and imposition aspects of authority and the social stratification (between ruled and ruler[s]) to which they lead may be regarded as ways of dealing with the ideological differences and relative scarcity of material and status resources that tend to characterize most societies. All that is necessary at this level is that the members of the system accept in general both the distributive scheme on which burdens and benefits are differentially apportioned and the legitimacy of those who supervise the distribution.

Once traditions are incorporated into formal state- and law-based politics and coercive legal penalties are attached to disobedience, so far as the legal system is concerned, they lose their status as traditions.[32] Traditions are enforced through informal and noninstitutionalized means, and their 'noninvented' beginnings, for the most part, are unwitting if not indeterminate. Law, by contrast, as something consciously contrived by states and their governments, is formal and institutionalized.[33] In the common law polities that continue the English practice, the judicial function is viewed in large part as a uniting of the past to the present by applying previous rulings to contemporary cases. Thus, while people correctly speak of 'political' and 'legal' traditions, they do so in ideological and not legalistic senses. The implicit references are to various ideals and principles that are presumed to be incorporated into the spirit of their laws and legal practices – the 'rule of law,' commitments to fairness and equity, a basis in reason, and so forth in most of the English-speaking world – and not to specific legal requirements or rules.

Codification of traditions is not the end of the story. Traditions are among the surest sources of social and political concord and approval; one of their primary functions, especially in multicultural societies, is to persuade the members that what they have in common unites them and is more important than their differences. Codification, enforcement, and even the 'invention' of traditions can thus be understood as attempts to institute unity. It often turns out that the integrating traditions are actually those of or are in the service of the dominant group or class, which is often in economic and political rather than overtly cultural control. Even relatively homogeneous societies have something equivalent to a ruling or dominant class that is ultimately in competition if not conflict with other groups.

In these terms, it is difficult to maintain a clear distinction between politics and law, on the one hand, and what I am calling 'culture,' on the other. Institutions and practices, even formal ones such as contractual economic exchanges, law, and public office, are embedded in the value systems and wider cultures that sustain them; at the same time, they are integral parts of and contribute to those surrounding cultures. Political scientists and anthropologists increasingly speak of the wider sphere within which political action occurs and against which it must be understood as 'political culture.'

The imposition of cultural values in the name of societal tradition and the manipulation of tradition function as important supports of social and political power as well as, rather more benignly, ways of minimizing discord. In these terms, it is often difficult and sometimes impossible to discern the differences between the intentional pursuit of what is presumed to be 'just' and/or in the 'public good' and the subtle maximization of one's own interests and the advantage of friends and neighbours.

The ease with which interest and advantage are confused with right and good is one of the classic starting points of moral and political philosophy. It comes into play at precisely the conceptual moment at which tradition is consciously transformed into law. Whatever the motivation of the leaders, those who reject the principles and tradition that are codified will feel oppressed and may resist what they see as unwarranted domination by asserting their own traditions. The clearest instances of this kind of discord are those provoked by religious conflicts, from the breakup of Roman Catholicism in the Reformation (which is still being played out in Northern Ireland) to the establishment of theocracies in twentieth-century Iran and Afghanistan, and including internal differences over religious questions in Israel (quite apart from conflicts with its Arab neighbours) and the Hindu–Muslim differences that led to the separation of Pakistan from India and continue to plague the Indian subcontinent.

In all these cases, much of what was perceived to be at stake by the ruling (or victorious) interests as well as by those they sought to dominate was the very existence of the practices and foundational beliefs on which their identities rested. It is a matter of being in charge or being extinguished. Toleration – forbearance toward one's neighbours despite the offensiveness of their lives – that very important but unique and difficult social virtue that allows people with differing ideologies and traditions to live together, is rarely seen as an option at the beginning of a conflict. It comes into play almost pragmatically: those who lose might seek to be tolerated rather than coerced or annihilated, or the 'winners' might determine that persecution has become too costly a policy to continue. It is limited and generally grudging – on all sides – at first, but however it is instituted and for whatever reasons, it is the necessary first step toward the peaceful coexistence of what are often rival if not incompatible traditions.

My claim is that formal states and law-based polities are no longer operationally traditional once coercive, legitimate penalties are attached to disobedience. Tradition, I have been arguing, works in informal and generally noninstitutionalized ways; states and their governments, by contrast, are formal, official, and institutional. But I have also argued that traditions persist in formal settings, in the sociological sense of providing part of what holds society together and in the ideological sense that is intended when we speak of 'the Western [or 'liberal'] political tradition.' To these should be added Michael Oakeshott's well-known insistence upon the importance of national traditions that must be allowed to operate without the resort to predetermined, 'rational' ends so popular among political theorists,[34] which is a variation on the 'social cement' thesis. Oakeshott contended that traditions are essential components of societies, even advanced, self-conscious, technological societies, that there is at least an aspect of tradition that defies rationality, and that attempts to reduce traditions to the rational principles they are presumed to contain is always destructive.

Oakeshott's attack on rational political theory was equally an admonition to public officials lest they act without understanding the traditions in which they 'participate.' The task of such officials is to attend to and maintain the 'arrangements' of their societies and to discover and repair the 'incoherences.' Their points of reference should always be the traditions and practices themselves, not abstract principles or goals.[35] In this respect, official actions are apparently to resemble those of members of cultures who 'participate' in their traditions and folkways without having full comprehension of the sources and implications of their behaviour. To understand and participate in tradition is to have a kind of knowledge that cannot be translated into rational principles, with this important difference: for the ordinary members of cultures, this knowledge is tacit, but political officials should be sufficiently self-conscious to know the traditions they are obliged to follow; acquiring that self-consciousness is difficult but essential.

In what is perhaps the central part of his argument, Oakeshott wrote:

> Now, a tradition of behaviour is a tricky thing to get to know. Indeed, it may even appear to be unintelligible. It is neither fixed nor finished; it has no changeless centre to which understanding can anchor itself; there is no sovereign purpose to be perceived or invariable direction to be detected; there is no model to be copied, idea to be realized, or rule to be followed. Some parts of it may change more slowly than others, but none is immune from change. Everything is temporary. Nevertheless, though a tradition of behaviour is flimsy and elusive, it is not without identity, and what makes it a possible object of knowledge is the fact that all its parts do not change at the same time and that the changes it undergoes are

potential within it. Its principle is a principle of *continuity*: authority is diffused between past, present, and future; between the old, the new, and
what is to come ...

It is clear, then, that we must not entertain the hope of acquiring this
difficult understanding by easy methods. Though the knowledge we seek
is municipal, not universal, there is no shortcut to it. Moreover, political
education is not merely a matter of coming to understand a tradition; it is
learning how to participate in a conversation: it is at once an initiation
into an inheritance in which we have a life interest, and the exploration of
its intimations.[36]

Accordingly, there is a deeply conservative quality to Oakeshott's
position, for an injunction to follow tradition is, on its face, an insistence that the present be built upon, if it does not actually replicate, the
past. But this is not so much an argument against change as it is a call
for change that is orderly. Oakeshott's essential conservatism, much
like that of Burke,[37] is part of an apparently descriptive political sociology and rests upon an implicit presumption that social policies that
depart from tradition will fail.[38] What this further illustrates is that an
internal resort to tradition in an advanced, self-conscious, that is, non-
traditional, society can appear to be descriptive and at the same time
function exhortatively. The identification of a practice or activity as a
cultural tradition is both a descriptive statement about the way things
have been done – the standards that have applied and have defined
legitimate actions – and a call to act in a particular way vis-à-vis those
standards, either in conformity with them, as Oakeshott wished, or
against them because they are overly inhibiting, as an advocate of
change or even a 'revolutionary' would desire.

Revolution, as usually understood, and the fervour it generates are
enemies to the position staked out by Burke and Oakeshott. This juxtaposition reveals the political poverty and the romanticized, almost
mystical, quality of those more characteristically 'conservative' doctrines. Neither theorist offered any guidance for overcoming the ideological and conceptual anomie that is brought about by the breaking of
tradition, other than going back and setting things right – which would
have been little solace for those who suffered under the crisis in France
that Burke described.[39] And neither writer had anything to say about
the relationship of tradition to authority, especially when tradition
becomes a tool for the manipulation of the members of society, through
falsification, hijacking, and invention. But almost any doctrine of revo-

lution, resting as it would have to on conflict, would be incapable of substituting itself for the stability or orderly change that inheres in the appeal to tradition. The two together leave a nagging concern about the ability of modernity to withstand the very forces that define it.

What is potentially a more fruitful avenue is suggested by Georgia Warnke's use of Bernard Williams's notion of 'confidence'[40] to open up the question of the 'orientations' members of diverse cultural traditions within a 'plastic and multicultural society' might take toward each others' orientations and understandings. 'Confidence' for Warnke means 'confidence in our [own] interpretations,' initially of texts and works of art, which then expands into confidence in our ethical judgments. Multiculturalism – seen as the ineliminability of diverse traditions – renders the issue of inclusion extremely difficult, especially on matters of judgment and response. Differing traditions provide varying and possibly discordant ways of dealing with abortion and surrogate motherhood, her principal examples.

Warnke is led by this route to a 'conversation' in which forbearance and ultimately a kind of tolerance[41] permit an amicable form of engagement from which everyone may benefit. The basic proviso is a mutual and continuing commitment to the avoidance of interpretations 'that suppress the interpretive voices of others.' This approach will work best in literature and art, but in politics and ethics, where rather more is at stake, people will, in all likelihood, have great difficulty showing the required restraint. What is necessary, then, is to lower the stakes there as well. Our goal, Warnke believes, is not 'knowledge but understanding, not conviction but confidence.' Like Williams, however, Warnke does not tell us how to bring about this transformation in the way people pursue their moral and political goals.

There is no question but that diversity of traditions can be a source of richness within a single society or state; it is one of the things that make complex, modern societies so interesting, if sometimes frustrating and potentially explosive. The multiplicity of traditions available to the members of modern societies can also increase their ideological and behavioural options, not in the sense that people necessarily *choose* among competing schemes or coexisting world-views but because the variety of legitimate alternatives is itself a source of personal and political liberty.

As Warnke's examples of abortion and surrogate motherhood illustrate and as I have previously observed, these traditions will often conflict with one another. It is all too frequently the case that people feel incapable of engaging in the discussions and 'conversations' that might prevent their conflicts from escalating beyond control, and when that happens, they lose a possible means of resolution. That resolution would require not simply a lowering of *voices* but a kind of other-regarding recognition of the validity of the claims of others.

Most disputes about what are taken to be fundamental values quickly become winner-take-all confrontations; they appear as nothing less than the timeless battle between 'good' and 'evil' in which no compromise is possible. Insisting that people show a willingness to accept less than or something different from that to which they feel entitled might actually be a call for the revision of at least part of their traditions, if not for their actual abandonment. Generally speaking, people are reluctant to surrender what they consider to be their fundamental interests and identities, and bringing tradition to the fore in this manner could be seen as calling for such a surrender and thereby provoke resistance. Thus, there is always a certain danger in urging that we fall back on our traditions.

Nonetheless, it is conceivable that raising tradition-based confidence to this level of consciousness in the context of other comparable traditions could introduce that willingness to compromise that is the foundation of social living. Part of what is necessary if this is to occur is that people appreciate that they all represent different perspectives and that they must somehow find ways of living together and sharing the benefits as well as the burdens of society. In terms of the society as a whole, no one tradition and the 'confidence' to which it gives rise is inherently more valuable or correct than any of the others. Coexistence, therefore, inevitably becomes irreducibly a matter of adopting the postures of civility and tolerance necessary for conversation and ultimately negotiation. And this can be done only by decreasing what one is willing to accept (if that were not the case, there would be no conflict to begin with).

The substantive weakness of this position is also one of its theoretical strengths, the presumption of sufficient rationality and other-regardingness to support the entire process.[42] The ultimate challenge is to create and maintain a society that incorporates meaningfully diverse traditions and is built upon the kind of cooperative spirit that would permit them to flourish. That noble if paradoxical goal has always been the core objective of liberalism, sustaining within a single, unified community the diversity that calls forbearance and toleration into existence.[43]

NOTES

It is a pleasure to acknowledge my indebtedness to Jonathan McFall, as usual, and Amy Lynch for their close readings and valuable suggestions; to Mark Phillips for helping as I attempted to work my way through these issues over the past few years; to John Pocock, Lois Schwoerer, Lena Cowen Orlin, Linda Levy Peck, David Armitage, and Kathleen Lynch, my friends and colleagues at the Folger Library's Center for the History of British Political Thought; and especially to Peter Laslett, Ellen Wood, and Neal Wood for having constantly forced me to confront these questions; and to Louise Haberman and Rumm, also as usual.

1 I am indebted to my co-editor, Mark Phillips, for the use of the concepts 'police' and 'policing.' I will not comment upon – other than to point out – the obvious etymological relationship among 'police,' 'policy,' and 'politics' (and perhaps 'polite' and 'politesse' as well).

2 As translated from his *System des heutigen römanischen Rechts*, I, xv, in Richard Zimmerman, *Roman Law, Contemporary Law, European Law: The Civilian Tradition Today* (Oxford, 2001), 188.

3 *Stare decisis* is not, of course, ironclad, for the United States Supreme Court does overrule earlier decisions from time to time. Moreover, the criteria for determining (sufficient) similarity – that is, when one case is sufficiently like another to be controlling – are left to judicial discretion.

4 See Cass Sunstein, 'Against Tradition,' *Social Philosophy and Policy*, 13 (1996): 207–28.

5 See John Rawls, *The Law of Peoples* (Cambridge, MA, 1999), esp. 82–5 and 113–20, for a useful discussion of cosmopolitanism.

6 At least since the Reformation, the territorial nation-states of Western Europe have included diverse religious faiths, each with its own stories and traditions. Once it was clear that this denominational variety was ineliminable, debates about religious toleration (as the alternative to annihilation) raised what has become the issue of heterogeneity within a single society.

7 I have intentionally omitted critical race theory only because the groups with which it is concerned already qualify as tradition- and identity-bearing cultures on conventional grounds. In the United States, where it seems first to have emerged, critical race theory applied primarily to people of African and Spanish-speaking American descent and went hand in hand with a new 'ethnic' consciousness that celebrated 'multiculturalism.' The sociological consequence of multiculturalism was to undermine the assimilationist, 'melting pot' model of society, which had long been a prominent feature of the American social tradition. The vehicle for this assimilation was pre-

sumed to be the educational system, which had worked to incorporate Europeans but was not serving the comparable needs of Blacks and Latinos. Not only did this suggest that 'race' and 'ethnicity' functioned differently from one another in the United States, it raised questions about whether Americans could ever be brought together as a 'people' who shared a single set of traditions. There is a huge and growing literature on this subject, and the educational issues are pointedly dealt with in Nathan Glazer *We Are All Multiculturalists Now* (Cambridge, MA, 1997), esp. 122–46.

The arguments about oppression and domination are politically similar in all three cases of race, class, and gender, and each of these categories includes members of the other two. For an excellent illustration of the complexities of this cross-cutting, see Patricia Williams, *The Alchemy of Race and Rights: Diary of a Law Professor* (Cambridge, MA, 1991). 'Tradition' does not appear in Williams's index; her book is more overtly about categories and boundaries of identity, but it is replete with tales of 'transmission.'

8 There is a conflict between the celebratory endorsement of identity and the distrust of tradition in that so much of identity is built upon cultural traditions. This conflict is rendered problematic by the fact that the two positions often issue from the same sources.

9 John Locke, *Two Treatises of Government* (1690), II, §103, text from the edition by Peter Laslett, Cambridge Texts in the History of Political Thought (Cambridge, 1988), 336.

10 Or, conversely, the recitation of historical grievances as grounds for restorative or rehabilitative actions. Although not usually seen as related to the ordinary senses of tradition, such claims work the same way, implicitly appealing to what could be called 'traditions of deprivation.' The list of grievances in the United States Declaration of Independence and the demands by expropriated Native peoples are equally historical claims.

11 Unadorned historical narration, or putatively factual storytelling about the past, does not move people to act; 'facts' alone are descriptive, not normative. There must be some triggering mechanism in the built-in response of the intended audience or in an exhortation by the narrator/storyteller, both of which generally transform the history into legend or myth that should guide or inspire behaviour. See, for instance, Yael Zerubavel, 'The Historic, the Legendary, and the Incredible: Tradition and Collective Memory in Israel,' in John Gillis, ed., *Commemorations: The Politics of National Identity* (Princeton, 1994), 105–23, and at greater length in *Recovered Roots: Collective Memory and the Making of Israeli National Tradition* (Chicago, 1995).

12 While this resort to a vague and somewhat illusory history is not necessarily the unique preserve of the United States – other nations certainly cele-

brate their pasts – it is difficult to think of states in which the practice is so constitutive of public life. It is part of a preoccupation with loyalty and an illusive national identity that reached a zenith during the Cold War era, when a committee to investigate 'Un-American Activities' was established by the United States House of Representatives. Apparently, civic loyalty was seen to be attached to deeply rooted, traditional American values. The very notions of 'Un-Canadian,' 'Un-British,' etc. investigations make the point because they are unimaginable in precisely the ways that 'Un-American' is not.

13 It is, as a rule, much easier to justify acting in conformity with tradition than to urge its overthrow. The concept itself normally functions as part of a vocabulary of commendation and approval, and for some, of grim inevitability (for instance, the character Tevye from *Fiddler on the Roof*, discussed below). More than that, however, the past has already been experienced; we know how it turned out and can more or less accurately point to its consequences. The future, on the other hand, is radically indeterminate, which is part of its appeal for some and precisely what makes it frightening for others.

Calls for the overthrow of tradition must somehow persuade their audiences both that the traditions they are being asked to abandon have had unacceptable results and that a better future is not only possible but likely. In this respect, virtually any 'reform' or 'liberation' movement that has as its goal the overthrow of entrenched rulers or long-established practices is an attack on tradition. An interesting and almost ironic variation on this mode of anti-traditionalism is the argument that an offensive practice, institution, or ruler has *interrupted* the flow of tradition, which must be restored.

14 From the perspective of the Natives, the issue was the loss of traditional folkways – hunting, migration, and ceremonies – as the cost of the material welfare that was promised to them in exchange. Their objections were not necessarily couched in the vocabulary of 'tradition,' but that is the conceptual language that their modern interpreters often use to express their sentiments. Peter Matthiessen has noted that 'a few years ago, the Inuit of Umingmakatok, in the remote Northwest Territories, chose to return the welfare checks of the Canadian government when they saw how fast their loss of independence had eroded the traditional skills and spirit of the band.' *Indian Country* (New York, 1992), 46.

The literature on this subject is legion; for excellent summary accounts that look beyond the initial period of white settlement and into the late twentieth century, see, in addition to Matthiessen, James Welch with Paul

Steckler, *Killing Custer: The Battle of the Little Big Horn and the Fate of the Plains Indians* (New York, 1994), and Peter Nabakov, ed., *Native American Testimony*, rev. ed. (New York, 1999).

15 Tevye is discussed in Jarislav Pelikan, *The Recovery of Tradition* (New Haven, 1984), 3–6.

16 An alternative interpretation of the ending of *Fiddler on the Roof* is that by leaving their *shtetl*, Tevye, his family, and his neighbours were in fact taking up an even older and perhaps more oppressive tradition, that of 'the wandering Jew.'

17 In his six-volume work (published in five volumes; volume 6 consists of fragments) of that title (New York, 1976–87); tradition itself is hardly discussed, but there are discussions of 'custom' throughout, most extensively in volume 3, *Safeguards of the Social Bond: Custom and Law*, in which the index entry for 'tradition' has a cross-reference to 'Custom, Tyranny of.' For other treatments of this once-popular subject from the perspective of grand social theory, see works by Charles Horton Cooley (who talked of the 'larger mind'), *Social Organization* (1909) and *Human Nature and the Social Order* (1902, 1922) both republished in *Two Major Works of Charles Horton Cooley*, intro. Robert Cooley Angell (Glencoe, IL, 1956); Robert Cooley Angell ('moral integration'), *Free Society and Moral Crisis* (Ann Arbor, 1958), esp. 61–104; R.M. MacIver ('myths'), *The Modern State* (Oxford, 1926), and *The Web of Government* (New York, 1947); and A.D. Lindsay ('operative ideals'), *The Modern Democratic State* (Oxford, 1944).

18 The notion 'collective memory' is part of a general theory of culture and to that extent belongs to (historical) anthropology. The phrase itself is associated with the work of the sociologist Maurice Halbwachs, who, in the words of his translator, Lewis A. Coser, believed that 'collective memory is a reconstruction of the past in light of the present.' Introduction to Halbwachs, *On Collective Memory*, ed. and trans. Coser (Chicago, 1992), 34; this translation conveniently provides a selection of Halbwachs's writings. Discussing the process by which, according to Halbwachs, 'individual recollections are integrated into the structures of collective memory as tradition,' Patrick H. Hutton argues that Halbwachs inevitably became a 'historian of collective memory.' *History as an Art of Memory* (Hanover, NH, 1993), 79, and chap. 5, passim.

For other, but not necessarily compatible, work on the subject, see – in addition to Coser's notes to his introduction – in order of publication, Robert Connerton, *How Societies Remember* (Cambridge, 1989); James Fentress and Chris Wickham, *Social Memory: New Perspectives on the Past* (Oxford, 1992); Gillis, ed., *Commemorations*; and Zerubavel, *Recovered Roots*.

Halbwachs seems to have claimed that presentist distortion of the past is inevitable – albeit not necessarily intentional – in the (re)construction of a society's or a culture's past, but unless the meaning of 'collective memory' is restricted to his usage, it is certainly possible to conceive of self-conscious processes whereby historically accurate accounts are sought. I have discussed some of this in 'Why Should History Matter? Political Theory and the History of Political Discourse,' in J.G.A. Pocock, Gordon Schochet, and Lois G. Schwoerer, eds, *The Varieties of British Political Thought, 1500–1800* (Cambridge, 1994), chap. 10.

19 Based on an understanding of society as a coherent and virtually organic structure, Burke claimed in his *Reflections on the Revolution in France* (1790) that consciously attempting to alter a people's (or a 'nation's') practices and institutions – or, worse yet, incorporating those from the outside that had no internal resonances or relevance – without due regard for the historical record and established traditions would always be unsuccessful. Moreover, that failure, in the process, would cause serious disruptions, careering off in disastrous, unanticipated, and ultimately uncontrollable directions. This can be read as a conceptual or even empirical assertion with no necessary normative implications, but Burke, of course, concluded not only that the French Revolution was doomed but that it was a political and social error.

20 There seems to be less difficulty with changes that cultures themselves introduce, although it is not unusual for outsiders to complain when a culture decides to sacrifice symbols of its heritage for the sake of progress or because they are deemed inappropriate. Concern about the building of the Aswan Dam in Egypt in the mid-twentieth century and international *aesthetic* objections to the destruction of ancient statues of Buddha by the government of Afghanistan in 2001 – coupled with unease about the construction of dams in China and India – suggest that we are moving to a point at which we are no longer willing to concede that cultures and nations are the sole determiners of the value of their own traditions.

21 The reference is Laslett's *The World We Have Lost* (London, 1965), the 2nd edition of which (1972) was subtitled 'England before the Industrial Age.'

22 See Hutton, *History as an Art of Memory*, 95.

23 Religions are somewhat anomalous in these terms, for they are not altogether voluntary associations. In many cases, people acquire their religious affiliations by birth, following the affiliations of their parents. From the perspective of a nontheocratic state, however, religious membership is optional, and people may leave or join as they see fit. Religions are perhaps second only to the state in their reliance upon member-sanctioned coercion

to maintain order. At the same time, they overtly rely on and claim the mantle of tradition and ritual far more than most states.

24 I have derived my understanding of this distinction from H.L.A. Hart, *The Concept of Law*, 2nd ed. (Oxford, 1994); Peter Winch, *The Idea of a Social Science and Its Relation to Philosophy* (London, 1958); and Winch, 'Understanding a Primitive Society,' *American Philosophy Quarterly*, 1 (1964): 307–24, frequently reprinted.

25 That distinction is rarely used today, largely because it tended to function teleologically and somewhat hierarchically, was seen as overly simplistic, and was regarded as implicitly demeaning of 'traditional' societies. The switch to 'underdeveloped,' 'developing,' and 'developed' did not fare much better, and the preferred terminology now seems to be 'preindustrial,' 'industrializing,' 'industrial,' and 'postindustrial,' which appears to be an improvement over the original 'traditional' and 'modern' differentiation only in that it adds two further categories. As will be seen below, for all its problems, I think there is still some analytic merit in the older scheme.

26 See Max Weber, *Economy and Society*, 2 vols., ed. Guenther Roth and Claus Wittich, trans. various (Berkeley and Los Angeles, 1978), 1: 212–301, esp. 215–16, for the barebones statement of distinction.

27 Two of the best-known but very different discussions of 'consciousness' of this sort as a hallmark of modernity are H. Stuart Hughes, *Consciousness and Society: The Reconstruction of European Social Thought, 1890–1930* (New York, 1959), and Charles Taylor, *Sources of the Self: The Making of the Modern Identity* (Cambridge, MA, 1989).

28 See the essay 'An Answer to the Question, What Is Enlightenment?' conveniently available in translation in James Schmidt, ed., *What Is Enlightenment: Eighteenth-Century Answers and Twentieth-Century Questions* (Berkeley and Los Angeles, 1996), 58–64; and in Immanuel Kant, *Political Writings*, 2nd ed., ed. Hans Reiss, trans. H.B. Nisbett, Cambridge Texts in the History of Political Thought (Cambridge, 1991), 54–60.

29 Making it, paradoxically perhaps, something of a 'tradition.' An important set of entrenched and generally unquestioned presuppositions about historical continuity must be in place before either of these responses will work.

'Practice' is part of that family of concepts I previously identified as including 'tradition.' It was employed as a term of art by one the great twentieth-century political theorist of tradition, Michael Oakeshott (see, in particular, *On Human Conduct* [Oxford, 1975], 54–88) and by the sociologist-philosopher Stephen Turner (see his *The Social Theory of Practices: Tradition, Tacit, Knowledge, and Presuppositions* [Cambridge, 1994].) For Wittgenstein-

ian treatments of the concept of 'practice' that retain its closeness to 'tradition,' see Richard Flathman, *The Practice of Rights* (Cambridge, 1976),
esp. chap. 1; and Theodore R. Schatzki, *Social Practices: A Wittgensteinian
Approach to Human Activity and the Social* (Cambridge, 1996). And for a more
general account, see J.C. Nyíri, 'Traditions and Practical Knowledge,' in
Nyíri and Barry Smith, eds, *Practical Knowledge: Outlines of a Theory of Traditions and Skills* (London, 1988), 17–52.

30 See Alasdair MacIntyre, 'A Mistake about Causality in Social Science,' in
Peter Laslett and W.G. Runciman, eds, *Philosophy, Politics, and Society,* 2nd
series (Oxford, 1962), 48–70.

31 My claim about 'transformation' is close to the reasoning of H.L.A. Hart
about the analytic separation of law and morals despite their substantive
overlaps. Hart too argues that 'acceptance' on whatever grounds provides a
motive for obeying the law. See *The Concept of Law,* passim, but esp. chaps 4
and 5 on acceptance and 9 on law and morals.

32 Or, speaking more strictly, acquire an additional and, from a legalistic perspective, more important status, and we might say that something is both
legally and traditionally required. The mandated practices or behaviours
themselves need not be transformed.

33 In the United States, one of the criteria of legal interpretation regularly
applied by judicial bodies is 'the *intentions* of the originators' (or 'framers').

34 See especially his inaugural address, 'Political Education' (1951), 'Rationalism in Politics' (1947), and 'Rational Conduct' (1950), all reprinted in his
Rationalism in Politics (London, 1962). Although he did not explicitly single
out for attack the conscious 'invention' of traditions for purposes of political control and manipulation and wrote before the publication of *The Invention of Tradition* (ed. Eric Hobsbawm and Terence Ranger [Cambridge,
1983]), Oakeshott's overall position was an implicit attack on the practices
famously identified and named in that volume.

35 Oakeshott, 'Political Education,' *Rationalism,* 122–5.

36 Ibid., 128 and 129.

37 In many respects, Burke's ideological opponents – the radical dissenter
Richard Price and the rational spirit of the French Enlightenment, which
summoned forth his *Reflections on the Revolution in France,* and the early
feminist Mary Wollstonecraft and the egalitarian defender of natural rights
Thomas Paine, who published extensive replies to the *Reflections* – gave
birth to Oakeshott's enemies.

38 Oakeshott did not attempt to disguise his own political conservatism, and
in an essay in *Rationalism in Politics* entitled 'On Being Conservative' he
spelled out the bases of his position. In all likelihood, he would have

objected to my application of the term 'political sociology' to his arguments.

39 To be fair to Burke, his goal was not to suggest remedies for France but to warn the British by example of the local and world-wide disasters they courted by supporting the appeal to the universal rights of the French Revolution. If Burke was correct about France, there was no hope for that nation until it restored its own traditions and gave up what Jeremy Bentham was to term the 'nonsense' of abstract rights. Even Bentham, the positivist and rationalist par excellence, turned to national or local tradition as embodied in the law when confronted by the spectre of abstract, natural rights. See his *Nonsense upon Stilts, or Pandora's Box Opened* (ca. 1795), in Bentham, *Rights, Representation, and Reform: Nonsense upon Stilts and other Writings on the French Revolution*, ed. Philip Schofield, Catherine Pease-Watkin, and Cyprian Blamires (Oxford, 2002), 319–401, a volume in *The Collected Works of Jeremy Bentham*. For an analysis – almost a caricature – of Bentham as the quintessential anti-traditionalist rationalist abhorred by Oakeshott, see D.J. Manning, *The Mind of Jeremy Bentham* (London, 1968).

40 Bernard Williams, *Ethics and the Limits of Philosophy* (Cambridge, MA, 1985), 171.

41 Her position is something of blend of the humanist rhetorical practice of 'sermo' with Habermassian conceptions of discourse. For the former, see Gary Remer, *Humanism and the Rhetoric of Toleration* (University Park, PA, 1996), esp. 1–41.

42 This is precisely the theoretical problem that confronted Hobbes in the construction of his leviathan-state and John Rawls is his derivation of the principles of 'justice as fairness' from the agreement of rationally self-interested individuals in *A Theory of Justice* (Cambridge, MA, 1971; rev. ed., 1999). Both resorted to a 'pre-political' condition – the state of nature for Hobbes and the 'original position' behind the 'veil of ignorance' for Rawls – with the important difference that Rawls's construct is thoroughly conjectural and heuristic with *stipulated* constraints, whereas the Hobbesian state of nature has at least the appearance of anthropological validity.

43 See, for instance, John Rawls, *Political Liberalism*, paperback ed. (New York, 1996), xxvi: 'The historical origin of political liberalism (and of liberalism in general) is the Reformation and its aftermath, with the long controversies over religious toleration in the sixteenth and seventeenth centuries.'

Contributors

Mieke Bal is Professor of the Theory of Literature at the University of Amsterdam and A.D. White Professor-at-Large at Cornell University. Among her most recent books are *Travelling Concepts in the Humanities: A Rough Guide* (2002), *Mieke Bal Kulturanalyse* (2002), *Louise Bourgeois' Spider: The Architecture of Art-Writing* (2001).

James Clifford teaches in the History of Consciousness Department, University of California, Santa Cruz. He is the author of *The Predicament of Culture* (1988), *Routes* (1997), and *On the Edges of Anthropology* (2003).

Patrick H. Hutton is Professor Emeritus of History at the University of Vermont, where he taught French history and European intellectual history. His recent books include *History as an Art of Memory* (1993) and *Philippe Ariès and the Politics of French Cultural History* (2004).

Andrea Laforet is Director of Ethnology and Cultural Studies at the Canadian Museum of Civilization. She is the author, most recently, with co-author Annie York, *Spuzzum, Fraser Canyon Histories, 1808–1939* (1998).

David Lieberman, the Jefferson E. Peyser Professor of Law at the University of California, Berkeley, is the author of several studies in the history of legal thought, including *The Province of Legislation Determined: Legal Theory in Eighteenth-Century Britain* (1989). He is currently preparing for publication a critical edition of Jean Louis DeLolme, *The Constitution of England*.

Michael McKeon teaches English literature at Rutgers University. He is the author of *Politics and Poetry in Restoration England* (1975) and *The Origins of the English Novel* (1987), and the editor of *Theory of the Novel* (2000). His forthcoming book is *The Secret History of Domesticity: Public, Private, and the Division of Knowledge*.

Mark Salber Phillips is Professor of History at Carleton University. He is the author of *Francesco Guicciardini: The Historian's Craft* (1978), *Marco Parenti: A Memoir of Medici Florence* (1987; 2000), and *Society and Sentiment: Genres of Historical Writing in Britain, 1740–1820* (2000). He is currently working on a book on the idea of historical distance.

Ruth B. Phillips holds a Canada Research Chair and is Professor of Art History at Carleton University. Her publications include *Trading Identities: The Souvenir in Native North American Art from the Northeast, 1700–1900* (1998); *Unpacking Culture: Art and Commodity in Colonial and Postcolonial Worlds*, co-edited with Christopher B. Steiner (1999); and, with Janet Catherine Berlo, *Native North American Art* (1998). She served as director of the Museum of Anthropology at the University of British Columbia from 1997 to 2003.

Daniel T. Rodgers teaches American cultural and intellectual history at Princeton University, where he is the Henry Charles Lea Professor of History. He is the author of *The Work Ethic in Industrial America* (1978), *Contested Truths: Keywords in American Politics since Independence* (1987), *Atlantic Crossings: Social Politics in a Progressive Age* (1998), and many essays on historiography.

Gordon Schochet teaches social and political philosophy and the history of political thought at Rutgers University and is a founding co-director of the Center for the History of British Political Thought of the Folger Shakespeare Library. He is the author of *Patriarchalism in Political Thought* (1975, 1988), the forthcoming *Rights in Contexts*, and numerous articles, editor of the *Proceedings of the Folger Center for the History of British Political Thought* (1990–3), and co-editor of *The Varieties of British Political Thought: 1500–1800* (1994).

Christopher B. Steiner is Lucy C. McDannel '22 Associate Professor of Art History and Director of Museum Studies at Connecticut College. He is the author of *African Art in Transit* (1994), and co-editor, with

Ruth B. Phillips, of *Unpacking Culture: Art and Commodity in Colonial and Postcolonial Worlds* (1999).

Georgia Warnke is Professor of Philosophy at the University of California, Riverside. Her most recent book is *Legitimate Differences: Interpretation in the Abortion Controversy and Other Public Debates* (1999). Currently, she is working on issues of race and gender.